THE
LATTER-DAY
SAINTS

THE LATTER-DAY SAINTS

A Contemporary History of the Church of Jesus Christ

William E. Berrett

Deseret Book

Salt Lake City, Utah

No part of this book may be reproduced in any
form or by any means without permission in writing
from the publisher, Deseret Book Company,
P.O. Box 30178, Salt Lake City, Utah 84130

Library of Congress Cataloging in Publication Data

Berrett, William E. (William Edwin)
    The Latter-day Saints.

    Bibliography: p.
    includes index
    1. Church of Jesus Christ of Latter-day Saints—
History. 2. Mormon Church—History. I. Title.
BX8611.B345   1985   289.3'32   84-25997
ISBN 0-87747-728-0

Photographs used by permission of
The Church of Jesus Christ of Latter-day Saints

First printing March 1985

Contents

Illustrations

Maps

Preface

The story of The Church of Jesus Christ of Latter-day Saints is the story of Jesus Christ, the resurrected Son of God, in our time, a time designated by him as the fulness of times. It is an account of a movement destined to convince all nations of the earth that Jesus Christ is divine; that he was indeed resurrected from the grave; that he lives; that his voice is heard in the earth; that authority from him has again been given to men on the earth to act in his name.

It is an account of his calling of Joseph Smith, Jr., and others as his servants in carrying out his designs. It is an account of the steps he has taken to restore his church upon the earth. It is an account of conviction in the hearts and minds of men and women that he lives, that he speaks, that he answers prayers, that he is concerned with the welfare of all the children of men. It is an account in which we witness the gifts of the Spirit that follow baptism and the laying on of hands by those called of God to do so.

It is a story of convictions so genuine that men and women were and are willing to forsake earthly possessions, homes, farms, and businesses, to forsake allegiance to the nations of their birth, to forsake even their lives, if necessary, to follow living prophets of the living Savior. It is a story of sacrifice, of physical hardships, of heartbreaking separation of family and friends. It is a story of the paying of tithes and offerings, of the building of chapels and temples, of voluntary service as teachers, missionaries, and administrators, of welfare programs for the sustenance and rehabilitation of Church members, of fast offerings for the poor, of a vast labor for those who have died without a knowledge of saving principles and ordinances.

In short, it is a story of faith in a living God. It is a story of the greatest movement in the history of mankind for the salvation of the human race.

In that story we see men and women rise to greatness under the inspiration of the Spirit. We see men and women who were before relatively unknown rise to positions of influence. And we see men and women fail when the pressures of society and the influence of skeptics overpower them.

In a study of the restoration we see how truth concerning God and man has enriched the world, and we can study the harmony of doctrine between ancient and present-day prophets. In the correlation of doctrines set forth in the messages of prophets in the Old and New Testaments, the Book of Mormon, the Doctrine and Covenants, and the Book of Abraham, we can discern the hand of Jesus Christ working for the salvation of all of God's children.

The story of the Church is not the story of Joseph Smith, Brigham Young, or their associates and successors, but the account of how Christ called and ordained them to disseminate the truth and promote his program for the advancement of mankind.

In the callings those leaders received and the part each played, there arise a multitude of individual stories, stories of merit, stories worth remembering and characters worthy of emulation. But this is all secondary to the overall account of Jesus Christ in our day.

Too often in a study of separate individuals in this great modern-day drama, the critic confuses the weaknesses and faults of the individual with the truths and principles that prompted the person to cleave to the Church. Thus the critic tends to search out and display such faults and weaknesses and to judge the Church thereby. This is to be deplored, as it blinds rather than edifies the student who delves into the critic's works.

1

A Growing, Vital Church

See them come—thousands of them! Men and women; young and old, all neatly dressed, all walking with purpose toward the large domelike building. It is a heterogeneous group, people of many nations: two young couples laughing and chattering; a gray-haired couple stopping to embrace some acquaintances; a family of Navahos, their unique jewelry designating their historic tribe; a family of blacks from far-off Nigeria; a group of Filipinos chatting with two young men who look like missionaries. They seem to be from a multitude of nations but they greet each other as brothers and sisters, with much enthusiasm and handshaking. They are a happy people, a friendly people. Yet they seem to have singleness of purpose as they enter the large building on Temple Square, a ten-acre block in the heart of downtown Salt Lake City. They have come to attend a general conference of The Church of Jesus Christ of Latter-day Saints. They have traveled to this assemblage from scores of nations around the globe to listen to a prophet of God and to receive instructions from apostles, seventies, and other officers of this fast-growing church. And these general officers, like those in the assembling throng, are from many lands—the United States, Canada, England, the Netherlands, Germany, Brazil, Argentina, Japan, Navaho-land, and the isles of the sea—for this is the Church of Jesus Christ, a world church that knows no boundaries of race or nation. It is a great melting pot of humanity where all people, black or white, bond or free, rich or poor, meet in a common bond of brotherhood, followers of Jesus Christ.

Let us enter that historic building, the Salt Lake Tabernacle, home of the world-renowned Tabernacle Choir. The Prophet of God is speaking. He is dressed like any ordinary businessman. There are no robes or badges of office, but there is dignity in his bearing and a sincerity in his voice. The thousands seated before him constitute but a few of a vast audience scattered throughout many lands and nations who are listening to his message carried by radio waves and by satellites orbiting 22,300 feet above the earth.

Who are these people, erroneously called by the media the "Mormons"? Why is that name applied? What are the principles of their faith? What is their program that is fast attracting the attention of thinking people throughout the world?

The objectives of the Church were set forth when it was restored in this dispensation by Jesus Christ. They are threefold: to strengthen the membership of the Church, to carry the gospel message to all the world, and to do the necessary work to save those who are dead. The programs to accomplish these objectives are so interwoven that one could not succeed without the other. The observer sees many separate facets but too often fails to discern how together they constitute the whole face of the Church today.

But what do we see? More than a million teachers and auxiliary workers called to their respective duties and teaching youth and adults in wards and stakes to follow the truths announced by Christ and to live them in their homes; a vast army of priesthood holders regularly visiting Church members in their homes and teaching them the principles of the gospel; women of the Relief Society visiting the female members of the Church to encourage them and to help them solve their problems.

We see Church members reserving each Monday night to be with their families—to plan together, to learn together, and to play together. And it is working. The family is being preserved; love and solidarity are being found.

We see families participating in a program of voluntary service to provide goods and services to those in need and to prepare to meet emergencies in home or community. In this vast welfare program, devoted Latter-day Saints tend and harvest crops on welfare farms; can meats and vegetables; produce soaps and other household necessities; make clothes; in short, prepare and store practically all things necessary to sustain life. We see huge trucks moving out from the Church storehouses to distribute these products to areas where fire, floods, earthquakes, and unemployment have created areas of need. Such help is rendered to Church members and others alike.

We see thousands of full-time missionaries serving without monetary reward, most of them supported by their own savings or by the support of their families, proclaiming a message of the living Christ to people throughout much of the world. But this is but the tip of the iceberg. Each convert is in turn converting family and neighbors in a never-ending circle. It is a vast and ever-expanding program to carry out the commandment of Christ: to carry the gospel truths to every nation and people in their own language.

We see huge printing presses producing copies of the Bible and the Book of Mormon, manuals, and other Church literature for distribution worldwide, in the languages of the nations where the church is established.

We see all of this activity bearing fruit the like of which has heretofore seldom been seen. Church membership passed the five million mark by 1984, having doubled in the preceding twelve years. And the rate of growth is accelerating, with statisticians foreseeing the possibility of the membership doubling and redoubling in ever-shorter periods of time.

We see the payment of honest tithes and offerings, attendance at Church meetings, and the fervor of missionary activity—all attesting to the prevalence of the Spirit of Christ and those gifts of the Spirit promised by Christ to those who enter his church by baptism and the laying on of hands by those having proper priesthood authority.

We see one or more new chapels being completed and dedicated each day, and the building of temples in nearly every land on the earth, so that the great millennial age will find the people and the place to do a work for the billions of the dead and that God's justice might be had for all who have lived, who are now living, and who will live in the future upon this planet.

We see members of the Church as well as many nonmembers from many nations searching for their ancestors in the largest repository of genealogical records in the world, aided by computers and other modern technology.

We see a people with an unusual commitment to learning and with a high literacy record. We see the largest church-operated university in the world, named after its founder, Brigham Young, a school that stresses high moral standards and excellence in scholarship and athletics. We see also elementary and high schools in nations where such schools might not otherwise be available to members of the Church.

We see a remarkable system of weekday religious education, known as the seminary program, where high school students can attend religion classes during released time from public schools or in an early morning hour before the opening of the public schedule. For those who, because of isolation, lack of transportation, or other unfavorable conditions, cannot attend regular religion classes, we find study courses in religion to be followed in the home, with weekly or monthly participation in activity with other youths.

We see college and university students attending religion classes at institutes of religion built by the Church adjacent to their campuses or in other available facilities.

Here is a people "in the world but not of the world." They include United States Senators and members of Congress, ambassadors, men and women who serve in departments of federal and state governments, governors of states, state and federal judges. The number of persons engaged in government service is far out of balance with the number of Church members, for this is a people concerned with the government of nations and the general welfare of people. But though they mingle thus with the world, these civil servants are distinctive in their continued Church activity and in their personal habits and moral conduct.

Here is a people known for their participation in youth organizations. Most Latter-day Saint boys are active in Scouting, and many Church leaders serve on national and local Boy Scout councils.

This is a people concerned not only about the development of the soul, but also about the care of the body. From the 1832 revelation when the Lord, in answer to the Prophet Joseph Smith's prayer, counseled Church members in the matter of foods and designated substances harmful to health and those beneficial to both body and soul, this people in quite remarkable numbers have adhered to these teachings. As the missionaries take the gospel message to the nations of the world, they take with them these teachings concerning the health of the body. And special missionaries, called from their professions and occupations because of their knowledge of such subjects as medicine, dentistry, and sanitation, are serving in areas where health has been a problem because of lack of understanding and skills.

One of the recent prophets of the Church, Joseph F. Smith, declared: "Any religion that does not make its members happier here and now is not worth having." All these activities, unbelievable as they may be to the observer, are not fiction. They are realities of a Church in action.

The observer might well ask, as indeed he usually does: How did it all begin? What is the source of the Church's power? How is it financed? Why do so many pay a tithe of their earnings to promote the cause? Why do so many contribute time and talent without thought of pay? What goes on in those temples and why?

2

A Remarkable Vision

The time is early spring in the year 1820. The place—a backwoods farm in western New York. A young boy of perhaps fourteen has just left the log farmhouse. He goes down the lane to the west across the small brook and then into a thick grove of trees. An hour later, or is it two, he emerges and returns slowly to his home.

What has happened to him? What is different? For there is a difference. Perhaps his very bearing, his apparent concentration in thought, his disregard of things about him, are outward evidences that the boy has been left in the grove and a man has emerged. His mother, noticing the change as he reenters the home and leans against the mantel, asks, "Joseph, what is wrong?" The boy, evidently recalling the church she had recently joined, replies, "Never mind, all is well—I am well enough off. I have learned for myself that Presbyterianism is not true."

That evening the young man, whose name was Joseph Smith, Jr., thrilled his family with the recounting of his unusual experience. This story was to be retold many times in future years. Let us follow the story as it was written for all the world to read:

> I was born in the year of our Lord one thousand eight hundred and five, on the twenty-third day of December, in the town of Sharon, Windsor County, state of Vermont. My father, Joseph Smith, was born July 12th, 1771, in Topsfield, Essex County, Massachusetts; his father, Asael Smith, was born March 7th, 1744, in Topsfield, Massachusetts; his father, Samuel Smith, was born January 26th, 1714, in Topsfield, Massachusetts; his father, Samuel Smith, was born January 26th, 1666, in Topsfield, Massachusetts; his father, Robert Smith, came from England. My father, Joseph Smith, Senior, left the state of Vermont and moved to Palmyra, Ontario (now Wayne) county, in the state of New York, when I was in my tenth year, or thereabouts. In about four years after my father's arrival in Palmyra he moved with his family into Manchester, in the same

Joseph Smith, the Prophet (1805–44)

county of Ontario, his family consisting of eleven souls, namely—my father, Joseph Smith, my mother, Lucy Smith, (whose name, previous to her marriage, was Mack, daughter of Solomon Mack,) my brothers, Alvin, (who died November 19th, 1824, in the 27th year of his age,) Hyrum, myself, Samuel Harrison, William, Don Carlos, and my sisters, Sophronia, Catherine, and Lucy.

Some time in the second year after our removal to Manchester, there was in the place where we lived an unusual excitement on the subject of religion. It commenced with the Methodists, but soon became general among all the sects in that region of country. Indeed, the whole district of country seemed affected by it, and great multitudes united themselves to the different religious parties, which created no small stir and division amongst the people, some crying, "Lo here!" and others, "Lo there!" Some were contending for the Methodist faith, some for the Presbyterian, and some for the Baptist. For notwithstanding the great love which the converts to these different faiths expressed at the time of their conversion, and the great zeal manifested by the respective clergy, who were active in getting up and promoting this extraordinary scene of religious feeling, in order to have everybody converted, as they were pleased to call it, let them join what sect they pleased—yet when the converts began to file off, some to one party and some to another, it was seen that the seemingly good feelings of both the priests and the converts were more pretended than real; for a scene of great confusion and bad feeling ensued; priest contending against priest, and convert against convert; so that all their good feelings one for another, if they ever had any, were entirely lost in a strife of words and a contest about opinions.

I was at this time in my fifteenth year. My father's family was proselyted to the Presbyterian faith, and four of them joined that church, namely—my mother Lucy; my brothers Hyrum and Samuel Harrison; and my sister Sophronia. During this time of great excitement, my mind was called up to serious reflection and great uneasiness; but, though my feelings were deep and often poignant, still I kept myself aloof from all these parties, though I attended their several meetings as often as occasion would permit. In process of time my mind became somewhat partial to the Methodist sect, and I felt some desire to be united with them; but so great were the confusion and strife among the different denominations, that it was impossible for a person young as I was, and so unacquainted with men and things, to come to any certain conclusion who was right and who was wrong. My mind at times was greatly excited, the cry and tumult were so great and incessant. The Presbyterians were most decided against the Baptists and Methodists, and used all the powers of both reason and sophistry to prove their errors, or, at least, to make the people think they were in error. On the other hand, the Baptists and Methodists in their turn were equally zealous in endeavoring to establish their own tenets and disprove all others.

In the midst of this war of words and tumult of opinions, I often said to myself, what is to be done? Who of all these parties are right, or, are they all wrong together? If any of them be right, which is it, and how shall I know it? While I was laboring under the extreme difficulties caused by the contests of these parties of religionists, I was one day reading the Epistle of James, first chapter and fifth verse, which reads:

"If any of you lack wisdom, let him ask of God, that giveth

to all men liberally, and upbraideth not; and it shall be given him."

Never did any passage of Scripture come with more power to the heart of man than this did at this time to mine. It seemed to enter with great force into every feeling of my heart. I reflected on it again and again, knowing that if any person needed wisdom from God, I did; for how to act I did not know and unless I could get more wisdom than I then had, I would never know; for the teachers of religion of the different sects understood the same passages of Scripture so differently as to destroy all confidence in settling the question by an appeal to the Bible. At length I came to the conclusion that I must either remain in darkness and confusion, or else I must do as James directs, that is, ask of God. I at length came to the determination to "ask of God," concluding that if He gave wisdom to them that lacked wisdom, and would give liberally, and not upbraid, I might venture. So, in accordance with this, my determination to Ask God, I retired to the woods to make the attempt. It was on the morning of a beautiful, clear day, early in the spring of eighteen hundred and twenty. It was the first time in my life that I had made such an attempt, for amidst all my anxieties I had never as yet made the attempt to pray vocally.

After I had retired to the place where I had previously designed to go, having looked around me, and finding myself alone, I kneeled down and began to offer up the desires of my heart to God. I had scarcely done so, when immediately I was seized upon by some power which entirely overcame me, and had such an astonishing influence over me as to bind my tongue so that I could not speak. Thick darkness gathered around me, and it seemed to me for a time as if I were doomed to sudden destruction. But, exerting all my powers to call upon God to deliver me out of the power of this enemy which had seized upon me, and at the very moment when I was ready to sink into despair and abandon myself to destruction—not to an imaginary ruin, but to the power of some actual being from the unseen world, who had such marvelous power as I had never before felt in any being— just at this moment of great alarm, I saw a pillar of light exactly over my head, above the brightness of the sun, which descended gradually until it fell upon me.

It no sooner appeared than I found myself delivered from the enemy which held me bound. When the light rested upon

The Sacred Grove, where Joseph Smith had first vision

me, I saw two personages, whose brightness and glory defy all description, standing above me in the air. One of them spake unto me, calling me by name, and said—pointing to the other—
"THIS IS MY BELOVED SON, HEAR HIM."

My object in going to inquire of the Lord was to know which of all the sects was right, that I might know which to join. No sooner, therefore, did I get possession of myself, so as to be able to speak, than I asked the personages who stood above me in the light, which of all the sects was right—and which I should join. I was answered that I must join none of them, for they were all wrong, and the personage who addressed me said that all their creeds were an abomination in His sight: that those professors were all corrupt; that "they draw near to me with their lips, but their hearts are far from me; they teach for doctrines the commandments of men: having a form of godliness, but they deny the power thereof." He again forbade me to join with any of them: and many other things did he say unto me, which I cannot write at this time. When I came to myself again, I found myself lying on my back, looking up into heaven. When the light had departed, I had no strength; but soon recovering in some degree, I went home.[1]

It would seem at first glance that we must depend upon the testimony of one man (or boy) as to what occurred in that grove of trees on that beautiful spring morning in 1820. No one accompanied him. No one saw him enter the grove and it is likely that no one observed his leaving.

It must be evident, however, to the biographer or the historian that something unusual had occurred. Three facts are of interest. First, whatever happened in the grove changed Joseph's outward bearing—he suddenly became less the boy and more the man. His mother was the first to notice it, but to many others it was also evident.[2] Second, Joseph came out of the grove with a set of definite ideas, ideas that he did not possess when he entered—indeed, ideas not to be found among the people with whom he associated or in the few books he had read. True, his ideas were not new. This idea, or that, might be found among the writings of his contemporaries; they were taught by the Christ eighteen hundred years before. But it seems plain that so far as Joseph Smith is concerned, those ideas were received in the grove on that spring morning. He had not possessed them before—he did not acquire them later. To the first person he met, his mother, he began to pronounce them. Within a week those ideas were known over an entire community.

The third fact is that Joseph had received a testimony. Whereas he had previously wavered as to where to place his allegiance, now the picture of a future church to embrace the gospel in its fullness was so real, and the existence of God so certain, that he would not deny it. Referring again from his journal:

> It caused me serious reflection then, and often has since, how very strange it was that an obscure boy, of a little over fourteen years of age, and one, too, who was doomed to the necessity of obtaining a scanty maintenance by his daily labor, should be thought a character of sufficient importance to attract the attention of the great ones of the most popular sects of the day, and in a manner to create in them a spirit of the most bitter persecution and reviling. But strange or not, so it was, and it was often the cause of great sorrow to myself. However, it was nevertheless a fact that I had beheld a vision. I have thought since, that I felt much like Paul, when he made his defense before King Agrippa, and related the account of the vision he had when he saw a light,

and heard a voice; but still there were but few who believed him; some said he was dishonest, others said he was mad; and he was ridiculed and reviled. But all this did not destroy the reality of his vision. He had seen a vision, he knew he had, and all the persecution under heaven could not make it otherwise; and though they should persecute him unto death, yet he knew, and would know to the last breath, that he had both seen a light, and heard a voice speaking unto him, and all the world could not make him think or believe otherwise. So it was with me. I had actually seen a light, and in the midst of that light I saw two personages, and they did in reality speak to me; and though I was hated and persecuted for saying that I had seen a vision, yet it was true; and while they were persecuting me, reviling me, and speaking all manner of evil against me falsely for so saying, I was led to say in my heart, Why persecute me for telling the truth? I have actually seen a vision, and who am I that I can withstand God, or why does the world think to make me deny what I have actually seen? For I had seen a vision; I knew it, and I knew that God knew it, and I could not deny it, neither dared I do it, at least I knew that by so doing I would offend God, and come under condemnation.[3]

It is not our purpose at this time to delve into a discussion with the critics of Joseph's story. The truth of the first vision is deeper than a mere discussion of a boy's truthfulness. The true test of his story is a test of a principle involved—a spiritual principle: Can one pray to God and receive an answer? Can a man go into a grove, or into his bedroom, and through prayer receive new ideas he did not before possess, new knowledge that to him, if not to the whole world, was before hidden? Is revelation and inspiration from God a reality? Can you or I have such an experience? Is the experience of the boy Joseph Smith an eternal verity that can be reproduced today and tomorrow? If we "lack knowledge," is there a channel that, with the requisite faith, we can open to God? If the answer is yes, God becomes suddenly, as to the boy Joseph Smith, a vital reality in our lives.

The answer is written in the hearts of thousands of men and women. Joseph Smith's testimony does not stand alone. In the years following his vision, many thousands of individuals, stirred to their depths by his story, have sought knowledge and testimony through the channel of prayer and have been converted. Converted to what? To a belief that Joseph Smith was an honest man? To the belief that he saw what he claimed to have seen? No. At least that is not the vital thing. The conversion is to the eternal truth that one might receive an answer to prayer, a testimony that God lives and that he speaks unto men. And this type of conversion is as strong as the conversion of Joseph Smith, or of Paul the apostle, or of Peter—the recipients are willing to die for it as Paul and Peter died for theirs, and as Joseph Smith was to die for his.

When Joseph came out of that grove and announced his experience to the world, Peter, Paul, and all the religious leaders of all ages really stood at his side to vouch for his story, for all had testified to similar experiences.

3

Why a Restoration

Why would Jesus Christ advise Joseph Smith to join none of the churches, saying, "They teach for doctrines the commandments of men: having a form of godliness, but they deny the power thereof"? Is there an answer?

Nineteen centuries ago John the Baptist called upon the Jews who had gathered about him on the banks of the Jordan River in Palestine to repent, for the kingdom of God was at hand. The kingdom was indeed at their very doors, for the Son of God was coming with authority to accept into his kingdom all who would prepare their hearts for that entrance. To those who had faith in God and sought to enter into the kingdom, John announced: "I indeed baptize you with water unto repentance: but he that cometh after me is mightier than I: . . . he shall baptize you with the Holy Ghost, and with fire." (Matthew 3:11.)

So when Jesus came, he established the kingdom of God upon the earth, that all who would, might enter and partake of the Spirit of God with him. To officiate in the kingdom upon the earth, Jesus ordained twelve men as apostles and gave them power and authority to preach the gospel and administer in all of its ordinances. They were instructed to carry the gospel first of all to the children of Israel. Later Christ chose seventy and commissioned them likewise to preach the gospel unto the people.

After the death and resurrection of the Savior, this nucleus of Church officers, acting according to the authority they possessed, perfected the organization. The vacancy in the quorum of the twelve apostles, caused by the death of Judas Iscariot, was filled by the ordination of Matthias. The offices of priest, teacher, deacon, evangelist, and bishop were added.

Of the people living in western Asia and in Europe at that day, the Israelites alone were prepared by training and tradition for the high standard of religion set forth by Christ. The moral laws of the Hebrews and the teachings of their prophets should have prepared that people for the gospel of Jesus Christ. So it was that the Savior commanded his disciples to carry the gospel first to the house of Israel and then to the Gentiles. By the Gentiles, we refer to those who had never accepted, or perhaps heard of, the God of Abraham, Isaac, and Jacob, but who believed in gods of nature to whom they built graven images and offered sacrifices.

A church can be no better than its people, and the immorality and licentiousness of the heathen peoples of that day were notorious. Those Jews who, with their background of Hebrew training and history, accepted the teachings of the Master became genuine followers of him and were indeed worthy of membership in his kingdom. But because the Jews as a nation had also drifted into immoral practices and had become subjected to a rigid priestly interpretation of their religious laws, the nation as a whole rejected the gospel.

It was with great disappointment that Jesus perceived the hardheartedness of his own people. One gets a glimpse into his great soul as, pausing with his disciples on the brow of the Mount of Olives on one occasion and gazing upon his beloved City of Jerusalem below them, he burst into tears, exclaiming: "O Jerusalem, Jerusalem, . . . how often would I have gathered thy children together, even as a hen gathereth her chickens under her wings, and ye would not!" (Matthew 23:37.)

As it became apparent to the Savior that the gospel would be rejected by those who by tradition and training should have been prepared for it, and that it must be taken to the heathen who were not prepared for its high moral requirements, he warned his few faithful followers of what the result would be: "Then shall many be offended, and shall betray one another, and shall hate one another. And many false prophets shall rise, and shall deceive many. And because iniquity shall abound, the love of many shall wax cold. But he that shall endure unto the end, the same shall be saved." (Matthew 24:10-13.)

Speaking of the period of apostasy and persecution that was to come, the Savior added: "Then shall they deliver you up to be afflicted, and shall kill you: and ye shall be hated of all nations for my name's sake." (Matthew 24:9.)

"Then if any man shall say unto you, Lo, here is Christ, or there; believe it not. For there shall arise false Christs, and false prophets, and shall shew great signs and wonders; insomuch that if it were possible, they shall deceive the very elect. Behold, I have told you before. Wherefore if they shall say unto you, Behold, he is in the desert; go not forth: behold, he is in the secret chambers; believe it not." (Matthew 24:23-26.)

It could hardly be hoped that the gospel would survive in purity among the heathen peoples of the Mediterranean world of that day, for the church can be no better than its members, and the people of that area had sunk into the depths of wickedness. This is evident from any extended study of the social conditions of the times. The heathen gods worshipped by these peoples were, with rare exceptions, immoral, given to excesses and indulgences, full of jealousy, motivated often by hate and seldom by love.

In the great Greek and Roman cities, sex relationships had reached a stage of license where marriage became a temporary convenience and immorality a virtue. Indeed, on certain festive occasions immoral relations were demanded as a part of public worship. Even the Jews had been affected by the lax conditions prevailing in the Greek and Roman world, and all sorts of fictions were devised to avoid the more rigid Jewish laws of marriage and divorce.

It was into this maelstrom of licentiousness that the intrepid apostle Paul and others carried the gospel of Jesus Christ, determined to save sinking humanity. The fire and enthusiasm of these great Hebrew leaders, together with the manifestations of the power and authority they possessed, caused the gospel to spread like a conflagration throughout the Mediterranean world whose mystic religions were on the verge of dissolution and decay. But while multitudes of the Greeks, and later of the Romans, were baptized members of the church of Christ, they did not always change their manner of living or follow the high standards set by the Master. Some did so, and of these, Justin Martyr, who lived in the second century, said:

> We, who were once slaves of lust, now have delight only in purity of morals; we, who once practised arts of magic, have consecrated ourselves to the Eternal and Good God; we, who once prized gain above all things, give even what we have to the common use, and share it with such as are in need; we, who once hated and murdered one another, who on account of differences of customs would have no common hearth with strangers, do now, since the appearance of Christ, live together with them; we pray for our enemies; we seek to convince those that hate us without cause, so that they may order their lives according to Christ's glorious doctrine and attain to the joyful hope of receiving like blessings with us from God, the Lord of all.[1]

The continued immorality of the majority of the newly baptized members caused Paul great concern. With almost superhuman effort he combated by letter and by visits these evils that were destroying the spirit of the church. Repeatedly he admonished the churches for their immoralities. An example of this is shown in his first letter to the Saints at Corinth: "It is reported commonly that there is fornication among you, and such fornication as is not so much as named among the Gentiles. . . . And ye are puffed up, and have not rather mourned, that he that hath done this deed might be taken away from among you." (1 Corinthians 5:1-2.)

Paul was aware that the continued existence of the church depended upon the members so living that the Holy Ghost would be their companion and comforter. Unless they lived lives of purity, the blessings of the Holy Ghost could not be had. Without the Holy Ghost there could not be that burning testimony of the Christ that Paul himself possessed and the possession of which caused men to devote their lives to God's kingdom. He warned the Corinthian Saints: "No man can say that Jesus is the Lord, but by the Holy Ghost." (1 Corinthians 12:3.)

Peter likewise admonished the Saints to live righteously so that they might receive the Holy Ghost as an instructor in the study of

the scriptures: "No prophecy of the scripture is of any private interpretation," he said. "For the prophecy came not in old time by the
will of man: but holy men of God spake as they were moved by the
Holy Ghost." (2 Peter 1:20-21.)

With the branches of the church so widely scattered and with
little written scripture other than the old Jewish Testament, the
church could not be kept in unity without the guidance of the Spirit.
Especially was this true in the face of Greek philosophies, which
were strongly entrenched in the minds of converts to Christianity.

Dr. Philip Smith wrote of the period: "The sad truth is that as
soon as Christianity was generally diffused, it began to absorb corruption from all the lands in which it was planted, and to reflect the
complexion of all their systems of religion and philosophy."[2]

Even while Paul lived, some of the churches he had established
in Asia turned from his leadership and doctrines. He predicted that
an apostasy from the true gospel would certainly occur. In speaking for the last time to the Saints of Ephesus, he said: "I know
this, that after my departing shall grievous wolves enter in among
you, not sparing the flock. Also of your own selves shall men arise,
speaking perverse things, to draw away disciples after them."
(Acts 20:29-30.)

In a letter written from a Roman prison to his beloved follower
Timothy, Paul said: "Now the Spirit speaketh expressly, that in the
latter times some shall depart from the faith, giving heed to seduc-
ing spirits, and doctrines of devils; speaking lies in hypocrisy; having their conscience seared with a hot iron; forbidding to marry,
and commanding to abstain from meats, which God hath created to
be received with thanksgiving of them which believe and know the
truth." (1 Timothy 4:1-3.)

In a later letter to Timothy, he added: "The time will come
when they will not endure sound doctrine; but after their own lusts
shall they heap to themselves teachers, having itching ears; and
they shall turn away their ears from the truth, and shall be turned
unto fables." (2 Timothy 4:3-4.)

It was the leadership of great Jews, men like Peter, James,
John, and Paul, who, by the sheer weight of personality and the
fervor of their testimony, held the churches in some semblance of

order during the first century. When these great Jewish leaders were silenced by death, there were none to replace them. The Jewish nation had rejected the gospel, and the Greek and Roman converts, though often exceedingly brilliant and capable, nevertheless lacked the fundamental foundations in tradition and training to comprehend the spiritual kingdom established by Jesus Christ. Immorality crept into all sections of the church, as a historian who lived in that period reported:

> When by reason of excessive liberty, we sunk into negligence and sloth, one envying and reviling another in different ways, and we were almost, as it were, on the point of taking up arms against each other and were assailing each other with words as with darts and spears, prelates inveighing against prelates, and people rising up against people, . . . some, indeed, like atheists, regarding our situation as unheeded and unobserved by a providence, we added one wickedness and misery to another. But some that appeared to be our pastors, deserting the law of piety, were inflamed against each other with mutual strifes, only accumulating quarrels and threats, rivalship, hostility, and hatred to each other, only anxious to assert the government as a kind of sovereignty for themselves.[3]

Under those conditions of unrighteousness the Holy Ghost could not operate, and men were left to quarrel over private interpretations of the scriptures and doctrines. Further, the gifts of the Holy Ghost, so evident in the period of the apostles, ceased to be manifest. As the gospel continued to spread among the heathen people, it began to be pervaded more and more with the nature of heathen practices. In the writings of Mosheim we read:

> Many rites were added, without necessity, to both public and private religious worship, to the great offense of good men; and principally because of the perversity of mankind who are more delighted with the pomp and splendor of external forms and pageantry than with the true devotion of the heart. There is good reason to believe that the Christian bishops purposely multiplied sacred rites for the sake of rendering the Jews and pagans more friendly to them. For both these classes had always been accustomed to numerous and splendid ceremonies, and believed them an essential part of religion. . . . To add further to the dignity of the Christian religion, the churches of the east feigned mysteries

similar to those of the pagan religions; and, as with the pagans, the holy rites of the mysteries were concealed from the vulgar: "And they not only applied the terms used in pagan mysteries to the Christian institutions, particularly baptism and the Lord's supper, but they gradually introduced also the rites which were designated by those terms."[4]

It must not be supposed that all of these changes in ordinances and doctrines came about in a short period of time. For the most part, several generations were involved. Nor did the changes occur uniformly throughout Christendom. Rather, until the fourth century widely divergent practices in the ordinances of the church existed; for example, two forms of baptism were often allowed in the same church.

During this period, frequent persecutions brought about the deaths of the Christian leaders and thereby weakened the church's resistance to pagan philosophies. The earliest persecutions were by the Jews who had rejected the gospel. To them, Christianity was a Jewish heresy whose very success seemed to strike at the foundations of the Jewish church. In A.D. 64 the Roman government under Nero took cognizance of the growing Christian church and commenced a bitter persecution against the sect. Later persecutions also occurred at intervals until the time of Constantine, who professed Christianity and constituted it the state religion. These persecutions were caused by two things:

> They dared to ridicule the absurdities of the Pagan superstition, and they were ardent and assiduous in gaining proselytes to the truth. Nor did they only attack the religion of *Rome,* but also all the different shapes and forms under which superstition appeared in . . . their ministry. From hence the Romans concluded, that the Christian sect was not only insupportably daring and arrogant, but, moreover, an enemy to the public tranquillity, and every way proper to excite civil wars and commotions in the empire. It is, probably, on this account that TACITUS reproaches them with the odious character of *haters of mankind,* and styles the religion of JESUS as a *destructive superstition;* and that SUETONIUS speaks of the Christians, and their doctrine, in terms of the same kind.[5]

However, while the persecutions drove many from the church, they did not seriously retard its growth; they may, in fact, have contributed to it. It was rather the internal weakness that caused a departure from the gospel of Jesus Christ.

It is not our purpose here to follow through, step by step, the growth of paganism in the rituals and ordinances of the church and the loss of priesthood that occurred. Reliable historians have done so with considerable skill. Nor can we here delve into the problem of determining when the apostasy was complete. Sufficeth to say, when we glimpse Christianity several hundred years after the Christian era began, we see few of the original ordinances established by Christ. The gifts of the Holy Ghost are no longer manifest, and the organization of the church is changed. Of this change Gibbon, the historian, writes:

> If, after all, the view of the early progress of Christianity be melancholy and humiliating, we must beware lest we charge the whole of this on the infidelity of the historian. It is idle, it is disingenuous, to deny or to dissemble the early deprivations of Christianity, its gradual but rapid departure from its primitive simplicity and purity, still more from its spirit of universal love. It may be no unsalutary lesson to the Christian world, that this silent, this unavoidable perhaps, yet fatal change shall have been drawn by an impartial, or even an hostile hand.[6]

The changes that had occurred in the Christian church might be summarized briefly as follows:

1. The ordinance of baptism, originally performed by immersion of the candidate beneath the waters,[7] was changed to the sprinkling of holy water by the priest upon the head of the convert. Many added ceremonies also changed the original simplicity of the ordinance, and baptism of infants commenced.[8]

2. The ordinance of the sacrament of the Lord's supper was changed. The original simplicity of partaking of the bread and wine in remembrance of the Savior gave way to an elaborate ceremony of pomp and mystery. The doctrine of transubstantiation became an essential doctrine of the Roman Church. This doctrine says, in effect, that the bread and the wine used in the sacrament

lose their character as bread and wine and become literally the flesh and blood of the crucified Christ. The change is assumed to occur mysteriously in a way beyond the power of mortals to perceive. These consecrated emblems then came to be worshipped of themselves and led to a pernicious practice of idolatry.

The celebration of the Mass, as the ordinance came to be called, was conducted at greater and greater intervals. Later the custom of administering only the bread was introduced, the assertion being that in some mystical way both the body and blood were present in the one emblem.[9]

3. Unauthorized changes occurred in church organization and government. The officers found in the primitive church, namely, apostles, pastors, high priests, seventies, elders, bishops, priests, teachers, and deacons, had largely disappeared. Further, the general membership of the church was not permitted to hold the priesthood; rather, a special class known as the clergy segregated themselves from the common people and professed to hold the authority of the priesthood.

The office of bishop had been retained, but unlike the order that prevailed in the primitive church, the bishops were not considered of equal rank. The Bishop at Rome, under the protection and sanction of the Roman government, had assumed jurisdiction over all other bishops and had acquired the title of pope, or "papa bishop." Mosheim says that the popes "carried their insolent pretentions so far as to give themselves out for lords of the universe, arbiters of the fate of kingdoms and empires, and supreme rulers over the kings and princes of the earth." [10]

4. The gifts of the Holy Ghost were no longer evident in the church. Indeed, the church was teaching that these gifts had been given during the period of the apostles for the purpose of aiding in the establishing of the church, and that after that establishment the gifts were withdrawn from the earth as being no longer necessary. Hence, such gifts as revelation, prophecy, tongues, the interpretation of tongues, healings, and discernment had wholly disappeared from the church.

5. The church had assumed the right to punish those who had broken church rules by giving them civil penalties. Further, the

church assumed the power to forgive men their sins upon evidence of repentance. This led to the shocking practice of selling indulgences, or pardons for money, which was one of the outstanding causes of the later rebellion of Martin Luther against the church.[11]

But the gospel of Jesus Christ was not defeated nor was the mission of the Savior to mankind a failure. Christ came at a period when the spiritual life of the world was at low ebb. Immorality, selfishness, hatred, love of money, cruelty, and slavery abounded. Into this sick soil he planted the seeds of the gospel, not with the idea that the whole world would immediately become righteous, but with the assurance that, like the leaven kneaded into the bread, a little leaven would enlighten the whole lump and eventually produce a better world in which to live. To his apostles he said: "The kingdom of heaven is like unto leaven, which a woman took, and hid in three measures of meal, till the whole was leavened." (Matthew 13:33.)

While the priesthood of Christ disappeared among men and the church ordinances and doctrines became corrupted, the leaven of the gospel survived through the Bible, which was preserved in the monasteries and convents during those trying times. The example Christ set in his life and the beauty of his teachings continued to touch the hearts of many people and to change their lives for good. Gradually mankind was being prepared for the restoration of the gospel in its fullness.

The effects of that leaven upon mankind are evident throughout the centuries of Christian history and attest the great love of God for all mankind and his hope that they would prepare for the great restoration of his kingdom. When one reads many of the dark pages of Christian history, one wonders if the leaven of Christ's words has not been wholly lost. For many individuals that was true, and at times the spirit of the Master was at low ebb among all peoples. Gradually, however, the leaven of righteousness began its work.

In order to understand the victory of Jesus Christ over the dark forces of sin and despair, it is necessary to keep in mind the condition of the world into which Jesus came. The Jewish historian

Josephus says of the Jews who lived in Jerusalem shortly after the death of Jesus "that a more wicked generation of men" had not been upon the earth since the days of Noah.[12]

In the great Greek city of Athens, at the time of Christ, three-fifths of the population were slaves, and a similar condition existed over the Mediterranean world. Individuals convicted of crimes were executed in the most brutal fashion, often being hung on crosses along public roads and in the marketplaces as examples to others. Fear was the chief restraining influence upon men. In parts of the Roman Empire the sick and aged were left upon mountainsides to perish. Starvation of the poor was commonplace. The natural affections for blood kin seemed woefully lacking. Brothers murdered brothers for gain; wives poisoned their husbands, and husbands destroyed their wives. Even the great Constantine murdered his wife and one of his sons without arousing much comment among a people depraved by sin.

There were, during this period, many righteous people, but they were comparatively few in number, and their very righteousness had become a reproach to them. The Greek writer Xenophanes, in depicting in one of his novels his ideal man, said of him, "No man ever did more good to his friends or more harm to his enemies."

It was a long step from this time of hatred to the high ideal of manhood portrayed by Tennyson in his character of King Arthur, who does not become the perfect knight until, realizing his Queen Guinevere has deeply wronged him, he generously forgives her. It was likewise a long step from the sick and aged dying on the mountains of Greece to the modern programs of civilized nations for the welfare and security of the sick and aged. It is likewise a long step from the time when victims of Roman justice were writhing upon the cross to the modern view of criminologists that the criminal is spiritually and mentally sick and must be treated with sympathy and understanding.

It was a slow process of development for the masses of mankind. The success was first manifest in the great reformations that began in the sixteenth century, when a great desire to receive and understand more of the gospel moved such individuals as Martin

Luther, John Calvin, and John Knox to rebel against restrictions on the gospel. While immorality has continued in many quarters during all the Christian ages, the exponents of righteousness have become more and more numerous. The little leaven has at least leavened a portion of mankind.

During the ages of Christian history, priesthood disappeared from the earth. It could neither function nor be perpetuated in unrighteousness. The best evidence of its absence is the total lack of those gifts which have accompanied priesthood in all ages of the world. Revelation, prophecy, speaking in tongues, healings, and other gifts of the Holy Ghost were not found among men. Without the Holy Ghost to guide men in the reading of scripture, diverse opinions and interpretations sprang up. Following the rebellion of Martin Luther against the Catholic Church, more than four hundred sects sprang up. All of these professed to have the true understanding of the gospel and assumed power and authority to officiate in the ordinances of the Master. The Christian world became a world of confusion.

Nevertheless, beneath this confusion were many fine Christian virtues. Men as a group were conforming more and more to those qualities exemplified by the Master. It was a long period of preparation, but the time came when God had fully prepared the way for his authority to be established again upon the earth and for the Gospel to be taught again in its fullness. The words of John the Revelator were ready to be fulfilled: "I saw another angel fly in the midst of heaven, having the everlasting gospel to preach unto them that dwell on the earth, and to every nation, and kindred, and tongue, and people." (Revelation 14:6.)

4

A Field Ready to Reap

Men's struggle for truth during the long period of the apostasy produced a crumbling of the political corruption, social injustices, and moral degradation that tended to destroy men's souls. It softened the prevailing emphasis on "otherworldness" and brought men to a deeper appreciation of the life here and now. As a result of this, there was an increase of intellectual freedom and enjoyment of this life. And as a result of this struggle for religious freedom, false practices and doctrines were, to a degree, corrected, the shackles of superstition and the church's worldly power were checked, and an opportunity to think freely and independently was afforded.

In this new world—where men did not crowd one another; where they were closer to nature, with time to meditate; where there were no corrupt prelates or jealous princes to issue unholy decrees—a new sense of the worth of the individual found root.

Joseph Smith was to write later: "The Constitution of the United States is a glorious standard; it is founded in the wisdom of God. It is a heavenly banner; it is to all those who are privileged with the sweets of liberty, like the cooling shades and refreshing waters of a great rock in a thirsty and weary land. It is like a great tree under whose branches man from every clime can be shielded from the burning rays of the sun."[1]

Where in Europe, or for that matter, where in the wide world, could six young men sit down together and organize a church without fear of hindrance by government and independent of political or governmental support and powers, and immediately receive legal sanction for it?

A kind providence had prepared a soil for new thinking. As Christ declared: "Behold, the field is white already to harvest; therefore, whoso desireth to reap let him thrust in his sickle with his might, and reap while the day lasts, that he may treasure up for his soul everlasting salvation in the kingdom of God." (D&C 11:3.) "Therefore, it is not right that any man should be in bondage one to another. And for this purpose have I established the Constitution of this land, by the hands of wise men whom I raised up unto this very purpose, and redeemed the land by the shedding of blood." (D&C 101:79-80.)

As a youth, Joseph Smith lived on the frontier. The frontier spirit was in the very air he breathed. It was a mighty force that was to transform the boy into a man and sweep him with it a thousand miles to the West, to immortal fame as a great American.

The physical frontier of America is gone—but the story of the frontier is a great epic that will never die. Entwined with that constantly shifting physical frontier has gone the religious frontier of America, so interlaced that a study of the one is impossible without the other. The boy Joseph was destined to play an important role in both and to wield an influence on the frontiers of America that has been felt and will yet be felt for many generations. From the first hardy English Pilgrims facing starvation on a bleak New England coast, even to the present day, the mass of immigrants pouring into America have been the discontented people of the earth. This discontent has arisen out of the economic, political, social, or religious conditions of the Old World.

The New World offered a new freedom—not because men and women transplanted to a new world suddenly became different and more tolerant, but because the American continent offered room to move away from one's neighbors when conflicts of opinion became oppressive. Thus, new ideas survived in American soil.

The story of the American frontier is a story of adventurous people; people seeking a change, fostering new and radical plans, throwing old ideas overboard. In the matter of religion, the frontier played a vital part. In the Old World of settled ideas, the religious liberal either recanted or was killed; in America, when the pressure became too great he moved. Because the West was practically virgin land, the movement was always in the one direction. The vast empty West encouraged the liberal thinker. It offered him safety and exile, if need be. Only if he refused its invitation was he martyred for his beliefs. So the story of the frontier is a story of new religious ideas—vital, challenging ideas, which often declared war on all existing creeds.

In Canada, the Huguenot immigrant, driven from France, defied the power of Catholicism and took refuge with his liberal ideas away from the arm of the law.

In New England, Roger Williams saved his radical religious views, and incidentally his life, by fleeing from Massachusetts and founding the colony of Rhode Island.

The Reverend Thomas Hooker, having incurred the wrath of the Boston Puritans, pushed southwest with his followers and the first "covered wagons" in America and founded the colony of Connecticut.

Always the liberal aroused persecution by his war on existing creeds and institutions—and always his safety lay in the west. The frontier was a constantly shifting fringe of civilization: poor in the comforts of home and rich in independence of thought.

No religious system was free of men and women too radical for it. The history of religion in America in the first half of the nineteenth century shows a constant spirit of rebellion from old creeds, resulting in the splitting of many churches and the establishment of some thirty new ones.

Eleven years before Joseph Smith went into the grove to pray, Alexander Campbell, having come to the conclusion that primitive Christianity was lost, "broke with mighty struggles the bonds of all creeds and made war upon them, whether they were true or false, with all the vigor of his giant mind."[2] His followers, known as "Disciples" or "Campbellites," although later regarded as Baptists, were independent thinkers of the frontier. From them Joseph Smith was to receive later a multitude of converts.

The early part of the nineteenth century witnessed a great revival in religious interests in America. In the first thirty years of the century most religious denominations doubled their membership, while the number of converts to new religions increased rapidly.

A Few of the Religious Pioneers

Among those people along the religious frontier of America, the Smith family played a prominent part. Joseph's grandfather had been discontented with existing creeds and forms of religious worship. This dissatisfaction with the religions in New England, coupled with a toleration toward all religious beliefs, brought him under suspicion of the orthodox Puritans. When he went so far as to shelter a despised and persecuted Quaker in his home, he so aroused the displeasure of the community of Topsfield, Massachusetts, where he then lived, that he resolved to sell his home and move to a more congenial society to the westward.[3]

The same freedom of religious thought is evident in the life of Asael Smith's son, Joseph Smith, Sr., father of the Prophet. He was vitally interested in religion and a firm believer in dreams, but his dissatisfaction with existing creeds prevented his joining any of them. His wife, Lucy Mack Smith, said of him, "About this time [March, 1811] my husband's mind became much excited upon the subject of religion; yet he would not subscribe to any particular system of faith, but contended for the ancient order, as established by our Lord and Savior Jesus Christ, and his Apostles."[4]

Joseph's mother also illustrates the independence of religious thinking along the frontier. An investigator in many religions, she early showed a discontent with the creeds of her time. None seemed to satisfy. She said of one occasion:

> I heard that a very devout man was to preach the next Sabbath in the Presbyterian church; I therefore went to meeting in the full expectation of hearing that which my soul desired—the Word of Life.
>
> When the minister commenced speaking, I fixed my mind with deep attention upon the spirit and matter of his discourse, but after hearing him through I returned home, convinced that he neither understood nor appreciated the subject upon which he spoke, and I said in my heart that there was not then upon the earth the religion which I sought.[5]

That Joseph Smith, Jr., should be disturbed in his mind in regard to the religions of his time could well be expected. That at the age of fourteen he had joined none of them shows that he early shared the religious independence of thought that characterized his parents. He had indeed been born on the religious frontier of America.

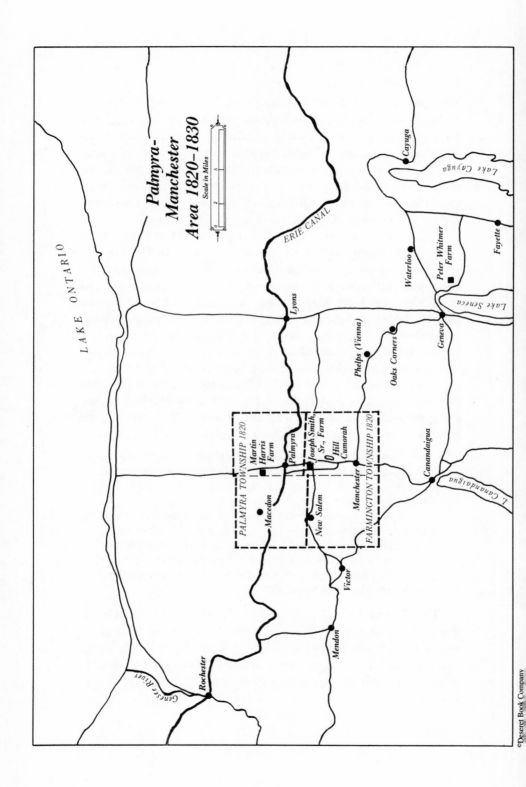

Palmyra-Manchester Area 1820–1830

Scale in Miles

LAKE ONTARIO

ERIE CANAL

Lyons

Cayuga

Lake Cayuga

Waterloo

Peter Whitmer Farm

Fayette

Lake Seneca

Geneva

Phelps (Vienna)

Oaks Corners

PALMYRA TOWNSHIP 1820

Martin Harris Farm

Palmyra

Joseph Smith, Sr., Farm

Hill Cumorah

Macedon

New Salem

Manchester

FARMINGTON TOWNSHIP 1820

Canandaigua

L. Canandaigua

Victor

Mendon

Rochester

Genesee River

© Deseret Book Company

The boy's announcement, "They are all wrong," is typical of the religious frontier. As previously mentioned, Alexander Campbell had openly declared war on all creeds a few years before. But while the usual free thinker often broke with the old church, he seldom had a new system to substitute. Rather, he left the old fold because of the perplexities and uncertainties in his own mind—and those perplexities continued to follow him into new creeds and religious organizations.

Joseph's break with the religions of his day was different. He came from the grove with definite, fixed ideas—ideas that were never changed in his subsequent life. He suddenly had something to offer the world, and those religionists who hated the usual liberals in thought were aroused to more than hatred against a boy who attempted to correct their established views of God.

It might be well at this point to mention other names along the religious frontier with which we will later become familiar. We find them, like the Smiths, dissatisfied with existing religious creeds and all looking and hoping for a religion to meet their need. We must constantly keep the picture of the frontier in mind and realize that the step these people later took into Mormonism was at times a very small one indeed. Before Joseph Smith had been heard of, these people were believing many of the doctrines he was later to advance.

In Mendon, New York, forty miles from Joseph Smith's home, three families were looking for a new religion. These were the Youngs, the Greenes, and the Kimballs. All were dissatisfied with existing creeds. Although some of the Kimballs joined the Baptists, and some of the Youngs and Greenes affiliated with the Reformed Methodists for a short time, the dissatisfaction only became the greater. In the journal of Heber C. Kimball we read:

> From the time I was twelve years old I had many serious thoughts and strong desires to obtain a knowledge of salvation, but not finding anyone who could teach me the things of God, I did not embrace any principles of doctrine, but endeavored to live a moral life. The priests would tell me to believe in the Lord Jesus Christ, but never would tell me what to do to be saved, and thus left me almost in despair.[6]

In Hartford, Connecticut, the Woodruff family was displaying the same unrest. We read in the journal of Wilford Woodruff:

> At an early age my mind began to be exercised upon religious subjects, but I never made a profession of religion until 1830 when I was twenty-three years of age. I did not then join any church for the reason that I could not find a body of people, denomination, or church that had for its doctrine, faith, and practices those principles, ordinances, and gifts which constituted the gospel of Jesus Christ as taught by Him and His apostles. Neither did I find anywhere the manifestations of the Holy Ghost with its attendant gifts and graces.[7]

In Burlington, Otsego County, New York, the Pratts showed a similar inclination. Parley P. Pratt wrote in his autobiography concerning his father:

> He taught us to venerate the Father in Heaven, Jesus Christ, His prophets and Apostles, as well as the Scriptures written by them; while at the same time he belonged to no religious sect, and was careful to preserve his children free from all prejudice . . . into which the so-called Christian world was then unhappily divided.[8]

Parley's dissatisfaction led him west to Kirtland, Ohio, where he joined a branch of the Campbellites under a man named Sidney Rigdon.

The Snow family has a similar history of dissatisfaction with religions of that day. In the *Biography of Lorenzo Snow,* written by his sister Eliza, we read: "In their religious faith our parents were by profession Baptists, but not of the rigid, iron-bedstead order; their house was a resort for the good and intelligent of all denominations." Concerning her brother Lorenzo, she writes: "Although religiously trained from infancy, up to this time [1830] my brother had devoted little or no attention to the subject of religion, at least not sufficiently to decide in preference of any particular sect."[9]

In Toronto, Ontario, Canada, John Taylor (who would later become the third president of the restored church) had become so dissatisfied with the Methodist Church, of which he was a minister, that, together with some of his congregation, he was expelled from office and condemned for his views. He and his followers firmly believed that the various religious sects of their day were wrong. They believed that men should be called of God as in former days and ordained by men having authority. They believed that the Church should have apostles, prophets, and teachers as in the primitive Church; that the gifts of the Holy Ghost should be manifest; that in the true Church of Christ there should be the gifts of healing, miracles, prophecy, faith, discerning of spirits, etc., as in the days of the early Christian Church.[10]

This condition was typical of the entire frontier. Great numbers had either broken away from existing denominations or were retaining their membership only in despair of finding something better, when the announcements by Joseph Smith began to spread from settlement to settlement.

Practically all who were later to become prominent in the organization established through Joseph Smith had previously broken with old faiths. Not a few of them were preaching from the pulpit many of the beliefs that Joseph was later to advance. These independent religious thinkers included four men who were to follow Joseph Smith successively as president of the Church, as well as nearly all those who were chosen as the first Quorum of Twelve Apostles.

Thus the field was ripe for the harvest. Joseph Smith, despite all the antagonism of the older churches, was to find a fertile soil in which the gospel of Jesus Christ would be planted. Men and women were eager for the doctrine he was to advance. All this had not come about in a day; it was a gradual growth in religious thinking that had its roots in the Old World and had flourished and blossomed in the free air of the American frontier. It was as if the mighty Director of human events had for centuries been preparing the stage for the principal actor to enter.

The Effect of the First Vision

We must not get the impression that the first vision of Joseph Smith in the grove near Palmyra had at that time any vital effect along the religious frontier. On the contrary, aside from the Smith family and the small community surrounding them, the incident was to remain relatively unknown for many years. Newspaper reporters did not flock to the village, nor was the experience heralded in the headlines of even the local papers. Distorted accounts, growing out of secondhand information and written in a jocular vein, did find their way into several eastern newspapers, but they created no particular stir. This was largely due to the fact that claims to visions, revelations, and dreams were common at that time. In the distorted fashion in which Joseph Smith's experience reached the majority of people along the frontier, it sounded very much like the experiences claimed by others.

The local ministers had become irritated by the boy's announcement to them, and to those who believed their words, that they were "all wrong" and that their creeds were an "abomination" in the sight of the Lord. In their irritation they turned from the boy and advised their people against him, so that he became ostracized in the community. This result was not strange. No learned man enjoys being told by a boy that he is "all wrong." Joseph's declaration made him a very lonely young man.

But although Joseph had declared the falseness of existing creeds, he did nothing further. He went about the usual pursuits of a young man of the frontier. He continued to labor on his father's farm, outwardly no different except for a sudden maturity that seemed to sober him.

While it is quite evident from the journals of both Joseph Smith and Lucy Mack Smith that Joseph's mother, father, brothers, and sisters believed in his related experience, it is not evident that the experience changed their lives or the manner of their living during the next few years. It was not, in fact, until seven years after the First Vision that the frontier began to pay attention to the young man in northern New York, and then it was in connection with something very tangible—a book that he was preparing for publication, translated from gold plates and containing in clearness the gospel for which the reformers of the frontier had been waiting. This book, published in 1830, was suddenly to elevate Joseph Smith to mighty leadership on the religious frontier of America. But in the meantime he had enjoyed other visions and visitations quite as vital as that in the grove near Palmyra.

5

Moroni's Mission to Joseph

Following his first vision, Joseph Smith reports, he "continued to pursue [his] common vocations in life" until September 21, 1823—"all the time suffering severe persecution at the hands of all classes of men, both religious and irreligious, because I continued to affirm that I had seen a vision." In his history as recorded in the Pearl of Great Price, he writes:

> During the space of time which intervened between the time I had the vision and the year eighteen hundred and twenty-three—having been forbidden to join any of the religious sects of the day, and being of very tender years, and persecuted by those who ought to have been my friends and to have treated me kindly, and if they supposed me to be deluded to have endeavored in a proper and affectionate manner to have reclaimed me—I was left to all kinds of temptations; and, mingling with all kinds of society, I frequently fell into many foolish errors, and displayed the weakness of youth, and the foibles of human nature; which, I am sorry to say, led me into divers temptations, offensive in the sight of God. In making this confession, no one need suppose me guilty of any great or malignant sins. A disposition to commit such was never in my nature. But I was guilty of levity, and sometimes associated with jovial company, etc., not consistent with that character which ought to be maintained by one who was called of God as I had been. But this will not seem very strange to any one who recollects my youth, and is acquainted with my native cheery temperament.
>
> In consequence of these things, I often felt condemned for my weakness and imperfections; when, on the evening of the above-mentioned twenty-first of September, after I had retired to my bed for the night, I betook myself to prayer and supplication to Almighty God for forgiveness of all my sins and follies, and also for a manifestation to me, that I might know of my state and standing before him; for I had full confidence in obtaining a divine manifestation, as I previously had one.
>
> While I was thus in the act of calling upon God, I discovered

a light appearing in my room, which continued to increase until the room was lighter than at noonday, when immediately a personage appeared at my bedside, standing in the air, for his feet did not touch the floor.

He had on a loose robe of most exquisite whiteness. It was a whiteness beyond anything earthly I had ever seen; nor do I believe that any earthly thing could be made to appear so exceedingly white and brilliant. His hands were naked, and his arms also, a little above the wrist; so, also, were his feet naked, as were his legs, a little above the ankles. His head and neck were also bare. I could discover that he had no other clothing on but this robe, as it was open, so that I could see into his bosom.

Not only was his robe exceedingly white, but his whole person was glorious beyond description, and his countenance truly like lightning. The room was exceedingly light, but not so very bright as immediately around his person. When I first looked upon him, I was afraid; but the fear soon left me.

He called me by name, and said unto me that he was a messenger sent from the presence of God to me, and that his name was Moroni; that God had a work for me to do; and that my name should be had for good and evil among all nations, kindreds, and tongues, or that it should be both good and evil spoken of among all people.

He said there was a book deposited, written upon gold plates, giving an account of the former inhabitants of this continent, and the source from whence they sprang. He also said that the fulness of the everlasting Gospel was contained in it, as delivered by the Savior to the ancient inhabitants;

Also, that there were two stones in silver bows—and these stones, fastened to a breastplate, constituted what is called the Urim and Thummim—deposited with the plates; and the possession and use of these stones were what constituted "seers" in ancient or former times; and that God had prepared them for the purpose of translating the book.

After telling me these things, he commenced quoting the prophecies of the Old Testament. He first quoted part of the third chapter of Malachi; and he quoted also the fourth or last chapter of the same prophecy, though with a little variation from the way it reads in our Bibles. Instead of quoting the first verse as it reads in our books, he quoted it thus:

For behold, the day cometh that shall burn as an oven, and

*all the proud, yea, and all that do wickedly shall burn as stubble;
for they that come shall burn them, saith the Lord of Hosts, that it
shall leave them neither root nor branch.*

And again, he quoted the fifth verse thus: *Behold, I will reveal unto you the Priesthood, by the hand of Elijah the prophet,
before the coming of the great and dreadful day of the Lord.*

He also quoted the next verse differently: *And he shall plant
in the hearts of the children the promises made to the fathers, and
the hearts of the children shall turn to their fathers. If it were not
so, the whole earth would be utterly wasted at his coming.*

In addition to these, he quoted the eleventh chapter of
Isaiah, saying that it was about to be fulfilled. He quoted also the
third chapter of Acts, twenty-second and twenty-third verses,
precisely as they stand in our New Testament. He said that that
prophet was Christ; but the day had not yet come when "they who
would not hear his voice should be cut off from among the
people," but soon would come.

He also quoted the second chapter of Joel, from the twenty-
eighth verse to the last. He also said that this was not yet fulfilled,
but was soon to be. And he further stated that the fulness of the
Gentiles was soon to come in. He quoted many other passages of
scripture, and offered many explanations which cannot be mentioned here.

Again, he told me, that when I got those plates of which he
had spoken—for the time that they should be obtained was not
yet fulfilled—I should not show them to any person; neither the
breastplate with the Urim and Thummim; only to those to whom
I should be commanded to show them; if I did I should be destroyed. While he was conversing with me about the plates, the
vision was opened to my mind that I could see the place where the
plates were deposited, and that so clearly and distinctly that I
knew the place again when I visited it.

After this communication, I saw the light in the room begin
to gather immediately around the person of him who had been
speaking to me, and it continued to do so until the room was
again left dark, except just around him; when, instantly I saw, as
it were, a conduit open right up into heaven, and he ascended till
he entirely disappeared, and the room was left as it had been
before this heavenly light had made its appearance.

I lay musing on the singularity of the scene, and marvel-
ing greatly at what had been told to me by this extraordinary

messenger; when, in the midst of my meditation, I suddenly discovered that my room was again beginning to get lighted, and in an instant, as it were, the same heavenly messenger was again by my bedside.

He commenced, and again related the very same things which he had done at his first visit, without the least variation; which having done, he informed me of great judgments which were coming upon the earth, with great desolations by famine, sword, and pestilence; and that these grievous judgments would come on the earth in this generation. Having related these things, he again ascended as he had done before.

By this time, so deep were the impressions made on my mind, that sleep had fled from my eyes, and I lay overwhelmed in astonishment at what I had both seen and heard. But what was my surprise when again I beheld the same messenger at my bedside, and heard him rehearse or repeat over again to me the same things as before; and added a caution to me, telling me that Satan would try to tempt me (in consequence of the indigent circumstances of my father's family), to get the plates for the purpose of getting rich. This he forbade me, saying that I must have no other object in view in getting the plates but to glorify God, and must not be influenced by any other motive than that of building his kingdom; otherwise I could not get them.

After this third visit, he again ascended into heaven as before, and I was again left to ponder on the strangeness of what I had just experienced; when almost immediately after the heavenly messenger had ascended from me for the third time, the cock crowed, and I found that day was approaching, so that our interviews must have occupied the whole of that night.

I shortly after arose from my bed, and, as usual, went to the necessary labors of the day; but, in attempting to work as at other times, I found my strength so exhausted as to render me entirely unable. My father, who was laboring along with me, discovered something to be wrong with me, and told me to go home. I started with the intention of going to the house; but, in attempting to cross the fence out of the field where we were, my strength entirely failed me, and I fell helpless on the ground, and for a time was quite unconscious of anything.

The first thing that I can recollect was a voice speaking unto me, calling me by name. I looked up, and beheld the same messenger standing over my head, surrounded by light as before. He then again related unto me all that he had related to me the previous night, and commanded me to go to my father and tell him of the vision and commandments which I had received.

I obeyed; I returned to my father in the field, and rehearsed the whole matter to him. He replied to me that it was of God, and told me to go and do as commanded by the messenger. I left the field, and went to the place where the messenger had told me the plates were deposited; and owing to the distinctness of the vision which I had had concerning it, I knew the place the instant that I arrived there.[1]

The Hill Cumorah

If one travels today on New York State Highway 21 from Palmyra south toward Manchester, he will pass directly by the most impressive monument in the northern part of that state. If the journey be made at night, the sight is doubly impressive, for then one sees from a distance a veritable pillar of light ascending from the open plain. On closer approach the phenomenon becomes an illuminated monument on the very apex of a hill that rises approximately 150 feet above the surrounding country. Surmounting the huge granite shaft is a representation of the Angel Moroni. The hill lies to the east of the highway, its north end rising abruptly from the surrounding plain, and slopes gradually to the level terrain on the south. This is the hill Cumorah, known locally as "Mormon Hill."[2]

When Joseph Smith ascended this hill, somewhat excited and stirred by his expectations, he little dreamed of the multitudes who would one day follow in his path, or of the tremendous consequences of his visit. The hill then lay as it had lain for centuries, untouched by human gardeners—its very name buried within it, its great secrets locked from the minds of men. Through faith and prayer a young man had received a key to hidden centuries. A voice from the dust would soon stir the religious frontier of America and eventually the whole world.

Ascending the hill on its western side, Joseph walked directly to the spot near the top that he had seen in his vision. Even with the ground surrounding it was the rounded upper surface of a large stone, its outer edges covered with soil and grass. Joseph removed

The Hill Cumorah, near Palmyra, New York

these and then, using a pole as a lever, raised the stone, which he found had a flat undersurface. Beneath the stone, which outwardly appeared much like other stones strewn over the hillside, was a box or container. Joseph writes of this experience:

> I looked in, and there indeed did I behold the plates, the Urim and Thummim, and the breastplate, as stated by the messenger. The box in which they lay was formed by laying stones together in some kind of cement. In the bottom of the box were laid two stones crosswise of the box, and on these stones lay the plates and the other things with them.[3]

When the young man, eager to handle the treasure, reached into the cavity to remove the contents, a shock like that produced by electricity rendered his arm powerless. Three times he reached out, and each time he received a shock, each one greater than the previous one. Joseph cried aloud in his anguish, "Why cannot I obtain this book?" A voice by his side replied, "Because you have not kept the commandments of the Lord."[4]

As Moroni stood by him, his presence reminded Joseph of the injunction of the night before: "Have no other object in view in getting the plates but to glorify God." In that journey to the hillside, wild dreams of wealth, ease, and fame had flashed through the young man's mind. A desire for a share of what wealth could offer momentarily overpowered him—it all lay within reach—but he was powerless to touch it. Now he knelt, humbled and repentant, before the heavenly instructor. In his humility and sincere repentance, the power of his soul again awakened. "The heavens were opened and the glory of the Lord shone round about, and rested upon him." Then the angel said, "Look!" and Joseph beheld "the 'Prince of Darkness,' surrounded by his innumerable train of associates." The heavenly messenger told him:

> All this is shown, the good and the evil, the holy and impure, the glory of God and the power of darkness, that you may know hereafter the two powers and never be influenced or overcome by that wicked one. Behold, whatever entices and leads to good and to do good, is of God, but whatever does not is of that wicked one: It is he that fills the hearts of men with evil, to walk in darkness and blaspheme God; and you may learn from henceforth, that his ways are to destruction, but the way of holiness is peace and rest. You now see why you could not obtain this record; that the commandment was strict, and that if ever these sacred things are obtained they must be [obtained] by prayer and faithfulness in obeying the Lord. They are not deposited here for the sake of accumulating gain and wealth for the glory of this world: they were sealed by the prayer of faith, and because of the knowledge which they contain they are of no worth among the children of men, only for their knowledge. On them is contained the fullness of the gospel of Jesus Christ, as it was given to his people on this land, and when it shall be brought forth by the power of God it shall be carried to the Gentiles, of whom many will receive it, and after will the seed of Israel be brought into the fold of their Redeemer by obeying it also.
>
> Those who kept the commandments of the Lord on this land, desired this at his hand, and through the prayer of faith obtained the promise, that if their descendants should transgress and fall away, that a record might be kept and in the last days come to their children. These things are sacred, and must be kept so, for the promise of the Lord concerning them, must be fulfilled. No man can obtain them if his heart is impure, because they contain that which is sacred; and besides, should they be intrusted in unholy hands the knowledge could not come to the world, because they cannot be interpreted by the learning of this generation; con-

sequently, they would be considered of no worth, only as precious metal. Therefore, remember, that they are to be translated by the gift and power of God. By them will the Lord work a great and marvelous work: the wisdom of the wise shall become as naught, and the understanding of the prudent shall be hid, and because the power of God shall be displayed those who profess to know the truth but walk in deceit, shall tremble with anger; but with signs and with wonders, with gifts and with healings, with the manifestations of the power of God, and with the Holy Ghost, shall the hearts of the faithful be comforted. You have now beheld the power of God manifested and the power of satan: you see that there is nothing that is desirable in the works of darkness; that they cannot bring happiness; that those who are overcome therewith are miserable, while on the other hand the righteous are blessed with a place in the kingdom of God where joy unspeakable surrounds them. . . .

I give unto you another sign, and when it comes to pass then know that the Lord is God and that he will fulfill his purposes, and that the knowledge which this record contains will go to every nation, and kindred, and tongue, and people under the whole heaven. This is the sign: When these things begin to be known, that is, when it is known that the Lord has shown you these things, the workers of iniquity will seek your overthrow: they will circulate falsehoods to destroy your reputation, and also will seek to take your life: but remember this, if you are faithful, and shall hereafter continue to keep the commandments of the Lord, you shall be preserved to bring these things forth; for in due time he will again give you a commandment to come and take them. . . . Your name shall be known among the nations, for the work which the Lord will perform by your hands shall cause the righteous to rejoice and the wicked to rage: with one it shall be had in honor, and with the other in reproach; yet, with these it shall be a terror because of the great and marvelous work which shall follow the coming forth of this fulness of the gospel.[5]

One must be prepared in order to do the work of God. Mere willingness is not enough. The angel made this perfectly clear to the young man. Additional years must be spent in preparation, years of hard study, of living the commandments of God, of receiving instruction from the glorious personage before him who would meet him annually at this same spot.

"Accordingly, as I had been commanded," Joseph wrote, "I went at the end of each year, and at each time I found the same messenger there, and received instruction and intelligence from him at each of our interviews, respecting what the Lord was going to do, and how and in what manner his kingdom was to be conducted in the last days."[6]

The four years during which Joseph waited for the privilege of taking possession of the plates was indeed a period of preparation—preparation such as few or any prophets before ever had. It was a period of instruction at the hands of an angel sent by Jesus Christ for that purpose. But it was also a time for some other events. Joseph had to accept employment to assist his family, who had been deeply grieved and impoverished by the death of Joseph's older brother, Alvin. It was during these years of employment that he met and married Emma Hale. Joseph continues:

> At length the time arrived for obtaining the plates, the Urim and Thummim, and the breastplate. On the twenty-second day of September, one thousand eight hundred and twenty-seven, having gone as usual at the end of another year to the place where they were deposited, the same heavenly messenger delivered them up to me with this charge: that I should be responsible for them; that if I should let them go carelessly, or through any neglect of mine, I should be cut off; but that if I would use all my endeavors to preserve them, until he, the messenger, should call for them, they should be protected.
>
> I soon found out the reason why I had received such strict charges to keep them safe, and why it was that the messenger had said that when I had done what was required at my hand, he would call for them. For no sooner was it known that I had them, than the most strenuous exertions were used to get them from me. Every stratagem that could be invented was resorted to for that purpose. The persecution became more bitter and severe than before, and multitudes were on the alert continually to get them from me if possible. But by the wisdom of God, they remained safe in my hands, until I had accomplished by them what was required at my hand. When, according to arrangements, the messenger called for them, I delivered them up to him; and he has them in his charge until this day, being the second day of May, one thousand eight hundred and thirty-eight.[7]

6

The Book of Mormon Comes Forth

The manner in which the restoration of the Church of Jesus Christ came about reveals God's delegation of authority and power, his foresight, and his concern for his children. In answering Joseph Smith's humble prayer, God revealed the delegation of power over this earth that had been given to the Son. Joseph's vision established the reality of the Father and the Son as living individuals in whose form man had been created; it established the truth of the resurrection; it proclaimed that there was a work for Joseph to do. This event was to be followed by other events that were equally astounding, for Christ sent one of his resurrected servants after another to assist in the restoration. The astonishing appearance of Moroni, a prophet who had lived upon the western continent some four hundred years after the resurrection of Christ, was to be followed by others, including John the Baptist, Peter, James, and John, who had lived and served Jesus when he was upon the earth in the flesh. The world had seemingly forgotten the reality of the resurrection and the nature of resurrected beings; how the resurrected Christ walked and talked and ate with his apostles; how he had invited them to touch his body and to observe for themselves, for, he said, "a spirit hath not flesh and bones, as ye see me have." (Luke 24:39.)

The recorded testimony of Matthew, that when Christ arose from the dead many others also arose and appeared unto many (Matthew 27:52-53), had been forgotten. In a great letter to the saints of his day, the apostle Peter declared: "Moreover I will endeavor that ye may be able after my decease to have these things always in remembrance. For we have not followed cunningly devised fables, when we made known unto you the power and coming of our Lord Jesus Christ, but were eyewitnesses of his majesty." (2 Peter 1:15-16.)

After the apostles had died, philosophers scoffed and most

44

Christians began to look upon the resurrection as an imagination of the mind. It is little wonder, then, that the account of the restoration in modern times was met with disbelief. But the history of The Church of Jesus Christ of Latter-day Saints cannot be understood apart from the reality of resurrected beings and their part in the restoration of the gospel. The important part the resurrected Moroni played in the restoration of sacred records we have seen.

From the time of Adam, records have been kept of God's revelations to man. We read: "A book of remembrance was kept, in the which was recorded, in the language of Adam, for it was given unto as many as called upon God to write by the spirit of inspiration." (Moses 6:5.) The children of Israel kept scriptures containing the words of Jehovah to them, but many of the plain and precious things were lost. Jesus frequently rebuked the Pharisees: "Ye do err, not knowing the scriptures." (Matthew 22:29.) He also admonished the scribes: "Search the scriptures; for in them ye think ye have eternal life: and they are they which testify of me." (John 5:39.)

With the recorded word of God available, it is not necessary that each man seek direct revelation from God in such matters as have already been made plain. As Christ later explained to Joseph Smith: "To some it is given by the Holy Ghost to know that Jesus Christ is the Son of God, and that he was crucified for the sins of the world. To others it is given to believe on their words, that they also might have eternal life if they continue faithful." (D&C 46:13-14.)

To the Latter-day Saints, Joseph Smith advised:

> Search the Scriptures—search the revelations which we publish, and ask your Heavenly Father, in the name of His Son Jesus Christ, to manifest the truth unto you, and if you do it with an eye single to His glory, nothing doubting, He will answer you by the power of His Holy Spirit. You will then know for yourselves and not for another. You will not then be dependent on man for the knowledge of God; nor will there be any room for speculation. . . . You stand then in these last days, as all have stood before you, agents unto yourselves, to be judged according to your works.[1]
>
> We never inquire at the hand of God for special revelation only in case of there being no previous revelation to suit the case;

and that in a council of High Priests. . . . It is a great thing to inquire at the hands of God, or to come into His presence; and we
feel fearful to approach Him on subjects that are of little or no
consequence, to satisfy the queries of individuals, especially
about things the knowledge of which men ought to obtain in all
sincerity, before God, for themselves, in humility by the prayer
of faith; and more especially a Teacher or a High Priest in the
Church.[2]

In keeping with this principle, the first major step taken by the
Lord was to restore to earth lost scriptures that, with the Holy
Bible, would bring mankind to a fullness of the gospel.

With the plates of the Book of Mormon now in Joseph Smith's
hand, Jesus, the Son of God, now instructed him:

And you have a gift to translate the plates; and this is the first
gift that I bestowed upon you; and I have commanded that you
should pretend to no other gift until my purpose is fulfilled in this;
for I will grant unto you no other gift until it is finished. . . .

For hereafter you shall be ordained and go forth and deliver
my words unto the children of men.

Behold, if they will not believe my words, they would not
believe you, my servant Joseph, if it were possible that you
should show them all these things which I have committed unto
you. (D&C 5:4, 6-7.)

This generation shall have my word through you;

And in addition to your testimony, the testimony of three of
my servants, whom I shall call and ordain, unto whom I will
show these things, and they shall go forth with my words that are
given through you. (D&C 5:10-11.)

The truth regarding the existence of the Book of Mormon
plates was not to be left solely to the testimony of those who actually saw and felt them, but, as Christ promised, "whosoever believeth on my words, them will I visit with the manifestation of my
Spirit; and they shall be born of me, even of water and of the
Spirit." (D&C 5:16.)

Joseph Smith said of the ancient record:

These records were engraven on plates which had the appearance of gold, each plate was six inches wide and eight inches

long and not quite so thick as common tin. They were filled with engravings, in Egyptian characters and bound together in a volume, as the leaves of a book with three rings running through the whole. The volume was something near six inches in thickness, a part of which was sealed. The characters on the unsealed part were small, and beautifully engraved. The whole book exhibited many marks of antiquity in its construction, and much skill in the art of engraving. With the records was found a curious instrument which the ancients called "Urim and Thummim," which consisted of two transparent stones set in the rim of a bow fastened to a breastplate. Through the medium of the Urim and Thummim I translated the record by the gift, and power of God.[3]

While we have no other description of the Urim and Thummim, we do have a record of an instrument called Urim and Thummim that was used in the time of Moses while he was leading the children of Israel out of Egypt. This was also used for divine communication. When Moses consecrated his brother Aaron, he placed a "breastplate" on him, and in it he placed the "Urim and Thummim."[4] How this instrument was used by Joseph Smith in translating the record of the Nephites is not fully known. The only description of the breastplate that we now have is taken from an account written by Joseph's mother, who claimed to have been shown it by her son:

> It was wrapped in a thin muslin handkerchief, so thin that I could feel its proportions without any difficulty. It was concave on one side, and convex on the other, and extended from the neck downwards, as far as the center of the stomach of a man of extraordinary size. It had four straps of the same material, for the purpose of fastening it to the breast, two of which ran back to go over the shoulders, and the other two were designed to fasten to the hips. They were just the width of two of my fingers, (for I measured them,) and they had holes in the end of them, to be convenient in fastening. After I had examined it, Joseph placed it in the chest with the Urim and Thummim.[5]

It is not known what part, if any, the breastplate played in the subsequent translation of the ancient records.

The Translation of the Record

The attempts of various persons to get possession of the plates proved unsuccessful, but they did prevent Joseph from beginning immediately the important work of translation.

In December 1827, Joseph received an invitation to the home of his father-in-law, Isaac Hale, in Harmony, Pennsylvania. Desiring a place where he could find the necessary peace and quiet for his work, he accepted the invitation. Joseph was without means to make the journey and commence the translation, but at this time a prosperous farmer of Palmyra proved a friend indeed. Martin Harris had heard and believed the account of Joseph's visions and was especially interested in the "gold book." As Joseph was preparing to depart for Harmony, Martin came to the Smith home and presented fifty dollars as a gift for "the work of the Lord."

When Joseph arrived in Harmony with his wife, he made an agreement to purchase a small house and some farm land belonging to members of the Hale family. It was here that he began to make a real study of the ancient records. Between December 1827 and February of the following year, he made a copy of some of the characters on the plates and translated some of them "by means of the Urim and Thummim."[6]

Sometime in February Martin Harris arrived in Harmony and, securing a transcription of the characters Joseph had made, took them to New York—evidently determined to check on Joseph's story concerning them.

In New York Martin showed two papers to Professor Charles Anthon of Columbia University and a Dr. Mitchell (probably Samuel L. Mitchell, M.D.): a transcript of characters without a translation and a sheet with both characters and translation.[7] According to the story told by Martin Harris, Professsor Anthon gave him a writing certifying that the characters shown to him were genuine and that the translation of the part was fairly accurate. Upon hearing from Martin that the ancient records had been obtained from an angel, the professor asked for the certificate and tore it into shreds. The reason for this is quite obvious. Neither Professor Anthon nor any other man could read the characters. The char-

acters were in a language that, as Moroni informs us in Mormon
9:32, had developed from the Egyptian. Even had they been in
close harmony with ordinary Egyptian hieroglyphics, it is improbable that Professor Anthon could have read them, as that language
was then little known and no single American was as yet skilled in
its reading.[8]

Bearing these facts in mind, we must arrive at the following
conclusions: Professor Anthon knew nothing as to the correctness
of the translation or the genuineness of the characters and was
either scheming to get possession of the plates or was not willing to
confess his ignorance of the ancient language. Hence he fabricated
the certificate. After finding the nature of the origin of the ancient
records and what might happen to his certificate, he was wise
indeed to destroy it before his pretended knowledge made him the
laughingstock of other learned men. If Dr. Mitchell, to whom Martin Harris also showed his copies, agreed as to the genuineness of
the characters, he at least was wise enough to refrain from writing
that which he could not possibly have known.

Suffice it to say that the two learned men were visibly impressed by the characters and the translation. Returning from his
encounters, Martin Harris was ready to devote much time to the
work as well as to borrow money to pay for the publication of the
translation.

This incident fulfilled the following words of the Book of Mormon:

> It shall come to pass that the Lord God shall bring forth
> unto you the words of a book, and they shall be the words of
> them which have slumbered. And behold the book shall be
> sealed. . . .
>
> Wherefore, because of the things which are sealed up, the
> things which are sealed shall not be delivered in the day of the
> wickedness and abominations of the people. Wherefore the book
> shall be kept from them.
>
> But the book shall be delivered unto a man, and he shall de-
> liver the words of the book, which are the words of those who
> have slumbered in the dust, and he shall deliver these words unto
> another; but the words which are sealed he shall not deliver,
> neither shall he deliver the book. . . .

But behold, it shall come to pass that the Lord God shall say unto him to whom he shall deliver the book: Take these words which are not sealed and deliver them to another, that he may show them unto the learned, saying: Read this, I pray thee. And the learned shall say: Bring hither the book, and I will read them.

And now, because of the glory of the world and to get gain will they say this, and not for the glory of God.

And the man shall say: I cannot bring the book, for it is sealed.

Then shall the learned say: I cannot read it.

Wherefore it shall come to pass, that the Lord God will deliver again the book and the words thereof to him that is not learned; and the man that is not learned shall say: I am not learned. Then shall the Lord God say unto him: The learned shall not read them, for they have rejected them, and I am able to do mine own work; wherefore thou shalt read the words which I shall give unto thee. (2 Nephi 27:6-10, 15-20. Compare Isaiah 29:11-12.)

This prophecy was the primary factor that led Joseph Smith to prepare the transcript of characters he gave to Martin Harris, and its fulfillment accordingly had a great effect upon the latter.

Martin Harris as Scribe

Martin Harris went to Harmony about April 12, 1828, to act as scribe for Joseph Smith. Sometime after he began his work as scribe, Martin began to importune Joseph Smith for the privilege of carrying home the writings he had made, in order to convince his wife and skeptical friends of the nature of the work in which he was engaged. Joseph inquired of the Lord and received an answer that he should not do so. A second inquiry produced a like answer. Martin continued his pleading, and Joseph continued his inquiries to the Lord, until he felt that the Lord had acceded to his request.

On June 14, 1828, Martin Harris left Harmony with 116 pages on foolscap of the translation of the ancient plates. It was the last the Prophet saw of it. Martin broke his solemn promise to Joseph to show it to none other than a designated few, with the result that the manuscript was stolen or destroyed.

As a consequence of the incident, Moroni took from Joseph the Urim and Thummim and the ancient records. These were returned only after he had humbled himself before the Lord. And Martin Harris was denied the privilege of further acting as scribe.

The rebuke of the Lord to Joseph Smith at this time contains a message for all mankind: "Although a man may have many revelations, and have power to do many mighty works, yet if he boasts in his own strength, and sets at naught the counsels of God, and follows after the dictates of his own will and carnal desires, he must fall and incur the vengeance of a just God upon him." (D&C 3:4.)

The Lord made clear to Joseph that the work, the designs, and the purposes of God cannot be frustrated. After chastizing Joseph for listening to men rather than to God, he warned him: "Behold, thou art Joseph, and thou wast chosen to do the work of the Lord, but because of transgression, if thou art not aware thou wilt fall. But remember, God is merciful; therefore, repent of that which thou hast done which is contrary to the commandment which I gave you, and thou art still chosen, and art again called to the work; except thou do this, thou shalt be delivered up and become as other men, and have no more gift." (D&C 3:9-11.)

In the revelations that followed, the Lord indicated that he would not let enemies destroy the Nephite record or prevent the establishment of his church.

Joseph did not immediately resume his work of translating. He now had no scribe and, further, he was under the necessity of working on the small farm he had purchased in order to earn a livelihood for his family.

In the midst of these events, deep sorrow came to the Prophet's home. In July 1828 a son was born to Emma; he soon died, and Emma also was very near death's door. Caring for his wife and laboring on his farm prevented further work on the ancient records at that time. As the months passed and Emma began to convalesce, she sometimes took up the work of scribe while her young husband, after a hard day's labor, devoted further hours to the slow task of translation. Often he prayed that circumstances might again allow him to devote full time to his mission.

Oliver Cowdery Enters the Scene

On a Sabbath evening, April 5, 1829, a young schoolteacher named Oliver Cowdery knocked on Joseph Smith's door in Harmony, Pennsylvania. Joseph considered the young man's arrival as an answer to his prayers, and two days later the work of translation continued with Oliver as scribe.

In the autumn of the preceding year Oliver had filled a teaching appointment in the township of Manchester, New York. He heard of the young prophet, his visions, and his alleged receipt of sacred records. The accounts took serious hold of his mind. Were they true? He took his problem to the Lord and came from his prayer with a firm conviction that Joseph Smith was engaged in the work of God. So firm was that conviction that he obtained a release from all his teaching labors, journeyed to the Smith home, and volunteered his time and service. There was no hope of monetary reward, for the job paid no salary and there would be no royalties. In fact, the task would bring ridicule and hatred upon him.

But there are rewards greater than gold or silver, and one of these is an association with a prophet of God. Oliver later wrote of this period: "These were days never to be forgotten—to sit under the sound of a voice dictated by the *inspiration* of heaven, awakened the utmost gratitude of this bosom! Day after day I continued, uninterrupted, to write from his mouth, as he translated, with the *Urim and Thummim,* or, as the Nephites would have said, 'Interpreters,' the history, or record, called 'The Book of Mormon.'"[9]

The work of translation went forward rapidly, but opposition in Harmony gradually increased, and only the determined stand of Isaac Hale that law and order should prevail prevented open mob violence. Oliver had been writing for some time to his friend David Whitmer, acquainting him with the work of the Prophet. Of this period Joseph Smith writes:

> Shortly after commencing to translate, I became acquainted with Mr. Peter Whitmer, of Fayette, Seneca County, New York, and also with some of his family. In the beginning of the month of June, his son, David Whitmer, came to the place where we were residing, and brought with him a two-horse wagon, for the

purpose of having us accompany him to his father's place, and there remain until we should finish the work. It was arranged that we should have our board free of charge, and the assistance of one of his brothers to write for me, and also his own assistance when convenient. Having much need of such timely aid in an undertaking so arduous, and being informed that the people in the neighborhood of the Whitmers were anxiously awaiting the opportunity to inquire into these things, we accepted the invitation, and accompanied Mr. Whitmer to his father's house, and there resided until the translation was finished and the copyright secured. Upon our arrival, we found Mr. Whitmer's family very anxious concerning the work, and very friendly toward ourselves. They continued so, boarded and lodged us according to arrangements; and John Whitmer, in particular, assisted us very much in writing during the remainder of the work.[10]

The work was rapidly completed, with David Whitmer and Emma Smith at times relieving Oliver Cowdery in his task as scribe. The great task was brought to a close some time in July or August, 1829.

Having learned the folly of trusting to a single manuscript, Joseph instructed Oliver to make a copy of the entire translation, which he did. It was this copy from which the Book of Mormon was finally published.[11]

The Method of Translation

As previously mentioned, the ancient records were written in a language entirely unknown in modern times. Had Joseph Smith been schooled by the greatest tutors of his time, had he been the peer of all the modern readers of ancient languages, the records before him would have remained a blank page so far as his own human ability to decipher them was concerned. Had all the learned linguists of the world been called into conference and the ancient records of the Nephites placed before them, they would have been unable to read one single sentence.[12]

How, then, was the translation effected? The Prophet was emphatic in his claim to divine aid, which was received by means of an instrument that he called Urim and Thummim. The exact method by which the strange device was used is not known. Joseph Smith has left us little or no information in regard to it. Aids to the senses are common in our own day. The telephone and the radio are mechanical aids to the human ear. The microscope, sensitized films, and television instruments are aids to the human eye. The Urim and Thummim seems to have been an instrument designed to aid the senses and enable prophets to communicate readily with divine powers. This device has been used in both ancient and modern times. The Prophets of Israel possessed a Urim and Thummim by which the will of the Lord could be obtained.[13] The particular one used by Joseph Smith was found deposited with the plates. According to the translated record, it was first given by the Lord to an ancient prophet called in the account "the brother of Jared." In Ether 3:23-24 we read: "And behold, these two stones will I give unto thee, and ye shall seal them up also with the things which ye shall write. For behold, the language which ye shall write I have confounded; wherefore I will cause in my own due time that these stones shall magnify to the eyes of men these things which ye shall write."

It is quite evident that the translation of the record, even with the use of the mechanical device, was not a simple accomplishment. At times, when Joseph's mind was in a turmoil over family disagreements or other matters, he was unable to translate at all. Faith in God and purity of soul seemed, as in the case of any communication with God, to be the prime requisites.

A key to the problem of translation is found in section 9 of the Doctrine and Covenants. When Oliver Cowdery had asked if he could do some translating, his request was apparently granted, and the Urim and Thummim, together with an ancient writing, was placed in his hands. His attempt, however, was an utter failure. The Lord, through the Prophet Joseph Smith, said to him:

> Behold, you have not understood; you have supposed that I would give it unto you, when you took no thought save it was to ask me.
>
> But, behold, I say unto you, that you must study it out in your mind; then you must ask me if it be right, and if it is right I

will cause that your bosom shall burn within you; therefore, you shall feel that it is right.

But if it be not right you shall have no such feelings, but you shall have a stupor of thought that shall cause you to forget the thing which is wrong; therefore, you cannot write that which is sacred save it be given you from me. (D&C 9:7-9.)

Thus the Lord set forth the method of translation that certainly applied to Joseph Smith or any other translator, including Oliver Cowdery. The Prophet, from his study of the characters that were "magnified" before him, "thought it out in his mind"; and when he had the assurance that the thought was right, he spoke the thought in his own words and language to the scribe, from whom he was separated during the process of translation by a curtain. The translation was thus subject to the imperfections of language and grammar that characterized the early writings of the Prophet, and to the mistakes in spelling to which the scribe was addicted.[14]

There is no doubt that, as the Prophet progressed with translation, he became familiar with the ancient manner of writing and with the interpretation of the symbols so that he need not always resort to the Urim and Thummim, but could immediately state the meaning previously found for the same characters. As in ancient languages, a single character might have many shades of meaning according to the particular use; some of the beauty of the original might therefore have been lost in the translation. Further, as all who have made translations know, there are often no equivalents in the translated language for the expression or shade of meaning in the original. These are regrettable and unavoidable factors in translation.

It is also evident that the Prophet had his Bible by his side during the translation. Where he found the ancient writers quoting from the Hebrew scriptures, a copy of which they possessed (see 1 Nephi 5:10-16), he undoubtedly called the King James Version of the Bible to his aid in fashioning the thoughts into the English tongue. Such a use of the Bible was recognition of his own lack of literary ability and of the beauty of expression in that early English translation. He did not hesitate, however, to correct the English

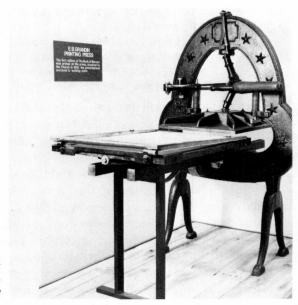

E. B. Grandin
printing press
on which Book
of Mormon was
printed

translation when the meaning failed to agree in any vital way with
his interpretation of the quotations on the plates before him.

The exact amount of time occupied in the translating will
perhaps never be known. The Prophet spent many, many hours
with the records when scribes were not present. In the first two
months of intensive study, December 1827 to February 1828, very
little was set forth in the English tongue, indicating something of
the tremendous work involved. If the work of translation appears
to be rapid later, when Oliver Cowdery was the scribe, it must be
remembered that the foundations for the final work were laid by
many months of previous labor.

The Publication of the Book of Mormon

The Prophet's difficulties did not end when the translation was
complete and the sacred record had been returned once more to the
keeping of the Angel Moroni. The publication of the book presented many problems. Joseph Smith was without funds for its

publication, and so great was the feeling against the unseen volume that publishers hesitated to undertake the task.

Martin Harris, the one-time scribe of the Prophet, now came to the rescue. Borrowing money on his farm, he induced Egbert B. Grandin, a printer in Palmyra, to print five thousand copies of the Book of Mormon at a price of three thousand dollars. The contract was signed on August 25, 1829.

Extreme caution was taken by the Prophet to protect the publication. He kept the original manuscript, and only the copy made by Oliver Cowdery was entrusted, a few pages at a time, to the printer. Oliver, in going to and from the printing establishment with a portion of the translation, was always accompanied by a guard. The house where the manuscript was kept was also under guard day and night.

Notwithstanding these precautions, a garbled account of the Book of Mormon story very nearly reached publication before the Book of Mormon itself. One Squire Cole was found to have access to Grandin's printing office for the publication of a weekly periodical called *Dogberry Paper on Winter Hill*. Hyrum Smith and Oliver Cowdery discovered that Cole was about to publish mutilated extracts of the Book of Mormon obtained from the printer's copy. Only the threat of suit for the infringement of the copyright law caused him to desist.

The first copies of the Book of Mormon issued from the press March 18 through 25, 1830.

7

Authority Is Restored

During the translation of the plates, Joseph Smith and Oliver Cowdery encountered some problems that were solved by Joseph inquiring of the Lord through use of the Urim and Thummim. The answers were recorded by Joseph, but there are too many to be all cited in this brief history. Several passages on baptism found on the records, especially the following, led to further inquiry of the Lord:

> And again the Lord called others, and said unto them likewise; and he gave unto them power to baptize. And he said unto them: On this wise shall ye baptize; and there shall be no disputations among you.
>
> Verily I say unto you, that whoso repenteth of his sins through your words, and desireth to be baptized in my name, on this wise shall ye baptize them—Behold, ye shall go down and stand in the water, and in my name shall ye baptize them.
>
> And now behold, these are the words which ye shall say, calling them by name, saying:
>
> Having authority given me of Jesus Christ, I baptize you in the name of the Father, and of the Son, and of the Holy Ghost. Amen.
>
> And then shall ye immerse them in the water, and come forth again out of the water. (3 Nephi 11:22-26.)

On May 15, 1829, Joseph and Oliver went to a small grove of trees on the bank of the Susquehanna River, near Joseph's residence in Harmony, and sought through prayer further enlightenment of this passage. In the midst of their prayers a bright light overspread them and a messenger of the Lord confronted them. He announced himself as John, the Baptist, who held the keys of baptism in the days of Jesus of Nazareth. After giving them instructions concerning those topics uppermost in their minds, he laid his hand upon their heads and conferred upon them that priesthood and authority which he himself held. His words, as received by Joseph

Smith, are significant: "Upon you my fellow servants, in the name of Messiah I confer the Priesthood of Aaron, which holds the keys of the ministering of angels, and of the gospel of repentance, and of baptism by immersion for the remission of sins; and this shall never be taken again from the earth, until the sons of Levi do offer again an offering unto the Lord in righteousness." (D&C 13.)[1]

Joseph wrote in his journal:

> He [John] said this Aaronic Priesthood had not the power of laying on hands for the gift of the Holy Ghost, but that this should be conferred on us hereafter; and he commanded us to go and be baptized, and gave us directions that I should baptize Oliver Cowdery, and afterwards that he should baptize me. Accordingly we went and were baptized. I baptized him first, and afterwards he baptized me—after which I laid my hands upon his head and ordained him to the Aaronic Priesthood, and afterwards he laid his hands on me and ordained me to the same Priesthood—for so we were commanded.
>
> The messenger who visited us on this occasion, and conferred this Priesthood upon us, said that his name was John, the same that is called John the Baptist in the New Testament, and that he acted under the direction of Peter, James and John, who held the keys of the Priesthood of Melchizedek, which Priesthood, he said, would in due time be conferred on us, and that I should be called the first Elder of the Church and he (Oliver Cowdery) the second. . . .
>
> Immediately on our coming up out of the water after we had been baptized, we experienced great and glorious blessings from our Heavenly Father. No sooner had I baptized Oliver Cowdery, than the Holy Ghost fell upon him, and he stood up and prophesied many things which should shortly come to pass. And again, so soon as I had been baptized by him, I also had the spirit of prophecy, when, standing up, I prophesied concerning the rise of this Church, and many other things connected with the Church, and this generation of the children of men. We were filled with the Holy Ghost, and rejoiced in the God of our salvation.[2]

What joy must have been theirs! The power to act in God's name had been conferred upon them! A power that had been manifest in the days of Christ was again restored! Oliver Cowdery said of this event:

> I shall not attempt to paint to you the feelings of this heart, nor the majestic beauty and glory which surrounded us on this occasion; but you will believe me when I say, that earth, nor men, with the eloquence of time, cannot begin to clothe language in as interesting and sublime a manner as this holy personage. No; nor has this earth power to give the joy, to bestow the peace, or comprehend the wisdom which was contained in each sentence as it was delivered by the power of the Holy Spirit! . . . The assurance that we were in the presence of an angel, the certainty that we heard the voice of Jesus, and the truth unsullied as it flowed from a pure personage, dictated by the will of God, is to me, past description, and I shall ever look upon this expression of the Savior's goodness with wonder and thanksgiving.[3]

The Melchizedek Priesthood Is Restored

Some time later, perhaps in late May or early June 1829 (the exact date is not recorded), Joseph and Oliver again sought knowledge from the Lord in regard to the higher authority that had been promised them. In answer to their petition, another remarkable occurrence took place. Peter, James, and John, the ancient apostles of Jesus, appeared, gave them the gift of the Holy Ghost by the laying on of hands, and conferred upon them the Holy Melchizedek Priesthood. Thus was restored to earth that priesthood so distinctive of The Church of Jesus Christ of Latter-day Saints today.

The effect of the Holy Ghost upon Joseph and Oliver is portrayed in the Prophet's journal: "Our minds being now enlightened, we began to have the scriptures laid open to our understandings, and the true meaning and intention of their more mysterious passages revealed unto us in a manner which we never could attain previously, nor ever before had thought of." (Joseph Smith–History 1:74.)

The spirit of missionary work that they had not previously experienced came upon them. Despite the opposition which was gathering against them and the necessity for secrecy in their work, the Spirit would not be stilled. Joseph says: "After a few days, however, feeling it to be our duty, we commenced to reason out of the Scriptures with our acquaintances and friends, as we happened to meet them."[4]

In a revelation given at Harmony, Pennsylvania, in August 1830, the Lord confirmed the restoration of his authority and the ordination of Joseph and Oliver as apostles:

> The hour cometh that I will drink of the fruit of the vine with you on the earth, and with Moroni, whom I have sent unto you to reveal the Book of Mormon, containing the fulness of my everlasting gospel, to whom I have committed the keys of the record of the stick of Ephraim. . . .
>
> And also with Peter, and James, and John, whom I have sent unto you, by whom I have ordained you and confirmed you to be apostles, and especial witnesses of my name, and bear the keys of your ministry and of the same things which I revealed unto them;
>
> Unto whom I have committed the keys of my kingdom, and a dispensation of the gospel for the last times; . . . in the which I will gather together in one all things, both which are in heaven, and which are on earth. (D&C 27:5, 12-13.)

The close relationship between Jesus Christ and Joseph Smith in the translation of the Book of Mormon is shown by the many revelations given to the Prophet during that work. The following reflects that great concern: "Behold, I am Jesus Christ, the Son of God. I came unto mine own, and mine own received me not. I am the light which shineth in darkness, and the darkness comprehendeth it not. I am he who said—Other sheep have I which are not of this fold—unto my disciples, and many there were that understood me not. And I will show unto this people that I had other sheep, and that they were a branch of the house of Jacob; and I will bring to light their marvelous works, which they did in my name; yea, and I will bring to light my gospel which was ministered unto them." After reemphasizing that the Nephite record would establish the true points of his doctrine, the Lord adds: "And this I do that I may establish my gospel, that there may not be so much contention; yea, Satan doth stir up the hearts of the people to contention concerning the points of my doctrine; and in these things they do err, for they do wrest the scriptures and do not understand them." (D&C 10:57-62.)

The Three Witnesses

Joseph Smith records in his journal, "In the course of the work of translation, we ascertained that three special witnesses were to be provided by the Lord, to whom He would grant that they should see the plates from which this work (the Book of Mormon) should be translated; and that these witnesses should bear record of the same."[5] In June 1829, the Prophet received a revelation addressed to Oliver Cowdery, David Whitmer, and Martin Harris. In it the Lord declared:

> Behold, I say unto you, that you must rely upon my word, which if you do with full purpose of heart, you shall have a view of the plates, and also of the breastplate, the sword of Laban, the Urim and Thummim, which were given to the brother of Jared upon the mount, when he talked with the Lord face to face, and the miraculous directors which were given to Lehi while in the wilderness, on the borders of the Red Sea.
>
> And it is by your faith that you shall obtain a view of them, even by that faith which was had by the prophets of old.
>
> And after that you have obtained faith, and have seen them with your eyes, you shall testify of them, by the power of God; and this you shall do that my servant Joseph Smith, Jun., may not be destroyed, that I may bring about my righteous purposes unto the children of men in this work.
>
> And ye shall testify that you have seen them, even as my servant Joseph Smith, Jun., has seen them; for it is by my power that he has seen them, and it is because he had faith. And he has translated the book, even that part which I have commanded him, and as your Lord and your God liveth it is true. (D&C 17:1-6.)

Joseph Smith writes in his journal that immediately after the completion of the translation, "Martin Harris, David Whitmer, Oliver Cowdery and myself, agreed to retire into the woods, and try to obtain, by fervent and humble prayer, the fulfilment of the promises given in the above revelation—that they should have a view of the plates.

> We accordingly made choice of a piece of woods convenient to Mr. Whitmer's house, to which we retired, and having knelt down, we began to pray in much faith to Almighty God to bestow upon us a realization of these promises.

Martin Harris   *David Whitmer*   *Oliver Cowdery*

According to previous arrangement, I commenced by vocal prayer to our Heavenly Father, and was followed by each of the others in succession. We did not at the first trial, however, obtain any answer or manifestation of divine favor in our behalf. We again observed the same order of prayer, each calling on and praying fervently to God in rotation, but with the same result as before.

Upon this, our second failure, Martin Harris proposed that he should withdraw himself from us, believing, as he expressed himself, that his presence was the cause of our not obtaining what we wished for. He accordingly withdrew from us, and we knelt down again, and had not been many minutes engaged in prayer, when presently we beheld a light above us in the air, of exceeding brightness; and behold, an angel stood before us. In his hands he held the plates which we had been praying for these to have a view of. He turned over the leaves one by one, so that we could see them, and discern the engravings thereon distinctly. He then addressed himself to David Whitmer, and said, "David, blessed is the Lord, and he that keeps His commandments;" when, immediately afterwards, we heard a voice from out of the bright light above us, saying, "These plates have been revealed by the power of God, and they have been translated by the power of God. The translation of them which you have seen is correct, and I command you to bear record of what you now see and hear."

I now left David and Oliver, and went in pursuit of Martin Harris, whom I found at a considerable distance, fervently engaged in prayer. He soon told me, however, that he had not yet prevailed with the Lord, and earnestly requested me to join him in prayer, that he also might realize the same blessings which we had just received. We accordingly joined in prayer, and ultimately obtained our desires, for before we had yet finished, the same vision was opened to our view, at least it was again opened to me, and I once more beheld and heard the same things; whilst at the same moment, Martin Harris cried out, apparently 'in an ecstasy of joy, "'Tis enough; 'tis enough; mine eyes have beheld; mine eyes have beheld;" and jumping up, he shouted, "Hosanna," blessing God, and otherwise rejoiced exceedingly.[6]

In the years of trial and persecution that followed, all three of these men were found outside the Church, with feelings of bitterness toward it or its leaders. But not one of them denied at any time his testimony, although they were afforded ample opportunity and inducement to do so.

The declaration of these three witnesses appears in the opening pages of the Book of Mormon:

> Be it known unto all nations, kindreds, tongues, and people, unto whom this work shall come: That we, through the grace of God the Father, and our Lord Jesus Christ, have seen the plates which contain this record. . . . And we also know that they have been translated by the gift and power of God, for his voice hath declared it unto us. . . . And we also testify that we have seen the engravings which are upon the plates; and they have been shown unto us by the power of God, and not of man. And we declare with words of soberness, that an angel came down from heaven, and he brought and laid before our eyes, that we beheld and saw the plates, and the engravings thereon; . . . wherefore, to be obedient unto the commandments of God, we bear witness of these things."

The Testimony of Eight Witnesses

Remarkable and convincing as is the testimony of the three witnesses as to the divine origin and translation of the Book of Mormon, such evidence is further supported by the testimony of eight additional men. These witnesses were shown the plates in a grove near the Smith residence in Palmyra, New York, two or three days after the experience of the three witnesses at Fayette. They declared:

Be it known unto all nations, kindreds, tongues, and people, unto whom this work shall come: That Joseph Smith, Jun., the translator of this work, has shown unto us the plates of which hath been spoken, which have the appearance of gold; and as many of the leaves as the said Smith has translated, we did handle with our hands; and we also saw the engravings thereon, all of which has the appearance of ancient work, and of curious workmanship. . . . And we give our names unto the world, to witness unto the world that which we have seen. And we lie not, God bearing witness of it.

Of the eight men whose signatures appear after this declaration, five lived and died members of the Church established through Joseph Smith: Christian Whitmer, Peter Whitmer, Joseph Smith, Sr., Hyrum Smith, and Samuel H. Smith. The remaining three—Jacob Whitmer, John Whitmer, and Hyrum Page—left the Church or were excommunicated from it during the trying days of 1838 in Missouri. But like the three witnesses, each of these eight men remained true to his testimony. Even those who left the Church and had every opportunity to renounce their testimony did not do so; on the contrary, they repeatedly declared it to be the sober truth, and they died with that testimony unchanged and unrefuted. John Whitmer, for example, who was excommunicated from the Church in 1838, had a bitter quarrel with Joseph Smith and sought in many ways to bring him into disrepute, but never would he retract one single word of his sworn testimony concerning the plates of the Book of Mormon.

The experience related by both sets of witnesses occurred in the bright light of day, under the open sky. All were honest and God-fearing men and were so recognized by the communities in which they lived. They were practical men, used to the hard realities of the frontier. They were men who had at that early date acquainted themselves with Joseph Smith's account concerning the plates and who had believed.

During the period of translation of the Book of Mormon a number of individuals were baptized. Filled with the Spirit, some, like Hyrum Smith, desired to go forth and proclaim the restoration. The answer of the Lord given through revelation to Hyrum is instructive:

Behold, I command you that you need not suppose that you are called to preach until you are called. Wait a little longer, until you shall have my word, my rock, my church, and my gospel, that you may know of a surety my doctrine. . . .

Seek not to declare my word, but first seek to obtain my word, and then shall your tongue be loosed; then, if you desire, you shall have my Spirit and my word, yea, the power of God unto the convincing of men.

But now hold your peace; study my word which hath gone forth among the children of men, and also study my word which shall come forth among the children of men, or that which is now translating, yea, until you have obtained all which I shall grant unto the children of men in this generation, and then shall all things be added thereto. (D&C 11:15-16, 21-22.)

Joseph the Prophet also received by revelation many instructions concerning the reestablishment of Christ's church on the earth. He commented that all the steps to be taken in the organization of the Church had been received by revelation at the home of Peter Whitmer, Sr., in Fayette in early June 1829:

In this manner did the Lord continue to give us instructions from time to time, concerning the duties which now devolved upon us; and among many other things of the kind, we obtained of Him the following, by the spirit of prophecy and revelation; which not only gave us much information, but also pointed out to us the precise day upon which, according to His will and commandment, we should proceed to organize His Church once more here upon the earth.[7]

8

Messages of the Book of Mormon

The preface of the Book of Mormon, which Joseph Smith testifies was written by the hand of Moroni, proclaims that the account was written by commandment of God, "Which is to show unto the remnant of the House of Israel what great things the Lord hath done for their fathers; and that they may know the covenants of the Lord, that they are not cast off forever—And also to the convincing of the Jew and Gentile that Jesus is the Christ, the Eternal God, manifesting himself unto all nations."

The book begins with an announcement from God and ends with an invitation to the reader to test its truth by an appeal to the Almighty through prayer. (See Moroni 10:4-5.)

Only through a study of the truths announced by Christ and recorded in the Book of Mormon can the history of the Church of Jesus Christ be understood, for these truths have led the Latter-day Saints to do what they have done and are now doing in the world. Before we relate the account of the official organization of the Church and of the leaders and followers in their missionary zeal, their migrations and sufferings, and their present purposes, programs, and achievements in carrying the gospel to the world, we need to set forth some of the words of Christ and his prophets as recorded in the Book of Mormon, which lie at the root and foundation of it all. The brevity of this short history precludes more than a brief glimpse at the words of Christ to his people, and those set forth here are those that so clearly restore the truth about God and his relationship to his people. The darkness that enveloped the mind of man regarding God the Father and his Son, Jesus Christ, at the time Jesus Christ reestablished his church makes this necessary to our understanding.

The philosopher John Locke presents the orthodox Christian view of God at the time of Joseph Smith: "God, every one easily allows, fills eternity; and it is hard to find a reason why anyone should doubt that he likewise fills immensity. His infinite being is certainly as boundless one way as the other; and methinks it ascribes a little too much to matter to say, where there is no body there is nothing. . . . Motion cannot be attributed to God; not because he is an immaterial but because he is an infinite spirit."

Spinoza, the Jewish philosopher of the seventeenth century, wrote: "All who have in anywise reflected on the divine nature, deny that God has a body. Of this they find excellent proof in the fact, that we understand by body a definite quantity, so long, so broad, so deep, bounded by a certain shape, and it is the height of absurdity to predicate such a thing of God, a being absolutely infinite."

Such vagueness had come to be adopted by Christianity. But the experience of the brother of Jared as recorded in the Book of Mormon puts to shame the doubt and uncertainty of the philosopher, for here we find the direct words of Jesus Christ:

> Behold, the Lord stretched forth his hand and touched the stones one by one with his finger. And the veil was taken from off the eyes of the brother of Jared, and he saw the finger of the Lord; and it was as the finger of a man, like unto flesh and blood; and the brother of Jared fell down before the Lord, for he was struck with fear.
>
> And the Lord saw that the brother of Jared had fallen to the earth; and the Lord said unto him: Arise, why hast thou fallen?
>
> And he saith unto the Lord: I saw the finger of the Lord, and I feared lest he should smite me; for I knew not that the Lord had flesh and blood.
>
> And the Lord said unto him: Because of thy faith thou hast seen that I shall take upon me flesh and blood; and never has man come before me with such exceeding faith as thou hast; for were it not so ye could not have seen my finger. Sawest thou more than this?
>
> And he answered: Nay; Lord, show thyself unto me.
>
> And the Lord said unto him: Believest thou the words which I shall speak?
>
> And he answered: Yea, Lord, I know that thou speakest the truth, for thou art a God of truth and canst not lie.
>
> And when he had said these words, behold, the Lord showed himself unto him, and said: Because thou knowest these things

ye are redeemed from the fall; therefore ye are brought back into my presence; therefore I show myself unto you. Behold, I am he who was prepared from the foundation of the world to redeem my people. Behold, I am Jesus Christ. (Ether 3:6-14.)

After pointing out how to become sons and daughters of God, Christ continued:

> I am the Father and the Son. In me shall all mankind have light, and that eternally, even they who shall believe on my name; and they shall become my sons and my daughters.
>
> And never have I showed myself unto man whom I have created, for never has man believed in me as thou hast. Seest thou that ye are created after mine own image? Yea, even all men were created in the beginning after mine own image.
>
> Behold, this body, which ye now behold, is the body of my spirit; and man have I created after the body of my spirit; and even as I appear unto thee to be in the spirit will I appear unto my people in the flesh. (Ether 3:14-16.)

The appearance of the resurrected Christ in America as recorded in the Book of Mormon clarifies the relationship of God the Father and his Son, Jesus Christ. When the Nephites were gathered at the temple in the land Bountiful, they heard a voice "as if it came out of heaven," saying, "Behold my Beloved Son, in whom I am well pleased, in whom I have glorified my name—hear ye him." As they looked up,

> behold, they saw a Man descending out of heaven; and he was clothed in a white robe; and he came down and stood in the midst of them; and the eyes of the whole multitude were turned upon him, and they durst not open their mouths, even one to another, and wist not what it meant, for they thought it was an angel that had appeared unto them.
>
> And it came to pass that he stretched forth his hand and spake unto the people, saying:
>
> Behold, I am Jesus Christ, whom the prophets testified shall come into the world. And behold, I am the light and the life of the world; and I have drunk out of that bitter cup which the Father hath given me, and have glorified the Father in taking upon me the sins of the world, in the which I have suffered the will of the Father in all things from the beginning.
>
> And it came to pass that when Jesus had spoken these words

the whole multitude fell to the earth; for they remembered that it
had been prophesied among them that Christ should show himself unto them after his ascension into heaven.

And it came to pass that the Lord spake unto them saying:
Arise and come forth unto me, that ye may thrust your hands into
my side, and also that ye may feel the prints of the nails in my
hands and in my feet, that ye may know that I am the God of Israel, and the God of the whole earth, and have been slain for the
sins of the world.

And it came to pass that the multitude went forth, and thrust
their hands into his side, and did feel the prints of the nails in his
hands and in his feet; and this they did do, going forth one by one
until they had all gone forth, and did see with their eyes and did
feel with their hands, and did know of a surety and did bear record, that it was he, of whom it was written by the prophets, that
should come.

And when they had all gone forth and had witnessed for
themselves, they did cry out with one accord, saying: Hosanna!
Blessed be the name of the Most High God! And they did fall
down at the feet of Jesus, and did worship him. (3 Nephi 11:6-
17.)

The direct words of Jesus Christ in his instructions to the
Nephites in the Book of Mormon are almost as voluminous as all
the direct words of Jesus in the Gospels, and these verify, clarify,
and add to the Bible account.

"The Fall"

The long-standing fallacy of Christendom concerning the fall
of Adam is set forth in both Catholic and Protestant writings.
Nearly all churches, and certainly those in the time of Joseph
Smith, looked upon the fall of Adam and Eve as a calamity, upset-
ting the plans of God and responsible for all the miseries of the
human race.

What was the viewpoint of the Nephite prophets?

And now, behold, if Adam had not transgressed he would
not have fallen, but he would have remained in the garden of
Eden. And all things which were created must have remained in
the same state in which they were after they were created; and
they must have remained forever, and had no end. And they

would have had no children; wherefore they would have remained in a state of innocence, having no joy, for they knew no misery; doing no good, for they knew no sin.

But behold, all things have been done in the wisdom of him who knoweth all things. Adam fell that men might be; and men are, that they might have joy. And the Messiah cometh in the fulness of time, that he may redeem the children of men from the fall. And because that they are redeemed from the fall they have become free forever, knowing good from evil; to act for themselves and not be acted upon, save it be by the punishment of the law at the great and last day, according to the commandments which God hath given. (2 Nephi 2:22-26.)

The effect of this doctrine upon the ideas of men concerning Adam is revolutionary. It is supported by revelations that Joseph Smith received in response to his prayers while he was revising the account of Moses as contained in the Bible:

In that day Adam blessed God and was filled, and began to prophesy concerning all the families of the earth, saying: Blessed be the name of God, for because of my transgression my eyes are opened, and in this life I shall have joy, and again in the flesh I shall see God.

And Eve, his wife, heard all these things and was glad, saying: Were it not for our transgression we never should have had seed, and never should have known good and evil, and the joy of our redemption, and the eternal life which God giveth unto all the obedient.

And Adam and Eve blessed the name of God, and they made all things known unto their sons and their daughters. (Moses 5:10-12.)

The truth thus set forth in the Book of Mormon respecting the Fall does away with the Christian fallacy that because of the Fall all, including infants, would be forever lost without baptism. The matter of infant baptism is further clarified by direct revelation of Jesus Christ to the prophet Mormon:

Behold, I came into the world not to call the righteous but sinners to repentance; the whole need no physician, but they that are sick; wherefore, little children are whole, for they are not capable of committing sin; wherefore the curse of Adam is taken from them in me, that it hath no power over them; and the law of circumcision is done away in me.

And after this manner did the Holy Ghost manifest the word of God unto me; wherefore, my beloved son, I know that it is solemn mockery before God, that ye should baptize little children.

Behold I say unto you that this thing shall ye teach—repentance and baptism unto those who are accountable and capable of committing sin; yea, teach parents that they must repent and be baptized, and humble themselves as their little children, and they shall all be saved with their little children.

And their little children need no repentance, neither baptism. Behold, baptism is unto repentance to the fulfilling the commandments unto the remission of sins. But little children are alive in Christ, even from the foundation of the world; if not so, God is a partial God, and also a changeable God, and a respecter to persons; for how many little children have died without baptism! (Moroni 8:8-13.)

The Reality of Satan

That Satan exists as a real person is taught in the New Testament. Those references are considered by many as being unreliable and are classified as myths. But the words of the prophets and of Christ in the Book of Mormon clarify the matter:

> I, Lehi, according to the things which I have read, must needs suppose that an angel of God, according to that which is written, had fallen from heaven; wherefore, he became a devil, having sought that which was evil before God. And because he had fallen from heaven, and had become miserable forever, he sought also the misery of all mankind. Wherefore, he said unto Eve, yea, even that old serpent, who is the devil, who is the father of all lies, wherefore he said: Partake of the forbidden fruit, and ye shall not die, but ye shall be as God, knowing good and evil. (2 Nephi 2:17-18.)

The Lord verifies the work of Satan in his words to the Nephites: "Ye must watch and pray always lest ye enter into temptation; for Satan desireth to have you, that he may sift you as wheat." (3 Nephi 18:18. See also Abraham 3:15-25; Moses 1:1-16; 4:1-4.)

The Gospel of Salvation

While appearing as a resurrected being to the Nephite people, Christ defined his gospel:

> Behold I have given unto you my gospel, and this is the gospel which I have given unto you—that I came into the world to do the will of my Father, because my Father sent me.
>
> And my Father sent me that I might be lifted up upon the cross; and after that I had been lifted up upon the cross, that I might draw all men unto me, that as I have been lifted up by men even so should men be lifted by the Father, to stand before me, to be judged of their works, whether they be good or whether they be evil—and for this cause have I been lifted up; therefore, according to the power of the Father I will draw all men unto me, that they may be judged according to their works.
>
> And it shall come to pass, that whoso repenteth and is baptized in my name shall be filled; and if he endureth to the end, behold, him will I hold guiltless before my Father at that day when I shall stand to judge the world. (3 Nephi 27:13-16.)

The Church of Christ

The Nephites had the priesthood among them. Thus, we read: "In the commencement of the ninth year of the reign of the judges over the people of Nephi, Alma delivered up the judgment seat to Nephihah, and confined himself wholly to the high priesthood of the holy order of God, to the testimony of the word, according to the spirit of revelation and prophecy." (Alma 4:20.)

When the resurrected Christ appeared among the Nephites, he called twelve men and gave them power and authority to baptize. Then he spoke to the people:

> Blessed are ye if ye shall give heed unto the words of these twelve whom I have chosen from among you to minister unto you, and to be your servants; and unto them I have given power that they may baptize you with water; and after that ye are baptized with water, behold, I will baptize you with fire and with the Holy Ghost; therefore blessed are ye if ye shall believe in me and be baptized, after that ye have seen me and know that I am.
>
> And again, more blessed are they who shall believe in your words because that ye shall testify that ye have seen me, and that

ye know that I am. Yea, blessed are they who shall believe in your words, and come down into the depths of humility and be baptized, for they shall be visited with fire and with the Holy Ghost, and shall receive a remission of their sins. (3 Nephi 12:1-2.)

Concerning those not of the house of Israel, Christ proclaimed: "If they will repent and hearken unto my words, and harden not their hearts, I will establish my church among them, and they shall come into the covenant and be numbered among this the remnant of Jacob." (3 Nephi 21:22.)

At one point the Nephites asked Christ, "Lord, we will that thou wouldst tell us the name whereby we shall call this church; for there are disputations among the people concerning this matter." He replied:

Why is it that the people should murmur and dispute because of this thing? Have they not read the scriptures, which say ye must take upon you the name of Christ, which is my name? For by this name shall ye be called at the last day; and whoso taketh upon him my name, and endureth to the end, the same shall be saved at the last day.

Therefore, whatsoever ye shall do, ye shall do it in my name; therefore ye shall call the church in my name; and ye shall call upon the Father in my name that he will bless the church for my sake. And how be it my church save it be called in my name? For if a church be called in Moses' name then it be Moses' church; or if it be called in the name of a man then it be the church of a man; but if it be called in my name then it is my church, if it so be that they are built upon my gospel. (3 Nephi 27:3-8.)

The Ordinances

The resurrected Christ taught the Nephites concerning the ordinance of baptism. He told Nephi, "I give unto you power that ye shall baptize this people when I am again ascended into heaven." Then he called others,

and said unto them likewise; and he gave them power to baptize. And he said unto them: On this wise shall ye baptize; and there shall be no disputations among you.

Verily I say unto you, that whoso repenteth of his sins

through your words, and desireth to be baptized in my name, on this wise shall ye baptize them—Behold, ye shall go down and stand in the water, and in my name shall ye baptize them.

And now behold, these are the words which ye shall say, calling them by name, saying: Having authority given me of Jesus Christ, I baptize you in the name of the Father, and of the Son, and of the Holy Ghost. Amen. And then shall ye immerse them in the water, and come forth again out of the water. . . .

And whoso believeth in me, and is baptized, the same shall be saved; and they are they who shall inherit the kingdom of God. And whoso believeth not in me, and is not baptized, shall be damned.

Verily, verily, I say unto you, that this is my doctrine, and I bear record of it from the Father; and whoso believeth in me believeth in the Father also; and unto him will the Father bear record of me, for he will visit him with fire and with the Holy Ghost. (3 Nephi 11:21-26, 33-35.)

Christ also introduced the sacrament to the Nephites:

And when the disciples had come with bread and wine, he took of the bread and brake and blessed it; and he gave unto the disciples and commanded that they should eat. And when they had eaten and were filled, he commanded that they should give unto the multitude.

And when the multitude had eaten and were filled, he said unto the disciples: Behold there shall one be ordained among you, and to him will I give power that he shall break bread and bless it and give it unto the people of my church, unto all those who shall believe and be baptized in my name.

And this shall ye always observe to do, even as I have done, even as I have broken bread and blessed it and given it unto you. And this shall ye do in remembrance of my body, which I have shown unto you. And it shall be a testimony unto the Father that ye do always remember me. And if ye do always remember me ye shall have my Spirit to be with you.

And it came to pass that when he said these words, he commanded his disciples that they should take of the wine of the cup and drink of it, and that they should also give unto the multitude that they might drink of it. And it came to pass that they did so, and did drink of it and were filled; and they gave unto the multitude, and they did drink, and they were filled.

And when the disciples had done this, Jesus said unto them: Blessed are ye for this thing which ye have done, for this is fulfilling my commandments, and this doth witness unto the Father that ye are willing to do that which I have commanded you.

And this shall ye always do to those who repent and are baptized in my name; and ye shall do it in remembrance of my blood, which I have shed for you, that ye may witness unto the Father that ye do always remember me. And if ye do always remember me ye shall have my spirit to be with you. (3 Nephi 18:3-11.)

Life after Death

The confusion that exists among the churches regarding life after death is clarified by an angel sent by Christ to the prophet Alma in answer to his prayer. Alma records:

Now, concerning the state of the soul between death and the resurrection—Behold, it has been made known unto me by an angel, that the spirits of all men, as soon as they are departed from this mortal body, yea, the spirits of all men, whether they be good or evil, are taken home to that God who gave them life.

And then shall it come to pass, that the spirits of those who are righteous are received into a state of happiness, which is called paradise, a state of rest, a state of peace, where they shall rest from all their troubles and from all care, and sorrow.

And then shall it come to pass, that the spirits of the wicked, yea, who are evil—for behold, they have no part nor portion of the Spirit of the Lord; for behold, they chose evil works rather than good; therefore the spirit of the devil did enter into them, and take possession of their house—and these shall be cast out into outer darkness; there shall be weeping, and wailing, and gnashing of teeth, and this because of their own iniquity, being led captive by the will of the devil.

Now this is the state of the souls of the wicked, yea, in darkness, and a state of awful, fearful looking for the fiery indignation of the wrath of God upon them; thus they remain in this state, as well as the righteous in paradise, until the time of their resurrection. (Alma 40:11-14.)

9

The Church Is Organized

The time: April 6, 1830. The place: the living room of the humble log home of Peter Whitmer, Sr., in Fayette, New York. The participants: six young men and about twenty-five of their followers. The occasion: a meeting to organize a church.

This was not to be a church like some others being organized in the same general area and time. This was to be the church of Christ—the Church of Him who had been slain; who had arisen from the grave; who had spoken anew from the heavens; who had commanded these people to gather at this place, at this time, and for this purpose; who had given direction as to the procedure to be followed, and the purpose to be proclaimed.

The six young men—Joseph Smith, Oliver Cowdery, Samuel H. Smith, Hyrum Smith, David Whitmer, and Peter Whitmer, Jr.—were not ordinary men; all had been baptized by authority given by an angel, even John, the Baptist. All had been shown the plates containing the record of God's dealings with the Nephite people and had borne record of that experience, and their testimonies had been published in the front of the Book of Mormon, just off the press. Two of these men were already ordained apostles of Jesus Christ, ordained by Peter, James, and John, who held the keys of presidency.

After the meeting was called to order, Joseph Smith records,

we proceeded, according to previous commandment, to call on our brethren to know whether they accepted us [Joseph Smith and Oliver Cowdery] as their teachers in the things of the Kingdom of God, and whether they were satisfied that we should proceed and be organized as a Church according to said commandment which we had received. To these several propositions they consented by a unanimous vote. I then laid my hands upon Oliver Cowdery, and ordained him an Elder of the "Church of Jesus Christ of Latter-day Saints;" after which, he ordained me also to the office of an Elder of said Church. We then took bread,

77

blessed it, and brake it with them; also wine, blessed it, and drank it with them. We then laid our hands on each individual member of the Church present [they had all been previously baptized], that they might receive the gift of the Holy Ghost, and be confirmed members of the Church of Christ. The Holy Ghost was poured out upon us to a very great degree—some prophesied, whilst we all praised the Lord, and rejoiced exceedingly.[1]

After appropriate songs and prayer, revelations concerning the organization of the Church were read to the assembled people. These revelations, which set forth fundamental doctrines, ordinances, and government, were later included in the Doctrine and Covenants, section 20. The revelations seem to be a series of instructions received prior to the organization of the Church, combined by Joseph Smith and couched in terms of narration—"We, the elders of the Church, have heard and bear witness," "And we know," and so forth—such language being in a form suitable for articles of incorporation as required by the state in the organization of a charitable society. While the articles of incorporation signed by the six elders of the Church have not been found in the archives of the State of New York (most of the early records of such matters have been lost or destroyed), it is likely that the articles so signed and filed would of necessity be comparable to, if not the same as, those now in the Doctrine and Covenants as section 20. A document called "The Articles" circulated in the early Church, and this was likely the name given to section 20, which we know was circulated before the Doctrine and Covenants was published.

As the state law of New York required six signatories to the articles of incorporation of a religious body, the first six persons baptized in this dispensation affixed their signatures in the order of their baptism: Oliver Cowdery, Joseph Smith, Jr., Samuel H. Smith, Hyrum Smith, David Whitmer, and Peter Whitmer, Jr.

Thus was the Church of Jesus Christ restored to earth in this dispensation.[2] The priesthood had been restored, and the Church was the creation of the priesthood. It was the means for the efficient and orderly functioning of the priesthood and for carrying the gospel to the world.

Before the meeting closed, Joseph received another revelation

Peter Whitmer Home, Fayette, New York

directing that a record should be kept and that in it, Joseph should be called "a seer, a translator, a prophet, an apostle of Jesus Christ, an elder of the church through the will of God the Father, and the grace of your Lord Jesus Christ." (D&C 21:1.)

In this manner Christ organized his church. But nothing was to be effective except by the consent and vote of the members, for the Lord said: "All things shall be done by common consent in the church, by much prayer and faith." (D&C 26:2.) Further, "no person is to be ordained to any office in this Church, where there is a regularly organized branch of the same, without the vote of that church." (D&C 20:65.)

Thus the members were taught that the Lord would give counsel and use persuasion in guiding the Church, but never compulsion. Further, he expects his officers in the Church to follow the same high moral principle. A short time later the high standard by which the priesthood should govern the affairs of the Church was revealed:

> The rights of the priesthood are inseparably connected with the powers of heaven, and . . . the powers of heaven cannot be controlled nor handled only upon the principles of righteousness.
> That they may be conferred upon us, it is true; but when we

undertake to cover our sins, or to gratify our pride, our vain ambition, or to exercise control or dominion or compulsion upon the
souls of the children of men, in any degree of unrighteousness,
behold, the heavens withdraw themselves; the Spirit of the Lord
is grieved; and when it is withdrawn, Amen to the priesthood or
the authority of that man. . . .

No power or influence can or ought to be maintained by virtue of the priesthood, only by persuasion, by long-suffering, by
gentleness and meekness, and by love unfeigned. (D&C 121:36-
37, 41.)

Nearly all great religious movements have had humble beginnings, but none more so than that which began in the humble
dwelling of Peter Whitmer, Sr., in the western borders of New
York in 1830. Founded by divine command, like "the stone which
is cut out of the mountain without hands,"[3] it has rolled forth until it
has branches in every state of the Union, in nearly every civilized
nation of the earth and upon the isles of the sea. The roster of six
members has grown to many millions, and the movement is still in
its infancy.

10

Missionaries Go Forth

The restoration of the gospel of Jesus Christ through the coming forth of the Book of Mormon and the many revelations to Joseph Smith; the ordination of apostles; the organization of the Church and designation of officers and duties of the priesthood—these all had a marked effect on those who came to know of and believe these things. They sought baptism and, having had hands laid upon their heads for the bestowing of the Holy Ghost by those now having authority, felt a conviction that changed their lives in a remarkable way. They manifested a new joy and a new commitment to action. This was shown by a desire to carry the message of the restoration to friends and neighbors. Many asked Joseph Smith to inquire of the Lord as to what they should do for the Church. In a general message to the Church, Christ proclaimed by revelation:

> A great and marvelous work is about to come forth unto the children of men. Behold, I am God; give heed to my word, which is quick and powerful, sharper than a two-edged sword, to the dividing asunder of both joints and marrow; therefore give heed to my word.
>
> Behold, the field is white already to harvest; therefore, whoso desireth to reap let him thrust in his sickle with his might, and reap while the day lasts, that he may treasure up for his soul everlasting salvation in the kingdom of God. (D&C 14:1-3.)

Some members sought special revelations through the Prophet for their individual guidance. Typical of these was Peter Whitmer, who received an answer by revelation: "The thing which will be of the most worth to you will be to declare repentance unto this people, that you may bring souls unto me, that you may rest with them in the kingdom of my Father." (D&C 16:6.)

As a reward for the members' missionary labors, the Savior promised: "If it so be that you should labor all your days in crying repentance unto this people, and bring, save it be one soul unto me, how great shall be your joy with him in the kingdom of my Father! And now, if your joy will be great with one soul that you have brought unto me into the kingdom of my Father, how great will be your joy if you should bring many souls unto me!" (D&C 18: 15-16.)

Great as the enthusiasm was to go forth with their message, all were to wait until the Church was established and they should be called and ordained as missionaries by those in authority. On Sunday, April 11, 1830, "Oliver Cowdery preached the first public discourse that was delivered by any of our number."[1] In these few simple words, Joseph Smith relates the beginning of a missionary movement that in time was to sweep over the whole world. At the close of his discourse Oliver baptized six new members into the Church. A week later he baptized seven more. The work was underway.

Shortly after the organization of the Church, Samuel Smith was called by revelation to go into northern New York. He traveled by foot some four hundred miles and distributed a number of copies of the Book of Mormon, one of which was directly responsible for the later conversion of Brigham Young and Heber C. Kimball.

Other missionaries followed in the work. David Whitmer, preaching to friends in the vicinity of Fayette, baptized eleven persons about the middle of June. The Church membership increased rapidly, with little branches soon organized at Fayette, Palmyra, Manchester, and Colesville in New York and at Harmony in Pennsylvania.

The Mission to the Western Border

The first extended mission, and one that was destined to influence the Church for many years, followed the conference of September 26, 1830. At this conference Oliver Cowdery and Peter Whitmer were called to go and preach to the Lamanites, or American Indians. In October Parley P. Pratt and Ziba Peterson were called to accompany them. During their mission they would travel on foot for more than fifteen hundred miles.

After visiting the Indian tribe of Catteraugus, near Buffalo,

New York, with meager results, the missionaries pushed on to Kirtland, Ohio. Elder Pratt had previously lived in that vicinity and had received a commission from the Campbellites there as a minister. He now sought out his former pastor, Sidney Rigdon, a preacher in the Church of the Disciples (Campbellites), and was well received. He was allowed to speak to the congregation of the church, and Sidney Rigdon promised that he would read and study the Book of Mormon. The gospel sermon appealed to the congregation, and the Book of Mormon won over the scholarly and intelligent pastor. The roots of the Church were spreading with amazing rapidity. When the missionaries departed from Kirtland to continue on to their original goal, they took with them Dr. Frederick G. Williams, a new convert. They left a thriving branch of the Church with twenty members who would, in succeeding weeks, bring into the Church practically all of the so-called Disciples.

Walking day after day westward, the five intrepid missionaries came to the Wyandot tribe of Indians near Sandusky, Ohio, where they spent several days. Parley P. Pratt writes: "We were well received, and had an opportunity of laying before them the record of their forefathers, which we did. They rejoiced in the tidings, bid us God speed, and desired us to write to them in relation to our success among the tribes further west, who had already removed to the Indian territory, where these expected soon to go."[2]

On December 20, the missionaries took passage on a steamer for St. Louis. Reaching the mouth of the Ohio, they found the Mississippi blocked with ice and were compelled to walk the remaining two hundred miles to St. Louis. The weather was severe and the snow sometimes three feet deep. In January 1831, the little party left St. Louis for a journey of 306 miles on foot through a trackless waste to Independence, Missouri. It was a journey accompanied by much hardship, with deep snow and little wood for fires. Elder Pratt writes: "We carried on our backs our changes of clothing, several books, and corn bread and raw pork. We often ate our frozen bread and pork by the way, when the bread would be so frozen that we could not bite or penetrate any part of it but the outside crust."[3]

A Visit to the Delaware Indians

In February the group reached Independence, some fifteen hundred miles from the beginning of their mission, with most of the distance being traversed on foot. But still they had not reached their destination. While two of them hired out as tailors in Independence in order to secure funds to continue the missionary labors, the other three crossed over the frontier into the Indian country. They visited the powerful Shawnees and then crossed the Kansas River into the region of the Delawares.

After considerable difficulties, Chief Anderson (as the whites called him), head of the ten nations of Delawares, granted them an opportunity to speak to the united council of the ten nations. Forty chieftains met in the chief's council chambers. The council fires were lighted, and the pipe of peace was passed around. Then Oliver Cowdery, with a copy of the Book of Mormon in his hand, addressed them through an interpreter:

> Aged Chief and Venerable Council of the Delaware Nation, we are glad of this opportunity to address you as our red brethren and friends. We have travelled a long distance from toward the rising sun to bring you glad news; we have travelled the wilderness, crossed the deep and wide rivers, and waded in the deep snows, and in the face of the storms of winter, to communicate to you great knowledge which has lately come to our ears and hearts; and which will do the red man good as well as the pale face.[4]

Oliver Cowdery then told them of the Book of Mormon and of their ancestors who had written it, and how the book had come again to the knowledge of men. After a pause and some discussion among the council, the venerable old chief replied:

> "We feel truly thankful to our white friends who have come so far, and been at such pains to tell us good news, and especially this new news concerning the Book of our forefathers; it makes us glad in here"—placing his hand on his heart. "It is now winter, we are new settlers in this place; the snow is deep, our cattle and horses are dying, our wigwams are poor; we have much to do in the spring—to build houses and fence and make farms; but we

will build a council house and meet together, and you shall read to us and teach us more concerning the Book of our fathers and the will of the Great Spirit."[5]

Elder Pratt in his report of the experience adds:

We continued for several days to instruct the old chief and many of his tribe. The interest became more and more intense on their part, from day to day, until at length nearly the whole tribe began to feel a spirit of inquiry and excitement on the subject. We found several among them who could read, and to them we gave copies of the Book, explaining to them that it was the Book of their forefathers. Some began to rejoice exceedingly, and took great pains to tell the news to others, in their own language. The excitement now reached the frontier settlements in Missouri, and stirred up the jealousy and envy of the Indian agents and sectarian missionaries to that degree that we were soon ordered out of the Indian country as disturbers of the peace, and even threatened with the military in case of noncompliance. We accordingly departed from the Indian country, and came over the line, and commenced laboring in Jackson County, Missouri, among the whites. We were well received, and listened to by many, and some were baptized and added to the Church.[6]

That work among the dark-skinned Lamanites was destined to wait many years for its accomplishment, during which time the scene of Mormonism was to shift twenty-five hundred miles west from the place of beginning, into the mighty Rockies. But the spirit of the little group of missionaries was undaunted. Without money or supplies, and depending upon the hospitality of the few red and white inhabitants, they had traversed sixteen hundred miles of wilderness and opened the way for thousands to hear the message of the restored gospel. When Elder Pratt returned east in the spring of 1831, he found that the little branch he and his companions had organized in Kirtland, Ohio, had grown to a membership well over a thousand.

This one missionary journey, so rich in results, is but typical of many, and the spirit in which it was carried out is the spirit of all missionary activities in the Church from the beginning. There was no thought of pay; no expectations of earthly rewards; no hope of earthly fame. A great urge to teach had come upon the members of the Church, and the enthusiasm was contagious. Men who had but recently received the gospel themselves found such comfort and joy in its message that they could not rest until they had taught the good news to relatives and friends.

While Oliver Cowdery, Parley P. Pratt, and their companions were journeying to the west, Ezra Thayre and Northrop Sweet were called to labor in the east. (D&C 33.) In November 1830, Orson Pratt, who had been converted by his brother Parley, was called to labor as a missionary. (D&C 34.) In December, Sidney Rigdon and Edward Partridge received a similar call. (D&C 35, 36.) At a conference in June 1831, twenty-eight missionaries were called to labor in pairs, the majority to work westward to Independence, Missouri, where already the seeds of the gospel had been planted.

Whence Comes this Missionary Zeal?

What spirit prompted the new converts to the Church to leave home, friends, and comforts in order to carry the gospel to others?

If we can understand what prompted the ancient apostle Paul to encompass land and sea, endure privations, beatings, shipwreck, prisons, and even walk cheerfully to his death in order that men might hear the message of Jesus, and if we can answer why Jesus himself trod the certain road to the cross when he realized so clearly what lay ahead, then we can understand the spirit of the missionaries in early Mormonism. To them, privation and sufferings were nothing compared to the priceless joy they attest to having received.

In each case the individual testifies to a happiness in the work, a newfound joy in the service of humanity and God that becomes an irresistible driving power. Obstacles may be met; barriers and pitfalls may be thrown in their paths; but as well attempt to stop the flow of Mt. Vesuvius in its eruptions as to stem the tide of the restored church. The movement had all the energy of a Vesuvius, all the fire and irresistibleness of the lava flow. Men and women everywhere caught the contagion of it. The discontented in religion felt its pull and severed the few remaining ties with their old creeds, for the new religion breathed power and attained results.

Prayer had again become a vital force, and many who had previously prayed with doubts and misgivings now received the needed bolstering that brought the Spirit of God. Men and women prayed for a testimony concerning Joseph Smith's message, and their prayers were answered. Men and women read the Book of Mormon with a prayer in their hearts that they might know of its truth, and the Lord remembered his promise.

People are always lifted by the faith of their associates. Confidence inspires confidence. When the Savior walked the earth, his presence, his voice, and his touch dispelled fear and doubt; the sick arose from their beds of affliction and the blind opened their eyes. His apostles finally acquired that same faith and confidence and rejoiced in the power they possessed. So in this new dispensation, Christ had revealed himself. The confidence and faith of Joseph Smith had opened the heavens, and prayers were being answered. Others caught the same faith and, having been vested with the powers of priesthood, went forth to instill faith in all who would listen.

The fire and enthusiasm of the movement dwarfed all other motives in life. The desire for gain or power seemed to disappear. In the giving of service to others, self was forgotten and a new social brotherhood began—a true kingdom of God. The principle that he who "loseth his life" in the service of others "shall find it" is still the fundamental principle of Mormon missionary activity at home or abroad. It cools when service cools and bursts into new flame when service is resumed. In the early Mormon society it permeated everything and enriched all that it touched. The spirit of service and brotherhood entered into home life and community life and brought dreams of a new Zion—a place where one could find brotherly happiness and service to one another, where there should be no rich and no poor, where greed and selfishness should be banished forever.

Effects of the Restoration on Disbelievers

The account that God the Father and his Son, Jesus Christ, had appeared to an unknown young man; that they had bodies like unto those of men; that a succession of angels and other heavenly beings had followed; that the Book of Mormon contained a gospel so different from the prevailing views of theologians of that day—all this was quite too much for most of the older generation to accept, for if these events proclaimed by Joseph Smith and his associates were true, then the old established churches were indeed wrong.

People don't like to be wrong. Most ministers trained to accept Christianity as set forth by councils such as the Nicean Council and the Council of Trent were not ready to do an about-face, lose their means of a livelihood, and lose their flocks. The story of God and angels appearing on earth might be set aside as a dream or hallucination that might, given time, die of itself; but the Book of Mormon could not. It was tangible evidence that had to be destroyed. Challenged it must be, and was, and continues to be. But it has not been destroyed. It still divides its readers into enemies and friends. Scores of books have been published by authors seeking to refute its claims and to find an explanation for its existence other than that related by Joseph Smith. One such attempt after another has failed and passed into oblivion. Joseph Smith's account remains as the only plausible answer. The Book of Mormon stands next to the Bible alone in the number of volumes published over so long a period of time. Translated into all the major languages of the world, it comes to the attention of more millions of people each year.

The Constitution of the United States contains the provision to guarantee freedom of speech and religious beliefs, but the provisions were quite thrust aside by those who sought to crush the restored church and its adherents.

The Latter-day Saints were not the only religious group to suffer from persecution during the early half of the eighteenth century. The Catholics, the Jews, and small groups such as the Campbellites and the Shakers, which had broken away from parent churches, also met with stiff opposition, but on none was the persecution so severe and so long-lasting as that against The Church of Jesus Christ of Latter-day Saints. Dr. Milton V. Backman, Jr., has written:

> Writers of the 1830s were quick to criticize the doctrines of
> the Latter-day Saints, especially those that differed most mark-

edly from popular beliefs espoused by the major Protestant faiths. Most Protestants of that period believed that the Bible was the sole guide of faith; that visions, revelations, and gifts of the spirit, such as prophecy, speaking in tongues, and interpretation of tongues, had ceased with the death of the apostles; that all believers were priesthood bearers; and that anyone who received an internal call and was called by a congregation had the authority to preach and to administer the sacraments. Many further believed that since men were saved by the grace of God and the church was a congregation of believers, it was improper to say that any one particular faith was the only way leading to eternal life with God. According to the creeds of the major Protestant denominations, all believers who were either elected by God or who did not fall would enter heaven, while the unregenerates, or those who fell, would suffer everlasting damnation.

It is not surprising, therefore, that the doctrines most frequently denounced by the critics related to the Church's beliefs concerning the Book of Mormon, the visions and revelations of Joseph Smith, the restoration of the priesthood, gifts of the spirit, and the reestablishment of the one and only true church of Christ on the earth. These teachings were perceived as a threat to all other religious institutions. Even though Protestants quarreled among themselves concerning some interpretations of the Bible, many united in opposition to this new faith, which, in their minds, was an unacceptable form of religious exclusiveness.[7]

Many of those seeking to attack the new Church published libelous accounts about the Smith family. Concerning these, Dr. Backman writes:

> From an examination of the various primary sources available, it is evident that most of the men who circulated tales about Joseph and his family were but casual acquaintances of the Smiths. Many of the derogatory character references were gathered by D.P. Hurlbut, who was excommunicated from the Restored Church for immorality and traveled throughout the town of Palmyra in the early 1830's gathering disparaging statements about the Smith family. Although those who purportedly signed affidavits, many of which Hurlbut evidently wrote, constituted a very small percentage of the settlers in Palmyra, it is questionable whether any one of these men could be classified as an authority on the character of members of the Smith family.[8]

Few of the anti-Church writings of the twentieth century contain any attack on the character of Joseph Smith or his family, the good character of the Smiths having been well established by careful historians.

Newspapers in the near vicinity, the *Palmyra Reflector* and the *Painesville Telegraph,* led the attack from the press. As the headquarters of the Church moved to Kirtland, Ohio, in 1831, the *Buffalo Gazette* and the *Cleveland Herald* joined the attack. Ministers of other churches, especially those who were beginning to lose members to the new faith, became loud in their denunciations. Writers began to seize upon the opportunity to write for the various newspapers and to seek publication of their own books against the Church. In the archives of the Latter-day Saint Church today are found some eighteen hundred books written by individuals who have sought to destroy or explain away the Book of Mormon. These books have in general passed into oblivion, only two or three ever reaching a second edition. The Church has not attempted to refute these writings. The Book of Mormon itself stands as the refutation, no one having successfully found the book or Joseph Smith's account of its coming to the Church to be false. The reason for the continued attack by many of the so-called Christian churches is not hard to find. The central questions are simply these: Does God have a body? Was Jesus Christ, His Son, resurrected with a body of flesh and bone? Does he appear and speak to men today? Does he send angels to carry messages to his prophets? Joseph Smith and his associates and all of the subsequent leaders of the Church of Jesus Christ say yes. Orthodox Christian churches say no.

The Latter-day Saints follow the admonition of Christ, "Contend against no church." Joseph Smith set the pattern: "We claim the privilege of worshiping Almighty God according to the dictates of our own conscience, and allow all men the same privilege, let them worship how, where, or what they may." (Article of Faith 11.)

11

The Church Moves West

By late 1830, the growth of the Church in upper New York State had been steady but slow, and the work there was being greatly hampered by persecution. Mobs gathered to molest the Saints in their meetings as well as in their travel to and from meeting places. Fictitious charges were being made against Joseph Smith, and he was subjected to trials in courts of law. The first such trial, held in the town of South Bainbridge, was on the charge that he was a "disturber of the peace." He was acquitted. Other trials followed on various trumped-up charges, all ending in acquittals, but they were time-consuming and hindered his work in revising the Bible and other important work he had been commanded to do.

Meanwhile, Parley P. Pratt and his missionary companions, both on going west in their appointed mission to the Indian nations and on their return, had stopped at Kirtland, Ohio, and found receptive listeners for the gospel message. The growth of the Church in Kirtland and outlying areas was rapid, and by the spring of 1831 the center of Church population had shifted from Fayette, New York, to Kirtland, Ohio, with the number of members living in that vicinity being several times the number residing in New York and Pennsylvania branches.

Joseph Smith recorded that after prayer to the Lord, he received the following revelation on January 5, 1831: "Thou art not called to go into the eastern countries, but thou art called to go to the Ohio. And inasmuch as my people shall assemble themselves at the Ohio, I have kept in store a blessing such as is not known among the children of men, and it shall be poured forth upon their heads. And from thence men shall go forth into all nations." (D&C 39:14-15.)

After advising the converts in New York and Pennsylvania to sell their properties and move to Ohio, Joseph prepared for his own departure. In the latter part of January 1831, in company with Sidney Rigdon and Edward Partridge, he and his wife, Emma, arrived in Kirtland, Ohio. There they were joyfully received. The Prophet and his wife were taken temporarily into the home of Newel K. Whitney, a member of the Church and a successful young merchant.

This was the beginning of a general exodus of the Saints from New York. As fast as they could dispose of their property and equip themselves for the journey, they moved into the frontier settlements of Ohio. They were attracted to those settlements where branches of the Church were already established. Kirtland and the nearby towns of Thompson and Hiram received the great majority. The Colesville, New York, branch moved en masse to Thompson, while the Palmyra branch settled in Kirtland and Hiram.

Before the message of the restored church had reached the vicinity of Kirtland, a group of Campbellites or Disciples had commenced the experiment of holding all property in common and living as one large family. After the visitation of Parley P. Pratt and his companions on their way to the Lamanite Mission, practically the entire group had embraced the new faith. They continued, however, their social experiment until the arrival of Joseph Smith. If they expected him to approve of the order, they were disappointed. Though he commended them for their brotherly spirit, he soon persuaded them to abandon the enterprise as not being patterned upon God's law. The Kirtland Saints were anxious to know what the law of God was in the matter, and so Joseph inquired of the Lord through prayer. On February 4 he received a revelation (D&C 41) in which Edward Partridge was called to "be appointed by the voice of the church, and ordained a bishop unto the church, to leave his merchandise and to spend all his time in the labors of the church." On February 9 the Prophet received another revelation (D&C 42), given in fulfillment of the promise the Lord had made earlier that the "law" would be given in Ohio, introducing what would be known as the law of consecration.

Under the plan, all of the members of the Church within a given community were to deed their property in fee to the bishop over that community. As trustee of the property for the entire community, the bishop would then, by special deed, convey back to each head of a family lands, store, mill, shop, or other property, subject to certain conditions. A person might not hold more land than he could properly use. Further, the surplus in goods or money produced from the land or other property over and above that required for the immediate well-being of the family, as well as the improvement of the property, should be turned over annually to the general fund or storehouse of the community. This community surplus was then to be used for the benefit of the whole group. Out of it the poor, the sick, the orphans, and the widows were to be provided for. Roads were to be built and an educational system maintained. Churches and community centers were to be erected, and all enterprises for the benefit of the whole group would be carried out. The system was designed to prevent the rise of class and to abolish hoarding, selfishness, and those elements that, in a modern community, tend to prevent a spirit of Christian brotherhood. Products and services were to be bought and sold as usual, and he that was idle should not "eat the bread nor wear the garments of the laborer." (D&C 42:42.)

The law of consecration was first followed among the Saints from the eastern states who settled in Kirtland and Thompson. Not all of the members of the Church in either place participated in the plan.

The settlements of the Saints in Ohio were considered by Joseph Smith as temporary. The permanent settlement was to be farther to the west, in a place unknown at that time. In a revelation received at Kirtland in May 1831, the Prophet was told: "I consecrate unto them this land for a little season, until I, the Lord, shall provide for them otherwise, and command them to go hence; and the hour and the day is not given unto them, wherefore let them act upon this land as for years, and this shall turn unto them for their good." (D&C 51:16-17.)

The spirit of community fellowship and cooperation that reached its finest expression in the law of consecration set the Latter-day Saints apart, socially and economically, from their neighbors. It struck deep at the roots of the American economic system and served notice upon the profit motive as a basis of human activity. This spirit bound the Mormon people closer together as units in the various communities. Though the law of consecration was short-lived, one must not interpret this as meaning that the spirit of brotherhood disappeared. That spirit was to grow stronger with the years. It was the very youth of the Church, coupled with the newness of the movement, that brought about the failure of a law they desired but had not sufficient experience to live. But the spirit of brotherhood continued and found expression in community enterprises and missionary activity.

The fact that the Mormons were animated by a different conception of community life aroused suspicion, and eventually persecution, among those who witnessed their numbers double and redouble with amazing rapidity. Ministers whose own flocks dwindled became alarmed as they saw converts by the score move away to the Mormon settlements or set up a new Mormon community in the same locality. Often they became embittered and active in stirring up feeling against the new religion.

A New Zion

The Mormon communities in Ohio were still in their infancy when Joseph Smith turned his attention farther west. In September 1830, while in New York State, he received a revelation in which the Lord revealed that a new Zion would be built somewhere in the West "on the borders by the Lamanites." (D&C 28:9.) From that time he had been besieged with inquiries as to its exact location. In the spring of 1831, Parley P. Pratt arrived in Kirtland with a glowing report of his mission to the west. The Indian mission had been brought to an abrupt close, but a small branch of the Church had been organized in Jackson County in the western part of Missouri. Elder Pratt's account of the country stirred the Prophet to make new inquiries of the Lord. During a conference of the Church at Kirtland in early June, he received by revelation the following:

> I, the Lord, will make known unto you what I will that ye shall do from this time until the next conference, which shall be held in Missouri, upon the land which I will consecrate unto my people, which are a remnant of Jacob, and those who are heirs according to the covenant.
>
> Wherefore, verily I say unto you, let my servants Joseph

Smith, Jun., and Sidney Rigdon take their journey as soon as preparations can be made to leave their homes, and journey to the land of Missouri. (D&C 52:2-3.)

In the same revelation, twenty-six other elders were called to serve missions to the West. They were to travel by twos, preaching the gospel on the way. All were to meet at Independence, Missouri, where the Lord would reveal the location of the new Zion.

The idea that there would be a new Zion upon the earth in the latter days may be obtained from a reading of the Bible. It was not the study of ancient prophecies, however, that so fired the Saints with a zeal for Zion. To them God had spoken anew. Zion was to be realized.

To Joseph Smith, the word *Zion* had two meanings: "the pure in heart," and "the place where the pure in heart dwell together in righteousness." It is quite evident that a successful "Zion community" is impossible without a "Zion people." Such an achievement could hardly be attained while the Saints were among people, in Ohio and elsewhere, who were not of their faith. Thus the Prophet contemplated a gathering place to which the pure in heart might gather from the four quarters of the earth and where a new society, patterned after God's law, might reach fruition. From that central Zion community the idea would spread until eventually Zion would embrace the whole of the American continent.

The distance from Kirtland, Ohio, to Independence, Missouri, was approximately one thousand miles. On June 19, 1831, Joseph Smith, accompanied by Sidney Rigdon, Martin Harris, Edward Partridge, William W. Phelps, Joseph Coe, and Algernon S. Gilbert and his wife, left Kirtland. They traveled by wagon, canal boat, steamer, and stage as far as St. Louis. From there Joseph and part of the company completed the journey to Independence on foot, arriving in mid-July. The rest went by boat up the Missouri River and arrived a few days later.

Shortly after he arrived in Missouri, the Prophet received a revelation announcing that Missouri was Zion, the gathering place for the Saints. "The place which is now called Independence is the center place; and the spot for the temple is lying westward, upon a lot which is not far from the courthouse. Wherefore, it is wisdom that the land should be purchased by the saints, and also every tract lying westward, even unto the line running directly between Jew and Gentile;[1] and also every tract bordering by the prairies, inasmuch as my disciples are enabled to buy lands. Behold, this is wisdom, that they might obtain it for an everlasting inheritance. (D&C 57:3-5.)

The land chosen for the new Zion was a land rich in those things needful to man. Joseph Smith, seeing it for the first time in midsummer, wrote of it:

> As far as the eye can reach the beautiful rolling prairies spread out like a sea of meadows; and are decorated with a growth of flowers so gorgeous and grand as to exceed description; and nothing is more fruitful, or a richer stockholder in the blooming prairie than the honey bee. Only on the water courses is timber to be found. There in strips from one to three miles in width, and following faithfully the meanderings of the streams, it grows in luxuriant forests. The forests are a mixture of oak, hickory, black walnut, elm, ash, cherry, honey locust, mulberry, coffee bean, hackberry, boxelder, and bass wood; with the addition of cottonwood, butterwood, pecan, and soft and hard maple upon the bottoms. The shrubbery is beautiful, and consists in part of plums, grapes, crab apple, and persimmons.
>
> The soil is rich and fertile; from three to ten feet deep, and generally composed of a rich black mould, intermingled with clay and sand. It yields in abundance, wheat, corn, sweet potatoes, cotton, and many other agricultural products. . . . Buffalo, elk, deer, bear, wolves, beaver and many smaller animals here roam at pleasure. Turkeys, geese, swans, ducks, yea a variety of the feathered tribe, are among the rich abundance that grace the delightful regions of this goodly land—the heritage of the children of God.[2]

Independence in 1831 was a small frontier town, the outfitting place for trapper and hunter, with a brick courthouse, two or three general stores, and some twenty log houses. The type of settlers presented a sharp contrast to the New England people who were now searching for a new Zion in that land. The old settlers were generally unschooled, ignorant of the ways of civilization, and unskilled in the arts of the newcomers.

On August 2, 1831, Joseph Smith and eleven other men, representing the twelve tribes of Israel, laid the first log for a Mormon dwelling in Jackson County. This scene was enacted in Kaw Township, twelve miles west of Independence (and now part of Kansas City). There the Saints who had migrated from Colesville, New York, to Thompson, Ohio, were now preparing to settle. As Sidney Rigdon dedicated the land for the gathering of Israel, he asked those assembled:

> Do you receive this land for the land of your inheritance with thankful hearts from the Lord?
> Answer from all, We do.
> Do you pledge yourselves to keep the laws of God on this land which you have never kept in your own land?
> We do.
> Do you pledge yourselves to see that others of your brethren who shall come hither do keep the laws of God?
> We do.
> After prayer, he arose and said, I now pronounce this land consecrated and dedicated to the Lord for a possession and inheritance for the saints, in the name of Jesus Christ, having authority from Him. And for all the faithful servants of the Lord to the remotest ages of time. Amen.[3]

On August 3, 1831, Joseph Smith, Sidney Rigdon, Edward Partridge, W. W. Phelps, Oliver Cowdery, Martin Harris, and Joseph Coe went to the place designated by revelation for the temple, and there the Prophet dedicated the temple site. The following day a conference was held at Kaw Township. Bishop Edward Partridge was appointed to remain in Independence "and divide unto the saints their inheritance." (D&C 57:7.) Sidney Gilbert, a young merchant, was appointed as agent of the Church to purchase lands for the Saints. (D&C 57:8.) William W. Phelps was named as a printer for the Church, with Oliver Cowdery to assist him. (D&C 57:11, 13.) Under the leadership of these men, the law of consecration was put into effect in Independence and other parts of Jackson County. The growth of the Mormon settlement was rapid. Funds from the Saints in Ohio for the purchase of lands in Missouri began to pour into the hands of the purchasing agent, and Bishop Partridge had to work feverishly to settle the constant stream of incoming Saints satisfactorily.

Two Centers of Activity and Influence

Thus, Mormon settlements in both Ohio and Missouri were developing at the same time. Though they were a thousand miles apart, with the country between them largely unsettled, Kirtland, Ohio, and Independence, Missouri, became the important centers of Church activity for a number of years.

By the summer of 1832, nearly all of the Saints from New York had migrated to Jackson County, Missouri. Some had stopped for a short time in Ohio, while others had made the fifteen-hundred-mile journey directly to the new Zion.

The converts in Ohio were content to remain in the vicinity of Kirtland. The Prophet, in fact, urged them to remain and build a temple to the Lord and reap the blessings God had promised them in that land.

Having announced the location for the new Zion and dedicated it as a gathering place for the Saints, Joseph Smith now devoted most of his time to the building up of the Church at Kirtland. This he did for several reasons. The main body of the Church membership were settled in and around Kirtland. The city offered a more convenient center for directing the affairs of the Saints everywhere, as well as for directing missionary activity in Canada and the eastern states. And God had given him commandments that necessitated his remaining at Kirtland until they were carried out.

Of the two communities, Independence offered the better opportunity for putting into effect God's complete law of consecration and for establishing a city that would serve as a model for all future centers of Zion. Practice of the law of consecration in Kirtland was soon abandoned, and at Thompson it came to an end when the Colesville Saints who had settled there moved in a body to Missouri. Joseph made no attempt to reestablish the law in Ohio. He did, however, insist that all who journeyed to the new Zion in Missouri must be willing to abide that law and that they enter into covenant with God that they would do so.

While the greater law of consecration was not continued in Kirtland, a very marked community spirit of cooperation developed there among the Saints. This segregated them from nonmembers and brought upon them both the envy and the hatred of many outside the new society. The Church demanded high standards of its members, resulting in the apostasy or falling away of those who were lukewarm in the faith or who had joined the Church for ulterior motives. These apostates did much to foment accusations and hatreds against the Latter-day Saints.

One of the most brutal of such mobbings was directed against Joseph Smith and Sidney Rigdon. At the time, both were living at Hiram, sixteen miles northwest of Kirtland, where the Prophet was working on a revision of the English Bible. About midnight of March 24, 1832, Joseph and Sidney were dragged from their beds by a mob estimated at forty or more, led by apostate Simonds Ryder. The Prophet was beaten into insensibility. When he came to, he was carried a distance from the house, stripped of his clothing, and covered with tar and feathers. Sidney was dragged by the heels over the frozen earth until he was unconscious.

This incident is typical of the opposition that, in time, rose against the early Saints wherever they settled and was to eventually culminate in their being driven from the confines of the United States.

A Model for Future Cities of Zion

In the spring of 1833, a general plan for building "cities in Zion" was evolved. In June the Prophet sent a copy of the city plan to the branch of the Church at Independence. The central city of Zion was to be laid out according to the model. Elder B. H. Roberts has condensed these elaborate instructions to the bishop in Zion as follows:

> The city plat is one mile square, divided into blocks containing ten acres each—forty rods square—except the middle range of blocks running north and south; they will be forty by sixty rods, containing fifteen acres, having their greatest extent east and west. The streets will be eight rods wide, intersecting each

other at right angles. The center tier of blocks forty by sixty rods will be reserved for public buildings, temples, tabernacles, school houses, etc.

All the other blocks will be divided into half-acre lots, a four rod front to every lot, and extending back twenty rods. In one block the lots will run from the north and south, and in the next one from east and west, and so on alternately throughout the city, except in the range of blocks reserved for public buildings. By this arrangement no street will be built on entirely through the street; but on one block the houses will stand on one street, and on the next one on another street. All of the houses are to be built of brick or stone; and but one house on a lot, which is to stand twenty-five feet back from the street, the space in front being for lawns, ornamental trees, shrubbery, or flowers, according to the taste of the owners; the rest of the lot will be for gardens, etc.

It is supposed that such a plat when built up will contain fifteen or twenty thousand population, and that they will require twenty-four buildings to supply them with houses for public worship and schools. These buildings will be temples, none of which will be less than eighty-seven feet by sixty-one, and two stories high, each story to be fourteen feet, making the building twenty-eight feet to the square. None of these temples will be smaller than the drawing of the one sent with the plat of the city to Independence; but of course there may be others much larger; the above, however, are the dimensions of the one the saints were commanded to build first.

Lands on the north and south of the city will be laid off for barns and stables for the use of the city, so there will be no barns or stables in the city among the homes of the people.

Lands for agriculturalists sufficient for the whole plat are also to be laid off on the north and south of the city plat, but if sufficient land cannot be laid off without going too great a distance, then farms are to be laid off on the east and west also; but the tiller of the soil as well as the merchant and mechanic will live in the city. The farmer and his family, therefore, will enjoy all the advantages of schools, public lectures and other meetings. His home will no longer be isolated, and his family denied the benefits of society, which has been, and always will be, the great educator of the human race; but they will enjoy the same privileges of society, and can surround their homes with the same intellectual life, the same social refinement as will be found in the home of the merchant or banker or professional man.

"When this square is thus laid off and supplied, lay off another in the same way," said the Prophet to those to whom the city plat was sent, "and so fill up the world in these last days, and let every man live in the city, for this is the city of Zion."[4]

Persecution prevented the carrying out of this plan. The general principles involved were later used in remodeling the city of Kirtland and became the basis for other Missouri settlements, for Nauvoo, and for Salt Lake City and practically all the Mormon settlements in the Rocky Mountain region.

12

Other Scriptures Come Forth

Scarcely had the Book of Mormon been published and the Church organized than Joseph Smith was directed by revelation to make some revisions and additions to the Bible. Comparisons of the writings of Isaiah and other Israelite prophets as recorded in the Bible with the Nephite records of the same had revealed some differences.

It appears that Joseph first made the necessary revisions in the Bible he used so that the Bible text might be in harmony with the Book of Mormon. In his study of the book of Genesis, he was aware of many problems. Resorting to prayer concerning them, he received a series of visions that he referred to as the "Vision of Moses." In June 1830, he received a revelation that is prefaced as follows: "The words of God, which he spake unto Moses at a time when Moses was caught up into an exceedingly high mountain, and he saw God face to face, and he talked with him, and the glory of God was upon Moses; therefore Moses could endure his presence." (Moses 1:1.)

These scriptures, which now appear in the Pearl of Great Price as "Selections from the Book of Moses," describe the creation of the earth and the placing of man upon it, the fall of Adam, and the plan of salvation as it was revealed to Adam. They make clear that the gospel of Jesus Christ was given to Adam in the beginning by that same Son of God who was later to live on the earth in the flesh. One of the series of visions contained what Moses wrote concerning a prophet named Enoch, who founded "a city that was called the City of Holiness, even Zion" (Moses 7), a city built on the principles of the law of consecration. Enoch also beheld in vision Noah and his family and the coming of the great flood; the coming of Jesus Christ, his atoning sacrifice and the resurrection of the saints; the restoration of the church of Christ; the gathering; the Second Coming; and the return of Zion.

The Book of Commandments

In the latter part of 1831, a council of Church leaders decided to compile the revelations concerning the origin of the Church and its organization. The collection, to be called the Book of Commandments, was presented to a conference of the priesthood at Hiram, Ohio, November 1, 1831. On the first day of the conference, Joseph Smith received a revelation that became the preface for the new volume and is now Section 1 of the book of Doctrine and Covenants. In this revelation an announcement is made to the whole world:

> Hearken, O ye people of my church; . . . hearken ye people from afar; and ye that are upon the islands of the sea, listen together. For verily the voice of the Lord is unto all men, and there is none to escape; and there is no eye that shall not see, neither ear that shall not hear, neither heart that shall not be penetrated. . . . And the voice of warning shall be unto all people, by the mouths of my disciples, whom I have chosen in these last days. . . .
>
> Behold, this is mine authority, and the authority of my servants, and my preface unto the book of my commandments, which I have given them to publish unto you, O inhabitants of the earth.
>
> Wherefore, fear and tremble, O ye people, for what I the Lord have decreed in them shall be fulfilled.
>
> And verily I say unto you, that they who go forth, bearing these tidings unto the inhabitants of the earth, to them is power given to seal both on earth and in heaven, the unbelieving and rebellious; yea, verily, to seal them up unto the day when the wrath of God shall be poured out upon the wicked without measure—unto the day when the Lord shall come to recompense unto every man according to his work, and measure to every man according to the measure which he has measured to his fellow man. (D&C 1:1-10.)

Concerning the language Joseph Smith used in recording these and other revelations, a language that had received criticism, the Lord said: "Behold, I am God and have spoken it; these commandments are of me, and were given unto my servants in their weakness, after the manner of their language, that they might come to understanding." (D&C 1:24.)

At the conference many of the brethren arose in turn and bore witness to the divine origin of the revelations. The Prophet challenged those who doubted that the revelations were of God to attempt to write such a revelation themselves. William E. McLellin made such an attempt, which ended in failure.

After accepting the collection as scripture, the conference voted to print ten thousand copies and to send Oliver Cowdery and John Whitmer with the manuscript to Independence, Missouri, where the Saints had set up a printing press for the publication of a newspaper, the *Evening and the Morning Star*. During the Prophet's next visit to Independence, authorization was given for W. W. Phelps, the Church printer there, to proceed with publication, but with the printing order reduced to three thousand copies. Preparations for printing the book were well underway in August 1833 when a mob destroyed the press and scattered the printed forms. Local members were able to retrieve some of the sheets that had already been printed, but the Book of Commandments as such was never again printed by the Church.[1]

With the Prophet continuing to receive revelations, the first collection was soon inadequate. In a high council meeting at Kirtland on September 24, 1834, a committee was appointed to bring the collection of revelations up to date. Members of the committee were Joseph Smith, Oliver Cowdery, Sidney Rigdon, and Frederick G. Williams. This collection was presented by Elder Cowdery at a general assembly of the Church at Kirtland on August 17, 1835, as the "Book of Doctrine and Covenants of the Church." After written testimony of the twelve apostles concerning the truthfulness of the book was read, the assembly voted to receive the collection of revelations as scripture. Publication followed that fall.

Subsequent revelations accepted by the vote of the Church were added to later editions until the book reached its present size. No attempt was made to place in the book all of the revelations the Prophet had received, but those that set forth in plain language the doctrines of the Church and the commandments of God to his people. Also, not all of the sections are revelations. Remarks given by the Prophet on several occasions so clearly set forth the principles of the gospel that they were received by vote of the Church as doctrine and included in the volume. An account of the martyrdom of the Prophet and his brother Hyrum was later added, as well as a revelation to Brigham Young concerning the organizing of the camps of Israel and a vision of the redemption of the dead, received by Joseph F. Smith in 1918 (now section 138).

The Origin of the Book of Abraham

In July 1835 Joseph Smith came into possession of some ancient records, the value of which is not even yet fully appreciated.

Sometime in 1828 a French explorer named Antonio Sebolo secured permission to make a certain excavation in Egypt. Three years later, having secured the proper license, he employed 433 men and began excavating a catacomb or tomb near the site of ancient Thebes. The tomb contained several hundred mummies, of which Sebolo took eleven, still encased. En route back to Paris, he put in at Trieste, where he died after a brief illness. The mummies were left by will to a nephew named Michael Chandler, who lived in Philadelphia, Pennsylvania. Some two years later Chandler took possession of them in New York. When he opened the caskets, he was disappointed to find no jewels or precious ornaments. But attached to two of the bodies were rolls of well-preserved linen, and within these coverings were rolls of papyrus bearing a perfectly preserved record in carefully formed black and red characters. When he could find no one in New York or Philadelphia who could translate the characters, Chandler began touring the country with the mummies. On July 3, 1835, he reached Kirtland, Ohio, where he sought an interview with Joseph Smith, who, he had been told, might be able to translate the characters.

When the Prophet was able to interpret some of the characters, Chandler responded with a letter of certification, stating: "This is to make known to who may be desirous, concerning the knowledge of Mr. Joseph Smith, Jun., in deciphering the ancient Egyptian hieroglyphic characters in my possession, which I have, in many eminent cities, showed to the most learned; and, from the information that I could ever learn, or meet with, I find that of Mr. Joseph Smith, Jun., to correspond in the most minute matters." He signed it: "Michael H. Chandler, Traveling with, and proprietor of, Egyptian mummies."[2] A comparison was apparently made with a transcript of characters from the Book of Mormon plates, "resulting in the discovery of some points of resemblance."[3]

Friends of the Prophet in Kirtland later purchased the four mummies together with the rolls of papyrus. Joseph Smith, assisted by W. W. Phelps and Oliver Cowdery as scribes, subsequently began to study ancient languages and to translate the papyrus. Under date of October 1, 1835, he wrote: "This afternoon I labored in the Egyptian alphabet, in company with brothers Oliver Cowdery and W. W. Phelps, and during the research, the principles of astronomy as understood by Father Abraham and the ancients, unfolded to our understanding."[4] On December 16, 1835, he noted that when three of the brethren visited him, "I exhibited and explained the Egyptian records to them, and explained many things concerning the dealings of God with the ancients, and the formation of the planetary system."[5]

From this, it would appear that considerable translating had been done before the end of 1835, but the difficulties that faced the Church and the Prophet during the years immediately following prevented him from completing the work. In addition, no grammar of the Egyptian language had appeared in America by 1835. Thus, the results of his labor became the more remarkable. In a letter dated December 25, 1835, Oliver Cowdery wrote to William Frye in Gilead, Illinois:

> The language in which this record is written is very comprehensive, and many of the hieroglyphics exceedingly striking. The evidence is apparent upon the face, that they were written by persons acquainted with the history of the creation, the fall of man, and more or less of the correct ideas of notions of the Deity. The representation of the god head—three, yet in one, is curiously drawn to give simply, though impressively, the writers views of that exalted personage. The serpent, represented as walking, or formed in a manner to be able to walk, standing in front of, or near a female figure, is to me, one of the greatest representations I have ever seen upon paper, or a writing substance; and must go far towards convincing the rational mind of the correctness and divine authenticity of the holy scriptures.[6]

The Prophet completed only part of the scrolls dealing with the life of Abraham. One of the rolls of papyrus containing the writings of Joseph, who was sold into Egypt, was apparently never translated sufficiently for publication.[7] Publication of the Book of Abraham began in the newspaper *Times and Seasons* in March 1842 at Nauvoo, Illinois, along with facsimiles of certain portions of the papyrus.[8]

A Continuing Search for Knowledge

In the early period of the Church, there was a thirst for knowledge among its members that was unusual for the time and conditions under which people lived. As a rule, the difficult struggle for sustenance along the frontier dwarfed all efforts to advance in the arts and higher fields of learning. Elementary schools were crude and adult education was unknown. In contrast to this general condition was the attitude of the Latter-day Saints toward education, led by the Prophet himself, who was indefatigable in his search for knowledge. The knowledge he acquired during his short lifetime did not come to any great extent from books. He recognized God as the source of all knowledge, and whatever he gleaned from books or evolved from the workings of his own mind or the association with men was generally presented before the Lord for approval or disapproval. He firmly believed in the maxim that "the Lord helps those who help themselves."

Joseph had been unable to translate the Book of Mormon without divine aid. But he did not expect the Lord to continue to aid him in understanding ancient languages. Thus, he began a study of Egyptian, Hebrew, and Greek to enable him to better understand the Bible and other ancient documents concerning God's people. This study continued at intervals until his death. Among his notable achievements was the development at Kirtland of a grammar for the Egyptian hieroglyphic form of writing, which he used, along with divine aid, in translating the ancient writings of Abraham, now published as the Book of Abraham in the Pearl of Great Price. This grammar was never published and was perhaps never used by any one other than Joseph Smith. It was, however, the first known Egyptian grammar in America and was developed entirely independent of Champollion's *Egyptian Grammar*. The latter, which is the basis for all modern scholarship on the subject, made its appearance in 1836.

The Prophet's zeal for learning soon permeated the Church. In December 1832 he received a revelation in which the Saints were commanded to "teach one another the doctrine of the kingdom . . . that you may be instructed more perfectly in theory, in principle, in doctrine, in the law of the gospel, in all things that pertain unto the kingdom of God, that are expedient for you to understand; of things both in heaven and in the earth, and under the earth; things which have been, things which are, things which must shortly come to pass; things which are at home, things which are abroad; . . . and a knowledge also of countries and of kingdoms." (D&C 88:77-79.) This revelation, known as the Olive Leaf and subsequently published in the Doctrine and Covenants as section 88, was apparently received on December 27 and 28, 1832, and January 3, 1833.[9]

In January 1833, according to divine counsel he had thus received, the Prophet established a seminary for Church leaders and missionaries, to be called the School of the Prophets. The school initially met in an apartment occupied by the Prophet's family in the upper story of Newel K. Whitney's store in Kirtland. Fourteen men attended the first meeting; others were later invited to join. Those participating in the school were required to keep fully the commandments of God and were received into full fellowship only after they had participated in prayer, the sacrament, and the ordinance of the washing of feet.[10]

Many spiritual manifestations were experienced while the brethren attended sessions at the school, which was a forerunner of adult education in America. And at least one revelation was given as a result of the Prophet's inquiry for light and knowledge. In February 1833, after his wife, Emma, had complained about the mess left in the school by the tobacco-chewing brethren, he sought the Lord in prayer for counsel and guidance. In answer, he received a revelation that has become known as the Word of Wisdom. In this revelation the Lord counsels the Saints against the use of wine and all strong drinks as well as against the use of tobacco. He also states that herbs, fruits, the flesh of animals and of fowls, and grains have been ordained for the use of man. The revelation concludes with this promise: "All saints who remember to keep and do these sayings, walking in obedience to the commandments, shall receive health in their navel and marrow to their bones; and shall find wisdom and great treasures of knowledge, even hidden treasures." (D&C 89:18-19.)

The numerous revelations Joseph Smith received in answer to his earnest inquiries for knowledge constitute a unique latter-day scripture. These revelations became standards for the Church only after each was received as such by the vote of the members—the law of common consent that is a fundamental principle of the government of the Church.

13

Conflict in Missouri

It was inevitable that conflict would arise between Latter-day Saints and other inhabitants in Missouri. The stage was set for conflict, and it would have been strange indeed had it not occurred. There were five underlying causes:

1. The Latter-day Saints were a different people from those already living in Missouri.

The early settlers in Missouri were mainly poor people from the mountain regions of the southern states who had been induced by politicians to move into Missouri before 1820 and swell the slave-holding population. The region was admitted to the Union as a slave state in 1820. These settlers were contented with a few acres of cleared land along the river bottoms. They had a few home comforts, little education, and a totally undeveloped appreciation of the arts. Hospitable and honest, they believed in the institution of slavery and were suspicious of all northerners.

Another class of people, found along the western border of Missouri near the Church settlements, were outcasts from society who found safety from the arm of the law in these western outposts. To these people the Saints presented a marked contrast, for the Saints were of New England stock, thrifty, ambitious, desirous of fine homes and broad acres. They had a strict respect for the law of the land and a reverence for the law of the Lord.

2. The Saints' zeal for Zion aroused the suspicions of the old settlers.

While the commandment to settle in Jackson County had included the injunction that the lands settled should be purchased, the assertion that all that land would become Zion, the property of the Church, was disturbing to the old settlers. The Saints were contemplating an exclusive Zion where only "the righteous" could dwell and from which all others must necessarily move. This attitude may have seemed innocent enough to those inspired to work for a new Zion, but it did not encourage the love of the old settlers.

3. The economic and social practices of the Saints aroused the suspicions and enmity of the old inhabitants.

The Saints, even among outsiders, lived apart, as a unit. They isolated themselves socially. Young people were discouraged from association with non-Church members. Marriage outside the Church was severely frowned upon. Buying and selling were done collectively. Homes, stores, and other buildings arose like magic under community cooperation. The Saints purchased the broad prairie lands that were ready for the plow without the clearing of timber, and they organized large cooperative farms. It was inevitable that the old settlers should find the economic competition too keen for them, or, sensing its coming, that they should seek to prevent it.

4. The unity and zeal of the Saints aroused jealousy and enmity among Protestant ministers in Jackson County.

These ministers had been sent into Missouri by their respective churches to build communities of members. But the zeal of the new Zion stole the whole show. It overshadowed and dwarfed their own movement and their individual importance. Their efforts to convert the rough border element to a religious life had not been encouraging, and funds for church building had not been forthcoming. In addition, the incoming Latter-day Saints were making inroads upon their small congregations. It is little wonder that the majority became embittered and sought to recover their influence by driving the new church out.

5. The great numbers of incoming Yankees aroused the slaveholders.

The movement of Saints to Missouri was surprisingly rapid. In the first two years their numbers increased to over a thousand—not a great number in a thickly populated community, but sufficient to alarm the few old settlers of Jackson County. Further, the stream of incoming members was growing. New wagon caravans were constantly on the way, and there were rumors that thousands of people in Ohio would soon join the Missouri group.

The Saints were not seeking to upset the slavery status of Missouri, but that would be the result if the migration continued. Missouri had been admitted as a slave state by a narrow margin, and whether or not these northerners preached the freedom of the slaves, it was a foregone conclusion that they would not vote for slavery at the polls.

As the slavery question was to pursue the Saints for the next thirty years, it is necessary that we understand the status of slavery at the time in question.

The Constitution of the United States, adopted in 1789, provided that Congress should pass no law against slavery prior to 1808.[1] As that date approached, the number of free states and slave states was the same, resulting in equal numbers of senators in Congress. This balance in the Senate prevented the passage of any antislavery law. After the Louisiana purchase in 1803, settlers began to push west into Missouri. Southern statesmen saw the possibility of a new free state and the destruction of slavery's safeguard. To the South, slavery was important—so important that they were willing, as later years proved, to spill their blood in its defense. It is not surprising, then, to find in the archives of the South that money was used freely to induce the poor whites of the mountain region to migrate to Missouri and later demand of Congress that Missouri be admitted as a slave state. This movement was successful. Missouri voted for slavery and was admitted to the Union.

But after 1831, the status of Missouri was threatened by an influx of northerners. True, they had not come to oust slavery and were careful to say nothing about it. They came out of a religious zeal for a new Zion. Nevertheless, slavery in Missouri was threatened. There were no slaves in the new Zion, and the Saints boasted that Zion would grow until it would encompass the whole of Missouri.

George Q. Cannon, well acquainted with the conditions prevailing in that period, writes:

> The Latter-day Saints were men from the eastern states—Yankees—and consequently open to the suspicion of being Abolitionists. In upper Missouri in those days no charge could be made that would arouse more intense hatred and violence than that of being an abolitionist. The mere whisper of such a suspi-

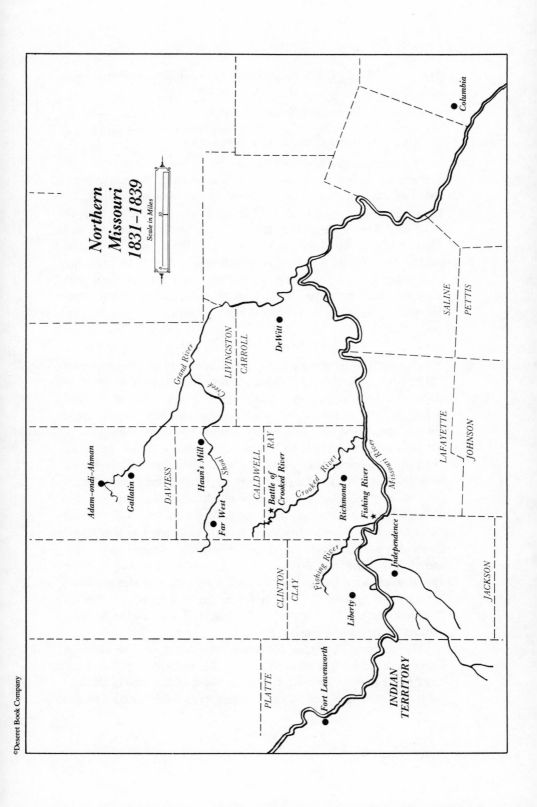

Northern
Missouri
1831–1839

Scale in Miles

©Deseret Book Company

Columbia

PETTIS

SALINE

JOHNSON

LAFAYETTE

LIVINGSTON

CARROLL

DeWitt

Grand River

Shoal Creek

DAVIESS

Adam-ondi-Ahman

Gallatin

Haun's Mill

Far West

CALDWELL

RAY

★ Battle of
Crooked River

Crooked River

Richmond

Fishing River

Missouri River

CLINTON

CLAY

Fishing River

Liberty

Independence

JACKSON

PLATTE

Fort Leavenworth

INDIAN
TERRITORY

cion was sufficient to inflame anger and arouse a mob. By such cries Pixley and others of his kind induced every dissolute idler in that region to join in an onslaught for plunder.[2]

How serious the South was in this struggle to defend slavery is well illustrated in the later settlement of the Kansas-Nebraska territory immediately west of the old Mormon homes in Missouri. There, in 1856, open warfare flamed. Slaveholders, seeking to drive non-slaveholders from the region, plundered, burned, and killed, and the northerners, unlike the Saints in Missouri, retaliated in kind until the total damage ran into millions of dollars and the loss of hundreds of lives. It is significant that many who took part in driving the Saints from Missouri were instrumental in fomenting the strife in the Kansas-Nebraska disturbance.

The Gathering Storm

The earliest rumblings of conflict occurred in the spring of 1832, when unknown individuals threw rocks through the windows of several Latter-day Saint homes. A few shots were fired into houses, with little damage. A number of stacks of hay were burned, and the Saints were being insulted by abusive language.

This was the prelude to the gathering storm. In the spring of 1833 the Reverend Finnis Ewing stirred opposition to the Saints by a publication that declared, among other things, that "Mormons were the common enemies of mankind, and ought to be destroyed."[3] Mass meetings were held. Early in July a document known as the "secret constitution" was circulated among non-Latter-day Saints, charging the Mormons with being "lazy, idle, and vicious," the very dregs of society, and as professing to have direct revelations from God "to perform all the wonder-working miracles wrought by the inspired Apostles and Prophets of old." This was declared "derogatory to God and religion, and to the utter subversive of human reason."[4]

The document, signed by many persons of note in Jackson County, called for a mass meeting July 20, 1833. As a result of the meeting, a committee was sent to demand of the Saints the immediate discontinuance of the printing press, the closing of the cooperative store, and the cessation of all mechanical labors. When the Saints refused to comply, a mob broke into the house of W. W. Phelps, where the printing press was located. The press was taken and many valuable documents were destroyed. Bishop Edward Partridge was tarred and feathered. He reported:

> I was taken from my house by the mob, George Simpson being their leader, who escorted me about half a mile, to the court house, on the public square in Independence; and then and there, a few rods from said court house, surrounded by hundreds of the mob, I was stripped of my hat, coat and vest and daubed with tar from head to foot, and then had a quantity of feathers put upon me; and all this because I would not agree to leave the county, and my home where I had lived two years.
>
> Before tarring and feathering me I was permitted to speak. I told them that the Saints had suffered persecution in all ages of the world; that I had done nothing which ought to offend anyone; that if they abused me, they would abuse an innocent person; that I was willing to suffer for the sake of Christ, but, to leave the country, I was not then willing to consent to it. . . . I bore my abuse with so much resignation and meekness, that it appeared to astound the multitude, who permitted me to retire in silence, many looking very solemn, their sympathies having been touched as I thought; and as to myself, I was so filled with the Spirit and love of God, that I had no hatred towards my persecutors or anyone else.[5]

On July 23 a crowd of non-Mormons gathered outside of Independence armed with rifles, old sabres, and other weapons, and bearing a red flag. To prevent bloodshed, the Saints entered into a treaty and agreed to leave the county by the first of the year. A committee of old settlers was appointed to help the Saints dispose of their property and to help prevent mob uprisings.

The treaty offered a temporary breathing spell, and Oliver Cowdery was sent on the thousand-mile journey to Kirtland to confer with the Prophet. A petition was also prepared and sent to "His Excellency, Daniel Dunklin, Governor of the State of Missouri," setting forth the grievances of the Saints and acquainting him with the true state of affairs. The petition asked that state troops be raised for the protection of property and that martial law be declared in the county. Meanwhile, depredations continued in direct violation of the agreement with the mob.

On October 18, 1833, Governor Dunklin replied to the petition. He regretted the Saints' difficulties and urged them to appeal to the courts of law to establish their rights, to preserve the peace, and to secure redress for their grievances.[6] As a result of this response, the Saints hired lawyers from Clay County, and a number of lawsuits were prepared and filed. This seemed the signal for a fresh attack. Officers of the courts were threatened with violence if the court actions were allowed.

On Thursday night, October 31, a mob armed with guns demolished ten homes of the Saints west of the Big Blue River, beat the male inhabitants, and drove the women and children into the woods. On November 1 one mob proceeded to attack a small prairie settlement while another stoned houses and shops in Independence and drove the men from their homes.

The next day the Saints in Independence, despairing of help from civil authorities, moved with some of their personal goods about one mile out of town and organized themselves for defense. Meanwhile, the mobs continued their work of turning the Saints out-of-doors and destroying their homes in the smaller settlements. The reign of terror lasted until the middle of November, by which time twelve hundred Saints had been driven out of Jackson County and 203 homes had been destroyed.

The Saints were not expelled without putting up some defense, but the opposition was not united. While some believed that God would justify them in defending their homes, the majority opposed the use of force as contrary to their religious beliefs.[7]

Some of the more militant Saints took up arms under the leadership of Lyman Wight and had several skirmishes with the mob, the main encounter being referred to as the battle of the Big Blue (after the river by that name). Wight's defensive movement was short-lived. On November 5 the militia was called out by Lieutenant-Governor Lilburn W. Boggs, a sympathizer of the mob and a slaveholder. Colonel Thomas Pitcher, a deputy constable of Jackson County and an energetic leader in the movement to oust the Saints, was placed in charge. Colonel Pitcher, promising that the mob would be forced to give up their arms, persuaded the Saints to turn over to the militia all their weapons of defense. They did so, with a feeling that they might then return to their homes in peace. Their hopes were soon dashed by a fresh series of mobbings that did not halt until every Latter-day Saint had left from Jackson County.

The exiles moved northward to the Missouri River and crossed as rapidly as possible on ferry boats into Clay County, the only county that had extended to them a welcome. Elder Parley P. Pratt, who was with the exiles, leaves a vivid picture:

> The shore began to be lined on both sides of the ferry with men, women and children; goods, wagons, boxes, provisions, etc., while the ferry was constantly employed; and when night closed upon us the cottonwood bottom had much the appearance of a camp meeting. Hundreds of people were seen in every direction, some in tents and some in the open air around their fires, while the rain descended in torrents. Husbands were inquiring for their wives, wives for their husbands; parents for children, and children for parents. Some had the good fortune to escape with their families, household goods, and some provisions; while others knew not the fate of their friends, and had lost all their goods. The scene was indescribable, and, I am sure, would have melted the hearts of any people on the earth, except our blind oppressors.[8]

The March of Zion's Camp

While the twelve hundred Saints of Jackson County were undergoing their trying experiences, the main body of the Church in Ohio was facing many difficulties of its own. A temple had been started at Kirtland, and the $60,000 cost had drained the treasury of the Church and most of the ready cash of its members. Also, persecution of the Saints in Ohio had broken out. The Prophet especially was harassed by lawsuits, which, though groundless, hampered his movements. Problems in organization constantly confronted him, as every little branch of the Church seemed to have its troubles.

It is not surprising, then, that in the midst of the enormous burden placed upon him, the Prophet did not realize the deep underlying causes of the Missouri persecutions. Twice in the two years following the dedication of Zion, he had made hasty journeys to Missouri to straighten out tangled matters that had arisen. In addition, a great deal of correspondence had been carried on between Independence and Kirtland. But many of the Saints in Missouri felt that the Prophet had deserted them. They fully expected him to move to the new Zion and could not reconcile themselves to his continued residence at Kirtland. News that a temple was being erected in Ohio, while the ground at the temple site in Independence was yet unbroken, aroused bitter feelings, which were ill-concealed. When the Saints were driven out of Jackson County, the Prophet looked no further than the apparent disobedience of the Saints as the chief cause. By letter he called them again to repentance and promised the reestablishment of Zion in the same place.

In looking back upon the events of the time, it is no reflection upon the greatness of Joseph Smith or upon his calling as a prophet of God that he saw only a part of the problem and not the whole of it in that fateful winter of 1833-34. He was, after all, a human being with human limitations, but faced with unusual problems. If the subsequent failure in reestablishing Zion at Independence caused a new bitterness in the hearts of some toward the Prophet, it was all the more bitter to the Prophet himself.

In their correspondence with Governor Dunklin during the months of November and December 1833 and January 1834, the Saints were encouraged to attempt to regain their rights by organizing as an armed militia. However, the mob in Jackson County would also be armed and would outnumber them two to one. It was useless to attempt to settle again in their homes without additional military aid. The courts seemed powerless to protect them.

To relieve the situation, early in the spring of 1834 Joseph Smith organized a group of some two hundred volunteers in Ohio to march to the aid of their brethren in Missouri. This organization came to be known as Zion's Camp. The men, heavily armed and well provisioned, were organized into companies of tens, fifties, and hundreds, with officers over each.

Letters of the Prophet to the brethren in Missouri indicate that the Ohio contingent was ready to fight for the rights of the Saints if that seemed feasible. Word of their coming reached the anti-Mormon settlers of Jackson County long before their arrival, and armed bands were directed to meet and turn them back.

As Zion's Camp neared Jackson County, Parley P. Pratt and Orson Hyde were dispatched to Governor Dunklin with a request that he carry out his promises to the Saints and call out the militia to aid in restoring the exiles to their homes. The governor, who had previously indicated great sympathy for the Saints and had appeared ready to champion their cause, refused. He expressed a fear of a civil war if the Saints were to resort to arms. In a later letter, dated July 18, 1836, the charge that the Saints were opposed to slavery appears as the chief accusation against them.[9] The question of slavery, coming before the governor in such force at this time, was unquestionably the factor that caused him to do an about-face in his attitude toward the Saints. Feelings on the slave question were tense and a civil war not at all improbable.

Several attempts were made to settle peaceably the difficulties between the Saints and the old settlers. Offers and counteroffers were made, but these proved fruitless. The Saints were not able to buy out all the old settlers of Jackson County at the terms offered, and they were unwilling to sell their own lands because of their belief that Zion would yet be established there. This latter attitude was heightened by a revelation Joseph Smith had received December 16, 1833, which stated: "It is my will that my people should claim, and hold claim upon that which I have appointed unto them, though they should not be permitted to dwell thereon." (D&C 101:99.) In addition, the Prophet had written to the Saints in Missouri in a letter dated December 10, 1833, and noted: "It is better in the eyes of God that you should die, than that you should give up the land of Zion, the inheritances which you have purchased with your moneys; for every man that giveth not up his inheritance, though he should die, yet, when the Lord shall come, he shall stand upon it, and with Job in his flesh he shall see God."[10]

On June 19, 1834, while Zion's Camp was settled for the night on a piece of elevated ground between Big and Little Fishing rivers, mobs sent to intercept them made an appearance. Sixty men from Ray County and seventy from Clay County were being joined by some two hundred men from Jackson County, directly across the Missouri River. A sudden and terrific storm scattered the mobs, however, and made it impossible for them to join forces. The next day the majority of them returned to their homes.

In a revelation received by Joseph Smith at Fishing River on June 22, the Saints were counseled to "wait for a little season for the redemption of Zion. . . . For behold, I do not require at their hands to fight the battles of Zion; . . . even so will I fulfil—I will fight your battles." (D&C 105:9, 14.)

With the governor turned against them and the strength of the opposition being realized, the Saints realized the wisdom of disbanding the camp and awaiting a future redemption. Zion's Camp continued peaceably into Clay County, where, on July 3, it was disbanded and the members were given leave to return home. Thus ended the attempts to restore the Saints to their lands in Jackson County. Henceforth they directed their energies to building up new communities in counties north of the Missouri River.

Though Zion's Camp had failed in its initial mission, it had nevertheless been of great value. The form of organization was later the pattern used in guiding the great exodus of the Saints to the Rocky Mountains. Brigham Young and others received in the Zion's Camp experience valuable for the leadership they were later to assume. From the members of this camp was chosen the first Quorum of Twelve Apostles. The willingness of two hundred men to give their all, even to their life's blood, to help establish Zion in her place, is a lasting monument to the faith and courage of the Saints.

Concerning the failure of the Saints to establish Zion in Jackson County, the Lord, through revelation, consoled them: "When I give a commandment to any of the sons of men to do a work unto my name, and those sons of men go with all their might and with all they have to perform that work, and cease not their diligence, and their enemies come upon them and hinder them from performing that work, behold, it behooveth me to require that work no more at the hands of those sons of men, but to accept of their offerings. . . . Therefore, for this cause have I accepted the offerings of those whom I commanded to build up a city and a house unto my name, in Jackson county, Missouri, and were hindered by their enemies." After indicating that he would bring justice and judgment upon the wrongdoers, he added: "And this I make an example unto you, for your consolation concerning all those who have been commanded to do a work and have been hindered by the hands of their enemies, and by oppression." (D&C 124:49, 51, 53.)

In the light of this revelation, Joseph Smith, after the Saints settled in Nauvoo, Illinois, sent a committee to Jackson County, Missouri, with instructions to sell properties there that were still owned by the Church or its members.

14

The Calling of Leaders

At his last supper with his disciples, the Savior made a significant announcement to the twelve apostles concerning leadership in his church: "Ye have not chosen me, but I have chosen you, and ordained you, that ye should go and bring forth fruit, and that your fruit should remain: that whatsoever ye shall ask of the Father in my name, he may give it you." (John 15:16.)

In the church of Jesus Christ in these latter days, as in his church in the days of the original Twelve, the leaders are called of Jesus Christ. In stating the doctrine of the Church in this matter, the Prophet Joseph Smith declared: "We believe that a man must be called of God, by prophecy, and by the laying on of hands by those who are in authority, to preach the Gospel and administer in the ordinances thereof." (Article of Faith 5.)

In all ages the true messengers of God have been called and ordained by him for their work, and this may be said to be one of the distinguishing features of the true church of Jesus Christ. Noah was thus called to preach repentance unto his generation. (Genesis 6:8.) Abraham was called to leave his former home and establish the true faith in a new land. (Abraham 2:6-11.) Moses was called out of bondage (Exodus 3:2-10), and Aaron was called of God to assist him (Exodus 4:14-16). When he was old, Moses pleaded with the Lord to call his successor, and Joshua was chosen. (Numbers 27:15-23.)

The apostles of Jesus Christ in the meridian of time were called directly by him, both those at Jerusalem and those chosen from among the Nephites on the American continent. In the restored church also, leaders are called of God and given authority to act in his stead upon the earth. Acting for God, the leaders of the Church call men and bestow upon them the offices and keys of priesthood necessary to their calling. It is the priesthood that leads the Church. Those who do not hold priesthood but are called as leaders and workers in various capacities are placed under those holding authority from God.

In the first vision to Joseph Smith, God identified his Son, Jesus Christ, and his authority when he said: "This is my Beloved Son. Hear him."

With that authority, Christ directed all that Joseph was to do. In calling others to assist Joseph Smith, Christ always identified himself to them. There was never any question of who it was that directed the restoration of the Church. Nor was there any question as to the authority given to Joseph Smith, his servant, for the Lord declared, "I will be with him, and I will sanctify him before the people; for unto him I have given the keys of this kingdom and ministry." (D&C 115:19.) Joseph Smith thus had authority to call and ordain those needed to help in the work. He took no credit unto himself for the doctrines he taught, for they came not of man but from God. Neither the Prophet nor any of his disciples ever claimed originality for these doctrines. Quite the contrary. Joseph claimed to be only a restorer of the gospel, the plan of life and salvation. He said on a number of occasions, "I was but a rough stone till the Lord took me in hand to polish me."

The Role of Priesthood Leadership

The period from 1831 to 1837, during which the headquarters of the Church remained at Kirtland, witnessed a rapid unfolding of Church organization. The foundation of Church government is the priesthood, and in that priesthood are two divisions—the Aaronic, or "Lesser," Priesthood and the Melchizedek, or "Higher," Priesthood. After the Melchizedek Priesthood had been given to Joseph Smith and Oliver Cowdery, and Joseph had received the keys of the kingdom, all of the authority existed that was necessary to bring the Church into being and to establish such offices and functions as needed. This power was subject, of course, to the common consent of those who had accepted the gospel and had been baptized into the kingdom of God.

On January 25, 1832, a conference of the Church was held in Amherst, Lorain County, Ohio, and here Joseph Smith was sustained as president of the High Priesthood of the Church and ordained to that office.[1] This ordination carries with it the office of president over the entire church. In a revelation we read: "And again, the duty of the President of the office of the High Priesthood is to preside over the whole church, and to be like unto Moses—behold, here is wisdom; yea, to be a seer, a revelator, a translator, and a prophet, having all the gifts of God which he bestows upon the head of the church." (D&C 107:91-92.)

Joseph Smith was sustained in that office by the vote of the Church in both Ohio and Missouri. He was as yet without counselors, and continued so for a little over a year. In response to a prayer on the matter of counselors, he received a revelation on March 8, 1833, calling Sidney Rigdon and Frederick G. Williams to serve in that capacity and to be equal with him "in holding the keys of this last kingdom." In the same revelation the Prophet was assured that "the keys of this kingdom shall never be taken from you, while thou art in the world, neither in the world to come; nevertheless, through you shall the oracles be given to another, yea, even unto the church." (D&C 90:6, 3-4.)

Ten days later the two counselors were ordained to that office by Joseph and were sustained by the vote of the Saints at their earliest conferences. Thus was brought into existence the First Presidency of The Church of Jesus Christ of Latter-day Saints. The president and his counselors constitute a quorum called the Quorum of the First Presidency.

On December 5, 1834, the quorum of the First Presidency met and ordained Oliver Cowdery as Assistant President of the Church. Later Hyrum Smith was ordained to this office. This is the only time in the history of the Church when there has been an Assistant President. However, more than two counselors have sometimes been called when more have been needed to care for the affairs of the Church. The organization of the Church is highly flexible and may be changed at any time to meet new conditions.

The Organization of Church Units

Early in the Church, provisions were made to organize the Saints into subdivisions called stakes and wards. The size of the territory comprising a ward usually depended upon its membership, and several wards formed a stake. The first stakes were organized at Kirtland, Ohio, and Clay County, Missouri. Zion, established at Independence, Missouri, was not organized as a stake but was the "center place," the Holy City, to be supported and strengthened by the stakes, like unto the stakes to which tent lines are tied.

In February 1834, a stake organization was effected at Kirtland with the First Presidency of the Church acting as the stake presidency. A high council consisting of twelve high priests was ordained to act within the stake "for the purpose of settling important difficulties which might arise in the church, which could not be settled by the church or the bishop's council to the satisfaction of the parties." (D&C 102:2.)

Later in 1834, a stake was organized in Clay County, Missouri, with David Whitmer as president and W. W. Phelps and John Whitmer as counselors. A high council for that stake was also chosen and ordained.

We must bear in mind that Joseph Smith and his counselors were acting in a double capacity. The office of "First Presidency of the High Priesthood," which is the First Presidency of the Church, was separate and distinct from their office as a stake presidency. In the former capacity they were at the head of the whole church. In the latter capacity their authority was limited to the stake at Kirtland. We will find that as the Church progressed in numbers, the First Presidency found their time fully occupied with that office, and, after the Church headquarters moved from Kirtland, a dual capacity was never held again by the First Presidency.

Twelve Apostles Are Chosen

As early as June 1829, it was known that twelve apostles would be chosen and ordained in the Church. Their nomination was to be made by Oliver Cowdery, David Whitmer, and Martin Harris, the three special witnesses of the Book of Mormon. The apostles were to be special witnesses of Christ to all the world, a traveling high council for the whole Church, officiating under the direction of the

First Presidency. This quorum was not organized, however, until the Church had grown to need it.

After the march of Zion's Camp, a special conference of the Church was called at Kirtland. On February 14, 1835, the three witnesses selected those to be apostles as follows: Thomas B. Marsh, David W. Patten, Brigham Young, Heber C. Kimball, Orson Hyde, William E. McLellin, Parley P. Pratt, Luke S. Johnson, William Smith, Orson Pratt, John F. Boynton, and Lyman E. Johnson.[2] These were unanimously sustained by the conference and later by the Saints in Missouri.

The Seventies Are Organized

Quorums of seventy were also to be chosen to assist the Quorum of the Twelve in bearing witness of Christ to all the world, acting under the direction of the Twelve. On February 28, 1835, the first quorum of the seventy was organized. Its seventy members, like the Twelve, were chosen from among those who had been members of Zion's Camp. Seven of them were ordained as presidents of the quorum: Hazen Aldrich, Leonard Rich, Joseph Young, Zebedee Coltrin, Levi W. Hancock, Lyman Sherman, and Sylvester Smith. The seventies were to constitute traveling quorums "to go into all the earth, whithersoever the Twelve Apostles shall call them."[3]

A second quorum of seventy was ordained shortly afterward. The number of quorums was later increased as the need arose. By January 1, 1845, there were fourteen quorums of seventy.

During this early period of the Church there were no auxiliary organizations. Sacrament meetings were held each Sunday, and priesthood meetings were also held on a regular basis. Quarterly conferences of the Church were held, with many special conferences to consider vital problems.

15

The Beginning of Temple Building

In December 1832, Joseph Smith received a revelation in which the Saints were commanded to "establish a house, even a house of prayer, a house of fasting, a house of faith, a house of learning, a house of glory, a house of order, a house of God." (D&C 88:119.)

A few months later, at a conference of high priests of the Church on May 4, 1833, a committee was named to begin making plans for a building to house a school for the elders. This committee was composed of Hyrum Smith, Jared Carter, and Reynolds Cahoon.[1] The same day the Prophet Joseph Smith was told by the Lord in revelation, "Ye have sinned against me a very grievous sin, in that ye have not considered the great commandment in all things, that I have given unto you concerning the building of mine house." The revelation went on to counsel,

> Let the house be built, not after the manner of the world, for I give not unto you that ye shall live after the manner of the world; therefore, let it be built after the manner which I shall show unto three of you, whom ye shall appoint and ordain unto this power. And the size thereof shall be fifty and five feet in width, and let it be sixty-five feet in length, in the inner court thereof. And let the lower part of the inner court be dedicated unto me for your sacrament offering, and for your preaching, and your fasting, and your praying, and the offering up of your most holy desires unto me, saith your Lord. And let the higher part of the inner court be dedicated unto me for the school of mine apostles. (D&C 95:3, 14-17.)

With these instructions in mind, the high priests again convened on June 3 to discuss the proposed house of the Lord. Joseph Smith, Sidney Rigdon, and Frederick G. Williams were appointed to draft plans for the "inner court."[2] Approval was given on June 6 to the committee appointed earlier to proceed immediately with building the structure.[3] The work would take three years at a cost of some sixty thousand dollars.

This was a courageous undertaking for a church that was itself only three years old. The treasury was virtually empty, and the members themselves were, for the most part, relatively poor. But courageous as the undertaking was, the remarkable thing was its accomplishment and the manner in which that accomplishment was brought about. No miracle was performed to produce funds. No millionaire endowed it. The beautiful colonial-style structure was a monument to cooperation—to the power of a people imbued with a common objective and inspired with a common faith. Greater and more costly temples would be erected by the Church later, but none so taxed the energies and resources of the people.

A letter from the First Presidency to the Saints in Missouri, dated June 25, 1833, contained this announcement: "We have commenced building the house of the Lord, in this place [Kirtland], and it goes on rapidly."[4]

Though the persecutions in Missouri at that time diverted some of the temple funds, they failed to divert the work. When Zion's Camp took the majority of the workmen on the temple, older men and young boys took their places. After Zion's Camp disbanded in Missouri, the men returned a thousand miles on foot to take up the mason's trowel and don the carpenter's apron anew. And all of this with no thought of pay, none of the rewards for which men ordinarily labor. The women also labored unselfishly. Heber C. Kimball, who devoted much of his own time to the temple construction, wrote in his journal:

> My wife had toiled all summer in lending her aid toward its accomplishment. She took a hundred pounds of wool to spin on shares, which, with the assistance of a girl, she spun, in order to furnish clothing for those engaged in building the temple; and although she had the privilege of keeping half the quantity of wool for herself, as a recompense for her labor, she did not reserve so much as would make a pair of stockings, but gave it for those who were laboring at the house of the Lord. Almost all the sisters in Kirtland labored in knitting, sewing, spinning, etc., for the same purpose; while we went up to Missouri to endeavor to

reinstate our brethren on the lands from which they had been driven.

Those who had not teams went to work in the stone quarry and prepared the stones for drawing to the house. The Prophet, being our foreman, would put on his tow [the coarse or broken part of flax or hemp] frock and tow pantaloons and go into the quarry. The Presidency, High Priests, and Elders all alike assisting. Those who had teams assisted in drawing the stone to the house. These all laboring one day in the week, brought as many stones to the house as supplied the masons through the whole week. We continued in this manner until the walls of the house were reared.[5]

The plan for the temple was given to Joseph Smith and the other members of the First Presidency, Sidney Rigdon and Frederick G. Williams, in vision. Orson Pratt later reported: "The Lord gave [the Saints] the pattern by vision from heaven, and commanded them to build that house according to that pattern and order; to have the architecture, not in accordance with architecture devised by men, but to have everything constructed in that house according to the heavenly pattern that he by his voice had inspired to his servants."[6]

The cornerstone was laid July 23, 1833, some six weeks after workers started digging the foundation, with twenty-four priesthood holders participating.

The committee composed of Hyrum Smith, Reynolds Cahoon, and Jared Carter continued to supervise the building and seek funds for its completion. In a letter sent to branches throughout the Church they wrote:

> We feel under obligations to write to you as well as to all the brethren of the different branches; and we do this, that you, with us, may exert yourselves to bring about the fulfilment of the command of the Lord concerning the establishing, or preparing a house, wherein the Elders who have been commanded of the Lord so to do, may gather themselves together, and prepare all things, and call a solemn assembly, and treasure up words of wisdom; . . . and now, in order to accomplish this, we are directed, yea, we are under the necessity, to call upon the whole Church as a body, that they may make every possible exertion to aid tempo-

rally, as well as spiritually, in this great work. . . . May the Lord
help you to exert yourselves with us, in raising the means to bring
about the glorious work of the Lord.[7]

As Church leaders visited branches in outlying areas, they
asked the Saints to contribute to the temple fund. A number of
individuals were also pressed into service on special fund-raising
missions. Some of the Saints contributed generously. For example, John Tanner loaned the Prophet money to help pay the
debt incurred for the temple site and also contributed about three
thousand dollars for supplies for the bishop's storehouse. To do
this, he had to sell his property in Bolton, New York, including
over two hundred acres of land, a sawmill, and a gristmill.[8] But
despite these efforts and the continual sacrifice of members in Kirtland, the committee was still thousands of dollars in debt when the
building was completed.

By the latter part of 1835, meetings were held in some of the
completed portions of the building. So urgent was the need for the
temple that, at its dedication on March 27, 1836, the second story
was still unfinished.

The first and second stories each had a large single hall, 55 feet
long by 65 feet wide and 22 feet high. At each end of each au-
ditorium were four tiers of pulpits, and within each pulpit were
three seats for the presidencies of the Melchizedek and Aaronic
priesthoods. White curtains were arranged on rollers so that, when
desired, they could be lowered to divide each room into two or four
rooms. Heber C. Kimball wrote: "The first story or lower room
was dedicated for divine worship alone. The second was finished
similar in form to the first, but was designed wholly for instructing
the Priesthood, and was supplied with tables and seats instead of
slips. In the attic, five rooms were finished for the convenience of
schools and for different quorums of the Church to meet in."[9]

The Saints could well be pardoned their pride in the building.
The historian Bancroft said of it: "The building of this structure
by a few hundred persons, who, during the period between 1832
and 1836, contributed voluntarily of their money, material, or
labor, . . . was regarded with wonder throughout all northern
Ohio."[10]

Kirtland Temple

The Temple Dedication

The dedication of the temple in March 1836 was a joyous event in the lives of the Saints. Those from nearby branches in Ohio and even a few from Missouri journeyed to Kirtland afoot, on horseback, or in wagons to witness the proceedings. By seven o'clock the morning of the dedicatory services, March 27, more than five hundred persons had lined up near the temple doors. When the doors were opened an hour later, more than eight hundred crowded into the building for the dedicatory service, and the doors had to be closed well before the service began at nine. Since hundreds could not get in, the Prophet recommended that the overflow crowd convene for a separate meeting in the schoolhouse west of the temple. The dedicatory services were repeated on Thursday, March 31, in order that all might be able to participate.

President Sidney Rigdon conducted the service on March 27. He also gave the opening prayer and delivered a two-and-a-half-hour sermon. This was followed by a sustaining vote for Joseph Smith as prophet and seer, first from the priesthood quorums and then from the congregation.

After a twenty-minute intermission, the service reconvened. President Joseph Smith delivered a short address and called upon the quorums and the congregation to "acknowledge the Presidency as Prophets and Seers, and uphold them by their prayers. They all covenanted to do so, by rising." He then called upon the quorums and congregation to acknowledge the Twelve Apostles as prophets, seers, and revelators and "special witnesses to all the nations of the earth." Other officers were also presented for sustaining vote, including the seventies, high councils, and bishops of Kirtland and Zion, and presidencies of the priests, teachers, and deacons quorums.[11]

The dedicatory prayer delivered by the Prophet on that occasion has become a model in thought for all succeeding dedicatory prayers for temples of the Church. (D&C 109.) These words contained in the prayer reflect its general spirit:

> Grant, Holy Father, that all those who shall worship in this house may be taught words of wisdom out of the best books, and that they may seek learning even by study, and also by faith, as thou hast said; . . . and that this house may be a house of prayer, a house of fasting, a house of faith, a house of glory and of God, even thy house; . . . and that no unclean thing shall be permitted to come into thy house to pollute it. . . .
>
> Remember the kings, the princes, the nobles, and the great ones of the earth, and all people, and the churches, all the poor, the needy, and afflicted ones of the earth; that their hearts may be softened when thy servants shall go out from thy house, O Jehovah, to bear testimony of thy name; that their prejudices may give way before the truth, and thy people may obtain favor in the sight of all; that all the ends of the earth may know that we, thy servants, have heard thy voice, and that thou hast sent us. (D&C 109:14, 16, 20, 55-57.)

In the journals of many who attended the services are testimonies that angels were present and heavenly choirs were heard. Historian Milton V. Backman writes:

> As the dedication services continued, the Prophet testified of his prophetic mission and of his being blessed with visitations from angelic beings, after which several others bore their testimonies. . . . Frederick G. Williams testified that during the

dedicatory service he had seen a heavenly messenger enter the temple and sit between himself and Father Smith. David Whitmer testified that he also had beheld heavenly beings during the services.

Some who attended the solemn assembly declared that the Savior was present. Truman O. Angell recorded in his journal that as Elder Rigdon was offering the opening prayer, "a glorious sensation passed through the House," and many felt a sensation that elevated their souls. During the afternoon meeting, he reported, Joseph Smith arose and informed the congregation that the personage whom President Williams had seen was the apostle Peter, who had come to accept the dedication. Heber C. Kimball also declared that apostle Peter attended and accepted the dedicatory service. He declared that the heavenly being who had sat near President Williams and Father Smith was a tall personage with white hair who wore a long garment that extended to his ankles.[12]

At the conclusion of the dedicatory services, the congregation "sealed the proceedings of the day by shouting hosanna, hosanna, hosanna to God and the Lamb, three times, sealing it each time with amen, amen, and amen."[13]

Over the following week, outpourings of the Spirit continued to be experienced by Saints attending meetings in the temple. This was climaxed by a lengthy service on April 3. At the conclusion of the service, Joseph Smith "retired to the pulpit, the veils being dropped, and bowed myself, with Oliver Cowdery, in solemn and silent prayer. After rising from prayer, the following vision was opened to both of us—

The veil was taken from our minds, and the eyes of our understanding were opened.

We saw the Lord standing upon the breastwork of the pulpit, before us; and under His feet was a paved work of pure gold in color like amber.

His eyes were as a flame of fire; the hair of His head was white like the pure snow; His countenance shone above the brightness of the sun, and His voice was as the sound of the rushing of great waters, even the voice of Jehovah, saying—

I am the first and the last, I am He who liveth, I am He who was slain, I am your advocate with the Father.

Behold, your sins are forgiven you; you are clean before me, therefore lift up your heads and rejoice. Let the hearts of your brethren rejoice, and let the hearts of all my people rejoice, who have, with their might, built this house to my name. For behold, I have accepted this house, and my name shall be here, and I will manifest myself to my people in mercy in this House. . . .

After this vision closed, the heavens were again opened unto us; and Moses appeared before us, and committed unto us the keys of the gathering of Israel from the four parts of the earth, and the leading of the Ten Tribes from the land of the north.

After this, Elias appeared, and committed the dispensation of the gospel of Abraham, saying, that in us, and our seed, all generations after us should be blessed.

After this vision had closed, another great and glorious vision burst upon us, for Elijah The prophet, who was taken to heaven without tasting death, stood before us, and said—

Behold, the time has fully come, which was spoken of by the mouth of Malachi, testifying that he [Elijah] should be sent before the great and dreadful day of the Lord come—

To turn the hearts of the fathers to the children, and the children to the fathers, lest the whole earth be smitten with a curse.

Therefore, the keys of this dispensation are committed into your hands; and by this ye may know that the great and dreadful day of the Lord is near, even at the doors.[14]

These statements were accepted as a revelation by the solemn assembly of the Church. The authority for doing temple work in the Church, which has grown to tremendous proportions today, is based upon this restoration of the keys of priesthood necessary to those functions, and especially upon the restoration of the keys held by Elijah.

The Kirtland Temple was not constructed for the ordinance referred to by Elijah. It contained no baptismal font for work for the dead, nor was it designed for other work now performed in temples of the Latter-day Saints. It was a holy meeting place, a place for instruction under the Spirit of God, a place of preparation for the great temple building era that followed.

16

The Saints Are Driven
Out of Missouri

From most appearances in the fall of 1837, the Church was rapidly approaching dissolution. Apostasy had rocked the organization to the very center. Even such great leaders as Oliver Cowdery, Martin Harris, and David Whitmer, the special witnesses of the Book of Mormon, had left the fold.

It is significant that, during this trying period, the optimism of Joseph Smith, and his assurance that the Church would stand forever, never faltered. In the darkest hours of apostasy he initiated two movements that strengthened the Church and illustrate his remarkable vision of the work ahead. He sent missionaries, with Heber C. Kimball at their head, to open a mission in England. Then he made a journey into northern Missouri and engineered the laying out of new towns to accommodate a great influx in population.

Both moves were timely. The British people were anxious for the gospel, and the Church's membership continued to grow despite the apostasies. And when the Saints in Ohio were forced to flee to a new land, that land was ready for them in Missouri.

Among the new towns laid out in northern Missouri were Adam-ondi-Ahman, Gallatin, and Millport in Daviess County, Far West and Haun's Mill in Caldwell County, and DeWitt in Carroll County. The Prophet's advice to the Saints in all of these settlements was to live within the cities with their farms on the outside. Small clusters of homes away from the central locations were discouraged. The centers were laid out as nearly as possible according to the plan for cities of Zion.

Some new social experiments are worthy of notice. Large farming corporations were organized for cooperative farming. One of these cooperative farms, the Western Agricultural Company, voted to enclose one field containing twelve sections of land, or 7,680 acres. A similar area was to be farmed by the Southern Agricultural Company, and one by the Eastern Agricultural Company. But the Saints were driven from the state before the plan could be carried out.

The Church population in Daviess, Caldwell, Ray, and Carroll counties was swelled rapidly by the steady stream of immigrants from the East as well as twelve hundred refugees who had been driven out of Jackson County. Long caravans of covered wagons cut deep ruts across the Missouri prairies. By the summer of 1838, the numbers in northern Missouri totaled fifteen thousand.

It was inevitable that persecution would follow. All the old causes of disquiet were intensified by numbers. One county would not hold the Saints; they were overflowing into all northwestern Missouri. In a few years they might conceivably dominate the state. Even the finest citizens became alarmed, and in that alarm all the wild and lawless element of the frontier found an opportunity to plunder and ravage.

The renewed persecution began at Gallatin on election day, August 6, 1838. A group of Latter-day Saint men appeared at the polls to vote. A much larger group of non-Mormons, led by Colonel William P. Peniston, a candidate for the state legislature, sought to prevent the casting of ballots, and a bitter fight ensued in which some heads were cracked. The Saints gained the upper hand, and Peniston's men withdrew to take up arms.

This was the beginning of the end for the Saints in Missouri. Once trouble began, misunderstandings grew apace. Distorted reports circulated rapidly; inflamed speeches against "Abolitionists" and "Yankees" were daily occurrences; and ministers renewed their charges against Latter-day Saint healings, signs, visions, and so forth. The whole population of northern Missouri became alarmed. Nor can the general populace be blamed. The Southerners' prejudice against Yankees was deep-seated. Reports of huge cooperative farms were disturbing to the agricultural element, and the competition of cooperative mercantile establishments was threatening disaster to non-Mormon merchants. The majority knew little of the Saints, nor had they any way of knowing, except from ministers and the press.

Among those well acquainted with the Saints, we find a

friendship for them that lasted throughout the persecution and manifested itself in many acts of kindness. But a certain lawless element had unfortunately found refuge from the law in the western part of Missouri, and it was this element that, under cover of the general feelings against the Saints, committed acts of wanton cruelty. Many of them saw a chance to profit by the misfortunes of others. To them, the improved farms and homes of the Saints offered a rich prize. Those of this class who had thus profited during the Jackson County persecutions now crossed into northern Missouri.

In addition, the office of governor was now held by a shrewd politician, Lilburn W. Boggs. He had been lieutenant governor during the expulsion of the Saints from Jackson County, and his course of action during that affair had been prompted by political ambition. As governor, he was well aware of public sentiment and was conscious that the voters were stirred against the Saints. From a politician an abused minority can expect no relief. The Saints expected none from Governor Boggs and received none.

The Conflict Around Far West

People who were most stirred up against the Latter-day Saints now congregated together in illegal groups or mobs, armed themselves with weapons of various kinds, and vowed that they would drive the Saints from the state. The earliest movements were against the outlying settlements, especially those unprotected by militia.

One mob, led by a Dr. Austin, besieged Adam-ondi-Ahman. But Lyman Wight was in that area, and he organized a resistance that was too much for them. Further, General Doniphan, who was in command of a group of state militia, was camped nearby, and he was a friend of the Saints.

Dr. Austin next moved against DeWitt in Carroll County. Under the leadership of Colonel George M. Hinkle, who had been authorized to raise a militia against the mobs, the Saints resisted. A state of siege followed, lasting from September 21 to October 11, 1838.

During this siege Joseph Smith risked his life to slip past

the guards at night into the city. He found the Saints destitute of food and suffering extreme hunger. A number had died. Few of the defenders possessed firearms, while the mob was growing constantly. General Parks, with a body of state militia, refused to interfere, and a petition to the governor had gone unheeded. Joseph counseled surrender. On the afternoon of October 11, the defenders filed out of DeWitt on the long road to Far West, leaving behind them all their earthly possessions except the few items that could be loaded into the available wagons.

The fate of DeWitt became the fate of all outlying settlements. From every direction, during the following month, refugees filed into the city of Far West. Their lands and homes were occupied by the mobbers or burned to the ground. Crops went unharvested, and cattle and hogs were wantonly killed to feed their pursuers.

Generals Atchison and Doniphan, with small forces of militia under their command, for a time exerted great energy in defense of the Saints, but public opinion was too powerful for them, and their appeal to the governor was met with rebuke. Superior officers, pledged to drive the Saints from Missouri, were placed over Atchison and Doniphan. Disgusted with the state of affairs, Atchison resigned. The last hope of protection from the military power of the state was gone.

In Caldwell County, centering around Far West, there was, for a time, a measure of protection. The county population was largely Latter-day Saint, and they had a county militia composed of their members and judges of their own faith.

After the fall of DeWitt, the Saints in outlying settlements were counseled to move into Far West. Many heeded the counsel. Some, however, failing to sense their danger and the tenseness of the situation, remained in their scattered communities. Upon them much of the brutality of the mobs fell.

Those of the Saints who had hoped for peace in Caldwell County were bitterly mistaken. The so-called "Mormon problem" had grown into a state issue. Slaveholders from Jackson and other counties south of the Mississippi River crossed into the troubled area to stir the mobs anew. The majority of those who fought against the Saints knew nothing of their real character and peaceful nature. False reports and propaganda had poisoned their minds. In a letter to Governor Boggs, dated September 25, 1838, General Parks wrote:

> Whatever may have been the disposition of the people called Mormons, before our arrival here, since we have made our appearance they have shown no disposition to resist the laws or of hostile intentions. . . . There has been so much prejudice and exaggeration concerned in this matter, that I found things on my arrival here, totally different from what I was prepared to expect. It is true that a great excitement did prevail between the parties, and I am happy to say that my exertions, as well as those of Major General Atchison, and the officers and men under my command, have been crowned with success. When we arrived here, we found a large body of men from the counties adjoining, armed and in the field, for the purpose, as I learned, of assisting the people of this county against the Mormons, without being called out by the proper authorities.[1]

As the disturbances grew worse, the state militia was increased until it finally reached a total of six thousand armed men. The militia was originally called out for the purpose of protecting property and to keep the peace, but in order to raise that number, thousands were enlisted who had previously taken part in the mobbings of the Saints, and these proved uncontrollable. Further, most of the officers themselves favored the mobs and did little to restrain them. Major General Parks repeatedly asserted that he could not control his troops or prevent them siding with the mob.[2]

Though the Saints did not continue to submit peaceably to these repeated outrages, they would not retaliate in kind. Two of their number, Colonel Lyman Wight and Colonel George M. Hinkle, held commissions in the state militia under the immediate command of General Parks. When their enemies began to burn and pillage, General Parks authorized the Saints to raise companies of militia and disperse the mobs. The companies were raised, but the number never exceeded five hundred. The settlements needing defense were widely scattered, and the mobbers outnumbered them by many thousands. This show of resistance, however, prevented a complete destruction of the Saints and their property.

The encounters of the Caldwell militia with the mobs only

served to fan the flames of persecution. Colonel Wight dispersed large mobs at Adam-ondi-Ahman and Millport. In the retreat of the mob from the latter place they burned some of their own dwellings and then spread the report that "the 'Mormons' had 'riz' and were burning the houses, destroying property, and murdering the 'old settlers.'"[3]

The chief clash between the Caldwell militia and their enemies is known as the Battle of Crooked River. A number of Saints had been carried away by a mob as prisoners, and a small detachment of the militia under Captain David W. Patten was sent in pursuit. At Crooked River he encountered some militia men of the state, under Captain Samuel Bogart, who fired upon him, and a battle occurred during the early dawn. Bogart and his men had formerly been in the mob that harassed the Saints in Carroll County. Captain Patten ordered a charge and put the enemy to flight. He was, however, mortally wounded in the fray, as were Gideon Carter and Patrick O'Banion. A number were wounded on both sides, and one of Bogart's men was killed. Reports were soon circulated that Captain Bogart and all of his company had been massacred by the Mormons. As a result, large mobs began to move toward Caldwell County.

A distorted report reached Governor Boggs. Without investigating any other reports, he issued an order to the commanding officer in the field, General John B. Clark, and others. The order, sometimes referred to as the "extermination order," said: "Your orders are, therefore, to hasten your operations and endeavor to reach Richmond, in Ray county, with all possible speed. The Mormons must be treated as enemies and *must be exterminated* or driven from the state, if necessary for the public peace. Their outrages are beyond all description."[4]

All hope of the Saints for peace in the state of Missouri was at an end. The militia sent to disperse the mobs had been ordered to aid them instead.

The day after this executive order was received, a company of so-called militia, under the command of Colonel William O. Jennings, fell upon the Saints at the Haun's Mill settlement. Seventeen were killed, while twelve escaped into the woods severely wounded.

On October 30, General Lucas, in the absence of his superior, General Clark, massed the state militia within firing distance of Far West. Some six hundred Latter-day Saint men and boys, with the news of the Haun's Mill Massacre still fresh in their minds, drew up in line of battle to defend their homes and loved ones in the last remaining city of the Saints.

Colonel George M. Hinkle, as the highest militia officer in Caldwell County, was in command of the defending forces. On October 31, he met with General Lucas, who was in command of the state militia forces, seeking a compromise. General Lucas proposed the following terms to the Saints:

> First, to give up their [the Church's] leaders to be tried and punished; second, to make an appropriation of the property of all who had taken up arms, for the payment of their debts, and indemnity for damage done by them; third, that the remainder of the Saints should leave the state, and be protected while doing so by the militia; but they were to be permitted to remain under protection until further orders were received from the commander-in-chief; fourth, to give up their arms of every description, which would be receipted for.[5]

For some unknown reason, Colonel Hinkle agreed to the terms. Not only that, he returned to Far West and reported to Joseph Smith that General Lucas desired a conference with him, together with Sidney Rigdon, Lyman Wight, Parley P. Pratt, and George W. Robinson. The brethren consented to the interview, but, on reaching the camp of Lucas, they were taken as prisoners of war and marched away to prison. The following morning, November 1, Colonel Hinkle led the militia out of Far West, and their arms were delivered to General Lucas. The city was now at the mercy of the mobs.

On the night of November 1, a court-martial was held in Lucas's camp. The officers of the militia sentenced the Prophet and the other prisoners to be shot at sunrise the next day on the public square at Far West.

Liberty Jail in Missouri

The order was never carried out. General Doniphan, to whom General Lucas sent the execution order, curtly refused, saying, "It is cold-blooded murder. I will not obey your order. My brigade shall march for Liberty tomorrow morning, at 8 o'clock; and if you execute these men, I will hold you responsible before an earthly tribunal, so help me God."[6]

Upon receiving the message, General Lucas refused to carry out the order. The prisoners were, however, marched into Far West that morning. Some, including the Prophet, were permitted to say goodbye to their loved ones. Then they were taken under guard to Independence. A score of other leaders were arrested and lodged in the jail at Richmond.

The Expulsion

When General Clark arrived at Far West, he endorsed all that General Lucas had done. In an address to the Saints he stated:

> Another article yet remains for you to comply with, and that is, that you leave the state forthwith; and whatever may be your

feelings concerning this, or whatever your innocence, it is nothing to me. . . . The orders of the governor to me were, that you should be exterminated, and not allowed to remain in the state, and had your leaders not been given up, and the terms of the treaty complied with, before this, you and your families would have been destroyed and your houses in ashes. . . .

I do not say that you shall go now, but you must not think of staying here another season, or of putting in crops, for the moment you do this the citizens will be upon you. . . . As for your leaders, do not once think—do not imagine for a moment—do not let it enter your mind that they will be delivered, or that you will see their faces again, for their *fate is fixed—their die is cast— their doom is sealed.*[7]

The hope for relief was gone. Nor were the Saints permitted to wait until spring. The expulsion from Missouri began immediately, so that the majority were forced to vacate their homes amid the snow and cold of winter.

The imprisonment of the majority of the Church leaders left the responsibility of directing the affairs of the people in the hands of Brigham Young and Heber C. Kimball. The remarkable executive ability of Brigham Young immediately came to the front. Under his leadership the greater portion of the Saints entered into a covenant "to stand by and assist each other to the utmost of our abilities in removing from this state, and that we will never desert the poor who are worthy, till they shall be out of reach of the exterminating order of General Clark, acting for and in the name of the state."[8] Two hundred and eighty men signed this covenant the first two days it was circulated.

The Saints appealed for aid to those Missourians who were not aligned with the mobs, and many came forward generously. Brigham Young sent agents down the Missouri River to cache corn for the Saints to use as they made their way out of the state. The agents were also to arrange for ferries and other necessary equipment.

The great activity of the Saints under Brigham Young aroused some of the enemies of the Church, and he was forced to flee for his life before the general exodus began. But so well had committees been organized that the work of removal went forward in an orderly fashion. A long line of covered wagons was soon trailing eastward, back over the long miles they had traversed but a few short years before. In charge of the sorrowful and poverty-stricken procession were Heber C. Kimball and John Taylor.

Brigham Young, with a few families, had found his way to Illinois, where inhabitants of Quincy encouraged him to settle the Saints in that vicinity. By April 20, 1839, nearly all the Saints had left Missouri and found temporary refuge in either Illinois or Iowa. Thousands lined the shores of the Mississippi in both Iowa and Illinois, living in tents or dugouts, sleeping on the ground, and subsisting chiefly on corn. Sickness and disease took a heavy toll. Practically all that the people possessed had been left behind. Property with an estimated value of two million dollars fell into the hands of their enemies. The Saints sent petitions to the governor and the legislature of Missouri, asking for reparation. Neither made any move to relieve the afflicted people; however, they did vote to pay two hundred thousand dollars, the expenses of the state militia in the "Mormon war."

Not all of the Saints moved from Missouri. The continued persecutions and the keen disappointment in failing to establish Zion destroyed the faith of many. Some of these became bitter against the Prophet and the Church and joined forces with the persecutors. Others, while remaining friendly, broke their affiliations with the Church and refused to undergo more for the sake of the gospel. These were generally left unmolested by the old citizens.

The Church Leaders in Prison

While the mobs were plundering the Saints in Far West and driving them from the state, the Church leaders who had been taken prisoner passed through many bitter experiences. They were first taken by General Wilson into Independence and paraded before the populace. Then they were marched under guard to Richmond, where they were placed in chains and abused by their guards. Parley P. Pratt wrote a graphic description of a scene in the Richmond jail:

> In one of those tedious nights we had lain as if in sleep till the hour of midnight had passed, and our ears and hearts had been

pained, while we had listened for hours to the obscene jests, the horrid oaths, and the dreadful blasphemies and filthy language of our guards, Colonel Price at their head, as they recounted to each other their deeds of rapine, murder, robbery, etc., which they had committed among the "*Mormons*" while at Far West and vicinity. They even boasted of defiling by force wives, daughters and virgins, and of shooting or dashing out the brains of men, women and children.

I had listened until I became so disgusted, shocked, horrified, and so filled with the spirit of indignant justice that I could hardly refrain from rising upon my feet and rebuking the guards; but had said nothing to Joseph or anyone else, although I lay next to him and knew he was awake. On a sudden he arose to his feet, and spoke in a voice of thunder, or as the roaring lion, uttering, as nearly as I can recollect, the following words:

"SILENCE, ye fiends of the infernal pit. In the name of Jesus Christ I rebuke you, and command you to be still; I will not live another minute and hear such language. Cease such talk or you or I die THIS INSTANT!"

He ceased to speak. He stood erect in terrible majesty. Chained, and without weapon; calm, unruffled, and dignified as an angel, he looked upon the quailing guards, whose weapons were lowered or dropped to the ground; whose knees smote together, and who, shrinking into a corner, or crouching at his feet, begged his pardon, and remained quiet till a change of guards.

I have seen the ministers of justice, clothed in magisterial robes, and criminals arraigned before them, while life was suspended on a breath, in the Courts of England; I have witnessed a Congress in solemn session to give laws to nations; I have tried to conceive of kings, of royal courts, of thrones and crowns; and of emperors assembled to decide the fate of kingdoms; but dignity and majesty have I seen but *once,* as it stood in chains, at midnight, in a dungeon in an obscure village of Missouri.[9]

On Tuesday, November 10, the prisoners were arraigned before Judge Austin A. King in the Court of Richmond. A great number of the Saints who had been arrested were tried at the same time. The trial lasted two weeks, at the end of which time all but the original prisoners were released or admitted to bail.

Joseph Smith, Lyman Wight, Caleb Baldwin, Hyrum Smith, Alexander McRae, and Sidney Rigdon were sent to the jail at Liberty, Clay County, to await trial for treason and murder. Parley P. Pratt, Morris Phelps, Lyman Gibbs, Darwin Chase, and Norman Shearer were placed in the Richmond jail to stand trial for the same crimes.

The testimony upon which Joseph and his companions were held for investigation before grand juries was the sworn testimony of apostates. Among these were Dr. Sampson Avard, John Corrill, W. W. Phelps, George M. Hinkle, and John Whitmer, all of whom had been prominent in Church affairs in Missouri.

Dr. Avard charged the Saints with having organized a band of avengers called "The Daughter of Zion," and afterwards called the "Danite Band." Joseph Smith was charged with being the prime instigator. Such a band as the "Danites" did exist, as historians affirm; but that Joseph Smith had nothing to do with it, and that he exposed the participants when he became aware of it, is equally well-confirmed. History further affirms that Dr. Avard himself was the author of the organization and that he was cut off from the Church when his guilt was discovered. The organization, whose purpose was to plunder and murder the enemies of the Saints, was foreign to the spirit of the Church. Joseph Smith declared: "Let no one hereafter, by mistake or design, confound this organization of the Church for good and righteous purposes, with the organization of the 'Danites' of the apostate Avard."[10]

Despite the lack of evidence against Joseph Smith and the other Church leaders, and despite the efforts of their attorneys, Doniphan and Reese, to secure their release, the imprisonment dragged on during the winter and into the summer.

From his prison cell at Liberty, the Prophet, through words of counsel and encouragement, kept faith and hope alive in the Church. It is characteristic of him that his mind did not dwell long on the afflictions of the moment, but turned toward a glorious future. To a people with every cause for bitterness and hatred, the Prophet counseled love and tolerance:

> We ought always to be aware of those prejudices which sometimes so strangely present themselves, and are so congenial to human nature, against our friends, neighbors, and brethren of the world, who choose to differ from us in opinion and in matters

of faith. Our religion is between us and our God. Their religion is between them and their God. There is a love from God that should be exercised toward those of our faith, who walk uprightly, which is peculiar to itself, but it is without prejudice; it also gives scope to the mind, which enables us to conduct ourselves with greater liberty towards all that are not of our faith, than what they exercise toward one another.[11]

In April the prisoners held at Liberty jail were removed for grand jury trial, first to Daviess County, and later to Boone County. While en route to the latter place, they were allowed by their guards to purchase two horses. Then the guards conveniently went to sleep, with the exception of one who helped them mount their horses and get away. Eventually they found their way out of the state and joined the Saints in Illinois.

While the escape was welcomed at the time, it was a source of embarrassment later. Their trial had been near at hand, and since they were innocent, no charges could have been sustained against them. But because of the escape, they were considered fugitives from justice, and their later arrest could be demanded whenever charges against them might be substantiated. Such demands for the Prophet's arrest would be made of the state of Illinois at a later period.

The leaders incarcerated in Richmond jail were given no such opportunity. Their escape was planned, however, and carried off successfully during the Fourth of July celebration of 1839. Eventually these men also fled Missouri and rejoined their loved ones in Illinois.

17

A Faith Stronger Than Steel

In the early summer of 1839, a man traversed a swampy terrain covered with underbrush and scattered trees in western Illinois. Around it on three sides, in a mighty horseshoe-like sweep, rolled the muddy waters of the Mississippi. The land was practically deserted, save for half a dozen stone and log houses squatting near the riverbank and mockingly designated as "Commerce." Swarms of mosquitoes, the then-unknown carriers of malaria fever, were everywhere.

The man was a fugitive from persecution, an escaped prisoner from the state of Missouri, haggard and pale from his long confinement. He was penniless. His people—those who called him "Prophet" and who had followed his leadership through nine eventful years—were as stripped and penniless as he. Twelve thousand of them lay in miserable encampments on both sides of the Mississippi and in the vicinity of Quincy, living in tents, in dugouts, and even shelterless under the open sky.

This mosquito-infested swamp over which Joseph Smith walked had just been purchased for the Saints' home. This land that nobody wanted was to be the dwelling place of this unwanted people. More attractive lands were to be had on the Iowa side, but the Saints had no money to purchase them. The owners of this land had been glad to take even promissory notes, payable over several years.

Little more than two weeks had passed since Joseph Smith had crossed the Mississippi into Illinois to escape further imprisonment. But those two weeks had been full of activity. On April 24, the second day after his arrival, a church committee comprised of the Prophet, Newel Knight, and Alanson Ripley had begun looking for land for a new gathering place. That purchase was made. A total sum of fourteen thousand dollars in promissory notes was paid to Dr. Isaac Galland and Hugh White for the initial tracts of land.

A scattered people suddenly had an objective again—a place of gathering—and a prophet as leader. Characteristic of the Prophet, he renamed the place to meet his desires—not what it was, but what, with the faith and work of man, the region might become: "Nauvoo, the City Beautiful."

On May 10, Joseph moved his family into a small log house on the bank of the river one mile south of Commerce. Following his example, the Saints began to arrive in numbers and were allotted lands according to their needs. Those who had previously gone to Quincy began to file into Nauvoo, while a large group remained on the opposite side of the river at Montrose, Iowa.

There was much sickness, the dreaded malaria taking a heavy toll of the weakened people. President Smith's home was crowded with the sick. Many of the newly arrived camped in his dooryard under tents. Joseph himself was stricken. Of the events occurring at this time Wilford Woodruff wrote:

After being confined to his house several days, and while meditating upon his situation, he [Joseph Smith] had a great desire to attend to the duties of his office. On the morning of the 22nd of July, 1839, he arose from his bed and commenced to administer to the sick in his own house and door-yard, and he commanded them in the name of the Lord Jesus Christ to arise and be made whole; and the sick were healed upon every side of him.

Many lay sick along the bank of the river; Joseph walked along up to the lower stone house, occupied by Sidney Rigdon, and he healed all the sick that lay in his path. Among the number was Henry G. Sherwood, who was nigh unto death. Joseph stood in the door of his tent and commanded him in the name of Jesus Christ to arise and come out of his tent, and he obeyed him and was healed. Brother Benjamin Brown and his family also lay sick, the former appearing to be in a dying condition. Joseph healed them in the name of the Lord. After healing all that lay sick upon the bank of the river as far as the stone house, he called upon Elder Kimball and some others to accompany him across the river to visit the sick at Montrose. Many of the Saints were living at the old military barracks. Among the number were several of the Twelve. On his arrival the first house he visited was that occupied by Elder Brigham Young, the President of the Quorum of the Twelve, who lay sick. Joseph healed him, then he arose and accompanied the Prophet on his visit to others who were in the same condition. They visited Elder Wilford Woodruff, also Elders Orson Pratt, and John Taylor, all of whom were living in Montrose. They also (arose and) accompanied him. [1]

The remarkable faith in the destiny of his people caused the Prophet to forget their poverty, their miserable homes, and their past bitter experiences. Faith is mightier than steel. While it lived in the hearts of men, Zion could never be destroyed.

Those people on the banks of the Mississippi, who like Jesus of Nazareth had nowhere to lay their heads, were nearer to Zion than they had ever been before. Their troubles had swept them clean of sordid desires. Those who were not pure in heart remained behind. For the first time it began to dawn upon the Church that a "Zion people" was infinitely more important than a "Zion place," for without a "Zion people," no spot in the world could remain holy.

While to the casual observer the Church seemed at its lowest ebb, the strength within was greater than before. The faith of the people, their loyalty to the Prophet, and the missionary zeal that swept over them has never been paralleled in history. That deep and abiding strength was to change a swamp into a great city; miserable shelters into splendid houses; penniless people into some of the most prosperous citizens of Illinois. That missionary zeal was to carry the gospel into many lands and double the membership of the Church. And all of this in the short time of five years!

Two thousand years ago Jesus of Nazareth said, "Seek ye first the kingdom of God, and his righteousness; and all these things shall be added unto you." (Matthew 6:33.)

Here was a people who believed those words. Here was a people who demonstrated that eternal truth.

Great Missionary Zeal

It is characteristic of the Church that its greatest missionary efforts have begun in its darkest hours. We saw a great expansion of missionary activity during the apostasy of 1837, when the gospel was carried to England. We witness another such outburst of missionary zeal in the dark hours following the expulsion from Missouri. We will witness still another following the great exodus to Utah. Stripped of worldly treasures, men's minds sense anew the eternal nature of spiritual values and readily respond to the call of the Spirit.

This missionary zeal in 1839 was especially manifest in the spirit among the Twelve. On April 26, the Twelve Apostles, or those of them who were not in Missouri prisons, returned to the city of Far West from which they had previously fled. In the early dawn they met upon the Temple Square and transacted the business of the quorum. In July, the Prophet gave, by way of revelation, the word of the Lord that the Twelve Apostles should depart upon missions to the world. (See D&C 118.) After that prophecy, mobs drove them from Far West and swore that here was one prophecy that would never be fulfilled.

The mission of the Twelve, starting from Far West, was delayed by the destitute conditions of the Saints in Montrose and Commerce. But the missionary spirit did not die. Between the first of August and the latter part of November, the majority parted from loved ones and started on the long journey to England. Never did missionaries begin their work under more heartrending conditions. Penniless themselves, with little extra clothing, they left their families equally destitute. The only assurance was the promise of neighbors, equally poor, that they would be cared for.

The first to start was Wilford Woodruff. In the early part of August he arose from a sickbed in Montrose, on the Iowa side of the Mississippi River, and was rowed across the river in a canoe by Brigham Young. Reaching the shore, he was so weak that he lay down upon a side of sole leather. Joseph Smith happened to see him there and said, "Well, Brother Woodruff, you have started on your mission."

"Yes, but I feel and look more like a subject for the dissecting room than a missionary," was the reply.

"What did you say that for?" asked Joseph. "Get up and go along, all will be well with you."

Wilford Woodruff got up and, joining Elder John Taylor, started north along the riverbank. They were on their way to the British Mission. They passed Parley P. Pratt, stripped to the waist, barefooted, and bareheaded, hewing logs for a cabin. He gave them a purse but had nothing to put in it. Elder Heber C. Kimball came up and said, "As Brother Parley has given you a purse, I have a dollar I will give you to put in it."

The others of the Twelve soon followed under similar circumstances. In the journal kept by Heber C. Kimball we find the following:

> September 14th, . . . President Brigham Young left his home at Montrose to start on the mission to England. He was so sick that he was unable to go to the Mississippi, a distance of thirty rods, without assistance. After he had crossed the river he rode behind Israel Barlow on his horse to my house, where he continued sick until the 18th. He left his wife sick with a babe only three weeks old, and all his other children were sick and unable to wait upon each other. Not one soul of them was able to go to the well for a pail of water, and they were without a second suit to their backs, for the mob in Missouri had taken nearly all he had. On the 17th, Sister Mary Ann Young got a boy to carry her up in his wagon to my house that she might nurse and comfort Brother Brigham to the hour of starting.
>
> September 18th, Charles Hubbard sent his boy with a wagon and span of horses to my house; our trunks were put into the wagon by some brethren; I went to my bed and shook hands with my wife, who was then shaking with a chill, having two children lying sick by her side; I embraced her and my children and bade them farewell. My only well child was little Heber P., and it was with difficulty he could carry a couple of quarts of water at a time to assist in quenching their thirst.
>
> It was with difficulty we got into the wagon, and started down the hill about ten rods; it appeared to me as though my very inmost parts would melt within me at leaving my family in such a condition, as it were almost in the arms of death. I felt as though I could not endure it. I asked the teamster to stop, and said to Brother Brigham, "This is pretty tough, isn't it; let's rise up and give them a cheer." We arose and swinging our hats three times over our heads, shouted, "Hurrah, hurrah for Israel." Vilate, hearing the noise, arose from her bed and came to the door. She

had a smile on her face. Vilate and Mary Ann Young cried out to us: "Good-bye, God bless you." We returned the compliment, and then told the driver to go ahead. After this I felt a spirit of joy and gratitude, having had the satisfaction of seeing my wife standing upon her feet, instead of leaving her in bed, knowing well that I should not see them again for two or three years.[2]

The success of these missionaries in England reminds us of the remarkable conversions of Paul in the early Church, when he went on a mission to the Greek world. A typical example of this power of conversion is illustrated in this account from Wilford Woodruff's journal. Elder Woodruff had called a meeting at the house of a Brother Benbow, whom he had previously baptized. He says:

When I arose to speak at Brother Benbow's house, a man entered the door and informed me that he was a constable, and had been sent by the rector of the parish with a warrant to arrest me. I asked him, "For what crime?" He said, "For preaching to the people." I told him that I as well as the rector, had a license for preaching the gospel to the people, and that if he would take a chair I would wait on him after meeting. He took my chair and sat beside me. For an hour and a quarter I preached the first principles of the everlasting gospel. The power of God rested upon me, His spirit filled the house, and the people were convinced. At the close of the meeting I opened the door for baptism, and seven offered themselves. Among the members were four preachers and the constable. The latter arose and said, "Mr. Woodruff, I would like to be baptized."

The baptisms followed. The journal continues:

The constable went to the rector and told him that if he wanted Mr. Woodruff taken for preaching the gospel, he must go himself and serve the writ; for he had heard him preach the only true gospel sermon he had ever listened to in his life. The rector did not know what to make of it, so he sent two clerks of the Church of England as spies, to attend our meeting, and find out what we did preach. They both were pricked in their hearts, received the word of the Lord gladly, and were baptized and confirmed members of the Church of Jesus Christ of Latter-day Saints. The rector became alarmed, and did not venture to send anyone else.[3]

Ministers and rectors in England attempted but failed to get through Parliament a bill that would prohibit the Mormons from preaching in the British dominions. Their petition stated that one Mormon missionary had baptized fifteen hundred persons, mostly members of the Church of England, in a period of seven months. This doubtless referred to Wilford Woodruff and is hardly an exaggeration. In his journal he gives a synopsis of his labors, which was duplicated by many of the other missionaries. This is for the single year of 1840 in southern England:

> I traveled 4,469 miles, held 230 meetings, established 53 places for preaching, and planted 47 churches and jointly organized them. . . . The baptisms of the year were 336 persons under my own hands, and I assisted at the baptism of 86 others. I baptized 57 preachers, mostly those connected with the United Brethren, also two clerks of the Church of England.[4]

In 1841, because of a threat of war between the United States and England, the majority of the brethren were called home to Nauvoo. Parley P. Pratt remained in charge of the Church publications in England, including the *Millennial Star*.

The great success of the Twelve's mission to England was felt in the Church. The converts became imbued with the spirit of gathering and desired to go to the central gathering place in America. The first shipload left Liverpool, England, on June 6, 1840. This was the beginning of a migration movement of such magnitude that the Church in America became predominantly English for the next fifty years. The rapidity of this movement, which greatly swelled the population of Nauvoo, can be realized from a notation in the *Autobiography of Parley P. Pratt* for one particular month:

> Between the middle of September [1840] and my own embarkation in October, I chartered three vessels for New Orleans, and filled them with the emigrating Saints, viz: The "Sidney," with one hundred and eighty souls; the "Medford," with two hundred and fourteen souls; and the "Henry," with one hundred and fifty-seven. I next chartered the "Emerald," on which I placed about two hundred and fifty passengers, including myself and family.[5]

The journey ordinarily took about three months—ten weeks to New Orleans and from seven to fourteen days by river steamer up the Mississippi to Nauvoo. The "Mormon metropolis" was a pleasing sight to these weary travelers, whose adaptation to the new society in a new world was an unusual accomplishment.

In the absence of the Twelve, tremendous changes had taken place in Nauvoo. Parley P. Pratt remarked on his return on February 4, 1843, "I was astonished to see so large a city all created during my absence, and I felt to rejoice."[6]

Palestine Is Dedicated

Another mission that was to have great significance began in the summer of 1840.

For eighteen centuries the Jewish people had been scattered throughout the world, driven from their native land of Palestine. Twelve million of them had congregated chiefly in great cities. They had found no opportunity to reestablish their nation and had given up all practical hopes of doing so. Elders Orson Hyde and John E. Page were called to carry the gospel to these people and to dedicate the Holy Land for their return.

The faith of Orson Hyde in his mission was unshakable. Even when Elder Page deserted him in New York and refused to go further, Elder Hyde did not waver. He carried on alone one of the longest missionary journeys ever undertaken, more than twenty thousand miles in all. Obedient to his calling, he visited the leading Jews in the principal cities of Europe. Finally he reached Jerusalem in the land of Palestine.

Early on Sunday morning, October 24, 1841, he went out alone to the top of the Mount of Olives and there, in the hearing of none but God, dedicated that land for the return of the Jewish people. In that beautiful prayer we read these words:

> Grant, therefore, O Lord, in the name of Thy well-beloved Son, Jesus Christ, to remove the barrenness and sterility of this land, and let springs of living water break forth to water its thirsty soil. Let the vine and olive produce in their strength, and the fig-tree bloom and flourish. Let the land become abundantly fruitful when possessed by its rightful heirs; let it again flow

with plenty to feed the returning prodigals who come home with a spirit of grace and supplication; upon it let the clouds distill virtue and richness, and let the fields smile with plenty. Let the flocks and the herds greatly increase and multiply upon the mountains and the hills; and let Thy great kindness conquer and subdue the unbelief of Thy people. Do Thou take from them their stony heart, and give them a heart of flesh; and may the sun of Thy favor dispel the cold mists of darkness which had beclouded their atmosphere. Incline them to gather in upon this land according to Thy word. Let them come like clouds and like doves to their windows. Let the large ships of the nations bring them from the distant isles; and let kings become their nursing fathers, and queens with motherly fondness wipe the tear of sorrow from their eye. . . .

Let that nation or that people who shall take an active part in behalf of Abraham's children, and in the raising up of Jerusalem, find favor in Thy sight. Let not their enemies prevail against them, but let the glory of Israel overshadow them, and the power of the Highest protect them; while that nation or kingdom that will not serve Thee in this glorious work must perish, according to Thy word—"Yea, those nations shall be utterly wasted."[7]

On the Mount of Olives and also upon Mount Moriah in Jerusalem, Elder Hyde built stone altars after the fashion of the early Israelites, as a memorial of his prayer.

The Prophet Writes His History

Despite the difficulties that Joseph Smith faced in evading the attempts of the Missourians to get him back into their custody for trial, as well as the many problems of the Church, which were a drain upon his time and energy, in the 1840s he wrote and published three documents that had profound effect upon the Church.

The first was his personal account of the rise and development of the Church, which he had begun writing in 1838 and continued during the Nauvoo period. This "History of the Church" was published in part in the *Times and Seasons,* and he continued to add to it until shortly before his death. As currently used in the Church, it consists of six large volumes, with extensive footnotes added by B. H. Roberts; a seventh volume has been taken from the manuscript history of Brigham Young and other documents.

The second document is the Book of Abraham, which the Prophet had begun to translate from the papyri while he resided in Kirtland. This was printed in sections in the *Times and Seasons* in 1841; later it became part of the Pearl of Great Price.

The third document was written in response to a request from John Wentworth, editor of the *Chicago Democrat*. The Prophet wrote a brief history of the rise of the Church, together with a condensed statement of doctrines, now known as the Articles of Faith. Generally known as the Wentworth Letter, this document was published in the *Times and Seasons* on March 1, 1842. The Articles of Faith also subsequently became part of the Pearl of Great Price.

The Prophet Plans a City

The story of the development of Nauvoo constitutes one of the most progressive chapters in social history. A people inspired by a great faith do not long remain in poverty. Swamps were soon drained, and with their disappearance went the mosquito and the dread malaria. Underbrush gave way to gardens. Tents and hastily devised shacks were replaced by beautiful dwellings.

Nauvoo did not develop in the usual haphazard way of cities. It was fashioned in the mind of its founder before a stone was laid or a ditch dug. As early as 1833 Joseph Smith had received revelations concerning the construction of cities of Zion. In that year he sent a plan for such a city to Independence, Missouri, but persecutions in that state prevented more than a partial conformity to the plan.

Nauvoo offered the first real opportunity to show what the Prophet might accomplish in solving the problems of city life. The city was laid out with streets, eight rods in width, running directly north and south, east and west, and crossing each other at regular intervals. Sections of the city were designated for the erection of public buildings and recreational centers. Building restrictions controlled the location of such businesses as manufacturing plants and mercantile establishments. In the residential sections, houses were erected a uniform distance from the street and were fronted with lawns and shrubs. Unsightly structures were prohibited. Nauvoo became the pattern for future cities built by the Saints in the Rocky Mountains.

The bitter lessons of the Missouri period had an important bearing upon the organization of the political government of the new city. To safeguard the people, Joseph Smith drew up the provisions for an unusual city charter and presented it to the Illinois legislature for approval. He said of it: "I concocted it for the salvation of the church, and on principles so broad that every honest man might dwell secure under its protecting influence, without distinction of sect or party."[8]

The charter provided for broad legislative powers resting in a city council elected by the qualified voters of the city and consisting of a mayor, four aldermen, and nine councilors. It provided for a municipal court, independent of any but the state supreme court and the federal courts. And it provided for a city militia to be known as the Nauvoo Legion, to be equipped by the state and officered by citizens of Nauvoo.

No other municipality in America before or since has enjoyed such complete control of its own affairs. The charter was a protection to the Church from mobs, illegal court proceedings, and the whims of higher governmental agencies.

Political circumstances aided the people of Nauvoo in getting the charter passed. The Saints were a numerous people in that sparsely settled state, and both political parties sought their friendship. The Mormon vote could easily sway a statewide election. Even political opponents like Stephen A. Douglas and Abraham Lincoln, then members of the Illinois legislature, joined hands to vote for the passage of the charter. In December 1840, Nauvoo began its official existence. John C. Bennett, who joined the Church at Nauvoo, was tireless in his efforts in securing its passage. For his work he was rewarded by being elected the first mayor.

The isolation of the Saints from those of other faiths, which had been attempted in Missouri, was abandoned. Indeed, people of all religious denominations were invited to dwell with the Saints in Nauvoo. In a proclamation from the First Presidency, dated January 15, 1841, we read:

> We wish it . . . to be distinctly understood, that we claim
> no privilege but what we feel cheerfully disposed to share with

our fellow citizens of every denomination, and every sentiment of religion; and therefore say, that so far from being restricted to our own faith, let all those who desire to locate themselves in this place [Nauvoo], or the vicinity, come, and we will hail them as citizens and friends, and shall feel it not only a duty, but a privilege, to reciprocate the kindness we have received from the benevolent and kind-hearted citizens of the state of Illinois.[9]

In keeping with this spirit, one of the first acts of the city council was to pass an ordinance protecting people in the undisturbed enjoyment of their several religions. Another early ordinance prohibited the sale of intoxicants and practically made Nauvoo a prohibition city.

In drawing up the proposed charter for Nauvoo, the Prophet granted power to the city to organize and control its own educational system, including a charter for a municipal university, the first of its kind in America. Thus, an educational system that included all grades from elementary to university classes was organized by the city council. University buildings and a campus were planned, but the plans could not be carried out before the people were driven from Nauvoo. Instructors were hired and university classes held, however, in such buildings as the city afforded. The organization for the university was later adopted in Utah for the University of Deseret, now the University of Utah. It was the Prophet's aim to educate his entire people, young and old.

One of the first priorities of the Prophet in planning Nauvoo was a site for a temple. A well-constructed city enjoying wise governmental powers would not alone make for a happy people. Even the addition of education would not assure success. The true Zion must have people who are pure in heart. So the City of Joseph, as Nauvoo came to be called, should be built around a temple of God and should also be provided with other suitable places of worship where the gospel of Jesus Christ might be taught.

The Growth of Nauvoo

As early as the summer of 1841, the St. Louis *Atlas* referred to Nauvoo as follows: "The population of Nauvoo is between 8000 and 9000, and of course the largest town in the State of Illinois.

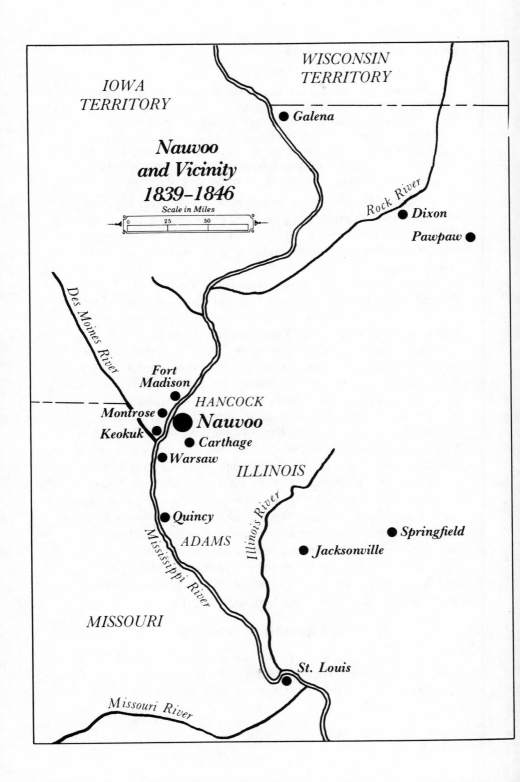

IOWA
TERRITORY

WISCONSIN
TERRITORY

● Galena

Nauvoo
and Vicinity
1839–1846

Scale in Miles

0   25   50

Rock River

● Dixon

Pawpaw ●

Des Moines River

Fort
Madison
●

HANCOCK

Montrose ●

Nauvoo

Keokuk ●

● Carthage

● Warsaw

ILLINOIS

Illinois River

● Quincy

ADAMS

● Springfield

● Jacksonville

Mississippi River

MISSOURI

St. Louis
●

Missouri River

How long the Latter-day Saints will hold together and exhibit their present aspect, it is not for us to say. At this moment, they present the appearance of an enterprising, industrious, sober and thrifty population, such a population, indeed, as in the respects just mentioned, have no rivals east, and we rather guess, not even west of the Mississippi."[10]

The city grew rapidly as it became the gathering place for the majority of the exiles from Missouri as well as converts migrating from eastern states and foreign lands. In June 1844 Franklin D. Richards, the Church Historian, placed the population at 14,000. No actual census was taken, and the number is variously estimated from twelve to twenty thousand. The growth of the city overshadowed that of the neighboring towns of Warsaw, Carthage, and Quincy, and caused considerable loss of prestige to the older places. This provoked jealousy and envy, especially among the speculators in lands.

The city attracted many visitors who came largely out of curiosity to see the Mormon metropolis. Eastern newspapers sent representatives to interview the founder of the city and make observations on unusual features of the Mormon center.

As Nauvoo grew, it became a social center, easily accessible to settlements up and down the river. Celebrations on the Fourth of July and other holidays attracted people for many miles. Excursion boats from Warsaw and even from St. Louis were common, the vessels docking at Nauvoo amidst much laughter and gaiety. Dances were held on such occasions, usually lasting until the early hours of the following morning.

A parade of the Nauvoo Legion was a colorful event that seldom failed to attract an audience. At its height the Legion had five thousand men, armed and in uniform. On many occasions mock battles were held, both to better train the soldiers and to entertain the people.

The most hospitable place in the city was the Mansion House, home of Joseph Smith. The residence also accommodated travelers stopping at Nauvoo. Men of renown visiting Nauvoo slept beneath its roof; the humblest were equally welcome. While the

Prophet was at home, he was accessible to all, and life in the city. gravitated about the Mansion.

To better accommodate travelers and converts who were constantly arriving in the city, a larger building, the Nauvoo House, was begun. The cornerstone was laid October 2, 1841, in obedience to a revelation that such a house should be erected. (See D&C 124.) Funds for construction were raised through an issue of stock to worthy Church members. Within the cornerstone Joseph Smith deposited the original manuscript of the Book of Mormon translation. The building, however, was never completed as originally designed, the martyrdom of the prophet and the contemplated exodus West causing a change in plans. The part that was completed is still standing in Nauvoo not far from the Mansion House, but it has been changed into a dwelling.

The temple, begun in 1841, was a never-failing source of interest to the visitor. Although it was not completed until 1846, its position on the highest point of the city made even the unfinished walls visible from the surrounding country.

Extending to the north, south, and east of the city were broad cultivated acres. One of the most advanced agricultural areas in that section of the nation, it was most unusual in that none of the people lived upon their farms, but resided in the city, going to and from their fields in the morning and evening. This gave to all the advantages of education and social contacts that the city afforded and also helped promote the unity of the people.

While the phenomenal growth of the Church, the rapid rise of the city, and the prosperity of the Saints were gratifying to the leaders of the church and city, these factors also attracted some persons who were quite undesirable, as one writer attested:

> Adventurers seeking for place and power and wealth; demagogues who by fulsome flattery of the people hoped to attain through their political influence a realization of their ambitious dreams; knaves who by falsely professing conversion, thought to cover up corrupt, licentious lives, and thrive by villainy; thieves and counterfeiters who saw their opportunity to live by roguery, and steal on the credit of the Mormons, of whom the people of Illinois were too ready to believe anything that savored of evil, be-

cause prejudiced against their religion—all these characters were
attracted to Nauvoo by the prosperity that reigned there; and their
ungodly conduct hastened the evil day of the city's destruction.[11]

Among these reckless adventurers, none was more skillful in
winning his way into the confidences of the people than John C.
Bennett, the city's first mayor. When his promiscuous sexual practices were discovered, he was excommunicated from the Church
and deprived of all his civic positions. Other men of the same
stamp as Bennett helped to bring discredit upon the community,
especially among those who were searching for charges against the
Saints.

The Church's enemies in Missouri also continued to harass the
Saints. It is doubtful if Joseph Smith, after the expulsion from Missouri, seriously expected to be reinstated in that state at that time or
even to receive compensation for the losses incurred. That hope
had not died out, however, among the Saints. Sidney Rigdon even
proposed a scheme to oust Missouri from the Union and worked up
considerable feeling over it. To allay this feeling and satisfy his
people, Joseph Smith started for Washington, D.C., on October
29, 1839, accompanied by Sidney Rigdon and Judge Elias Higbee,
to lay the cause of the people before the federal government. Elder
Rigdon, becoming ill, was left in Columbus, Ohio. The others
reached their destination.

A short time in Washington convinced the Prophet of the folly
of expecting help from that source. President Van Buren informed
them in a meeting, "Gentlemen, your cause is just, but I can do
nothing for you. If I take up for you I shall lose the vote of Missouri."[12]

While the Prophet returned to Nauvoo convinced that the
Saints must forget their cause against Missouri, the Missourians
were not willing to forget the Saints. Those responsible for the
Missouri mobbings seem to have been stirred to fresh determination by the hospitality displayed by the citizens of Illinois and the
blame poured upon Missouri by the eastern press. The Missourians
found legal justification for attempting to retake the Prophet and
others in the fact that the Mormon leaders had escaped from civil
authorities in Missouri while being taken to trial. Though Joseph

Smith was now in another state, he could be extradited; that is, the governor of one state may give up a person who has sought refuge in his state, upon the request of another governor for the arrest, when the other governor is convinced that a sufficient charge has been laid against the refugee. Missouri appealed to Governor Carlin of Illinois for such a writ, authorizing the arrest of Joseph Smith. Governor Carlin granted the request and issued the writ. The Prophet, though innocent of any crime, was convinced that if he fell into the hands of his Missouri enemies again, he would never return to Nauvoo alive. He and the other leaders named in the writ went into hiding, and the writ was returned unserved.

This was the beginning of a problem that was to last the remaining years of the Prophet's life and greatly hamper his work. Writs issued by Governor Carlin called for the arrest of all those who had escaped from Missouri prisons, but the real objective was to get hold of Joseph Smith. Some outrages were perpetrated, however, against some of the other brethren. On July 7, 1840, Alanson Brown, Benjamin Boyce, Noah Rogers, and James Allred were kidnapped by an armed mob of Missourians and taken into Missouri. They were severely handled before being released.[13]

In May 1842, someone in Missouri attempted to kill ex-Governor Boggs. He recovered from the assassin's bullet, but the assassin was never found. However, on July 20, 1842, Boggs swore out an affidavit that Orrin Porter Rockwell, a resident of Illinois, had done the shooting and that Joseph Smith was an "accessory before the fact." He asked Governor Reynolds of Missouri to demand that Governor Carlin of Illinois deliver the Prophet to be dealt with according to law. Governor Reynolds complied, and Governor Carlin issued a writ for Joseph Smith's arrest. On August 8, 1842, both he and Orrin Porter Rockwell were taken into custody. The Prophet demanded the right of *habeas corpus,* and the court of Nauvoo issued a writ requiring that the prisoners be brought before it. The sheriff, afraid either to obey or to disobey the order, rushed to Governor Carlin for instructions. When he returned, the prisoners were not to be found, nor could any threat against the people of Nauvoo cause them to disclose the hiding place.

On December 8, 1842, Governor Carlin's term of office expired and Thomas Ford took the gubernatorial seat. Affidavits were secured immediately to prove that Joseph Smith was not in Missouri at the time of the crime against Boggs; and on the basis of these, the Supreme Court of Illinois declared the writ to be illegal but decided that a trial should be held before the governor could interfere. The Prophet submitted to arrest, and in the subsequent trial on January 5, 1843, he was discharged.

For a brief period the Prophet was to enjoy peace. The respite was, however, short-lived. On June 13 a new conspiracy against him came to fruition. John C. Bennett, one-time friend of the Prophet and former mayor of Nauvoo, joined the Missouri forces. Bennett, who had been previously excommunicated from the Church, was bitter toward the Prophet for exposing him. But both Governor Reynolds of Missouri and Governor Ford of Illinois joined with him in his new scheme against the Mormon leader.

On June 13, 1843, a secret requisition was made to Governor Ford on the old charges. A writ was issued and repeated attempts were made by officers from Missouri to arrest the Prophet and whisk him across to Missouri. In each case, friends of the Prophet rose to his defense, brought him before impartial judges, and secured his release.

Tension ran high, as petitions were sent from Nauvoo to Governor Ford to dispel the false charges and calm the troubled waters. Fortunately Governor Ford recognized the jurisdiction of the courts that had discharged Joseph Smith, and the Prophet was again a free man—only to find the net of his enemies tightening further around him. To make matters worse, some of his own followers began to turn against him and lay plots to take his life.

18

The Temple in Nauvoo

On April 6, 1841, an unusual gathering took place on the brow of the highest eminence of land overlooking Nauvoo. A large rectangular excavation had been made. Near the edge of it Joseph Smith, Sidney Rigdon, and a score of Church leaders were gathered. Surrounding both the excavation and the leaders were sixteen companies of the Nauvoo Legion in full uniform. Beyond them, hundreds of men, women, and children had assembled.

This people, so lately impoverished, were laying the cornerstone for a million-dollar structure—a temple to the living God. A people of great faith, they were obeying the commandment of the Lord, who said, "Let this house be built unto my name, that I may reveal mine ordinances therein unto my people; for I design to reveal unto my church things which have been kept hid from before the foundation of the world, things that pertain to the dispensation of the fulness of times. . . . And ye shall build it on the place where you have contemplated building it, for that is the spot which I have chosen for you to build it." (D&C 124:40-43.)

The cornerstones were laid and the spot dedicated. A great undertaking had been commenced. Members of the Church gave in labor and money, in provisions and encouragement. Stone quarries were opened a short distance down the river and the gray sandstone blocks were transported to the temple site. By the end of the year, the foundations were visible from the surrounding country.

The Saints spent five years in erecting the building. When the capstone was laid, the Prophet and his brother were dead, the city lay practically deserted, and its inhabitants were spread out over the Iowa plain—exiles seeking another home. The story of those gray walls, once the glory of western Illinois, parallels that of the "City Beautiful." The rise and glory and fall of the temple was but typical of the city upon which it looked.

Near the walls of the temple the Saints erected a bowery, in

166

Nauvoo Temple

what they called "the Grove." There, in the open air, the people met in solemn worship. There they listened to the words of the Prophet and his associates. At times men of national renown sat there, and ministers of a dozen creeds, upon invitation, expressed their views there.

The Temple Ordinances

Within the walls of the temple were twelve bronze oxen, upon whose backs rested a great bowl filled with water, a baptismal font like that in the ancient temple of Solomon. Within this font, the living were baptized for their dead ancestors, a practice that prevailed in the early Church at the time of the apostle Paul.[1] The doctrine of baptism and ordinance work for the dead had been developing in the Church from the time of the visitation of the angel Moroni, when he quoted from the Book of Malachi as follows: "Behold, I will reveal unto you the Priesthood, by the hand of Elijah the prophet, before the coming of the great and dreadful day of the Lord. And he shall plant in the hearts of the children the promises made to the fathers, and the hearts of the children shall turn to their fathers. If it were not so, the whole earth would be utterly wasted at his coming." (D&C 2:1-3.)

Knowledge concerning this doctrine was received by Joseph Smith from time to time. On April 3, 1836, Elijah appeared to him and Oliver Cowdery in the Kirtland Temple and conferred upon them the keys of sealing. These keys included the authority necessary for temple ordinances for both the living and the dead. When the Saints were commanded to build a temple in Nauvoo, the Lord told them, "This ordinance belongeth to my house, and cannot be acceptable to me [that is, outside of the temple], only in the days of your poverty, wherein ye are not able to build a house unto me." (D&C 124:30.)

While the temple was in course of construction, some sealing ordinances were performed in the upper story of Joseph Smith's store in Nauvoo, while baptisms for the dead were performed in the Mississippi River. As soon as a portion of the temple was completed, the Lord, by revelation, commanded the Saints to cease performing those ordinances outside the proper house.

The work to be performed in the temple for both the living and the dead was for the salvation of men and consisted of those ordinances in the gospel which pertain to the mortal stage of existence.

For those who were already members of the Church, temple ordinances consisted of receiving endowments, a promise of blessings based on obedience to God's laws, and the "sealing of family ties." Within the temple walls was taught the beautiful doctrine of eternal marriage given by revelation from the Lord:

> If a man marry him a wife in the world, and he marry her not by me nor by my word, and he covenant with her so long as he is in the world, and she with him, their covenant and marriage are not of force when they are dead, and when they are out of the world; therefore, they are not bound by any law when they are out of the world.
>
> Therefore, when they are out of the world, they neither marry nor are given in marriage; but are appointed angels in heaven, which angels are ministering servants, to minister for those who are worthy of a far more, and an exceeding, and an eternal weight of glory. . . .

And again, verily I say unto you, if a man marry a wife, and make a covenant with her for time and for all eternity, if that covenant is not by me or by my word, which is my law, and is not sealed by the Holy Spirit of promise, through him whom I have anointed and appointed unto this power, then it is not valid neither of force when they are out of the world, because they are not joined by me, saith the Lord, neither by my word; when they are out of the world it cannot be received there, because the angels and the gods are appointed there, by whom they cannot pass; they cannot, therefore, inherit my glory; for my house is a house of order, saith the Lord God.

And again, verily I say unto you, if a man marry a wife by my word, which is my law, and by the new and everlasting covenant, and it is sealed unto them by the Holy Spirit of promise, by him who is anointed, unto whom I have appointed this power and the keys of this priesthood; and it shall be said unto them—Ye shall come forth in the first resurrection; and if it be after the first resurrection, in the next resurrection; and shall inherit thrones, kingdoms, principalities, and powers, dominions, all heights and depths—then shall it be written in the Lamb's Book of Life, that he shall commit no murder whereby to shed innocent blood, and if ye abide in my covenant, and commit no murder whereby to shed innocent blood, it shall be done unto them in all things whatsoever my servant hath put upon them, in time, and through all eternity; and shall be of full force when they are out of the world; and they shall pass by the angels, and the gods, which are set there, to their exaltation and glory in all things, as hath been sealed upon their heads, which glory shall be a fulness and a continuation of the seeds forever and ever.

Then shall they be gods, because they have no end; therefore shall they be from everlasting to everlasting, because they continue; then shall they be above all, because all things are subject unto them. Then shall they be gods, because they have all power and the angels are subject unto them. (D&C 132:15-20.)

Before the people were driven from Nauvoo, most of the adults had received their endowments, wives had been sealed to their husbands, and children had been sealed to parents by the power of God.

The second phase of the work was equally important. Millions upon millions of people had died in the world without hearing or

understanding the gospel of Jesus Christ. Joseph Smith said of
them:

> The great designs of God in relation to the salvation of the
> human family, are very little understood by the professedly wise
> and intelligent generation in which we live. Various and conflict-
> ing are the opinions of men concerning the plan of salvation, the
> requisitions of the Almighty, the necessary preparations for
> heaven, the state and condition of departed spirits, and the happi-
> ness or misery that is consequent upon the practice of righteous-
> ness and iniquity according to their several notions of virtue and
> vice.
>
> The Mussulman condemns the heathen, the Jew, and the
> Christian, and the whole world of mankind that reject his Koran,
> as infidels, and consigns the whole of them to perdition. The Jew
> believes that the whole world that rejects his faith and are not cir-
> cumcised, are Gentile dogs, and will be damned. The heathen is
> equally as tenacious about his principles, and the Christian con-
> signs all to perdition who cannot bow to his creed, and submit to
> his *ipse dixit* [dictum].
>
> But while one portion of the human race is judging and con-
> demning the other without mercy, the Great Parent of the uni-
> verse looks upon the whole of the human family with a fatherly
> care and paternal regard; He views them as His offspring, and
> without any of those contracted feelings that influence the chil-
> dren of men, causes "His sun to rise on the evil and on the good,
> and sendeth rain on the just and on the unjust." He holds the reins
> of judgment in His hands; He is a wise Lawgiver, and will judge
> all men, not according to the narrow, contracted notions of men,
> but "according to the deeds done in the body whether they be
> good or evil," or whether these deeds were done in England,
> America, Spain, Turkey, or India. He will judge them, "not
> according to what they have not, but according to what they
> have," those who have lived without law, will be judged without
> law; and those who have a law, will be judged by that law. We
> need not doubt the wisdom and intelligence of the Great Jehovah;
> He will award judgment or mercy to all nations according to their
> several deserts, their means of obtaining intelligence, the laws by
> which they are governed, the facilities afforded them of obtain-
> ing correct information, and His inscrutable designs in relation to
> the human family; and when the designs of God shall be made

manifest, and the curtain of futurity be withdrawn, we shall all of us eventually have to confess that the Judge of all the earth has done right.[1]

Joseph taught that all men would have equal opportunity to hear and embrace the laws of God whether in this life or in the life to come: "All who have died without a knowledge of this gospel, who would have received it if they had been permitted to tarry, shall be heirs of the celestial kingdom of God; also all that shall die henceforth without a knowledge of it, who would have received it with all their hearts, shall be heirs of that kingdom; for I, the Lord, will judge all men according to their works, according to the desire of their hearts." (D&C 137:7-9.) Those who in the spirit world accepted the gospel and wished to conform to its principles and ordinances would find a way provided. People upon the earth could perform by proxy the necessary things that they themselves had failed through lack of opportunity or understanding to do. This is temple work for the dead; it consists in the performance of all those ordinances which God ordained to be performed during man's mortal existence.

Thus, the temple at Nauvoo represented the beauty of that city, the purity of thought that actuated its people, the love of all mankind embraced in the Church doctrines.

19

A Clash of Social Orders

In the Ohio and Missouri settlements, the Saints acted as a unit politically, economically, and socially to the exclusion of others. In Nauvoo, this characteristic became even more pronounced. Practically all of the Saints congregated there, and while non-Mormons were invited and some came, nevertheless the city remained almost exclusively Mormon. The broad powers of the Nauvoo charter heightened this exclusiveness. It set the city apart, almost as a state within a state. It bestowed upon it powers that other cities did not possess. And it provoked jealousy and suspicion.

The solidarity of the Saints was felt especially at the polls. From the time the Saints began settling at Quincy, politicians sought favor with them. For a time they held the balance of power between the political parties of Illinois, registering a solid vote for candidates who promised to take an interest in their welfare. But as opposition against the Saints grew, this solidarity became a thorn in the flesh of those candidates who hoped to gain the Saints' vote while still retaining the vote of the non-Church members. And by 1843 the politicians of the state and nation were siding with the majority against the Saints in order to save their own political careers.

For the Saints, it soon became impossible to support candidates of either political party, a condition that meant the end of political protection for them in Illinois and eventually the repeal of those rights and privileges they had obtained. In fact, a repeal of the Nauvoo charter was attempted in 1843, with the bill for repeal passing the Illinois House of Representatives.

During the latter part of 1843, Joseph Smith communicated with the prospective political aspirants for the United States presidency. Candidates Henry Clay, John C. Calhoun, Lewis Cass, Richard M. Johnson, and Martin Van Buren were asked for their views toward the Latter-day Saints. Only two of them responded, and their answers were evasive. It was evident that the Saints could expect little help, whichever candidate was elected. Anxious to place their cause and views before the nation, the Saints then made a surprising move: they decided to place their own candidate in nomination. On January 29, 1844, Joseph Smith was named to run for the presidency on an independent ticket. Noting that he "would not electioneer" for himself, he called several members of the Twelve Apostles as well as other Church leaders and special missionaries to campaign in the East for his candidacy, telling them, "There is oratory enough in the Church to carry me into the presidential chair the first slide."[1]

On May 17, 1844, Nauvoo was the setting for a convention of the "National Reform" party, and Joseph Smith was officially nominated to run as the party's candidate for President of the United States. No one expected him to be elected, least of all himself. But his candidacy offered an opportunity to lay before the nation the cause of the Latter-day Saints. The press would publish the views of a candidate to the office of U.S. President whereas it would spurn those same views were they expressed by a prophet.

The political views that he set forth display the vast scope of his interests and something of his aggressive, fearless nature. In a document titled "Views of the Powers and Policy of the Government of the United States,"[2] he advocated the following:

1. A central banking system owned by the federal government, with the mother bank at Washington and branch banks in each state and territory.

2. The acceptance of Texas, Mexico, Canada, and any other "neighboring realm" that petitioned to become part of the United States.

3. The settlement of the Oregon territory, to "extend the mighty efforts and enterprise of a free people from the east to the west."

4. The reduction of Congress by up to two-thirds.

5. The freeing of slaves through reasonable payment to slaveholders, with funds obtained by the sale of public lands.

6. Reformation of the prison system, to make the prisons workhouses and "seminaries of learning."

7. Reformation of the military practice of trying men by court-martial for desertion in time of war.

8. A high tariff to protect young industries.

"In the United States the people are the government," he declared, "and their united voice is the only sovereign that should rule, the only power that should be obeyed, and the only gentlemen that should be honored at home and abroad, on the land and on the sea."

These views created wide interest, and many newspapers commented upon the new candidate, including the *Iowa Democrat*, which stated:

> We see from the *Nauvoo Neighbor* that General Joseph Smith, the great Mormon Prophet, has become a candidate for the next presidency. We do not know whether he intends to submit his claims to the National Convention, or not; but, judging from the language of his own organ, we conclude that he considers himself a full team for all of them.
>
> All that we have to say on this point is, that if superior talent, genius, and intelligence, combined with virtue, integrity, and enlarged views, are any guarantee to General Smith's being elected, we think that he will be a "full team of himself."[3]

The solidarity and exclusiveness of the Latter-day Saints was evident also in their economic practices. Although the law of consecration was never attempted at Nauvoo, the spirit of that social order was very manifest. Cooperation, rather than ruthless competition, was the core of the Mormon economic life. But the very success of the Mormon society drew the attention of its neighbors and aroused imaginary fears. Land speculators were perhaps the only persons directly affected. They found it virtually impossible to operate in and around Nauvoo. The Church purchased land in tracts and sold it to the Saints at nonprofit prices. While private land deals were made, the Church's land policy dominated the situation and discouraged profit-taking. Further, the rapid growth of Nauvoo had a retarding effect upon the growth of surrounding cities, a blow to speculators who had invested money in other towns with a view to profiting by their expected growth.

A New Doctrine Emerges

The religious beliefs of the Saints, as we have witnessed in the Missouri troubles, often clashed with those of their neighbors. Some new elements, however, were evident during the Illinois period. At Nauvoo the influence of the Prophet upon the people became increasingly evident, and belief in revelations affected almost all phases of community life. The assertion by the Saints that they possessed the gospel in its fullness, while all other denominations were wrong, continued to arouse opposition as it had done from the time of the First Vision. Further, in Nauvoo the Prophet proclaimed a number of additional doctrines, some of which set the Saints apart still further from the rest of the world.

One of these doctrines was especially responsible for bringing persecution upon the Church. That was the doctrine of plural marriage by divine sanction. As early as 1831, Joseph Smith claimed a revelation upon the subject and spoke of it to a few close associates. It was not, however, placed in writing, practiced, or generally made known at that time. In 1840, the Prophet taught the doctrine to a few leading brethren, and some of them, along with the Prophet, secretly married additional wives in the following year. This secrecy could not be long kept, though the doctrine was not openly discussed. Then, on July 12, 1843, the Prophet received the "Revelation on the Eternity of the Marriage Covenant, including the Plurality of Wives."[4] This revelation was subsequently set down in writing and read to the high council at Nauvoo.

For years after he had initially learned of the doctrine through revelation from God, Joseph Smith could not bring himself to practice it or to teach others to do so. The whole Anglo-Saxon training of the Church was opposed to plural marriage, although it had never been forbidden by either the state or the federal constitution. But the secrecy that surrounded the introduction of the practice led to gross misrepresentations and charges of adultery, an important factor in the embitterment of both Mormons and non-Mormons against the Prophet. None of the teachings of the Church clashed so directly with the social order of the day or aroused such resentment.

Plural marriage was never at any time a general law for the entire Church, and it was never practiced by more than a very small percent of the male population. The President held the keys to its practice, and only those deemed able to live the law in righteousness were permitted to enter into such relationships. That some of the finest people of the Church came from plural households is undeniable. But it is also true that a few abused the law and the trust placed in them and gave grounds for slander and ridicule against the Church.

Despite the social reasons which may be advanced in justification of plural marriage, it must be admitted that it was directly contrary to the traditions of persons both in and out of the Church. The very secrecy involved prevented any explanations to such persons, so the vaguest of rumors were multiplied and enlarged by the tongue of gossip.

The Prophet Anticipates the Crisis

The Prophet was aware that the social order he contemplated would arouse bitter opposition in Illinois; the experiences of the Church in Ohio and Missouri had made this apparent. The presence of the Mormons in a large body in any part of settled America at that time would have produced a similar story—not because the Mormons were hard to get along with, or because non-Mormons were wicked, but because the teachings of the Church and the existing social orders were so directly in conflict. It was to prepare for such an expected opposition and perhaps in a measure to avoid it that Joseph Smith had written the unusual Nauvoo charter and secured its passage. It was to prepare against illegal arrests that he insisted upon an independent municipal court at Nauvoo. It was to protect his people from expected mob violence that he organized and trained the famous Nauvoo Legion.

Nor did he believe that even these precautions would long protect his people. As early as 1842, he began to look for an unsettled section of America where his people might accomplish their "Zion" without conflict. In that year he uttered a famous prophecy to a group of Saints at Montrose, Iowa. In his journal for August 6,

1842, we read: "I prophesied that the Saints would continue to suffer much affliction and would be driven to the Rocky Mountains, many would apostatize, others would be put to death by our persecutors or lose their lives in consequence of exposure or disease, and some of you will live to go and assist in making settlements and build cities and see the Saints become a mighty people in the midst of the Rocky Mountains."[7]

From that time he anxiously gleaned such knowledge of the West as was available and began to lay plans for a westward exodus. These plans were hastened when the circle of his enemies began to tighten about him early in 1844. On February 20 of that year, he instructed the apostles to send out a delegation to explore Oregon and California (a region that at that time included the entire Rocky Mountain area) with a view to finding a suitable place for the Saints after the temple at Nauvoo was completed.[8]

Those who volunteered for the expedition were organized as the "Western Exploration Company." On February 25, 1844, the Prophet wrote in his journal: "I gave some important instructions, and prophesied that within five years we should be out of the power of our old enemies, whether they were apostates or of the world; and told the brethren to record it, that when it comes to pass they need not say they had forgotten the saying."[9]

On March 26, he wrote to Congress requesting that an ordinance be passed "for the Protection of the Citizens of the United States Emigrating to the Territories, and for the Extension of the Principles of Universal Liberty."[10] The ordinance would have empowered him to raise a force of one hundred thousand volunteers to safeguard and insure the settlement of the West under the principles suggested.

Congress rejected the proposed ordinance, partly because of existing treaties with England for the joint occupation of the Oregon territory and partly because of the personal nature of the ordinance and the great power it would have placed in the hands of one man.

Events in Nauvoo became so turbulent thereafter that those called for the western expedition were assigned other duties, and the proposed journey was postponed.

Apostates Within the Church

Among those who came into prominence during the Nauvoo period were some who lost their faith in the Prophet and sought his destruction. One of the early ones to fall was John C. Bennett, who had previously exerted great energy in securing the Nauvoo charter. On the eve of his intended marriage to a young woman in Nauvoo, it was learned that he had deserted a wife and children in the East. Other disclosures of immoral conduct followed, and he was excommunicated in May or June 1842. He had previously resigned from the office of mayor. In June he left Nauvoo and set about to undermine the Prophet. He later wrote a book, titled *The History of the Saints,* that was full of misrepresentations.

Many of those who were cut off from the Church remained in Nauvoo. In December 1843 the Prophet noted: "I am exposed to far greater danger from traitors among ourselves than from enemies without, although my life has been sought for many years by the civil and military authorities, priests, and people of Missouri. . . . I have had pretended friends betray me."[11]

On May 25, 1844, William Law, Robert D. Foster, and Joseph H. Jackson had Joseph Smith indicted at Carthage, Illinois, for adultery and perjury. When the Prophet appeared in court and demanded trial, his enemies, unwilling to press the charges against him, asked for a postponement of the case. A plot to take his life while he was at Carthage was disclosed by two of the conspirators, Charles A. and Robert D. Foster; they subsequently repented of their part in the proceedings and confessed to the Prophet in tears.

The apostates next purchased a printing press and prepared to publish a paper, the *Nauvoo Expositor,* for the avowed purpose of advocating "the unconditional repeal of the Nauvoo City Charter" and to expose immoral practices in the Church.[12] The only number, which appeared June 7, 1844, was filled with slander against Joseph Smith and the Church leaders in Nauvoo.

The Saints in Nauvoo were incensed. The city council met and declared the *Expositor* a public nuisance and ordered the city marshal, John P. Green, to forcibly enter the printing establishment, scatter the type, and destroy the printed papers.[13]

20

Martyrs for the Church

The destruction of the *Nauvoo Expositor* on June 10, 1844, proved to be the spark that ignited all the smoldering fires of opposition into one great flame. It offered the occasion for which apostates from the Church were waiting, a legal excuse to get the Prophet and other leaders into their hands. The cry that "freedom of the press" was being violated united the factions seeking the overthrow of the Saints as perhaps nothing else could have done. Protest meetings were held throughout Hancock and neighboring counties. On June 12 the *Warsaw Signal* published an account of the destruction of the *Expositor* press, adding: "We have only to state that this is sufficient! War and extermination is inevitable! *Citizens arise, One and All!!!!* Can you stand by, and suffer such *Infernal Devils* to rob men of their property and rights, without avenging them? We have no time to comment; every man will make his own. Let it be made with powder and ball!!!!"

On the same day this article appeared, Constable David Bettisworth came from Carthage to Nauvoo and arrested members of the Nauvoo city council on a charge of riot. Those arrested included Joseph Smith, Samuel Bennett, John Taylor, William W. Phelps, Hyrum Smith, John P. Green, Stephen Perry, Dimick B. Huntington, Jonathan Harmon, Jesse P. Harmon, John Lytle, and Levi Richards. Joseph Smith was released the next day after a habeas corpus hearing in the municipal court of Nauvoo. The following day, the same justice of the peace dismissed the other defendants. Harsh as the action in destroying the press was, it appeared, nevertheless, to be perfectly legal. On the advice of a circuit judge, a second trial was held before Judge Daniel H. Wells, a non-Mormon. Again the defendants were discharged. These trials failed to appease those of the opposing faction, who demanded that Joseph Smith and the others be tried at Carthage, the county seat. The Prophet, who felt that their lives would not be safe there, refused. Mobs were organizing in the neighboring towns, while anti-Mormon newspapers called for extermination of the Saints. Joseph Smith sent Governor Ford a statement of the situation and awaited his advice. None came. The situation only grew worse.

To protect his people, the Prophet called out the Nauvoo Legion and proclaimed martial law in Nauvoo on June 18. In what would be his last address to the Legion, he declared: "I call God and angels to witness that I have unsheathed my sword with a firm and unalterable determination that this people shall have their legal rights, and be protected from mob violence, or my blood shall be spilt upon the ground like water, and my body consigned to the silent tomb. While I live, I will never tamely submit to the dominion of cursed mobocracy."[1]

On June 20 Joseph wrote to the ten apostles who were on missions, bidding them return speedily to Nauvoo. The next day Governor Ford arrived at Carthage and immediately sent a letter to the Nauvoo city council asking that representatives be sent to present their case before him. That afternoon Willard Richards, John M. Bernhisel, and John Taylor were elected by the council for that mission. Richards was subsequently detained by Joseph Smith for other duties, and the next day Lucien Woodworth was sent in his place. He carried a letter to Governor Ford inviting him to come to Nauvoo and make a complete investigation.

The governor was apparently influenced by the feelings that prevailed at Carthage. In his reply, which Joseph Smith received late in the evening of June 22, he charged the Nauvoo city council with abuse of power and ordered the Legion disbanded and martial law discontinued. He also demanded that Joseph Smith submit to arrest and trial at Carthage. His letter ended with a promise and a threat:

> If it should become necessary to have witnesses on the trials, I will see that such persons shall be duly summoned, *and I will also guarantee the safety of all such persons as may be thus brought to this place from Nauvoo either for trial or as witnesses for the accused.*
>
> If the individuals accused cannot be found when required by the constable it will be considered by me as an equivalent to a refusal to be arrested, and the militia will be ordered accordingly.[2]

Joseph immediately dispatched a response in defense of the actions of the city council, noting:

> We would not hesitate to stand another trial according to your Excellency's wish, were it not that we are confident our lives would be in danger. We dare not come. Writs, we are assured, are issued against us in various parts of the country. For what? To drag us from place to place, from court to court, across the creeks and prairies, till some bloodthirsty villain could find his opportunity to shoot us. We dare not come, though your Excellency promises protection. Yet, at the same time, you have expressed fears that you could not control the mob, in which case we are left at the mercy of the merciless.[3]

A meeting of the leading brethren in Nauvoo was held at the Mansion House the evening of June 22. After reading Governor Ford's letter, the Prophet remarked, "There is no mercy—no mercy here." His brother Hyrum replied, "No; just as sure as we fall into their hands we are dead men." Suddenly the Prophet declared, "The way is open. It is clear to my mind what to do. All they want is Hyrum and myself; then tell everybody to go about their business, and not to collect in groups, but to scatter about. There is no doubt they will come here and search for us. Let them search; they will not harm you in person or property, and not even a hair of your head. We will cross the river tonight, and go away to the West."[4]

That night Joseph and Hyrum Smith, accompanied by Orrin Porter Rockwell and Willard Richards, secretly crossed the river into Iowa. At daybreak Rockwell was sent back to Nauvoo to get horses for the fugitives. He returned shortly after noon—without the horses. Accompanying him was Reynolds Cahoon, who brought a letter from Emma Smith entreating the Prophet to return. Cahoon reported that Governor Ford had threatened to send troops to Nauvoo unless Joseph surrendered, but that if the Prophet did give himself up, he would be protected while he underwent a "legal and fair trial." Cahoon also told him that the Saints in Nauvoo were accusing him of cowardice, likening him to a shepherd who has left his flock to the wolves. Stung by this accusation, Joseph replied, "If my life is of no value to my friends, it is of none to myself."[5]

Late that afternoon he returned to Nauvoo and sent word to Governor Ford that he would submit to arrest.

Joseph was confident that arrest would mean his death. Safety had lain within his grasp, and the Spirit had whispered to him the wisdom of flight. But safety without the faith and devotion of his beloved people was an empty shell.

Bound for Carthage

In Joseph's letter to Governor Ford, he asked that a posse be sent to conduct him safely into Carthage. The request was denied. Instead, Joseph was ordered to appear in Carthage by ten o'clock the next morning; otherwise "Nauvoo would be destroyed and all the men, women, and children that were in it."

Early on the morning of June 24, President Smith, members of the Nauvoo city council, and a few friends left Nauvoo, bound for Carthage to give themselves up for trial. It was a sorrowful procession. The Prophet's gaze rested long upon the uncompleted temple and upon his beloved city. Out of a heart full to bursting he exclaimed: "This is the loveliest place and the best people under the heavens; little do they know the trials that await them."[7] Later he commented, "I am going like a lamb to the slaughter, but my mind is calm as a summer's morning. I have a conscience void of offense towards God, and towards all men. . . . I am going voluntarily to give myself up, it shall be said of me that I was murdered in cold blood."[8]

About four miles west of Carthage, they were met by a company of sixty mounted militia. Captain Dunn, their commander, presented an order from Governor Ford for the Nauvoo Legion to give up all the state arms in their possession, which the Prophet countersigned. Captain Dunn, fearful of entering Nauvoo with his men, induced the Prophet to return with him and see that the governor's order was complied with. Reluctantly the people of Nauvoo surrendered their arms—their weapons of defense against mob violence.

As evening approached, the militia, with Joseph Smith and his party, again started for Carthage. It was midnight when they arrived, but the public square swarmed with troops known as the

Carthage Greys, who, with cursing and yelling, seemed ready to finish the Prophet then and there. The intervention of Governor Ford from his hotel window quieted them, and the company was permitted to retire to the Hamilton House for the night.

Early on the morning of June 25, Joseph and his companions voluntarily surrendered to Constable Bettisworth. At eight o'clock, Joseph and Hyrum were again arrested on the charge of treason against the State of Illinois. The alleged treason consisted in declaring martial law in Nauvoo.

Later in the day the two prisoners were paraded before the troops by Governor Ford, who seemed anxious to appease the militia. When they were introduced as Generals to the Carthage Greys, a near riot ensued. Shortly afterward, in the Hamilton House, militia officers complained that, although General Smith's appearance indicated a peaceful character, "We cannot see what is in your heart, neither can we tell what are your intentions." To this the Prophet replied:

> Very true, gentlemen, you cannot see what is in my heart, and you are therefore unable to judge me or my intentions; but I can see what is in your hearts, and I will tell you what I see. I can see you thirst for blood, and nothing but my blood will satisfy you. It is not for crime of any description that I and my brethren are thus continually persecuted and harassed by our enemies, but there are other motives, and some of them I have expressed, so far as relates to myself; and inasmuch as you and the people thirst for blood, I prophesy, in the name of the Lord, that you shall witness scenes of blood and sorrow to your entire satisfaction. Your souls shall be perfectly satiated with blood, and many of you who are now present shall have an opportunity to face the cannon's mouth from sources you think not of, and those people that desire this great evil upon me and my brethren, shall be filled with regret and sorrow because of the scenes of desolation and distress that await them. They shall seek for peace, and shall not be able to find it. Gentlemen, you will find what I have told you to be true.[9]

During the day members of the Nauvoo city council were brought before Robert F. Smith, a justice of the peace, and were bound over on bail to appear at the next term of the Circuit Court for Hancock County, on the charge of riot. The total bail was

Carthage Jail, where Joseph Smith was martyred

$7500, an excessive amount. To the surprise of their accusers, the bail was soon raised and the council members departed for Nauvoo that night. However, Joseph and Hyrum, while seeking an interview with Governor Ford, were arrested again by Constable Bettisworth and thrust into prison on a false mittimus[10] that declared that they had appeared on a charge of treason before Justice Smith and had been committed to prison to await trial. As no such appearance on that charge had been made, the imprisonment was illegal. But when the Governor was informed of the affair by John Taylor, he refused to interfere. That night Joseph and Hyrum, together with Willard Richards, John Taylor, Stephen Markham, Dan Jones, and John S. Fullmer, slept on the prison floor of the debtor's cell.

The following morning Joseph Smith again requested an interview with the governor, who came to the jail an hour or so later. A long conversation ensued, with the governor promising them protection. He said that if he marched his troops into Nauvoo the following day, Joseph and Hyrum would be taken along. Nothing was promised in regard to their false imprisonment.

As the day wore on, the prisoners wrote letters to friends and relatives, discussed plans with their attorney, and heard reports of public utterances against their lives. In the afternoon Justice of the Peace Smith sent for the prisoners, but the jailer refused to give them up. This caused considerable excitement. A mob gathered and a company of Carthage Greys was sent to bring the prisoners before the justice. Seeing the multitude and its threatening aspect, Joseph walked out of the prison into the midst of the Carthage Greys, locked arms with one of the men, and started for the courthouse. The brethren followed, surrounded by a guard. As witnesses could not be immediately procured, the court postponed the case until the following noon. The date was changed later that evening to June 29.

The prisoners were returned to the jail and placed in a room on the upper story. That evening they read and discussed passages from the Book of Mormon. Joseph also bore his testimony to the guards. As they lay on the floor of the cell, Joseph conversed with John S. Fullmer and Dan Jones, who were sleeping on either side of him. "I would like to see my family again," he said. "And would to God that I could preach to the Saints in Nauvoo once more." Later he was heard to whisper to Dan Jones, "Are you afraid to die?" Jones replied, "Has that time come, think you? Engaged in such a cause, I do not think death would have many terrors." The Prophet said, "You will yet see Wales, and fulfill the mission appointed you before you die."[11]

A Day of Infamy

Early on the morning of June 27, Governor Ford marched the militia toward Nauvoo—his promise to Joseph disregarded. Fifty men of the Carthage Greys were left to guard the prisoners at the jail.

The governor had planned a large display of military force in Nauvoo. However, he did send an order disbanding the regiment from Warsaw, telling them to return to their homes. Though most of them did so, some chose to follow the militia to Nauvoo while others went to Carthage.

Meanwhile the prisoners at Carthage jail spent the morning writing messages and preparing for their trial. John S. Fullmer was sent to Nauvoo to procure witnesses, and Dan Jones departed with a letter to O. H. Browning, an attorney, engaging him as counsel. Willard Richards was somewhat ill that morning, so Stephen

Markham left the jail to procure some medicine. He was not allowed to return, but was forced out of town by the Carthage Greys. This left but four men in the jail, Joseph and Hyrum Smith, Willard Richards, and John Taylor.

At four o'clock the guard at the jail was changed, with only eight men left to protect the prisoners. The jailer, noticing this, suggested to the prisoners that they would be safer in the cell on the lower floor. They promised to go there after supper. Suddenly loud cries and musket shots were heard as a mob of some one hundred men rushed the jail and overpowered the guards, who made a half-hearted attempt to protest. The assailants rushed up the stairs to the room where the prisoners waited. John Taylor and Willard Richards had stout canes with which to defend themselves, while Joseph Smith had a six-barrel revolver and his brother a single-shot pistol.

The prisoners tried to barricade the door, which had no lock, but shots rang out from the stairway. One ball struck Hyrum Smith in the face, and as he fell back, another shot from outside the window struck him in the back. He fell to the floor, mortally wounded, and cried, "I'm a dead man!"

Joseph, looking toward his brother, uttered "Oh, dear, Brother Hyrum." He then opened the door partway and shot into the hallway, but three of the six barrels misfired. Gunfire continued from the hallway, with several shots hitting Hyrum's body. John Taylor, cane in hand, tried first to knock down the bayonets and muskets that were discharging through the doorway, then rushed toward the window. A ball from the doorway struck his leg and one from outside the window smashed into his watch in his vest pocket, knocking him to the floor. As he lay motionless, the mob continued to fire upon him, hitting him in the wrist and the leg. Willard Richards joined him in the fray, knocking down muskets with his cane as he sought safety behind the door.

Joseph, his gun empty, was attempting to leap from the window when two balls hit him from the open door and another from outside the window. Mortally wounded, he fell out the window, exclaiming, "O Lord, my God!"

As the cry "He's leaped the window!" rang out, the attackers on the stairs rushed outside. Then someone cried that the Mormons were coming, and the mob quickly dispersed. Samuel Smith, the Prophet's brother, unexpectedly arrived on the scene and helped Willard Richards, who was uninjured, remove the bodies of Joseph and Hyrum to the Hamilton House. John Taylor was also carried there and given medical attention. A coroner's inquest was quickly convened by Justice of the Peace Robert Smith, after which Elder Richards sent a note to the Church at Nauvoo, informing them: "Joseph and Hyrum are dead."

21

The Church of Christ
or of Man?

On the morning of June 28, 1844, Nauvoo lay as in a pall. The sound of industry had ceased. The unfinished temple stood silent as the great sphinx. A hush, like death, enveloped the city. People spoke in whispers on the street corners and saluted one another in grave tones. All anger toward their persecutors and feelings of malice toward those who had killed their Prophet and his brother were forgotten for the moment as the anger turned into overwhelming grief.

In the Nauvoo Mansion, Joseph Smith's home, there was sorrow indeed. Emma Smith had maintained her courage, in the face of bitter slander, persecution, and forced migrations, while her husband lived. But now that sustaining strength had ebbed out with his lifeblood. Lucy Mack Smith, Joseph's mother, who had already lost one son and her husband in the past three years, was crushed by the sudden loss of two more sons. To these women there seemed nothing left for which to strive, nothing further for which to sacrifice.

The feeling of depression was not confined to Nauvoo. The apostles in the mission field sensed it even before news of the tragedy reached them. Parley P. Pratt wrote:

> A day or two previous to this circumstance I had been constrained by the Spirit to start prematurely for home, without knowing why or wherefore; and on the same afternoon I was passing on a canal boat near Utica, New York, on my way to Nauvoo. My brother, William Pratt, being then on a mission in the same state [New York] happened, providentially, to take passage on the same boat. As we conversed together on the deck, a strange and solemn awe came over me, as if the powers of hell were let loose. I was so overwhelmed with sorrow I could hardly speak; and after pacing the deck for some time in silence, I turned to my brother, William, and exclaimed—"Brother William, this is a dark hour; the powers of darkness seem to triumph, and the

spirit of murder is abroad in the land; and it controls the hearts of the American people, and a vast majority of them sanction the killing of the innocent. My brother, let us keep silence and not open our mouths. If you have any pamphlets or books on the fulness of the gospel lock them up; show them not, neither open your mouth to the people; let us observe an entire and solemn silence, for this is a dark day, and the hour of triumph for the powers of darkness. . . ." This was June 27, 1844, in the afternoon, and as near as I can judge, it was the same hour that the Carthage mob were shedding the blood of Joseph and Hyrum Smith, and John Taylor, near one thousand miles distant.[1]

About noon on June 28, the bodies of Joseph and Hyrum Smith were brought into the city of Nauvoo. Sorrowfully the people gathered behind the procession and filled the streets around the Mansion House. Several of their brethren addressed them and urged them to keep the peace and leave vengeance unto God.

On the 29th, thousands filed past the bodies as they lay in state in the mansion. At five o'clock in the evening the doors to the home were closed. The coffins were removed from the outer boxes. These outer boxes were then filled with bags of sand, taken to the cemetery, and buried with the usual ceremony. At midnight, the bodies were taken by trusted friends and buried in the basement of the Nauvoo House, then in course of construction.[2] This precaution was taken through fear that enemies of the martyrs would return to mutilate their remains.

A few days later, John Taylor, seriously and painfully wounded, was brought into Nauvoo. The sight of his suffering and the graphic nature of his account aroused in the Saints a new surge of anger and eagerness for revenge against the persecutors, but cooler heads prevailed, and the Saints returned to wisdom and forbearance.

What Would Happen to the Church Now?

Despite the tenseness of the times, members of the Church had not anticipated their Prophet's death. Time after time, a kind Providence had permitted him to escape his enemies, and they had felt that somehow he would be spared again. The blow that had fallen left them indeed like sheep without a shepherd. What would happen next? Would the solidarity of the Saints be forever broken? Many non-Mormon observers sincerely thought so. The enemies of the Church expected it. And the newspapers in Illinois proclaimed such a result. Had the Church been built solely around a charismatic personality, that result would certainly have followed. But this church was not the church of Joseph. It was the Church of Jesus Christ. The heart of the Church was not a great personality—it was the restored priesthood of the Lord and Master.

By the time of the Prophet's martyrdom, the "Ship of State" was ready to sail; the work of establishing the kingdom of God on earth had been completed. Prophets would follow, revelations would continue, but the important machinery had been installed; the Church's destiny was assured.

The Prophet had prepared for the event of his death better than the lay members of the Church knew. All the powers and rights of the priesthood had been conferred upon the Twelve, and this included the power to ordain a new President of the Church. But it took some time for the people to realize this.

Before the Prophet's death, Sidney Rigdon had become dissatisfied with the Church and had gone to live in Pittsburgh, Pennsylvania. Joseph Smith had recommended at the last conference he attended that the Saints reject Rigdon as first counselor in the First Presidency, but they had sustained him. Upon hearing of the death of the Prophet, President Rigdon returned to Nauvoo, arriving August 1. He had a plan for the government of the Church. No one, in his opinion, could be a prophet and take Joseph's place by mere appointment. Such a call must come from God. But in the meantime, a guardian was needed to act as the head of the Church. As first counselor in the Presidency, Sidney Rigdon should naturally be that guardian. Many of the Saints, including the Prophet's wife and mother, became staunch supporters of this proposal. However, the apostles who were in Nauvoo at the time—Willard Richards, John Taylor, and Parley P. Pratt—counseled the people to wait until the return of the remainder of the Twelve.

Sidney Rigdon, on his own initiative, called a meeting for August 8 to decide the matter of a guardian. By that time a number of

Brigham Young
(1801–77)

the Twelve, sufficient for a quorum, had arrived. The meeting was held in the Grove, or Bowery, with President Rigdon talking at great length during the morning. But he did not put the matter of a guardian to a vote. When he sat down, Brigham Young arose and announced that a meeting to be presided over by the Council of the Twelve would be held at two o'clock in the afternoon.

When that time arrived, a large congregation had gathered. Members of the priesthood were seated by quorums. Brigham Young, who was president of the Twelve, was the first speaker. He reminded the Saints that the Church was the Church of Jesus Christ and would continue until He should return to earth to reign in righteousness. All the powers of the priesthood were vested in the Twelve, he said. Upon the death of the President, the quorum of the First Presidency was dissolved and the governing power of the Church rested upon the Twelve until a new Presidency should be nominated by them through the spirit of revelation and sustained by the vote of the people.

Some of those present testified that as President Young spoke, the Prophet Joseph appeared to be standing before them and that his voice appeared to be speaking to them. When a vote was taken, the Twelve were sustained as the leaders of the Church.

The unity of opinion among the Twelve Apostles concerning the organization of Church government convinced the majority of the Saints that the organization had been so well laid that it was self-perpetuating. The Church was bigger than any man or set of men.

A few, however, remained unconvinced and drew away from the Church. After the August 8 meeting, Sidney Rigdon outwardly seemed to agree with the Twelve; he was, however, holding meetings with disgruntled members, telling them that he had been called by revelation of God to lead them. When he was called to account by the Quorum of the Twelve, he confessed to holding secret meetings and ordaining various officers. He refused, however, to correct his views or to be subordinated to the Twelve. At a subsequent hearing, which he refused to attend, he was excommunicated from the Church. Much disappointed, he returned to Pittsburgh, where he organized a church and gathered a few followers. The movement did not prosper and soon dissolved. Sidney Rigdon died in obscurity in Allegheny County, New York, in 1876.

Other Dissenting Groups

James J. Strang, a convert living at Voree, Walworth County, Wisconsin, also became dissatisfied with the new leadership of the Church and drew away. He laid claim to a letter from Joseph Smith under date of June 18, 1844, appointing him as the Prophet's successor. Several hundred of the discontented believed his claim, including William Smith, the only surviving brother of the Prophet; John E. Page, one of the Council of the Twelve; and John C. Bennett. Strang established himself and his followers on Beaver Island in upper Lake Michigan. There he organized a county, which he represented in the Michigan State Legislature, and had himself crowned as king of Beaver Island. In 1856 he was killed during an uprising on Manitou Island. His followers, generally nicknamed Strangites, disbanded.

Another person who led a group away from the Church was William Smith, brother of the martyrs and a member of the

Twelve. At the time of the martyrdom, he was in the East. When he returned to Nauvoo in the spring of 1845, he was ordained as Presiding Patriarch. Soon he was claiming authority over all of the priesthood in the Church. At a conference in October 1845, the congregation refused to sustain him either as an apostle or as the Presiding Patriarch. Later that month he was excommunicated. For a time William Smith associated with the movement started by James J. Strang. The spring of 1850 found him starting another movement. In that year he called a conference to assemble at Covington, Kentucky, where he effected a church organization with himself as president *pro tem* and Lyman Wight and Aaron Hook as counselors. He claimed that the office of President was a right of lineage in Joseph Smith's family, so Joseph Smith's eldest son should become President. But inasmuch as this son was then too young to take that office, it naturally followed that he, as the only surviving brother of the Prophet and the natural guardian of the "seed of Joseph," should act as President for the time being. His organization scarcely endured for a year. Later he became nominally connected with what became known as the Reorganized Church of Jesus Christ of Latter Day Saints, but he took little active part. He died at Osterdock, Iowa, 1893.

Lyman Wight was not among those who claimed the Presidency of the Church, but after the Prophet's death, no one could rule him. In the latter part of August 1844, he led a group of about 150 Saints into the sparsely settled territory of Wisconsin, where they settled on government lands, about 450 miles north of Nauvoo. For some years he had advocated the movement of The Church of Jesus Christ of Latter-day Saints to Texas. In 1845 he led his small colony there. His small company of Saints lived a form of the united order. On his death the order broke up and the Saints scattered. Lyman Wight was excommunicated from the Church at Salt Lake City in 1848.

While the Saints were in Kirtland, James C. Brewster, a youth of sixteen or seventeen years of age, claimed certain visions in connection with the books of Esdras in the Apocrypha. In 1840 he was severely rebuked by the Prophet at Nauvoo for advancing the claim that he had learned from the books of Esdras that the gathering place, or "place of refuge," was to be in the valleys of the Colorado and Gila rivers and on the shores of the Gulf of California. Four years after the Prophet's death, in 1848, Hazen Aldrich revived Brewster's views and organized a church at Kirtland, Ohio, with himself as president and James E. Brewster and Jackson Goodale as counselors. A small colony of believers moved west and established a colony on the Rio Grande. By 1852, the entire movement was broken up by internal disputes on doctrine. Brewster subsequently became a preacher of spiritualism in California.

Another dissenter was Granville Hedrick, who had joined the Church in Illinois prior to the death of the Prophet. After the martyrdom he followed several factions, but he soon became dissatisfied with all of them. In 1863 and 1864, claiming to be the true successor to Joseph Smith, he effected an organization called the "Church of Christ." He laid claim to revelations in which Joseph Smith was termed a fallen prophet. Hedrickite followers were to gather to Jackson County, Missouri, prior to "judgments" that would begin in 1871 and would destroy the nation in 1878. John E. Page, who had served as an apostle under Joseph Smith, joined this movement. The Hedrickites purchased plots of ground in Independence, and as of the 1980s they still own part of the plot designated by Joseph Smith as the temple site. Some time ago they began to construct a temple but abandoned the project for lack of funds. The membership of the group has never constituted more than a few hundred souls.

In 1847, three years after the death of the Prophet, William E. McLellin, formerly a member of the Twelve Apostles, and Martin Harris, one of the three witnesses of the Book of Mormon, started a church, designated as "The Church of Christ," at Kirtland, Ohio. McLellin visited David Whitmer at Richmond, Missouri, and induced him to join the movement together with the Whitmers in that vicinity. David Whitmer was sustained as president of the church. His claim was based on an alleged commandment of the Lord to Joseph Smith in 1834 to ordain David Whitmer as his successor. In 1838, at a meeting of the high council at Far West, the Prophet referred to this commandment and said that it was conditioned upon his own falling from the Church. At that time, Joseph approved of the action of the high council in excommunicating David Whitmer from the Church.[3] When Whitmer refused to move to Kirtland, where the new church had been organized by McLellin, a quarrel ensued between the two branches and the organization broke up. A second attempt to organize the Whitmerites occurred two years before David Whitmer's death, which occurred January 25, 1888. Nothing came of the movement, and in a few years' time the church was completely disorganized.

It must be remembered that the members of one faction that broke from the restored church often became members of succeeding factions, and that the total number of members breaking away from the Church was but a mere handful, considering the total membership. The failures of these factions and subfactions emphasize the prophecy of Brigham Young: "All that want to draw away a party from the Church after them let them do it if they can, but they will not prosper."

Sixteen years after Joseph Smith's death, one more church arose. On April 6, 1860, at Amboy, Illinois, Joseph Smith III, son of the Prophet, was accepted as the head of the Reorganized Church of Jesus Christ of Latter Day Saints, which had a membership of about three hundred. This group centered around those who believed that the principle of lineal descent should be applied to the presidency of the Church. William Smith, brother of the Prophet, was a leader in the movement. This organization drew to it many of those who had moved away from the main body of the restored church following the martyrdom. Headquarters of this church were established at Plano, Illinois, and later moved to Independence, Missouri.

22

The Persecution Resumes

On June 18, 1844, President Joseph Smith said in an address to the Nauvoo Legion: "It is thought by some that our enemies would be satisfied with my destruction; but I tell you that as soon as they have shed my blood they will thirst for the blood of every man in whose heart dwells a single spark of the spirit of the fullness of the Gospel. The opposition of these men is moved by the spirit of the adversary of all righteousness. It is not only to destroy me, but every man and woman who dares believe the doctrines that God hath inspired me to teach in this generation."[1]

This prophecy had a speedy fulfillment. The death of Joseph and Hyrum created but a brief breathing spell for the Saints in Illinois. As soon as it became apparent that under new leadership the Saints were as united as ever and that nothing had really been changed, opposition began anew.

Three lines of activity carried forward by the Saints under the leadership of the Twelve declared to the world that the Church of Christ was very much alive. First, the temple was pushed to completion. Under the direction of Brigham Young and the Twelve, this work moved forward with great rapidity. When the Prophet and his brother were killed, only one story of the temple had been completed. Eleven months later, on May 24, 1845, the capstone was laid.

Second, there was the increased missionary activity under the direction of the Twelve. The states of the Union and eastern Canada were divided into ecclesiastical divisions with a mission president placed over each. The number of missionaries was greatly increased. Wilford Woodruff was sent to Great Britain, while a number of missionaries were sent to Wales. In the next three years several thousand converts were baptized in Wales alone. Despite the heavy migration of Church members from England to Nauvoo, the Saints in that land in January 1846 numbered 12,247. Every month witnessed one or more shiploads of English Saints arriving at Nauvoo by river steamer. The Eastern States Mission, under the leadership of Parley P. Pratt, also took on renewed vigor.

Third, the Saints displayed increased vigor in industrial growth. Capitalists were invited to Nauvoo and encouraged to establish factories. Elder John Taylor took a prominent part in industrial affairs. On his recommendation and under his supervision a trade union was formed, with the objective of establishing industries to produce as far as possible everything the Saints at Nauvoo might need as well as a surplus for exportation.

These movements were successful and gave such impetus to industry that a new era of prosperity dawned upon Nauvoo. Factories sprang into existence and absorbed the population that was rapidly increasing through immigration. The material welfare of the Saints seemed assured.

Zion Must Flee

The great energy displayed by the Church and especially its activity along cooperative commercial lines also fed the fires of growing opposition. Mob violence was threatened as early as July 1844, and a movement was begun to have the charter granted to Nauvoo repealed. Unless the charter could be repealed, the Saints, with their powerful Nauvoo Legion, might prove too powerful for the factions aiming to overthrow them.

On July 22, 1844, Governor Ford addressed a letter to W. W. Phelps, acting editor of the *Times and Seasons,* setting forth the state of the public mind and that of the governor concerning the Saints.

> The naked truth then is, that most well-informed persons condemn in the most unqualified manner the mode in which the Smiths were put to death, but nine out of every ten of such accompany the expression of their disapprobation by a manifestation of their pleasure that they are dead. . . .
>
> The unfortunate victims of this assassination were generally and thoroughly hated throughout the country, and it is not reasonable to suppose that their death has produced any reaction in the public mind resulting in active sympathy; if you think so, you are mistaken.

Most that is said on the subject is merely from the teeth out; and your people may depend on the fact, that public feeling is now, at this time, as thoroughly against them as it has ever been.

I mention this, not for the purpose of insulting your feelings, but to show you clearly how careful your people ought to be in future to avoid all causes of quarrel and excitement, and what little reliance could be placed on any militia force which I could send in your favor.

I ought, perhaps, to qualify what I have said, by remarking that but few persons from the surrounding counties could now be procured to join a mob force against you, without further cause of excitement to be ministered by some misguided imprudence of your people. But what I mean to say, and to say truly, is, that in the present temper of the public mind I am positively certain that I cannot raise a militia force in the state who would be willing to fight on your side, or to hazard their lives to protect you from an attack of your enemies.[2]

Attempts on the part of state officials to bring the murderers of Joseph and Hyrum to justice were a farce. Nine known members of the mob were arrested, and at their trial, all were acquitted.

In September an armed movement to drive out the Saints was begun. Governor Thomas Ford, in his *History of Illinois*, wrote of it:

In the course of the fall of 1844, the anti-Mormon leaders sent printed invitations to all the militia captains in Hancock, and to the captains of militia in all the neighboring counties in Illinois, Iowa, and Missouri, to be present with their companies at a great wolf hunt in Hancock; and it was privately announced that the wolves to be hunted were the Mormons and Jack Mormons.[3] Preparations were made for assembling several thousand men, with provisions for six days; and the anti-Mormon newspapers, in aid of the movement, commenced anew the most awful accounts of thefts and robberies, and meditated outrages by the Mormons.[4]

To prevent this "wolf hunt," Governor Ford issued a proclamation calling for twenty-five hundred volunteers. Only five hundred responded. With these recruits he marched into Hancock County, and the malcontents abandoned their enterprise.

The anti-Mormons then concentrated their efforts on repeal of

the Nauvoo charter. In January 1845, the repeal measure passed
the state legislature, and Nauvoo was left without civil authority.
Only the Church organization and the respect of the members for
the law prevented an outbreak of confusion and crime.

The continued growth and prosperity of Nauvoo, despite the
repeal of her charter, aroused anti-Mormons to more drastic actions. In September 1845 they commenced mobbing the Saints in
outlying settlements and burning their homes. The Saints offered
no armed resistance, believing that any movement on their part
would be misjudged and bring upon them all the opposing forces.
They appealed to the sheriff of Hancock County for protection, and
he announced to the people of Hancock County that "the Mormon
community had acted with more than ordinary forbearance, remaining perfectly quiet, and offering no resistance when their
dwellings, their buildings, stacks of grain, etc., were set on fire in
their presence. They had forborne until forbearance was no longer
a virtue."[5]

Between September 10 and 25, the sheriff issued five procla-
mations setting forth the outrages against the Saints and calling
upon honest citizens to help put down mob violence. When his appeal to non-Mormons for a posse to aid him met with failure, he accepted a posse from among the Saints, led by Orrin Porter
Rockwell, and soon drove the mobbers from the county and broke
up their gatherings.

Anti-Mormons reported to Governor Ford that Sheriff Backenstos was overstepping the bounds of his authority, whereupon
Governor Ford sent a detachment of four hundred militia into Hancock County and declared the county under martial law. Sheriff
Backenstos, stripped of authority, left the county, his life in grave
danger from the mob.

On September 22, 1845, the citizens of Quincy held a mass
meeting. It was generally known that Joseph Smith had contemplated moving the Saints to the West, and a resolution was
passed demanding that that removal begin at once. A committee
from Quincy called upon the Quorum of Twelve to ascertain their
intentions. On September 24, 1845, a reply signed by Brigham
Young, president, was given as follows:

We would say to the committee above mentioned and to the Governor, and all the authorities, and people of Illinois, and the surrounding states and territories, that we propose to leave this country next spring, for some point so remote that there will not need to be any difficulty with the people and ourselves, provided certain propositions necessary for the accomplishment of our removal shall be observed, as follows, to-wit:

That the citizens of this and surrounding counties, and all men, will use their influence and exertion to help us to sell or rent our properties, so as to get means enough that we can help the widow, the fatherless and the destitute to remove with us.

That all men will let us alone with their vexatious lawsuits so that we may have time, for we have broken no law; and help us to cash, dry goods, groceries, good oxen, beef-cattle, sheep, wagons, mules, horses, harness, etc. in exchange for our property, at a fair price, and deeds given at payment, that we may have means to accomplish a removal without the suffering of the destitute to an extent beyond the endurance of human nature.

That all exchanges of property shall be conducted by a committee, or by committees of both parties; so that all the business may be transacted honorably and speedily.

That we will use all lawful means, in connection with others, to preserve the public peace while we tarry; and shall expect, decidedly, that we be no more molested with house-burning, or any other depredations, to waste our property and time, and hinder our business.

That it is a mistaken idea, that we have proposed to remove in six months, for that would be so early in the spring that grass might not grow nor water run; both of which would be necessary for our removal. But we propose to use our influence to have no more seed time and harvest among our people in this community after gathering our present crops; and that all communications to us be made in writing.[6]

On October 1 Brigham Young and other leaders of the Church met with General John J. Hardin, head of the governor's militia forces, Judge Stephen A. Douglas, and other delegates of the anti-Mormons to discuss the Saints' plans for leaving Illinois. The next day General Hardin and his associates wrote to "the First President and High Council" of the Latter-day Saints and reported that resolutions concerning the Saints had been adopted by delegates from nine counties. "It was resolved," they said, "to accept your proposition to remove in the spring. . . . We think that steps should be taken by you to make it apparent that you are actually preparing to remove in the spring. By carrying out, in good faith, your proposition to remove as submitted by us, we think you should be, and will be permitted to depart peaceably next spring for your destination, west of the Rocky Mountains." Should the Saints not proceed with this plan, the letter warned, "we are satisfied, however much we may deprecate violence and bloodshed, that violent measures will be resorted to, to compel your removal, which will result in the most disastrous consequences to yourselves and your opponents, and that the end will be your expulsion from the state."[7]

The enemies of the Saints did not wait until spring. Plundering began anew. Vexatious lawsuits were stirred up and officers with writs were constantly in Nauvoo seeking to arrest the Church leaders. Even Governor Ford attempted to hasten their departure by circulating a false story that the United States Secretary of War would send a force to prevent the Mormons from going to the Rocky Mountains for fear that they would join the British there and create more trouble than ever.

Throughout the winter of 1845-46 the work of preparation went forward for the Saints' removal to the West. Every available building in Nauvoo became a workshop, and the sounds of the hammer and anvil could be heard early and late. Timber was purchased and dried in a kiln. Wagons were sent into the surrounding counties to gather up scrap iron to be converted into wagon tires and axles. Piles of hides were purchased for harnesses, while horses were purchased in the surrounding territory until rises in price made such purchases prohibitive. Oxen were then purchased and yokes manufactured.

Meanwhile work on the interior of the temple continued, and temple work for the living and dead went forward feverishly. This continued until most of the Saints had started the long trek west. On May 1, 1846, after the majority had left, the completed temple was dedicated in the presence of about three hundred persons.

23

The Exodus from Nauvoo

Beginning February 4, 1846, an observer on the bank of the Mississippi River at Nauvoo would have witnessed an unusual succession of events. On that date a number of wagons drawn by horses and oxen, surmounted by great white canvas covers and loaded with household goods, provisions, and farm implements, drove off the wharf at Nauvoo onto flatboats and were ferried across the mighty Father of Waters. Reaching the Iowa side, the wagons struck west onto the prairie and disappeared in the distance, leaving a deep trail through the freshly fallen snow. About six and a half miles from the river the wagons came to a halt on the banks of Sugar Creek, where the snow was cleared away and tents were pitched. The wagons belonged to people who were exiles from their homes—the advance group of 15,000 men, women, and children who were being driven from their beloved city of Nauvoo.

On February 15, Brigham Young and members of the Twelve crossed the river with their families and moved on to Sugar Creek. The weather was extremely cold, the thermometer hovering below zero. On the 25th Charles C. Rich walked across the river on the ice near Montrose. Over the next few days long caravans streaked out across the mighty river over a solid floor of ice that stretched from bank to bank, a distance of one mile. A few days later this unique roadway cracked up, and the line of caravans was halted while great blocks of ice choked the river. The delay was but temporary. Soon ferryboats began to ply the river again and fresh caravans spotted the prairie. The great exodus of the Mormon people had begun.

Why were these people leaving their homes and heading west in the middle of a severe winter? Other people were also heading west, but not in the coldest and wettest part of winter. Also, they were going west for other reasons—to trap or barter with the Indians for furs; to find new and cheaper land; to preach to the

Indians; to escape debtors; or to search for gold. But the Saints were not on the move for any of these reasons. They had become relatively prosperous and happy in the Nauvoo area. Most had built comfortable homes; their industries were thriving; their great temple, the center of their religion, was just completed and awaiting full use. They did not look forward to the trials and hardships of a long trek into an unknown land. For the thousands of new converts from the British Isles who had become impoverished by the long trip to join the Saints in Nauvoo, expecting it to be Zion, the journey west seemed even more frightening and hopeless. Most had no means to buy horses, wagons, and supplies for the westward journey. Thus, these emigrants had to remain behind for a time.

No, the Saints were not moving westward for lands or gold. They were moving in order to survive and to perpetuate their church. As Brigham Young was to say later, "We came west because we had to." They might have dispersed from their community center, given up their zeal for a new Zion, and been left alone. Individually they could have been left alone; some were—and passed into oblivion.

The story of the exodus and of the people's endurance and privations on the western plains can only be explained when we remember that they had testimonies that God lives and that his Son, Jesus Christ, was directing their lives. Only such a people could sing while on such a journey, "And should we die before our journey's through, Happy day! all is well! We then are free from toil and sorrow, too; with the just we shall dwell!"

Over four hundred wagons congregated at Sugar Creek, awaiting the arrival of their leaders. Many were in want, their provisions gone, their shelter insufficient, and their clothing scanty. The antagonistic cries of the non-Mormons in Hancock and neighboring counties had become so insistent that the exodus began two months earlier than the Saints had anticipated. It had become absolutely vital that it begin if bloodshed were to be averted. Brigham Young had counseled the Saints to leave Nauvoo prepared with sufficient provisions for several months and with an adequate supply of tents and clothing. But this advice had not always been followed. For some families, there was not enough time to raise funds by the sale of property in Nauvoo. Others feared being left behind the Twelve and crowded into the vanguard despite their lack of preparation. Eight hundred men reported at Sugar Creek the last two weeks of February without more than a fortnight's provisions for themselves and their teams, whereas Brigham Young entered the camp with a year's supply of provisions in his wagons for his family. Within two weeks he had nothing left, so freely did he give to those in need. Before leaving Nauvoo, the leading brethren entered into a covenant that they would use all their means to aid the deserving poor. How quickly they were called upon to fulfill it! Brigham Young took upon himself the care of the poor and the destitute. Upbraid his people he did—many times—but never for their being poor.

Despite all the efforts of the leaders, the intense cold and the lack of preparation and organization produced much suffering at Sugar Creek. John R. Young wrote in his memoir:

> By the first of March over five thousand exiles were shivering behind the meager shelter of wagon covers and tents, and the winter-stripped groves that lined the Creek. Their sufferings have never been adequately told; and to realize how cruel and ill-timed was this forced exodus one has only to be reminded that in one night nine children were born under these distressing conditions. . . .
>
> By ascending a nearby hill we could look back upon the beautiful city and see the splendid temple we had reared in our poverty at a cost of one and a half million dollars; moreover, on a clear, calm morning we could hear:
> *The silvery notes of the temple bell*
> *That we loved so deep and well:*
> *And a pang of grief would swell the heart*
> *And the scalding tears in anguish start*
> *As we silently gazed on our dear old homes.*[1]

Violent storms and excessive cold sapped the energy and vitality of the people. Especially did the women and newborn infants suffer. Eliza R. Snow wrote:

> On the first night of the encampment, nine children were born into the world, and from that time as we journeyed onward

mothers gave birth to offspring under almost every variety of circumstances imaginable, except those to which they had been accustomed; some in tents, other in wagons—in rainstorms and in snow-storms. I heard of one birth which occurred under the rude shelter of a hut, the sides of which were formed of blankets fastened to poles stuck in the ground, with a bark roof through which the rain was dripping; kind sisters stood holding dishes to catch the water as it fell, thus protecting the new-comer and its mother from a shower bath as the little innocent first entered on the stage of human life.[2]

Reflecting upon the sufferings endured at Sugar Creek, Brigham Young recorded in his journal:

> The fact is worthy of remembrance that several thousand persons left their homes in midwinter and exposed themselves without shelter, except that afforded by a scanty supply of tents and wagon covers, to a cold which effectually made an ice bridge over the Mississippi River, which at Nauvoo is more than a mile broad.
>
> We could have remained sheltered in our homes had it not been for threats and hostile demonstrations of our enemies, who, notwithstanding their solemn agreements, had thrown every obstacle in our way, not respecting either life, or liberty, or property; so much so that our only means of avoiding a rupture was by starting in midwinter.[3]

On March 1, five hundred wagons moved out of camp and struggled five miles through snow and mud. Then, the wagons were stopped, the snow cleared away, and tents raised for the night. The journey continued daily until the wagons reached the Chariton River, when a halt was called for a few days.

The main camp, the camp of Brigham Young and most of the Twelve, was called the Camp of Israel. Ahead of this camp was a group sent to seek out the best roads, build bridges, and construct ferryboats. Meanwhile, the provisions of the camp were nearly exhausted. To supply the Saints with food, companies were organized to go north and south of the line of march to Iowa and Missouri settlements, to trade watches, featherbeds, shawls and other items that the Saints could dispense with in exchange for grain and flour. The season before, crops had been bountiful in Iowa and

Missouri, and the forests were full of hogs, so the farmers were glad for such an exchange. Many of the men also found employment on the farms and in the towns of Iowa and Missouri.

The exodus was not, however, without its bright side. John Taylor, after recounting the trials and hardships, wrote to the Saints in England:

> We outlived the trying scenes—we felt contented and happy—the songs of Zion resounded from wagon to wagon—from tent to tent; the sound reverberated through the woods, and its echo was returned from the distant hills; peace, harmony, and contentment reigned in the habitations of the Saints. . . . The God of Israel is with us. . . . And as we journey, as did Abraham of old, to a distant land, we feel that like him, we are doing the will of our Heavenly Father and relying upon His word and promises; and having His blessings, we feel that we are children of the same promise and hope, and that the great Jehovah is our God.[4]

Captain Pitt and his brass band accompanied the Camp of Israel, and after the toils of the day were over, music, dancing, and singing helped the people to forget their woes and look with hope to the future. Pitt's band was invited to play in towns on both sides of the line of march, often for pay, which helped the camps financially.

Before they left Nauvoo, the Saints had been organized into four companies, with captains of hundreds and fifties. This organization proved nearly useless, as people designated to belong to a particular company could not all leave Nauvoo at the same time, particularly since the exodus began two months earlier than originally planned. Further, many who had not been assigned to the advance companies crowded into the first encampments. Some independent persons pushed ahead without waiting for the main camp. This condition led Brigham Young to call a halt and reorganize the camps of Israel. He sent word to those who had pushed ahead and severely rebuked them, threatening to disfellowship them if they did not return to meet with the main camp on the Chariton River. They complied.

Brigham Young was unanimously chosen to preside over all

the camps. The Saints were reorganized into companies of hundreds and fifties, with captains over each. Each fifty appointed a clerk and two commissaries, one for the purpose of contracting for grain and work and one to distribute food in the camp. The captain of fifty further organized his camp by appointing captains of tens, with buglers, blacksmiths, and so forth, until every man had his assigned duties. William Clayton was named clerk for the entire camp. From the camp on the Chariton, the migration moved forward in orderly fashion.

The Vision of a Great Leader

Under the leadership of Brigham Young, the Saints early assumed the aspect of an industrial column on the march. From the first it was evident that sufficient provisions to last out the journey to the mountains could not be taken from Nauvoo, even had a sufficient supply been available. The migrating Saints must be self-sustaining during the march. To accomplish this, they took herds of cattle and sheep, hogs, and chickens with them across the plains. Further, the advance companies planted huge areas into grain that could be harvested by succeeding companies. The movement to the West might well continue for years after the Saints of Nauvoo reached the Rocky Mountains. Converts from the eastern states, Canada, and England would be following in their wake. With rare vision Brigham Young prepared for this continuing migration. He sent scouting parties ahead to select permanent camp sites that might be utilized for many years. As most of Iowa was still public land and unsurveyed, such selections and settlements could be made without great expense or difficulty.

The first of these encampments was located on a branch of the Grand River, 150 miles from Nauvoo. The Saints called it Garden Grove. Upon reaching this vicinity in late April, the Camp of Israel halted for a time. A council was called, and one hundred men were appointed to make rails, forty-eight to build houses, twelve to dig wells, ten to build a bridge, and the rest to plow the ground and plant grain.

Almost as if by magic an orderly town arose on the prairie, as

715 acres of sod were broken and planted to grain and other crops and enclosed by a neat rail fence. Log houses were built along hastily laid-out streets. Samuel Bent was appointed to remain at Garden Grove and preside over the settlement, with Aaron Johnson and David Fullmer as counselors. The harvested crops were to be put in a storehouse and distributed to the needy emigrants. Large flocks of sheep and herds of cattle were also to be maintained at the encampment.

The second permanent camp was made another hundred miles to the west. Parley P. Pratt, who had been sent ahead and who selected the location, said of it:

> I came suddenly to some round and sloping hills, grassy and crowned with beautiful groves of timber; while alternate open groves and forests seemed blended in all the beauty and harmony of an English park. While beneath and beyond, on the west, rolled a main branch of Grand River, with its rich bottoms of alternate forest and prairie. As I approached this lovely scenery several deer and wolves, being startled at the sight of me, abandoned the place and bounded away till lost from my sight amid the groves. Being pleased and excited at the varied beauty before me, I cried out, "this is *Mount Pisgah*."[5]

Upon reaching this place, the Camp of Israel halted again. Organized laborers went to work and soon produced another magic city, breaking ground and planting a farm of several thousand acres, and erecting scores of log cabins. William Huntington was made president of the encampment, with Ezra T. Benson and Charles C. Rich as counselors. They remained behind to supervise the flocks and herds, the harvesting of grain, and the care of incoming and outgoing Saints.

The main camp of Israel now moved forward again, and by June 14, they reached Council Bluffs, on the banks of the Missouri River, where a third permanent camp was made. It was too late in the season to plant, but preparations were begun for fencing, plowing, and planting. One group of men was detailed to build a ferry with which to cross the river.

A site across the river and a short distance above Council Bluffs was selected as a fourth permanent camp. Designated

"Winter Quarters," this encampment was located on the present site of Florence, Nebraska, about six miles from the present city of Omaha. The emigrants built 538 log houses and 83 sod houses before winter began. These were sufficient to shelter about three thousand persons. By spring, the numbers of houses and people had doubled. The buildings generally had a single room, twelve by eighteen feet, with sod floor and roof and a good chimney. Thousands of tons of prairie hay were cut with scythes and stacked for the winter, while the meat of wild game was salted down or dried. Hundreds of bushels of wild berries were gathered along the river bottoms and preserved in various forms for winter use. Scouting parties went out to find the best route to be followed in the spring. Wagons were sent to St. Louis to bring back much-needed supplies for the winter. Emptied of their loads, the wagons were then sent back over the prairies to aid other companies.

The city of Winter Quarters was divided into thirteen wards. A bishopric was appointed over each, with instructions to look after both the temporal and the physical welfare of the people, to supervise industrial activities, and to provide for sanitation in the community. The number of wards was later increased to twenty-two. High councils were selected for Winter Quarters and also for the other permanent camps.

During the winter, schools were held and most of the young people had an opportunity to gain some formal instruction. An improvised mail service was also instituted. Many men had gone ahead with the advance companies, and as they or others went back toward Nauvoo to get their friends, they took letters or messages to individuals in the various camps. Willard Richards became known as the general postmaster both for outgoing and incoming mail.

The Final Chapter at Nauvoo

During the spring and summer of 1846, Nauvoo rapidly assumed the appearance of a deserted city. Many Saints, of course, were too poor to provide themselves with the necessities of travel. These persons must wait until the advance wagons could be sent back for them. Further, there were some who were too sick to travel, and these persons must wait until health returned before undertaking the hard journey. Besides, the Saints had for the most part been unable to dispose of their property, so a number of people remained behind for this purpose.

As the mobs witnessed the departure of thousands of the Saints during the early spring, they ceased for a time their depredations. But when some of the remaining people began to plant grain, indicating that they might remain until another spring, new hostilities began. These hostilities were directed alike toward the Mormons and the non-Mormons who had purchased property of the Saints in Nauvoo. The mobs scoured the country outside the city limits, and it became dangerous to go into the fields without an armed guard.

Meanwhile the finishing touches were done on the interior of the temple. In the latter part of April 1846, Wilford Woodruff and Orson Hyde returned to Nauvoo from the British Mission. Under date of April 30, 1846, Elder Woodruff's journal contains the following:

> In the evening of this day I repaired to the Temple with Elder Orson Hyde and about twenty other elders of Israel. There we all clothed in our priestly robes and dedicated the Temple of the Lord, erected in His most holy name by the Church of Jesus Christ of Latter-day Saints. Notwithstanding the predictions of false prophets and the threat of the mobs that the building should never be completed or dedicated, their words had fallen to the ground. The Temple was now finished and dedicated to Him. After the dedication, we raised our voices in a united shout of "Hosanna to God and the Lamb."[6]

As the summer progressed, anti-Mormons held mass meetings in Hancock and neighboring counties and demanded the immediate evacuation of every Mormon in Nauvoo. In May, Governor Ford sent Major Warren to Nauvoo with a small military force to keep peace. He was empowered to enlist the aid of Nauvoo citizens to put down mob riots. For a time he was able to enlist public sympathy for the departing exiles by informing the people in the surrounding counties of the fact that the Saints were leaving with all possible speed. On May 14, he reported that 450 teams and 1,350 souls had left Nauvoo during the week. A week later he reported: "The Mormons still continue to leave the city in large numbers. The ferry at this place averages about 32 teams per day, and at Fort Madison, 45. Thus it will be seen that 539 teams have left during the week, which average about three persons to each, making in all 1,617 souls."[7]

The publishing of these facts did not stop the outrages of the mob. On June 6, a movement started at Warsaw to drive out the remaining Mormons at the point of the sword. A mob assembled at Golden Point, but when it was rumored that Stephen Markham had returned to Nauvoo with several hundred armed men, the mob dispersed. It was true that Markham had returned to Nauvoo, but only to remove some Church property, and he had brought no more than a few teamsters and wagons for that purpose.

The mob soon reassembled and issued an ultimatum against any Saints leaving the city limits except to go westward. In late July a group of Mormons and non-Mormons who went outside the city limits to harvest grain were captured and severely beaten. Attempts to bring the perpetrators to punishment failed.

Conditions went from bad to worse. Major Warren resigned, and on August 24, Major James R. Parker was sent with ten men and power to raise a posse to defend Nauvoo. His entreaties to the gathering mobs to disperse were met with contempt. He received a counterproclamation from the mob leader: "When I say to you the Mormons must go, I speak the mind of the camp and county. They can leave without force or injury to themselves or property, but I say to you, sir, with all candor, they shall go—they may fix the time within sixty days, or I will fix it for them."[8]

Parker, on behalf of the citizens of Nauvoo, agreed to the terms allowing sixty days for removal, but the mobs rejected the treaty made by their officers. The new leader of the mob, Thomas Brockman, marched a force of seven hundred men against Nauvoo. His propositions to the Saints were so outrageous that a force of 150 to 300 men was raised to resist him.[9] They threw up breastworks on the north side of Mulholland Street facing the mob camp and converted some steamboat shafts into crude cannons.

Firing on both sides ensued on September 10, 11, and 12. On the 13th, a real battle took place. The Nauvoo citizens' resistance was so determined that they drove the attacking force back to their encampment. Three of the defenders were killed and several wounded; it is not known how many of the mob were killed.

As the state made no move to aid the stricken city, the Saints in Nauvoo decided to surrender rather than to shed more blood in defending a city they were so soon to abandon anyway. The treaty of surrender guaranteed them protection until they could move across the river and provided for a committee of five Saints to remain in the city for the purpose of disposing of property. Under the terms of the treaty, the mob forces entered the city on September 17 and marched to camp on the southern side of the city. The constraints placed on them by the treaty, however, were not kept. Governor Ford reported what happened in his history:

> When the posse arrived in the city, the leaders of it erected themselves into a tribunal to decide who should be forced away and who remain. Parties were dispatched to hunt for Mormon arms and for Mormons, and to bring them to the judgment, where they received their doom from the mouth of Brockman, who there sat a grim and unawed tyrant for the time. As a general rule, the Mormons were ordered to leave within an hour or two hours; and by rare grace, some of them were allowed until next day, and a few cases longer. The treaty specified that the Mormons only should be driven into exile. Nothing was said in it concerning the new citizens, who had with the Mormons defended the city. But the posse no sooner obtained possession, than they commenced expelling the new citizens. Some of them were ducked in the river, being in one or two instances actually baptized in the name of the leaders of the mob, others were forcibly driven into the ferry boats, to be taken over the river, before the bayonets of armed ruffians; and it is believed that the houses of most of them were broken open and their property stolen during their absence. Many of these new settlers were strangers in the county from various parts of the United States, who were attracted there by the low price of property, and they knew but little of previous difficulties, or the merits of the quarrel. They saw with their own eyes that the Mormons were industriously preparing to go away, and they knew of their own knowledge that an effort to expel them with force was gratuitous and unnecessary cruelty.[10]

A Voyage of Ten Thousand Miles

When the ultimatum came to leave Nauvoo, not all the Saints were living in that vicinity. Thousands of converts were as yet in the eastern states, Canada, and England. In January 1846, Brigham Young advised the Saints in the East to join the Church in its western exodus the following spring or to charter ships and sail around South America to California.

Samuel Brannan, an energetic elder in the New York branch, was appointed to take charge of those who would go to California by water. The ship *Brooklyn* was chartered at a cost of $1,200 a month for the journey. Over three hundred Saints asked for places; 238 were finally taken at a cost of fifty dollars each.

The ship *Brooklyn,* by a coincidence, sailed on February 4, 1846, the same day the first wagons of the Saints left Nauvoo for the West. After a voyage of more than five months, the ship sailed through the Golden Gate in San Francisco harbor on July 29 and docked at Yerba Buena, now the city of San Francisco. To the surprise of the Saints, the Stars and Stripes were already floating over the city, having been raised some two weeks before.

The Saints had drawn up on board the *Brooklyn* a contract whereby they would give the proceeds of their labors of the next three years into a common fund from which all were to draw their living. This plan was soon abandoned. The people found work wherever they could. Twenty of them were detailed to select a place for settlement, put in crops, and build houses, preparatory to moving the entire colony to the site in the spring. The place selected, New Hope, was situated on the north bank of the Stanislaus River, about a mile and a half from the San Joaquin River. However, the uncertainty of where the main body of Saints would settle, as well as quarrels about the site of the settlement, prevented the project's being carried out. Brannan finally acquired title to the entire tract at New Hope.

In January 1847, Brannan began the publication of the *Yerba Buena California Star,* using the press on which the periodical *The Prophet* had been printed by the Saints in New York. This was the first newspaper printed in San Francisco and the second English paper in California.

Of the company of Saints who sailed on the *Brooklyn,* about 140 found their way to the Salt Lake Valley between 1848 and 1850 and joined the main body of the Church. Some of those who remained in California, together with Samuel Brannan, their leader, left the Church. Others later joined Mormon colonies in Arizona and at San Bernardino in southern California.

24

The Mormon Battalion

A visitor to the Utah State Capitol at Salt Lake City may see on the grounds, as he approaches from the south, a beautiful monument carved in enduring stone and bronze. On one side of the monument is the bronze figure of a soldier flanked by a group of pioneers enlisting as soldiers under the flag of the United States. On another side, recruits are on the march, some pulling wagons up a precipitous ascent, others widening a cut for the wagons between jutting rocks. On the third side of this triangular monument may be seen the dim and receding figure of a vanishing race, the American Indian. Over the bronze man and the thrilling scene on either side of him, symbolizing the brooding spirit of the mighty West, is chiseled the head and upper body of a beautiful woman.

The setting of this story takes us back to an exiled people camped on the Iowa plains—an unwanted people who are leaving the confines of the United States. It takes us back still further to the White House in Washington, D.C., into the presence of James K. Polk, President of the United States. Elder Jesse C. Little, representative of The Church of Jesus Christ of Latter-day Saints, and Amos Kendall, former Postmaster-General of the United States, have just completed a three-hour conference with the President on the subject of the Latter-day Saint migration to the West, which was then under way. President Polk assures Elder Little that he will aid the Saints in their journey to the West and protect them in their place of settlement. The date is June 3, 1846.

Before his death, Joseph Smith made some preparations for moving the Saints to the Rocky Mountains. He carried on negotiations with the federal government for governmental sanction and protection for the enterprise, and collected maps and other information of the West. After the martyrdom, Brigham Young carried the Prophet's plans forward. Before any government help could be obtained, however, the Saints were driven out of Nauvoo. Unable to dispose of much of their property, they were destitute of cash, so they sought a contract with the federal government to build a line of blockhouses to protect the Oregon migration. Such a contract would ease the financial problem and lend governmental sanction to the Saints' western movement.

On January 26, 1846, President Young wrote to Elder Jesse C. Little, then in New Hampshire, and asked him to go to Washington, D.C., to negotiate for "any facilities for emigration to the western coast" that the government could offer. By the time Elder Little reached Washington, the United States had declared war against Mexico. He carried letters of introduction from a number of notable men, including Judge John K. Kane and his son, Captain Thomas L. Kane. One of his first important contacts was with Amos Kendall, who had considerable influence in Washington. Of this meeting Elder Little reported: "We talked upon the subject of emigration, and he thought arrangements could be made to assist our emigration by enlisting one thousand of our men, arming, equipping and establishing them in California to defend the country."[1]

Elder Little, following Kendall's suggestion, wrote to President Polk asking for such a privilege. In a series of conferences with the President from June 1 to June 8, 1846, he secured the assurance that when the Saints reached the Rocky Mountains, a few companies would be received as volunteers by the United States Army to defend that area.

Elder Little, pleased with his success, forwarded his report to Brigham Young. President Polk seems to have been prompted by other motives than mere sympathy for the Saints. In his diary for June 2 he noted: "Col. Kearny was also authorized to receive into service as volunteers a few hundred of the Mormons on their way to California, with a view to conciliate them, attach them to our country, and prevent them from taking part against us."[2]

The Saints were becoming powerful enough that the President may have feared their allegiance to another nation. He also feared having a predominant force of Saints in the United States Army that occupied California. The War Department's final instructions to Colonel Stephen W. Kearny on this matter state:

It is known that a large body of Mormon emigrants are *en route* to California, for the purpose of settling in that country. You are desired to use all proper means to have a good understanding with them, to the end that the United States may have their co-operation in taking possession of, and holding, that country. It has been suggested here that many of these Mormons would willingly enter the service of the United States, and aid us in our expedition against California. You are hereby authorized to muster into service such as can be induced to volunteer; not, however, to a number exceeding one-third of your entire force. Should they enter the service they will be paid as other volunteers, and you can allow them to designate, as far as it can be properly done, the persons to act as officers thereof.[3]

Colonel Kearny sent Captain James Allen to intercept the Saints on their journey west and receive the enlistments.

Exiles Become Soldiers

Captain Allen reached the camps of the Saints before Elder Little. Thus, although Brigham Young and the other leaders were well aware of Elder Little's activities and expected some sort of enlistment in the government service, the exact nature of that service was not known until Captain Allen appeared. To the leaders, the call to raise a battalion that would leave the main body of the Saints and march by a totally different route to the West came as a surprise. Eighteen hundred wagons, with the attendant teamsters and families, were encamped in various places between Nauvoo and Council Bluffs. Many of the young unmarried men had gone into adjoining states to look for work, and five hundred teamsters, the majority with families, could hardly be spared. Brigham Young, upon hearing the enlistment order, said, "I would rather have undertaken to raise two thousand men a year ago in twenty four hours than one hundred in a week now."[4]

The Church leaders were, however, quick to see advantages of the enlistment. In the first place, they now realized that it was too late in the season to expect to move Saints with their families into the Rocky Mountains that year. The plan had suddenly been changed to finding a place suitable for spending the winter and sending a group of young men into the valleys of the mountains to prepare the way. Thus, although raising a battalion to serve for one year would interfere with the advance scout plan, it would not greatly hamper the western movement, which could not proceed until the following spring.

Second, the camps of Israel desperately needed funds. The committee left in Nauvoo to dispose of their properties had not succeeded in finding cash buyers. Surplus beds and bedding had been traded for corn and flour, but unless funds were forthcoming from some source, the Saints could not survive the coming winter. The battalion call presented an opportunity to get five hundred of the men to the West, feed them through the coming winter, and pay them a wage that would be a godsend to their families.

Third, the Saints, certain now that they must remain on the plains of Iowa and Nebraska during the winter of 1846-47, were facing perplexing problems that enlistment in the United States Army would help solve. The only suitable places for spending the winter were on Indian lands. While the Indians themselves were friendly to the Latter-day Saints, the Indian agents were not. It became increasingly evident, during the early summer of 1846, that an attempt to winter in Iowa or Nebraska would be fraught with trouble. If a battalion were raised to march in the cause of the United States, however, the government must protect the families of those men who wished to winter on the Indian lands.

Further, citizens in Missouri were deeply agitated by the presence of the Latter-day Saints along the state's northern borders, fearing that the Saints might attempt some sort of revenge against those who had driven them out or try to reestablish themselves there. Enlistment in the United States Army would help dispel these fears and give the government reason to act in the Saints' behalf.

Finally, Brigham Young desired that the Saints should not only have a part in settling the West but also in conquering it. This would assure them security and help them establish a right to the country.

All of these factors were known to President Young and prompted his reply that Captain Allen should have his battalion. But while the leaders of the Church saw advantages in raising a bat-

*Mormon
Battalion
Monument*

talion for the United States Army, their followers generally did
not. It took all the persuasion of Brigham Young, Heber C. Kimball, Parley P. Pratt, Orson Pratt, and others to change their suspicions of the government into gratitude. These brethren journeyed
from camp to camp with Captain Allen, explaining the call and its
advantages. In a letter written from Mount Pisgah to the Saints at
Garden Grove, Brigham Young pleaded for volunteers: "The U.S.
want our friendship, the President wants to do us good, and secure
our confidence. The outfit of these five hundred men costs us nothing, and their pay will be sufficient to take their families over the
mountains. There is war between Mexico and the U.S., to whom
California must fall prey, and if we are the first settlers, the old citizens cannot have a Hancock [county] or Missouri pretext to mob
the saints. The thing is from above for our good."[5] In a letter to the
Saints still in Nauvoo he added: "This is the first time the government has stretched forth its arm to our assistance, and we received
their proffers with joy and thankfulness. We feel confident they
[the Battalion] will have little or no fighting. The pay of the five
hundred men will take their families to them. The Mormons will

then be the old settlers and have a chance to choose the best locations."[6]

The final enrollment took place at Council Bluffs on July 13. An American flag was brought out and "hoisted to a tree mast," and under it the enrollment took place.[7] Colonel Thomas L. Kane, who was visiting Brigham Young at Council Bluffs, later wrote this description:

> There was no sentimental affection at their leave-taking. The afternoon before was appropriated to a farewell ball; and a more merry dancing rout I have never seen, though the company went without refreshments and their ball-room was of the most primitive. It was the custom, whenever the larger camps rested for a few days together, to make great arbors or boweries, as they called them, of poles and bush, and wattling, as places of shelter for their meetings of devotion or conference. In one of these, where the ground had been trodden firm and hard by the worshipers of the popular Father Taylor's precinct, was gathered now the mirth and beauty of the Mormon Israel.
>
> If anything told the Mormons had been bred to other lives, it was the appearance of the women, as they assembled here. Before their flight, they had sold their watches and trinkets as the most available resource for raising ready money; and, hence, like their partners, who wore waistcoats cut with useless watch pockets, they, although their ears were pierced and bore the loop-marks of rejected pendants, were without earrings, finger-rings, chains, or brooches. Except such ornaments, however, they lacked nothing most becoming the attire of decorous maidens. The neatly darned white stocking, and clean, bright petticoat, the artistically clear starched collar and chemisette, the something faded, only because too well washed, lawn or gingham gown, that fitted modishly to the waist of the pretty wearer—these, if any of them spoke of poverty, spoke of a poverty that had known its better days.[8]

Effects of the Enlistment

Some of the results of the enlistment were immediately felt. On July 1, Brigahm Young assured Captain Allen that the battalion would be raised. The following day ten Indian chiefs were brought before Captain Allen and induced to put their marks as signatures to a treaty guaranteeing to the Saints the right to stop upon the Indian lands, to cultivate the soil, and to pass through the area without molestation.[9] On July 16 Captain Allen gave a written approval for the Saints to reside in the Pottawattamie country, and a document was executed permitting the Saints en route to the West to make camp and fortifications as necessary. These documents were subsequently approved by President Polk.

A further benefit was soon realized. Members of the battalion were allowed to wear their regular clothing rather than uniforms and were paid in advance for this clothing when the companies reached Fort Leavenworth. A year's pay in advance for their clothing, at the rate of $3.50 per month, would mean $42.00 each, or $21,000 for the entire battalion. The greater part of this was sent back to their families, together with their first month's pay. The Saints also sent to Santa Fe secret agents to bring back to the camps of Israel the paychecks that would then have accrued. In a letter to the battalion, Brigham Young said: "We consider the money you have received, as compensation for your clothing, a peculiar manifestation of the kind providence of our Heavenly Father at this particular time, which is just the time for the purchasing of provisions and goods for the winter supply of the camp."[10]

The pay of the men ranged from seven dollars a month for privates to fifty dollars a month for captains. At the end of one year's service their equipment was to become the personal property of the men, on their discharge in California.

The raising of the battalion had been done from the Saints' advance companies, which left five hundred wagons without men as teamsters. To fill in the gaps, President Young wrote to the Saints camped at Garden Grove under date of July 7:

> The places of these five hundred teamster-soldiers must be immediately supplied, and we want you to gather up all the old men and boys and all the others who are capable of going into the army, driving oxen, herding cattle and sheep, milking cows, chopping wood, drawing water, cutting grass, pitching and stacking hay, etc., from the farm, and those who may be in Missouri at work and all others within your call, and dispatch them to Council Bluffs forthwith, or five hundred teams must be left

without drivers. . . . The demand we are making on you for every man and boy (only enough left to watch the farm crops and herds), we shall make immediately in all the regions of Nauvoo, and there must be no deafness on this subject.[11]

President Young promised the battalion members who left their families that he would see that all were provided for and either taken forward with the main camp or cared for in one of the stopping places. This promise was kept, Brigham Young later asserting that the families of the battalion men had fared even better than the others.

At the time the battalion was called, the plan was to winter the Saints on Grand Island in the Platte River. This island was fifty-two miles long, with an average width of a mile and three-quarters, and was well timbered. Near at hand were wide prairies covered with grass that might be cut for hay. This plan was later changed, and the Saints moved into Winter Quarters, across the river from Council Bluffs, not far from what is now Omaha, Nebraska.

Carving Out a Road

The route followed by the battalion led from Ft. Leavenworth, across the arid regions of the Southwest, to Santa Fe. Captain Allen, who was well liked by battalion members, died at Fort Leavenworth after having ordered the battalion to proceed on their journey without him. Lieutenant Andrew Jackson Smith succeeded him. As the battalion was part of the army of General Kearny, whom it was trying to overtake, battalion members felt that their own Captain Jefferson Hunt should command them until Kearny himself should appoint a command. Smith was accepted as commander, however, when the officers came to realize that their own commissions were not yet sanctioned by the U.S. War Department and they would thus be unable to draw on government supplies.

Day after day the march continued into the Southwest. Feet blistered by the hot sands and shoulders galled by the heavy packs, the men found no time to rest. Some of the battalion had been allowed to bring their families, but it soon became apparent that this was no march for women and children, even where private wagons had been brought for them. On September 16, at the last crossing of the Arkansas River, the commanding officer insisted that the families accompanying the battalion, twelve or fifteen in number, should be detached and sent under guard up the Arkansas to Pueblo, Colorado. There were many protests, but future events proved the wisdom of this order.

During the days that followed, there was much to discourage the soldiers. The journal of James A. Scott, under date of September 26, reads:

> March, march, march, is the daily task. Day break brings the reveille, sick or well must go either to roll call or to the doctor; next boys get your breakfast and strike your tents with all possible speed; then left, left, all day over the sand, through dust, over hills and across valleys, sometimes twelve, fifteen and eighteen miles. Halt, stack arms, pitch tents, run all over creation gathering buffalo chips or a little brush and getting water, draw rations, cook supper, eat, then roll call, and by the time the evening chores are finished it is dark. Attend to evening duties, go to bed and sleep on the rough, cold ground, with only one blanket and a thin tent to shelter from the cold. Say, sympathetic reader, is not the condition of the Mormon soldier hard? But dwell not my mind on these things; gloom, perhaps repentance at having started the journey, might overcome thee. Cheer up, drooping Saint, and look forward to green fields, pleasant gardens and neat farm houses that will soon adorn the valleys of California and think thou hadst had a part in the accomplishment of this.[12]

On October 9, the first detachment of the battalion reached Santa Fe, a city of six thousand inhabitants. General Kearny had previously entered Santa Fe without opposition and taken the city in the name of the United States. Leaving Colonel Alexander Doniphan in charge, he had then gone on west. Colonel Doniphan had earlier shown friendship for the Saints in the Missouri troubles, so when the Mormon Battalion entered the city, he ordered a salute of a hundred guns fired in their honor.

At Santa Fe Lieutenant-Colonel Philip St. George Cooke took over command of the battalion. The battalion was now inspected, and eighty-six men who were found to be too sick to endure the march ahead were detached and sent to Pueblo for the winter. It was understood that in the spring the Pueblo detachment would be able to join the main body of the Saints and move with them to the West at government expense. Five wives of battalion officers were reluctantly allowed to remain with the expedition, but they had to furnish their own transportation.

On October 10, the battalion left Santa Fe behind. The difficulties had just begun. The long journey to California across the roadless waste was enough to test the endurance of the strongest of men. Often wells had to be dug before water of any sort could be obtained.

The march took the army 220 miles down the Santa Fe River and then west to the San Pedro. At this place the only fighting in which the battalion engaged took place—a fight with wild bulls.

Leaving the San Pedro, the command marched northeasterly to Tucson, a Mexican town of four or five hundred inhabitants. When they were within sixteen miles of the town, they sent word to Captain Comanduran, who commanded a Mexican force of some two hundred men, demanding that his men give up their arms and agree that the inhabitants would not fight against the United States. Captain Comanduran declined, and the battalion prepared for battle. But when they arrived at Tucson the next day, they found that the Mexican garrison had fled. The battalion marched through the town without firing a shot.

Three days out of Tucson, the command reached the Gila River. Attempting to lighten the load by floating provisions down the river on a raft, the battalion lost most of its supplies, which had to be unloaded to get the craft over frequent sandbars.

From the mouth of the Gila the journey lay for a hundred miles across the desert beyond the Colorado River in southern California. Daniel Tyler wrote of this part of the journey:

> We found here the heaviest sands and hottest days, and coldest nights, with no water and but little food. At this time the men were nearly barefooted; some used, instead of shoes, rawhide wrapped around their feet, while others improvised a novel style of boots by stripping the skin from the leg of an ox. To do this a ring was cut around the hind leg above and below the gambrel

joint, and then the skin was taken off without cutting it length-
wise. After this the lower end was sewed up with sinews, when it
was ready for the wearer, the natural crook of the hide adapting
it somewhat to the shape of the foot. Others wrapped cast-off
clothing around their feet to shield them from the burning sand
during the day and the cold at night.

Before we arrived at the garrison many of the men were so
nearly used up from thirst, hunger and fatigue, that they were unable to speak until they reached the water or had it brought to
them. Those who were strongest reported, when they arrived,
that they had passed many lying exhausted by the wayside.[13]

The battalion was scheduled to join General Kearny at San
Diego, but reports reached them that the enemy was concentrated
at Los Angeles, so they changed direction to come upon the city
from the east. Then, finding that all of California was already in the
hands of the Americans, the company turned south to San Diego.
They reached the end of their journey on January 29, 1847. They
had conquered the desert and made a wagon road of sorts over one
of the most difficult sections of North America.

The march of the Mormon Battalion has been called the greatest march of infantry in the history of the world. At the end of the
journey, Lieutenant Colonel Philip St. George Cooke wrote: "The
Lieutenant Colonel commanding congratulates the Battalion on
their safe arrival on the shores of the Pacific ocean, and the conclusion of their march of over two thousand miles. History will be
searched in vain for an equal march of infantry."[14]

Duty Versus Wealth

Since no fighting remained to be done in California, the battalion was divided and assigned to garrison duty at the San Luis Rey
Mission and in San Diego and Los Angeles. On July 16 they were
discharged. Great inducements were offered to get them to reenlist
when their term of service had expired. Eighty-one did reenlist for
an additional six months, but the majority were anxious to rejoin
their families. Some of the families were by that time nearing the
Salt Lake Valley, while others were still in encampments on the
plains. The majority of the former battalion members hurried on to

the Salt Lake Valley, traveling over the Sierra Nevadas and cutting a wagon road on that route. They were in constant danger from attack by Indian bands, and three men who volunteered to go ahead of the rest were killed by Indians. Meanwhile, those who had been sent to Pueblo earlier in the battalion's march followed the pioneer Saints into the Salt Lake Valley. There, their term of enlistment having expired, they were mustered out of the service with full pay.

A few of the returning battalion members remained in northern California for the winter. They found employment at Sutter's Fort in the Sacramento Valley and were present at the time of the discovery of gold. It is from the journal of one battalion member, Henry Bigler, that the authentic date for the discovery of gold in California is learned. On Monday, January 24, 1848, Bigler wrote: "This day some kind of metal was found in the tail race that looks like gold." A short time later battalion members discovered gold on an island in the American River. They had, however, hired out to Sutter by contract, and they kept that contract despite the fact that many times the amount of their wages could be obtained digging for gold. Spring found these battalion members heading for the Great Basin with their savings.

25

Pioneers

During the trying winter of 1846-47, one thought dominated the encampment of the Saints: "West in the spring." The expression became a symbol of hope that lightened people's loads, eased their sorrows, and assuaged their griefs. Colonel Thomas L. Kane, who spent much time among them, said: "The Mormons took the young and hopeful side. They could make sport and frolic of their trials, and often turn right sharp suffering into right round laughter against themselves. I certainly heard more jests and 'Joe Millers' while in this Papillion camp than I am likely to hear again in all the remainder of my days."[1]

Yet underneath the great hope for the future were hearts mellowed by grief and sorrow that few people have known. Before the cold of winter prevented the spread of disease, some three hundred fresh graves appeared in the cemetery outside Winter Quarters. Weakened by the long trek from Nauvoo and the lack of sufficient vegetables in their diet, the Saints became easy victims of malaria, scurvy, and other then little-known maladies. Scurvy, called by the Saints "blackleg," caused the greatest sufferings and the majority of deaths. When the disease became rampant, wagons were sent to Missouri to bring back potatoes, which proved effective in checking and curing the disease. Horseradish, found in an abandoned fort some distance from the camp, proved an excellent antidote. The disease was totally checked during the winter, but not until it had made inroads upon nearly every family.

The Indians, especially the Omahas wintering in the river bottoms, though they professed the greatest of friendship for the Latter-day Saints, lived either by gift or theft upon cattle belonging to the Saints. Many of the thieves were caught and severely punished, but this did not greatly lessen the loss of cattle. It was during this winter that Brigham Young became well acquainted with Indian nature and formulated the policy for which he became famous—"It is cheaper to feed the Indians than to fight them." In the war that occurred during the winter between the Omahas and the Sioux and Iowas, the Saints kept aloof.

Long months before the movement west could begin again, preparations were under way. Wagons were repaired and some new ones made. Canvas was sewed into covers and tents. Shoes were fashioned and socks knitted. A gristmill was constructed, and all the grain, except that which was needed for the animals, was ground into flour. Those who had no other tasks set about gathering willows and weaving them into baskets and half-bushel measures. Some of the men manufactured washboards to sell to the people of Iowa and Missouri.

On January 14, 1847, Brigham Young gave to the Saints the only revelation he ever set down in writing: "The word and will of the Lord," which dealt with the organization of the Camp of Israel in its march to the West. In it the Saints were commanded:

> Let all the people of the Church of Jesus Christ of Latter-day Saints, and those who journey with them, be organized into companies, with a covenant and promise to keep all the commandments and statutes of the Lord our God.
>
> Let the companies be organized with captains of hundreds, captains of fifties, and captains of tens, with a president and his two counselors at their head, under the direction of the Twelve Apostles.
>
> And this shall be our covenant—that we will walk in all the ordinances of the Lord. (D&C 136:2-4.)

As spring approached, Brigham Young selected those who were to go west with the advance company to make roads and prepare the way. This company was to consist of able-bodied men who could travel quickly and without their families, so as to be less handicapped in the hard work that lay ahead. They were to be the vanguard of the movement. The remainder of the people were to march by families under appointed leaders when the grass became high enough for their cattle and sheep.

The unity and cooperation of the people in preparing for the long trail west is one of the remarkable elements of the exodus. This unity was marred, however, by a few defections. Bishop

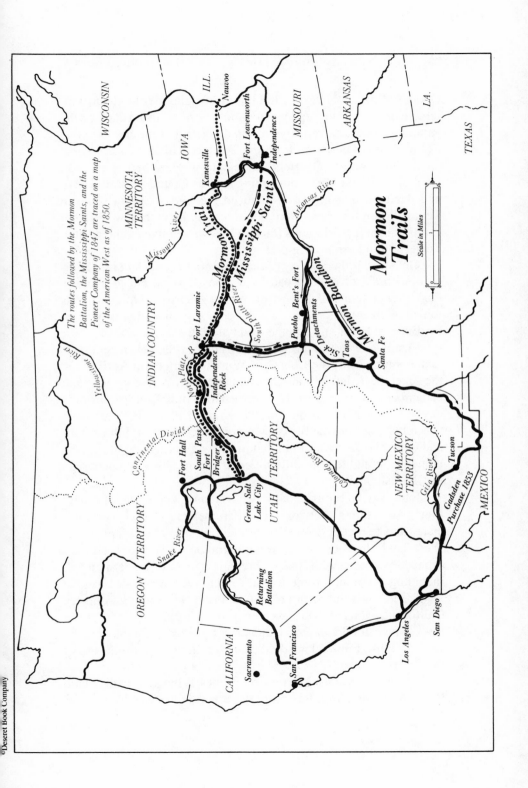

The routes followed by the Mormon Battalion, the Mississippi Saints, and the Pioneer Company of 1847 are traced on a map of the American West as of 1850.

Mormon Trails

Scale in Miles

©Deseret Book Company

WISCONSIN
ILL.
Nauvoo
IOWA
MINNESOTA TERRITORY
Kanesville
Fort Leavenworth
Independence
MISSOURI
ARKANSAS
LA.
TEXAS
Missouri River
Arkansas River
Mormon Trail
Mississippi Saints
Pueblo
Bent's Fort
Sick Detachments
Taos
Santa Fe
Mormon Battalion
INDIAN COUNTRY
Yellowstone River
North Platte R.
Fort Laramie
South Platte River
Independence Rock
South Pass
Continental Divide
Fort Bridger
Fort Hall
OREGON TERRITORY
Snake River
Great Salt Lake City
UTAH TERRITORY
Colorado River
NEW MEXICO TERRITORY
Gila River
Tucson
Gadsden Purchase 1853
MEXICO
Returning Battalion
CALIFORNIA
Sacramento
San Francisco
Los Angeles
San Diego

George Miller, contrary to the advice of Brigham Young, had wintered with sixty-two wagons, including those of Anson Call, on the Running Water, eleven days' drive due north of the line of travel of the Saints. On orders from the Twelve, Miller's encampment moved into Winter Quarters in the spring. Here he came out in open opposition to Brigham Young and the Council of the Twelve and declared that he was convinced the Saints should settle in Texas. When his views were not accepted, he withdrew from the camp, took a few followers (mostly his own relatives), and went to Texas to join Lyman Wight.

On April 5, the journey of the pioneers began. Heber C. Kimball, with six of his company's wagons, moved out to Cutler's Park, about four miles west of Winter Quarters. Other wagons joined as they were ready, and the company moved westward to the Elkhorn River and commenced building a ferry.

Meanwhile President Young presided at the seventeenth annual conference of the Church at Winter Quarters on April 6. On the seventh, he left Winter Quarters with twenty-five wagons and encamped ten miles west. He returned to Winter Quarters the next day, with members of the Twelve, to meet Parley P. Pratt, who was returning from the British Mission. Together with John Taylor and Orson Hyde, Elder Pratt had journeyed to England during the winter to straighten out difficulties in the mission and encourage the English Saints.

John Taylor brought back two sextants, one circle of reflection, two artificial horizons, two barometers, several thermometers, and telescopes. He also brought a number of maps of the West that he had obtained in Washington, D.C. The brethren were especially pleased with John C. Fremont's maps of western routes, including Fremont's route to California, via Great Salt Lake, in 1843, and one of his return from California "in 1844, *via* southern California, Mohave river, Las Vegas, Rio Virgin, the Sevier, Utah Lake, Spanish Fork canon, Uintah river, and so to Pueblo and the east."[2] Thomas Bullock made sketches of these maps for the use of the Saints.

The real start of the Mormon pioneers was made from the Platte River April 16. From this point there was but one objective: the valleys of the Rocky Mountains. The first company numbered 143 men, 3 women, and 2 children. No women or children were to have gone with this company, but Harriet Page Wheeler Young, wife of Lorenzo Young, had been stricken with malaria, and she persuaded the leaders to let her go with the camp and get away from the river bottoms. Her two children accompanied her. Clara Decker Young, wife of Brigham Young, and Ellen Sanders Kimball, wife of Heber C. Kimball, were also added to the company. The outfit included 73 wagons, 93 horses, 52 mules, 66 oxen, 19 cows, 17 dogs, and some chickens.

The camp had a dual organization, one following the revelation received at Winter Quarters and the other a military organization. Under the first, the camp was divided into hundreds, fifties, and tens; Stephen Markham and Albert P. Rockwood were appointed captains of hundreds, with five captains of fifties, and fourteen captains of tens. In the military organization Brigham Young was elected commander of the camp; Stephen Markham, colonel; John Pack and Shadrach Roundy, majors.

The Westward Movement

The Mormon exodus to the West was unique in that it was a movement of an entire people under unfavorable circumstances to a land that had been uninviting to other emigrants. It was not, however, the only movement of people to the West nor by any means the first.

The Lewis and Clark expedition, which in 1804-1806 traversed the western regions to the Oregon country and back, turned the attention of America to the West. Adventurous spirits saw in the unsettled region a golden opportunity for a life of freedom and profit.

The first adventurers to push into the little-known region were fur trappers, first as individuals and then part of organized companies. Both American and British companies penetrated the Rocky Mountain area, visiting nearly every stream and lake and leaving a lasting imprint on the names of streams, mountains, and places of rendezvous. Further, these so-called mountain men carried back to civilization valuable information concerning the

unsettled mountainous regions. Forts established by them for protection from hostile Indians became guideposts for caravans of
emigrants who later came west. By the time of the Mormon exodus, fur-bearing animals were rapidly disappearing and the fur
trade was swiftly declining. Most of the trading posts in the Great
Basin had been abandoned. Fort Bridger, about one hundred miles
east of the Great Salt Lake, was one of the last outposts of the fur
trade; it was abandoned in 1853.

The fur hunter was followed by missionaries to the Indian.
Aside from the efforts of early Catholic priests, who pushed northward from Mexico into California, Arizona, and southern Utah,
little work had been done among the Indians. In the Northwest, a
Protestant movement began in 1834, when Jason and Daniel Lee
were sent to that region by the missionary board of the Methodist
Episcopal church. They journeyed to Oregon via the Oregon Trail.
A year later they were followed by the Reverend Samuel Parker
and Dr. Marcus Whitman of the Presbyterian church. Their party,
which was under the protection of sixty trappers of the American
Fur Company, traveled in wagons as far as Fort Laramie. In 1836,
Dr. Whitman took his wife west and induced the Reverend H. H.
Spaulding and his wife to join them. The wives of these mis-
sionaries were the first white women to make the overland journey
to the Northwest.

After 1836, small companies of settlers headed west each year
over the Oregon Trail. In 1841 the John Bartleson company, consisting of forty-eight men and women, joined by seventeen missionaries, teamsters, hunters, and others, traveled via the Oregon
Trail to Fort Hall, then down the Bear River, through Cache Valley
in Utah, around the north end of the Great Salt Lake to the sinks of
the Humboldt, and thence to California.[3] The next year Elijah
White led a company of 112 men, women, and children from
Jackson and Platte counties, Missouri, to Oregon. In 1843, a large
company made up of emigrants from various states left Independence, Missouri. This company, which was comprised of about
one thousand people, one hundred and twenty wagons, and five
thousand cattle, went west from Fort Laramie as far as Fort Bridger
before turning north to Fort Hall and thence to Oregon. The follow-

ing year, fourteen hundred people migrated to Oregon, and in 1845 over three thousand persons passed over the Oregon Trail to the Columbia River Valley. By the end of that year seven thousand Americans had reached Oregon. In 1846, about twenty-five hundred persons migrated to the West. Nearly half of these journeyed to California, some passing through Salt Lake Valley by way of Echo and Weber canyons and around the south end of Great Salt Lake. One company, the Donner party, turned left at the head of Weber Canyon, climbed what is now known as East Canyon, and descended Emigration Canyon to the valley. They then headed around the south end of the Great Salt Lake and continued on across the desert. The next year the Mormon migration followed the wheel tracks of the Donner party into Salt Lake valley.

Thus, by the spring of 1847 the Oregon Trail had become a great national highway that had been in use for forty years. The exodus of the Saints was part of a great surge to the West of adventurous groups pushing the confines of the nation to the Pacific Ocean. Of all the emigrant trains that passed to the west, the Mormons alone went because they were forced. They alone were seeking a home where they might preserve their faith. A search for wealth and fame did not prompt their journey. Therefore it was easier for them to prepare homes in barren valleys and to find contentment in seclusion.

The Mormon Trail

Strangely enough, the Mormon pioneers did not start westward on the Oregon Trail. They made a new road that came to be known as the Mormon Trail. This road ran to the north of the Platte River, while the Oregon Trail was on the south. The two routes nearly paralleled each other, often with no more than the width of the river between. The reasons for this deviation from the established route are not at first clear. After all, the Oregon Trail was easy to follow, with no road to make or bridges to build; south of the river the grass was green, while the Saints passed for days through blackened stubble, where prairie fires had left scarcely a vestige of feed for cattle or horses.

It was the vision of the leaders that prompted the making of the

Mormon Trail. Had the first group under Brigham Young been the only company of Saints traveling west, they would certainly have crossed the Platte and followed the Oregon Trail, saving weeks in travel and hard labor. But they were not looking for easy travel for themselves. They had in mind the moving of fifteen thousand people in their wake, and probably countless other thousands as the years progressed. The route they chose was somewhat shorter than the Oregon Trail, with a better grade.[4] The grass, though scanty for the Mormon pioneer company, would be plentiful by the time the larger companies should follow.[5]

Further, the greater part of the emigrants going west on the Oregon Trail were from Missouri, and many were old enemies of the Mormons. A trail to the north of the Platte would avoid contacts that might have proved unpleasant. Many times in the trek from Winter Quarters to Fort Laramie, when the going was difficult, the men in the first company called a council to consider the advisability of crossing the river to the Oregon Trail. Each time consideration of the camps to follow outweighed any present inconveniences.

As the company moved forward each day, the monotony was broken by unusual sights and experiences. Buffalo herds created considerable interest. At one time a herd that extended for several miles was seen. Thomas Bullock noted:

> The prairie was literally a dense, black mass of moving animals. Our camp had to stop two or three times while the droves went around us. As soon as they had passed many would stop and look at us, as if amazed at such a sight. We caught several calves alive. Remember, catching a buffalo calf and a domesticated one, are two different things. A swift horse is sometimes pushed to catch up with him. They are as swift as horses, and although the old animals are the ugliest racers of any brutes, they get over the ground very fast, and an inexperienced rider is soon left to admire their beauty in the distance.[6]

Indians often visited the camp, and they were generally given gifts of tobacco, beads, and fishhooks. While the Saints were passing through the country of the Pawnees, some of their animals were stolen. Often a double guard was kept at night for fear of an Indian attack. Much of the Mormon exodus occurred at a time when the Indians of the plains were at peace with the whites, and the Mormon emigrants' friendly attitude toward their "red brothers" caused them to gradually distinguish between Mormons and other white men, resulting in immunity from attack for later Mormon emigrant trains.

The pioneer camp took on some of the nature of a scientific expedition. Orson Pratt, who had a keen scientific mind, made almost daily observations of the latitude, longitude, and altitude of the camping places. He also noted atmospheric conditions and changes in flora and fauna along the way. William Clayton kept a record of distances traveled each day and the total distances between landmarks. For a time the estimates were a matter of guesswork. Then Clayton devised a method of tying a red rag on the spoke of a wheel and computing the miles traveled by the number of revolutions of the wheel. This was a tiring job, but its very tiresomeness led to the invention of an instrument to do the counting. The instrument, invented by Clayton and Appleton M. Harmon, a skilled mechanic, was made on the principle of the endless screw; by a system of wooden wheels and cogs, it registered the miles and tenths of miles traveled.[7] After its installation, mileage information was kept until the company reached Salt Lake Valley. Data concerning the route was also carved into the trunks of trees or on posts set in the ground for the benefit of companies following. For example, on May 8 a cedar post was planted on a north bluff of the Platte Valley, near the river, on which was written:

From Winter Quarters, 295 miles
May 8th, '47. Camp all well
W. Clayton

West of Fort Laramie the pioneers planted posts every ten miles. Sometimes a letter was sealed in a groove sawed into a board or post, with a sign to indicate where it was. On the open plain, whitened buffalo skulls were commonly used as bulletins.[8] Letters were often sent back to the Saints with trappers and guides who were on their way east.

The pioneering Saints observed the Sabbath except for such necessary chores as keeping the camp in order and the stock tended, or when the need to reach water or feed made camping impractical. Most of the members of the camp were high-spirited young men who sometimes wasted their time in such frivolities as dancing, checkers, dominoes, playing cards, scuffling, wrestling, telling jokes, loud laughter, and playing practical jokes. When these amusements seemed to threaten the welfare of the camp, Brigham Young gave his severest rebuke of the journey. On May 29, as the camp was preparing to move, he called the men together, and according to Wilford Woodruff, told them:

> I had rather risk myself among the savages with ten men that are men of faith, men of mighty prayer, men of God, than to be with this whole camp when they forget God and turn their hearts to folly and wickedness. Yes, I had rather be alone; and I am now resolved not to go any further with the camp unless you will covenant to humble yourselves before the Lord and serve him and quit your folly and wickedness. For a week past nearly the whole camp has been cardplaying, and checkers and dominoes have occupied the attention of the brethren, and dancing and "hoeing down"—all this has been the act continually. Now, it is quite time to quit it. And there has been trials of law suits upon every nonsensical thing; and if those things are suffered to go on, it will be but a short time before you will be fighting, knocking each other down and taking life. It is high time it was stopped.[9]

He continued to admonish the camp for some time, after which the brethren voted to abstain from the offensive practices. The following day, Sunday, was set apart for fasting and prayer. The repentance of the camp was genuine, and not a single complaint of their conduct is thereafter mentioned.

On June 1, the company reached Fort Laramie; they had covered one-half the distance to Salt Lake Valley. Four hundred miles of new road had been broken and the Mormon Trail begun. Fort Laramie was situated on the Laramie River just west of its confluence with the North Platte. Finding that the north bank of the North Platte could no longer be followed, the pioneers obtained the use of a flatboat from the American Fur Company, which owned the fort, and spent three days in ferrying the wagons over to the south side.

At Fort Laramie the Saints met a company of Church members from Mississippi who had been waiting for them to arrive. The Mississippians were converts to the Church from Monroe County, Mississippi, who had started westward in April 1846, planning to join the main body of the Church in their journey to the mountains. At Independence, Missouri, they were joined by some Saints from Illinois, and the company journeyed west to within a few miles of Fort Laramie. When they learned that the main body of the Church had not yet come west, they went south to Fort Pueblo, Colorado, for the winter. There they were joined by the members of the Mormon Battalion who had been sent there because of illness. The group eventually totaled 287 men, women, and children. In the spring of 1847 an advance party of the combined groups returned to Fort Laramie to meet Brigham Young's company. The rest followed within a few days and then continued on to Salt Lake Valley, arriving there just a few days after President Young's group.

On June 8 Brigham Young's company met a small number of wagons loaded with pelts, traveling east from Fort Bridger under the leadership of James H. Grieve. President Young records that from Grieve he learned "that Mr. Bridger was located about 300 miles west, that the Mountaineers could ride to Salt Lake from Bridgers in two days and that the Utah country was beautiful."[10] The next day they were overtaken by a pack train of fifteen to twenty horses en route to San Francisco via the Great Salt Lake.[11] They reached the area where the Oregon Trail crossed the Platte River on June 12. An advance company who had been sent ahead to the crossing were busy ferrying Oregon emigrants, using a leather boat called the "Revenue Cutter" that they had carried across the plains in a wagon. For the work of crossing the emigrant party the Saints received "1,295 lbs. flour at 2½¢ per lb., also meal, beans, soap and honey at corresponding prices, likewise two cows, total bill for ferrying $78.00."[12] Seeing the possibility of conducting a profitable ferry at that place, the Mormons constructed a large one and left a company of ten men under the leadership of Thomas Grover.[13]

The pioneer company now followed up the Sweetwater to South Pass, a broad expanse of country some 7,080 feet above sea level. Orson Pratt wrote in his journal, "It was with great difficulty that we could determine the dividing point of land which separates the waters of the Atlantic from those of the Pacific. . . . This country called the South Pass, for some 15 or 20 miles in length and breadth, is a greatly undulating plain or prairie, thickly covered with wild sage from one to two feet high."[14]

Near South Pass the company met Major Moses Harris and a party from Oregon. Major Harris had an extensive knowledge of the mountains, and he told the Saints about the Salt Lake Valley. Elder Pratt noted: "He had acquired an extensive and intimate knowledge of all the main features of the great interior basin of the Salt Lake, the country of our destination. His report, like that of Captain Fremont's, is rather unfavourable to the formation of a colony in this basin, principally on account of the scarcity of timber. He said that he had traveled the whole circumference of the lake and there was no outlet to it."[15]

Near the South Pass the company also met Thomas L. Smith, who had a trading post on the Bear River. He described Bear Lake, Cache, and Marsh valleys, in all of which he had trapped. Erastus Snow later wrote:

> He earnestly advised us to direct our course northwestward from Bridger, and make our way into Cache Valley; and he so far made an impression upon the camp, that we were induced to enter into an engagement with him to meet us at a certain time and place some two weeks afterwards to pilot our company into that country. But for some reason, which to this day has never to my knowledge been explained, he failed to meet us; and I have ever recognized his failure to do it as a providence of the allwise God. The impressions of the Spirit signified that we should bear rather to the south of west from Bridger than to the north of west.[16]

Two days later the pioneers met that picturesque character of the West, Jim Bridger. The Saints had desired to interview him but had expected to find him at his home—Fort Bridger. Having previously heard that the Mormons wished to see him, he suggested that they call a halt and camp for the night together. Various versions of this interview have been given. Orson Pratt records: "Being a man of extensive acquaintance with this interior country, we made enquiries of him in relation to the great basin and the country south. His information was rather more favourable than that of Major Harris."[17] Brigham Young in his journal adds: "Bridger considered it imprudent to bring a large population into the Great Basin until it was ascertained that grain could be raised; he said he would give one thousand dollars for a bushel of corn raised in the basin."[18] President Young replied, "Wait a little and we will show you."[19]

Bridger's statement concerning corn being raised in the Great Basin was not intended to discourage the Saints from settling there, but to express a hope that it might be done successfully. This view is expressed by Wilford Woodruff in his journal: "He [Bridger] spoke more highly of the Great Basin for a settlement than Major Harris had done. He said it was his paradise and that if this people [i.e. the Saints] settled in it he would settle with them. . . . There was but one thing that could operate against it becoming a great grain country, and that would be frost, as he did not know but the frost might affect the corn."[20] From the time of this meeting, there seems to have been but one place for settlement in the minds of the Mormon pioneers: Salt Lake Valley.

From the South Pass to the Green River was the most pleasant part of the journey. The grass was high and game plentiful, and the downhill grade eased the teams and rested the men. At the Green River it was necessary to build another ferry. While the Saints were camped there, Samuel Brannan rode into camp, having crossed the mountains from California to meet the Church leaders and persuade them to go to California. He brought news of the ill-fated Donner party, the greater number of whom had perished in the mountains, while many of the survivors had turned to cannibalism.[21]

Brannan's efforts to convince Brigham Young that the Saints should go on to the Sacramento Valley were unavailing. President Young had made up his mind—he knew where he was going. Brannan remained with the pioneers until they reached Salt Lake

Valley. Then, disappointed, he returned to California and soon left the Church.

The company reached Fort Bridger July 9. From here they left the Oregon Trail and followed the fading trail left by the wagons of the Donner party the year before. This route was the most direct route into Salt Lake Valley. On July 10 they met Miles Goodyear, who was acting as guide for a party traveling east from San Francisco. He had what he called a farm at the mouth of Ogden Canyon, on the site of the present city of Ogden, Utah. Respecting Salt Lake Valley as a promising place of settlement, "he, too, was unable to give us any hope," says Erastus Snow. "On the contrary, he told us of hard frosts, cold climate, that it was difficult to produce grain and vegetables in any of this mountain region. The same answer was given to him as to Mr. Bridger—'Give us time and we will show you.'"[22]

From the Green River the camp had considerable sickness from "mountain fever." President Young was severely stricken and remained behind at Bear River while the main company moved forward. Orson Pratt was sent ahead with twenty-three wagons and forty-two men to lay out the route. The route chosen followed closely that which the Donner party had taken into Salt Lake Valley, for Miles Goodyear had reported the Weber Canyon was impassable with wagons. Elder Pratt's group moved down Echo Canyon and, after some difficulty, passed through East Canyon and over Big Mountain into the head of what is now called Parley's Canyon. From here the road led over Little Mountain to Emigration Canyon, which they called "Last Creek." From the top of Big Mountain, on July 19, they had their first view of Salt Lake Valley.

The main body of pioneers was now close behind Elder Pratt's group. President Young sent word to Elder Pratt to proceed on into Salt Lake Valley, bear northward, and begin to plant potatoes, as the season was late and he wanted to raise seed for another year. Accordingly, Orson Pratt moved forward, accompanied by Erastus Snow. From a hill at the mouth of Emigration Canyon they obtained an unobstructed view of the valley on July 21. Elder Pratt recorded: "After issuing from the mountains among which we had been shut up for many days, and beholding in a moment such an extensive scenery open before us, we could not refrain from a shout of joy which almost involuntarily escaped from our lips the moment this grand and lovely scenery was within our view."[23]

The next day the advance company entered the valley, and on July 23, Elder Pratt called the camp together, dedicated the land, and asked God's blessing upon the seed they were about to plant. Following the dedication, the men were divided into groups, some to clear the sagebrush from the land preparatory to plowing, some to unpack the wagons and do the plowing, and others to make an encampment and care for the stock. A company was set to work to put a dam in a creek at the northern end of the valley to flood the land, to begin to transform the desert into a garden. Several acres were plowed the first day and some potatoes planted.

The following day, July 24, 1847, Brigham Young and the main company entered the valley. There was no special demonstration in the camp on their arrival. Brigham Young's own narrative simply says: "July 24th: I started early this morning and after crossing Emigration Canyon Creek eighteen times, emerged from the kanyon. Encamped with the main body at 2 p.m. About noon, the five acre potato patch was plowed, when the brethren commenced planting their seed potatoes. At five, a light shower accompanied by thunder and stiff breeze."[24]

Wilford Woodruff later wrote, "When we came out of the canyon in full view of the valley I turned the side of my carriage around open to the West, and President Young arose from his bed and took a survey of the country. While gazing on the scene before us, he was enrapt in vision for several minutes. He had seen the valley before in vision, and upon this occasion he saw the future glory of Zion and of Israel, as they would be, planted in the valleys of these mountains. When the vision had passed, he said: 'It is enough. This is the right place. Drive on!'"[25]

26

The New Gathering Place

It is easy to forget that the rich valleys of Utah with their fine irrigated fields were, in 1847, part of the Great American Desert; that Salt Lake Valley was then considered worthless for the raising of crops and entirely unfit for the habitation of large populations.

When the early pioneers drove their wagons onto the site of the present Salt Lake City, the valley floor was a dry and treeless plain. The hot July sun had scorched the grass and baked the earth. Had the Saints arrived while the freshness of spring was in the air, the prospect might have been more pleasant, but a dry blistering heat greeted them and smote on the thin canvas coverings of their wagons.

For centuries the hot rays of the sun in summer and the cold blasts of wind in winter had ruled in this vast inland basin. A few Indian tribes here eked out an existence, while a few intrepid trappers had drained the area of its only apparent wealth—its furs. But the Great Basin was unconquered. It presented a challenge to civilization—to the ingenuity of man and his ability to survive. When the Latter-day Saints accepted this challenge, many predicted that the desert would come off victor in the struggle. Samuel Brannan, in meeting the returning members of the Mormon Battalion in the Sierra Nevadas in September 1847, reportedly said that

> the Saints could not possibly subsist in the Great Salt Lake Valley, as, according to the testimony of the mountaineers, it froze there every month in the year, and the ground was too dry to sprout seeds without irrigation, and if irrigated by the cold mountain streams, the seeds planted would be chilled and prevented from growing, or, if they did grow, they would be sickly and fail to mature. He considered it no place for an agricultural people and expressed his confidence that the Saints would emigrate to California the next spring. On being asked if he had given his views to President Brigham Young, he answered that he had. On further inquiry as to how his views were received, he said, in sub-

stance, that the President laughed and made some rather insignificant remark; "but," said Brannan, "when he has fairly tried it, he will find that I was right and he was wrong, and will come to California."[1]

To persons of vision, the Salt Lake Valley did present possibilities, the realization of which would involve years of toil and hardship. But to many of the women, it was a picture of utter desolation. Many a tear came to the eyes of brave women who found only a barren waste at the end of their long journey. Clara Decker Young is reported to have said, "I have come twelve hundred miles to reach this valley and walked much of the way, but I am willing to walk a thousand miles farther rather than remain here."

Not only the Salt Lake Valley was chosen to be the new home of the Saints—they were to inhabit the whole Great Basin, of which the valley was a small part. Dr. James E. Talmage described the area as follows: "The region to which this name [Great Basin] is applied is of outline roughly triangular. . . . It extends about 880 miles in greatest length running east of south and west of north, and 572 miles in extreme width from east to west. The area thus included is about 210,000 square miles, comprising the western half of Utah, the greater part of Nevada, and portions of eastern California, south-eastern Oregon, south-eastern Idaho, and south-western Wyoming."[2] This vast area has no external drainage—all the water of the region loses itself in the sands, evaporates, or finds its way into streams emptying into inland lakes or seas that have become salty through years of evaporation.

The Spanish priest Escalante came into the Great Basin in 1776, the same year that the American Colonies declared their independence from England. In a four-month journey, Escalante's party left Santa Fe, crossed through western Colorado, traveled up the Uintah, Duchesne, and Strawberry valleys and down Spanish Fork Canyon, then entered Utah Valley, which the Catholic priest called "The Valley and Lake of Our Lady of Mercy of the Timpanogotsis."

After preaching to the Indians and making some observations, the group headed south, looking for Monterey, California. When snow overtook them, Escalante returned to Santa Fe, where he arrived January 2, 1777. The Great Basin again became lost to mankind, bearing new names of lakes and rivers but as forbidding and unconquered as before.

Nearly half a century passed before white men again reached the heart of this vast inland area. Beginning about 1820, trappers entered the Great Basin. Powerful fur companies struggled for control of the rich harvest of furs, while diplomats of three nations politely asserted the claims of their respective countries to the disputed region. But when the fur-bearing animals had largely disappeared two decades later, the area had hardly seemed worth dispute, and it remained barren and unoccupied.

The trapping period did leave its stamp on the basin. Peter Skeen Ogden, working for the British Hudson Bay Fur Company, trapped throughout what is now northern Utah. He made several large caches of furs in what is now called Cache Valley and in the area where the city of Ogden now stands. His name was given to the trading post there. Another adventurer, Etienne Provost, left his name to a river and later a city that stands on the spot where seventeen of his men lost their lives through Indian treachery. General Ashley, founder of the Rocky Mountain Fur Company, left his name to a valley and a river. And of James Bridger, who was one of the first and the last of the Mountain Men, we have already heard. None of these men came into the basin to make their homes or to conquer the soil. Nor did Colonel John C. Fremont or Captain B.L.E. Bonneville, who came into the valley prior to the Saints, do more than add to the world's store of information of the barren area.

The Saints came into the Great Basin to establish homes, to subsist from the soil, to preserve a faith, even though that preservation would require the conquering of a desert. Except for their desire to exercise their faith unmolested, the Great Basin would likely not have been settled in 1847 or perhaps for many years afterward. The history of attempts at establishing agricultural communities in similar areas of the United States, where settlement was not prompted by such religious faith, had been a story of failure.

Founding a City

When the Saints erected their tents on the site of present-day
Salt Lake City, the land into which they had come technically belonged to Mexico. The treaty of peace with that country, whereby
the Great Basin became part of the United States, was not signed
until February 2, 1848. Actually, the region belonged to no nation.
No governmental officers had ever lived in the territory nor had the
administration of any law been attempted there. The Mexicans
called the region Upper California, and the Mexican governor at
Monterrey was technically its administrative officer, but that is as
far as the attempt of government had gone. Miles Goodyear had
obtained from the Mexican government a grant of land of considerable extent where Ogden is now situated, but he lived alone with
his gardens, undisturbed by government or law.

The Saints must of necessity establish their own law and their
own government. On the first Sabbath day in the valley, they held
religious services in the forenoon and afternoon and administered
the sacrament of the Lord's Supper. Several of the apostles spoke
and declared the law of the Lord to be the law of the land. Brigham
Young laid down the principles that should govern the appropri-
ation of property in the valley. Out of fairness to the thousands of
Saints who were yet upon the plains, he was determined that none
should seize upon and monopolize the resources of the valley. "No
man should buy or sell land," he said. "Every man should have his
land measured off to him for city and farming purposes, what he
could till. He might till it as he pleased, but he should be industrious and take care of it."[3]

The law was laid down that the timber in the mountains belonged to the community and could not be appropriated by individuals. It must be conserved, with only the deadwood cut for fuel.
Water in the streams and rivers also belonged to the community. A
man might appropriate that which he could profitably use on his
land for irrigation, but no more.

Before the Saints definitely selected the site of the city, exploration parties were sent out in each direction for short distances.
Some went into the canyons and located splendid timber. Others

investigated the river flowing into the Great Salt Lake. Some bathed in the salt water of the lake and were amazed at its buoyancy.

President Young, in company with several of the Twelve and others, ascended a peak in the north. Someone suggested that this peak was a fitting ensign to the nations, so President Young named it Ensign Peak.

To the Saints gathered upon the peak it seemed that the ancient prophecy of Isaiah was about to be fulfilled: "It shall come to pass in the last days, that the mountain of the Lord's house shall be established in the top of the mountains, . . . and all nations shall flow unto it. And many people shall go and say, Come ye, and let us go to the mountain of the Lord, to the house of the God of Jacob; and he will teach us of his ways, and we will walk in his paths: for out of Zion shall go forth the law, and the word of the Lord from Jerusalem." (Isaiah 2:2-3.) No flag was raised on Ensign Peak, but in the minds of the people a new standard had been unfurled to all the world.

The results of the brief exploration satisfied the Saints with the selection of the site for the city and filled them with optimism for the future. On July 28 members of the Twelve met and designated the site for a temple block between the two forks of City Creek. By motion of Orson Pratt, it was unanimously voted that a temple should be built upon the site so designated. At the same time the apostles voted to lay out the city in blocks of ten acres each with streets eight rods wide running at right angles. The blocks were to be divided into lots each containing one and one-quarter acres. One house was to be built on a lot and must be twenty feet back from the street line. Upon every alternate block, four houses were to be built on the west side and four on the east. The intervening blocks were to have four houses on the north side and four on the south. Thus, no houses confronted each other across the street, and those on the same side were eight rods apart. Four squares of ten acres each were designated for public grounds. This plan followed Joseph Smith's plan for cities of Zion.

On August 2, 1847, Orson Pratt began a survey of the city. The base line of his survey was on the southeast corner of the temple block. Government officials later adopted this as the base meridian line for the survey of the entire intermountain area. The city was originally named City of the Great Salt Lake. It was subsequently changed to Salt Lake City.

During the first month after they reached the valley, the pioneers plowed eighty-four acres of land and planted buckwheat, corn, beans, potatoes, turnips, and other vegetables. The season was too late, however, to secure much of a crop; the potatoes got just large enough to be used for seed the following spring. At the same time, twenty-seven log houses were built, and a portion of a fort was erected on a ten-acre plot where 160 families could winter until they built on their own land. The Old Fort was built on what is now Pioneer Park. Later in the year two additional blocks, one on the north and one on the south, were joined to the original Old Fort. A bowery twenty-eight feet by forty feet was erected as a place for public worship and served as the first community center.

At the suggestion of Brigham Young, the majority of the Saints were rebaptized beginning August 6, as a renewal of their covenants with the Lord to keep his commandments. Their former baptisms were perfectly valid, but many records had been lost and some previous ordinances had been unrecorded.

In the founding of the city, the heroism of the pioneer women played a large part. Nine women entered Salt Lake Valley with Brigham Young's company on July 24, 1847—three with the pioneer company, and six among the Mississippi Saints who had joined Brigham Young's party at Green River. The main body of the Mississippi Saints and the Pueblo detachment of the Mormon Battalion entered the valley on July 29. This greatly increased the number of pioneer women and swelled the population of the settlement to 400. By the close of the year the majority of the 2,095 who had entered the valley were women.

The first birth in the valley was that of Elizabeth Steel, a daughter of John and Katherine Campbell Steel, on August 9. A second child, Hattie A. Therlkill, was born August 15 in the family of George W. Therlkill. The first death was also in this family, a three-year-old child who fell into City Creek and was drowned on August 11.

Of the pioneer women, Dr. Charles William Elliott, then president of Harvard University, said in a speech in the Salt Lake Tabernacle on March 17, 1892:

> Did it ever occur to you what is the most heroic part of planting a colony of people which moves into a wilderness to establish a civilized community? You think perhaps, it is the soldier, the armed man or the laboring man. Not so, it is the women who are the most heroic part of any new colony. Their labors are less because their strength is less. Their anxieties are greater, their dangers greater, the risks they run are heavier. We read that story in the history of the Pilgrims and Puritan Colonies of Massachusetts. The women died faster than the men; they suffered more. Perhaps their reward was greater, too. They bore children to the colony. Let us bear in our hearts veneration for the women of any Christian folk going out in the wilderness to plant a new community.

The Main Body of the Church

While the early pioneers were building a road across plains and mountains and founding a new city, the main body of the Church, comprised of some 13,000 persons, was still upon the Indian lands of Iowa and Nebraska. In addition, ten companies were on the plains en route to their new home. These ten companies were comprised of over sixteen hundred souls, with women and children greatly predominating. They were bringing with them large herds of sheep, cattle, hogs, and chickens, and necessarily moved slowly along the route laid out by the earlier party. Aside from the occasional letters which trappers carried to them, and the signposts erected to mark the way, the companies on the plains knew nothing of their final destination.

Ezra T. Benson and three companions started from Salt Lake Valley on August 2 to meet the Saints on the plains and give them the news that a gathering place had been found. Since many of the Saints already in the Salt Lake Valley had families still at Winter Quarters, preparations were made to return there to prepare for their removal in the spring. Accordingly, on August 16, a company of sixty men organized for the return journey, taking with them thirty-four wagons, seventy-two yoke of oxen, eighteen horses, and fourteen mules. This company started ten days ahead of a second company, composed of 107 persons, 71 horses, and 49 mules. Brigham Young and other members of the Council of Twelve in the valley headed this company. John Smith, uncle of the Prophet Joseph, was left in charge of the colony at Salt Lake City.

On September 4, Elder Benson and his companions met the first of the westbound companies, under the direction of Parley P. Pratt and Perregrine Sessions. Two days later they encountered the companies of John Taylor and Joseph Horne on the Sweetwater. On September 9, the last westbound company for 1847, led by Jedediah M. Grant, was met. All of these companies arrived safely in Salt Lake Valley by October 10.

Brigham Young and his eastbound party reached Winter Quarters on October 31. When they were one mile from the settlement, Brigham Young told them,

> Brethren, . . . I am satisfied with you; you have done well. We have accomplished more than we expected. Out of one hundred forty-three men who started, some of them sick, all of them are well; not a man has died; we have not lost a horse, mule, or ox, but through carelessness; the blessings of the Lord have been with us. If the brethren are satisfied with me and the Twelve, please signify it, (which was unanimously done). I feel to bless you all in the name of the Lord God of Israel. You are dismissed to go to your own homes.[4]

The reunion of the men with their families at Winter Quarters was a happy one. Brigham Young and the Twelve were relieved to find that the Saints in Winter Quarters, Council Bluffs, Mount Pisgah, and Garden Grove had enjoyed an abundant harvest and would have ample food for the winter.

Organizing the First Presidency

On December 4, 1847, in a meeting at the home of Elder Orson Hyde, Brigham Young was chosen and sustained by the Quorum of the Twelve to be the President, Prophet, Seer, and Revelator to

The Church of Jesus Christ of Latter-day Saints, with Heber C. Kimball and Willard Richards as his first and second counselors. For three and one-half years the Church had been without a First Presidency. The Twelve with Brigham Young as their president had successfully directed the Church throughout that period, but now it was thought proper to perfect the Church organization.

The action of the council was ratified by the unanimous vote of a general conference held in the Log Tabernacle at Winter Quarters on December 27, 1847; in the eighteenth annual conference of the Church at Kanesville, Iowa,[5] on April 6, 1848; and in England by a general conference of the English branches on August 14, 1848.

Spring found Brigham Young and Heber C. Kimball leading two large companies of Saints toward the distant valley in the mountains. President Young says in his journal: "On the 26th (May) I started from Winter Quarters on my journey to the mountains, leaving my houses, mills and the temporary furniture I had acquired during our sojourn there. This was the fifth time I had left my home and property since I embraced the gospel of Jesus Christ."[6] He arrived in Salt Lake Valley on September 20, 1848, with his company of 1,229 persons. President Kimball arrived with his company a few days later. By the end of the year there were 5,000 Saints in the valley.

27

The Spirit of Gathering

In 1849, when the feverish haste for gold drew men in a steady stream across the nation to California, the strangest sight in all that dreary march was the Mormon missionary threading his way against that tide. It was so strange an event that few historians of the West have passed it by without comment. It was not that the Mormon missionary looked different from the gold seeker, nor that the manner by which each traveled was different. The startling difference lay in the fact that, while the illusive luster of the yellow metal was drawing all other men toward it, the missionary, who often had been at the very scene of the discovery and felt the thrill of the golden dust in his hands, was turning his back against it all and was traveling out into the world to give two or three years of his time for the salvation of his fellowmen.

It is significant that a religion might be found upon the earth promoting in its followers a faith so strong and with a feeling of duty toward mankind so insistent that worldly considerations sink into insignificance beside it. Yet that is the story of the great missionary movement of the Church during the very years when the Saints were most in need of money, when they were attempting to make a new start in a barren desert, while wealth in abundance was beckoning from the hills and streams of a neighboring land.

This great missionary movement, the third of its kind in the history of the Church, had its beginning, like those that preceded it, in the darkest days of trouble and persecution. It began during the spring of 1846, while the Saints were impoverished exiles on the plains of Iowa. A young man named Orson Spencer had just lost his wife; the privations and hardships had been too much for her frail body. She had sacrificed her life for the gospel, and now her husband resolved to devote his life to that same gospel. The summer of 1846 found him in England, appointed to preside over that mission of the Church. His remarkable work there was the begin-

ning of a missionary movement that in the next few years would
double the membership of the Church and do much toward accomplishing the Church's goal of carrying the gospel to every tongue
and people. During the next two years the number of converts in
England increased by 8,467 souls, and when Orson Pratt replaced
Elder Spencer in 1848, the total number of Saints in the British
Isles was 17,902.

At Winter Quarters in the winter of 1847-48, Brigham Young
called seventeen elders to serve missions, and this number was
greatly enlarged in the spring. Jesse C. Little was sent to preside
over the Eastern States Mission. Ezra T. Benson and Amasa M.
Lyman were sent to visit the Saints in the eastern and southern
states. Orson Pratt was sent to England, while Wilford Woodruff
was called to preside over the Canadian Mission. The effect upon
the missions was remarkable. New members joined the restored
church by the tens, hundreds, and finally the thousands.

The missionary zeal reached its greatest height in 1849-50.
Charles C. Rich was called to assist Amasa M. Lyman in the
California Mission. They succeeded in organizing the scattered
Saints in that region. In 1851 they purchased the San Bernardino
Rancho of 80,000 acres for the settlement of the Saints. Five
hundred migrated there from Utah in 1851 and commenced build-
ing a Mormon colony.

Elders Addison Pratt, James Brown, and Hiram H. Blackwell
were sent to the Society Islands in the South Pacific in 1849, to extend the mission established there by Addison Pratt a few years earlier. Church membership in those islands soon numbered many
thousands. In the same year, Lorenzo Snow, Joseph Toronto, and
Thomas B. H. Stenhouse were sent on a mission to Italy. A branch
of the Church was formally organized in Italy on September 19,
1850. Elder Snow, like Paul of old, catching the spirit of his calling, earnestly desired to carry the gospel into the whole Mediterranean world. The year 1850 found him and Elder Stenhouse organizing a flourishing branch in Switzerland. Leaving Elder
Stenhouse to preside over the mission there, Elder Snow sailed to
the island of Malta, where he established another branch.

Already Elder Snow was looking for new lands in which to

preach, and he set his heart on going to India, circumnavigating the globe from there, and returning to Utah via the Mormon settlements in California. Returning from Malta to London, he sent Elder William Willis by ship to Calcutta, India, to open the way. Hugh Findlay was sent to Bombay. Before Elder Snow could follow and begin his trip around the globe, however, he was recalled to Utah for other duties. The mission to India met with temporary success. Elder Willis baptized 309 natives and 40 English residents and established a branch at Calcutta. Before Elder Snow left England, he sent Joseph Richards to assist Elder Willis.

The zeal of Lorenzo Snow and his companions had resulted in four new missions being opened. In addition, Elder Snow had published a pamphlet, *The Voice of Joseph,* in the French language. Meanwhile, John Taylor had been sent to open a mission in France and had been successful in establishing a branch of the Church there.

Erastus Snow was sent to open missions in Scandinavia. He journeyed to Denmark accompanied by Peter O. Hansen and John Forsgren, and on September 15, 1850, they organized a branch of fifty members in Copenhagen. Elder Forsgren was then sent to open the ministry in Sweden. At Geffle, in the northern part of that nation, he baptized twenty persons and was about to organize a branch when he was arrested and placed on a ship for deportation to America. En route, the ship docked for a few days at Elsinore, Denmark, and Elder Forsgren managed to escape. He rejoined Elder Snow and continued his mission in Denmark.

Erastus Snow sent Elder George P. Dykes to Jutland, Denmark, in October 1851 and within six months ninety-one persons had been baptized and a branch had been organized there. In September 1851, Hans F. Peterson was sent from Aalborg, Jutland, to open the gospel door to Norway. Gudmund Gudmundson, a native Icelander who had been converted in Denmark, was sent to Iceland, where he laid the foundation for future proselytizing there.

When Elder Snow left Denmark to return to Salt Lake City at the end of twenty-two months, the Church in Denmark numbered six hundred members. The Book of Mormon and the Doctrine and Covenants had been translated and published in the Danish language, and a number of missionary pamphlets were available in both Danish and Swedish.

The Hawaiian Mission was opened in 1850-51 under the direction of Elder Charles C. Rich, then presiding over the Church in California. The first branch was organized at Kula, on the island of Maui, by George Q. Cannon. Elder Cannon translated the Book of Mormon into the Hawaiian language, and it was published at San Francisco in 1855. A letter from Elder F. A. Hammond dated March 1, 1852, indicates the success of missionary work in Hawaii. He wrote: "The Missionaries [that is, of other denominations] succeeded at first in putting a stop to our labors, until we sent to the heads of Government to know whether we should have the same privileges as other sects upon the Islands. The Government gave their full consent to our laboring here. The U.S. Consul took an active part in getting granted to us the same rights as the other denominations, since that time the work has been increasing rapidly, we now number about 600 members upon all the Islands, about 450 of them upon this Island [Maui]. We baptized about 250 since Christmas and the work still going ahead."[1]

Parley P. Pratt was set apart in February 1851, "to a mission to open the door and proclaim the Gospel in the Pacific Islands, in Lower California, and in South America." Under his direction, the mission to Hawaii was expanded, and the mission to the Society Islands, under Addison Pratt, was extended to the Friendly Islands. Elder Pratt sent Elders John Murdock and Charles W. Wandell to Australia in 1851, and in 1852 nine other missionaries were assigned to Australia, New Zealand, and Tasmania. Branches were established in each of these lands. At Sydney, Australia, a Church periodical called *Zion's Watchman* was published. Elder Pratt, accompanied by his wife and by Rufus Allen, journeyed to South America and commenced laboring at Valparaiso, Chile. However, civil war in that land brought an end to their labors, and they returned to California.

Not all of the missionary efforts were successful. An attempt by Elders Orson Spencer and Jacob Hortiz to establish a mission in Prussia in January 1853 failed, and the missionaries were ordered to leave the country. On the island of Gibralter and in Spain, Elders

Edward Stevenson and Nathan T. Porter were forced to leave because of intolerant attitudes of the authorities. An attempt to establish the Church in China in 1853 was cut short by the spread of revolution in that land. In Siam and Burma, the elders were rejected, and one of them was stoned in Bangkok. The mission in India also met with eventual failure; in 1855 the mission was closed by an order from Brigham Young, who told the missionaries to return home and bring with them all the converts who could conveniently come. In the West Indies and British Guiana, missionaries withdrew after not a single meeting was allowed to be held. And it was only after many difficulties that Elders Jesse Haven, William Walker, and Leonard I. Smith succeeded in establishing some small branches in South Africa.

Thus a heroic attempt was made to carry the gospel to "every kindred, nation, tongue and people." In many parts of the world the time was not ripe for the success of the movement, but in the main, the foundation for a great work was laid. The missionary expansion of these years brought converts from many lands into the Church. As the numbers grew, the Church was rapidly becoming a melting pot of nationalities, and the predominance of the English membership gradually began to diminish.

A Worldwide Gathering

With the selection of the valleys of the mountains as home of the Saints, an ensign was raised under which converts were called to gather from every land and clime. In a general epistle sent by Brigham Young and the Twelve from Winter Quarters on December 23, 1847, the Saints scattered from Nauvoo and those in Canada and the British Isles were advised to gather to the eastern bank of the Missouri River, preparatory to further migration to the Rocky Mountains. They were to settle temporarily on U.S. government land formerly inhabited by the Pottawattamie Indians. Kanesville was to be the jumping-off point for the western migration. The gathering Saints were urged to bring

> all kinds of choice seeds, of grain, vegetables, fruits, shrubbery, trees, and vines—every thing that will please the eye, gladden the heart, or cheer the soul of man; that grows upon the face of the

whole earth; also, the best stock of beast, bird, and fowl of every kind; also, the best tools of every description, and machinery for spinning, or weaving, and dressing cotton, wool, flax, and silk, &c., &c., or models and descriptions of the same, by which they can construct them; and the same in relation to all kinds of farming utensils and husbandry, such as corn shellers, grain threshers and cleaners, smut machines, mills and every implement and article within their knowledge that shall tend to promote the comfort, health, happiness or prosperity of any people. So far as it can be consistently done, bring models and drafts, and let the machinery be built where it is used, which will save great expense in transportation, particularly in heavy machinery, and tools and implements generally.[2]

The Saints in California were instructed to remain where they were, if they so chose; likewise the Saints on the islands of the Pacific, "until further notice." The Saints in Australia and the East Indies were urged to ship to the "most convenient part in the United States" and thence to the Great Basin. The missionaries were then instructed in regard to the new converts:

Teach them the principles of righteousness and uprightness between man and man; administer to them bread and wine, in the remembrance of the death of Jesus Christ, and if they want further information, tell them to flee to Zion.—There the servants of God will be ready to wait upon them, and teach them all things that pertain to salvation. . . . Should any ask, Where is Zion? tell them in America; and if any ask, What is Zion? tell them the pure in heart.[3]

The epistle closed with a stirring appeal to all of the Saints in the world:

We are at peace with all nations, with all kingdoms, with all powers, with all governments, with all authorities under the whole heavens, except the kingdom and power of darkness, which are from beneath, and are ready to stretch forth our arms to the four quarters of the globe, extending salvation to every honest soul; for our mission in the gospel of Jesus Christ is from sea to sea, and from the river to the ends of the earth. . . .

The kingdom which we are establishing is not of this world, but is the kingdom of the Great God. It is the fruit of righteousness, of peace, of salvation to every soul that will receive it, from

Adam down to his latest posterity. Our good will is towards all men, and we desire their salvation in time and eternity; and we will do them good so far as God will give us power, and men will permit us the privilege; and we will harm no men. . . .

Come, then, ye Saints of Latter-day, and all ye great and small, wise and foolish, rich and poor, noble and ignoble, exalted and persecuted, rulers and ruled of the earth, who love virtue and hate vice, and help us to do this work, which the Lord hath required at our hands; and inasmuch as the glory of the latter house shall exceed that of the former, your reward shall be an hundred fold, and your rest shall be glorious.[4]

At the time the epistle was issued, fewer than two thousand souls were gathered in Salt Lake Valley. Upwards of fifteen thousand were in temporary settlements in Iowa and Nebraska, and a greater number were in the Eastern States, Canada, England, and the islands of the sea. It was a colossal program to gather them to Zion. The appeal for the Saints to gather struck a responsive chord in the hearts of converts, whether those converts were on the plains of Iowa or in foreign lands.

The Perpetual Emigrating Fund

Of all the members of the Church in the late 1840s, those who were most in need were probably those who had been driven from Nauvoo and had spent two winters as exiles on the Indian lands of Iowa. Before they left Nauvoo, Brigham Young and other Church leaders had pledged themselves to use all their influence and, if necessary, their property, to remove all the Saints of that city to the Rocky Mountains. Accordingly, in September 1849 President Young and his counselors proposed the creation of a revolving fund for the purpose of helping Saints who were in need to reach the Salt Lake Valley. Willard Snow, John S. Fullmer, Lorenzo Snow, John D. Lee, and Franklin D. Richards were appointed to raise the nucleus of an emigrating fund. At general conference in Salt Lake in October, the congregation voted unanimously to support the emigration fund by their contributions. Destitute as many of the Saints were, having barely reached the valley themselves, they gave liberally of their means to aid the needy emigrants.

Lorenzo Snow relates: "One man insisted that I should take his only cow, saying that the Lord had delivered him, and blessed him in leaving the old country and coming to a land of peace; and in giving his only cow, he felt that he would only do what duty demanded, and what he would expect from others, were the situation reversed."[5]

About five thousand dollars was raised that fall and forwarded by Bishop Edward Hunter to Kanesville, to relieve the Saints residing on the Pottawattamie lands. Bishop Hunter had been appointed general agent of the Perpetual Emigrating Fund Company, under which name the enterprise had been incorporated. The Presidency sent a letter to Orson Hyde, who was in charge of the membership in Iowa, setting forth the plan for aiding the emigrants:

> We write you more particularly at this time, concerning the gathering, and the mission of our general agent for the Perpetual Emigrating Fund for the coming year, Bishop Edward Hunter, who will soon be with you, bearing the funds already raised in this place, and we will here state our instructions to Bishop Hunter, so that you may the more fully comprehend our designs.
>
> In the first place this fund has been raised by voluntary donations, and is to be continued by the same process, and by so managing as to preserve the same and then to multiply. . . .
>
> As early in the spring as it will possibly do, on account of feed for cattle, Brother Hunter will gather all his company, organize them in the usual order, and preside over the camp, traveling with the same to this place; having previously procured the best teamsters possible, such as are accustomed to driving, and be gentle, kind and attentive to their teams. When the Saints thus helped, arrive here, they will give their obligations to the Church to refund to the amount of what they have received, as soon as circumstances will permit, and labor will be furnished to such as wish on the public works, and good pay; and as fast as they can procure the necessaries of life, and a surplus, that surplus will be applied to liquidating their debt, and thereby increasing the Perpetual Fund. By this it will be readily discovered that the funds are to be appropriated in the form of a loan, rather than a gift; and this will make the honest in heart rejoice, for they love to labor and be independent by their labor, and not live on the charity of friends.[6]

The immediate purpose of the revolving fund was to help the exiles in Iowa to reach the valley. The ultimate object was to help the needy converts throughout the world gather to Zion.

In 1850, there were 7,828 Saints on the Indian lands of Iowa. The movement of these Saints to the West was too slow to suit the presiding authorities of the Church. On September 21, 1851, the First Presidency issued a sharp order to all those remaining in Iowa to bestir themselves and remove to the mountains the following spring. Ezra T. Benson and Jedediah M. Grant were sent to organize them and lead the caravans west. By 1852, the Pottawattamie lands were practically deserted, and the Nauvoo Saints were at last removed to the Rocky Mountains. The population of Utah Territory in 1850 was 11,380. By the close of 1852, the number was between 25,000 and 30,000.[7]

In the migration of the Saints from Europe, there were two important functions: first, the work of the shipping office in England, charged with chartering ships and organizing the prospective emigrants; and second, the work of the outfitting agent at the landing place on the Missouri River, whose duty was to provide the proper equipment for the journey across the plains.

The shipping agent in England made his announcements through the *Millennial Star*. One such item announced that a ship would be sailing in January, 1853. "Every application should be accompanied by names, age, occupation, country where born, and £1 deposit for each one named, except for children under one year old. . . . Passengers must furnish their own beds and bedding, their cooking utensils, provision boxes, &c."[8]

Charles Dickens, the famous novelist, visited a ship loaded with Mormon converts to observe the general procedure. He later wrote:

> Two or three Mormon agents stood ready to hand them [the emigrants] on to the Inspector, and to hand them forward when they had passed. By what successful means, a special aptitude for organisation had been infused into these people, I am, of course, unable to report. But I know that, even now, there was no disorder, hurry, or difficulty. . . . I afterwards learned that a Despatch was sent home by the captain before he struck out into

the wide Atlantic, highly extolling the behavior of these Emigrants, and the perfect order and propriety of all their social arrangements. . . . I went on board their ship to bear testimony
against them if they deserved it, as I fully believed they would; to
my great astonishment they did not deserve it, and my predispo-
sitions and tendencies must not affect me as an honest witness. I
went over the Amazon's side, feeling it impossible to deny that,
so far, some remarkable influence had produced a remarkable
result, which better known influences have often missed.[9]

The efficiency of the Church shipping agent is described in an
article in the *Edinburgh Review,* January 1862:

The Select Committee of the House of Commons on emigrant ships for 1854 summoned the Mormon agent and passenger-
broker before it, and came to the conclusion that no ships under
the provisions of the "Passengers' Act" could be depended upon
for comfort and security in the same degree as those under his administration. . . . The Mormon ship is a Family under strong
and accepted discipline, with every provision for comfort, de-
corum, and internal peace. . . . As the emigration season came
round, from every branch and conference the Saints would be
gathered and taken by their elders, who saw them on shipboard in
vessels chartered for their use. Not a moment were they left to the
mercy of "runners" and shipping agents. When on board, the
companies, which in some cases amounted to more than a
thousand souls per ship, were divided into wards, each ward
under its president or bishop, and his two councilors, and each
company under its president and councilors; and besides these
there were the doctor, steward, and cook, with their assistants.
During the passage, regular service was daily observed,—morning and evening prayers, preaching meetings and councils. Besides these were numerous entertainments, concerts, dances,
etc.[10]

An idea of the procedure of the outfitting agent on the Missouri
may be obtained from a letter written by Erastus Snow, then frontier agent, published in the *Luminary* in St. Louis on February 16,
1855:

My assent will not be given for any Saint to leave the Missouri River, unless so organised in a company of at least fifty ef-

fectual *well armed* men, and that too under the command of a
man appointed by me. . . .

I will furnish at the point of outfit, for such as desire it, wagons, oxen, cows, guns, flour, bacon, &c. Choice wagons made
to be order and delivered at the point of outfit, with bows, projec-
tions, &c. will be about $78, without projections, $75. Oxen,
with yokes and chains, from $70 to $85 per yoke; cows from $16
to $25 each. My experience, derived by six journeys over the
plains, enables me to know what kind of teams and outfits are
wanted for the plains. . . .

One wagon, two yoke oxen and two cows will be sufficient
(if that is the extent of their means) for a family of eight or ten
persons, with the addition of a tent for every two or three
families. Of course with that amount of teams only the necessary
baggage, provisions and utensils can be taken, and then the persons ride but little.[11]

The period from 1852 to 1855 forms the first period of European emigration under the Perpetual Emigrating Fund. In those
years over 125,000 pounds ($650,000) was expended by the com-
pany in helping poor converts to emigrate. A total of 6,753 emigrants sailed during that period, with 2,885 aided entirely by the
fund, 1,043 traveling under special rate arrangements, and 2,825
helped by purchasing agencies and the general organization of the
company.[12]

So successful were the efforts to aid the emigrating Saints during this period that Brigham Young wrote to the Church in England: "Let all who can procure a bit of bread, and one garment on
their back, be assured there is water plenty and pure by the way,
and doubt no longer, but come next year to the place of gathering,
even in flocks, as doves fly to their windows before a storm."[13]

Handcart Emigrants

The costs of transporting emigrants from England to Salt Lake
Valley rose so rapidly during the early 1850s that a new experiment
was inaugurated to cut down the cost. Wagons and carts made entirely of wood, the wheel looped with hickory or rawhide, had been
used by some of the Saints in crossing the plains earlier than 1851,

Artist's sketch of the handcart pioneers

and it was now proposed that light carts be made entirely of wood and pulled or pushed by hand across the plains. The first emigrants to use the handcarts came from England in 1856. By this means of travel the emigrant could journey from Liverpool, England, to the Salt Lake Valley for about forty-five dollars.

One company, led by Edmund Ellsworth and numbering 266 people, left Iowa City on June 9, 1856. Another followed two days later, under the leadership of Daniel D. McArthur. A third company, under Edward Bunker, left on June 23. The first two companies arrived in the Salt Lake Valley on September 26. They were met at the foot of Little Mountain, Emigration Canyon, by the First Presidency, a large number of people, and a brass band, and were escorted into the city. Captain Bunker and his company received an enthusiastic welcome on October 2.

Two other handcart companies were fitted out in 1856. These were composed of British and Scandinavian Saints who arrived in Iowa City in June only to find that the tents and carts for the journey had not been provided, which delayed them for a few weeks. The first company, under James G. Willie, finally left Iowa City on July 15 and reached Florence, Nebraska (Winter Quarters) on August 19. The second, under Edward Martin, left nearly two weeks later. At Florence the companies, contrary to the advice of eastbound missionaries they met there, voted to continue the journey that year, despite the lateness of the season.

It was an unfortunate decision. The wood in the carts had not been properly seasoned, and under the burning August sun they dried and fell apart. Precious days had to be taken, time and again, for repairs. An extraordinarily early winter shortened the season still further. By the middle of September, heavy frosts made the nights uncomfortable, and winter was fast approaching. Because of the delays, restrictions were placed on food rations. Some of the handcarts became so useless they had to be left by the wayside. The remainder were so heavily loaded that as the Saints climbed the steep sandy slopes west of Fort Laramie, they had to cache articles of clothing and bedding by the wayside. Improperly clad for the winter weather and weakened by the meager rations, many of the Saints fell sick and were buried along the trail in hastily dug graves.

Martin's company, coming later than Captain Willie's, suffered even greater hardships and loss of life. They encountered heavy snows on the Sweetwater, and during one of the severe storms, fifteen died in one day.

Missionaries returning to Salt Lake Valley from the East passed the companies on the Sweetwater, and on reaching Salt Lake Valley, they informed President Young of the emigrants' condition. Relief parties were immediately formed and started east with provisions and bedding. Joseph A. Young and Stephen Taylor traveled ahead in a light wagon to inform the companies that help was on the way. They found the Martin company encamped in a ravine between the Platte and the Sweetwater, now called "Martin's Ravine." The company's food was gone, and the Saints had about given up hope and were waiting for the inevitable end. When word of relief arrived, they took new courage and pushed forward again to meet the relief parties. But even with the relief provisions and clothing, their troubles were not over. Snow-covered mountains had to be crossed and icy streams had to be forded.

It was November 9 before Willie's company entered Salt Lake

City, and the close of the month before Martin's survivors arrived. Of the first company of over 400 persons, 75 had perished. Of Martin's company of 576, about 150 had been buried in wayside graves.

The handcart as a method of crossing the plains had not failed, but the tragedy of 1856 had the effect of lessening the number of emigrants who relied on that method of transportation. Never again were handcart companies allowed to leave the outfitting point so late in the season or under such conditions. Handcarts continued to be used by a portion of the emigrants until 1860. Beginning in 1861, the Church, acting through its emigration agency, began to send teams east each year to meet Utah-bound emigrants. These teams and teamsters were supplied by volunteers, who responded readily to calls from the First Presidency.

The method of crossing the plains and mountains with covered wagons and handcarts was to continue until the coming of the railroad in 1869. From 1846 to 1869, some six thousand Saints lost their lives over those weary miles, and most of them were laid to rest in unmarked graves.

28

Conquering the Desert

The outcome of great military battles has often decided the destiny of nations, but few battles have so affected the destiny of a people and the fate of a vast inland empire as the battle fought between man and desert in the quiet valleys of the Rockies between the fall of 1847 and the spring of 1849. Upon the outcome of that battle depended the future of the Great Basin. If one large colony could survive in that barren land, others could be established. But for the first two years, the result was uncertain. Only a mighty faith in a Divine Providence and a wise leadership tipped the scales in favor of civilization and the establishment of a commonwealth.

Two thousand people had gathered in Salt Lake Valley by the fall of 1847. For these people there had been no harvest, as the summer had been spent traversing the plains. The food they had brought from Winter Quarters was nearly exhausted, and it could not be replenished. As the heavy snows closed the mountain passes and shut off all contact with the outside world, fear of starvation entered many a heart. And who knew there would be a harvest? To their knowledge, no large amount of food had ever been produced there. Then, too, the coming summer would see thousands more of the Saints pouring into the valley, depending upon that uncertain harvest for the preservation of their lives. Before the first winter was over many families were destitute. Their flour was gone— their meat was gone. There were no vegetables or fruits. The oxen were needed for the plowing, and the few cows for the milk they produced.

At a public meeting that winter, the Saints expressed the spirit of brotherly love and cooperation by which they had become unconquerable. So long as one pound of flour remained in the community, no person would be allowed to starve. If there was to be hunger unsatisfied, then all would hunger together. Bishop Edward Hunter and Tarlton Lewis were appointed to receive food from those who had it and to distribute it to those who were destitute. By spring the hunger of many was intense. John R. Young wrote:

> By the time the grass began to grow the famine had waxed sore. For several months we had no bread. Beef, milk, pigweeds, segoes, and thistles formed our diet. I was the herd boy, and while out watching the stock, I used to eat thistle stalks until my stomach would be as full as a cow's. At last the hunger was so sharp that father took down the old bird-pecked ox-hide from the limb; and it was converted into most delicious soup, and enjoyed by the family as a rich treat.[1]

In the spring the roots of the sego lily, which adorned the hills, were used for food, as were weeds and watercress. A few deaths occurred when people ate the poisonous roots of the wild parsnip.

Fortunately for the Saints, the winter was a mild one, and they were able to plow the fields throughout the winter months. The Saints rejoiced to see the first green grain that had been planted in the fall covering nearly two thousand acres of land. Between three thousand and four thousand acres more were planted into spring grain. But wait!—Had the Saints forgotten those hordes of black crickets they had observed in the foothills when they entered the valley? They had then been amused, watching the Indians gathering the black insects for winter food. Now they were painfully reminded of their existence, as the usually insignificant cricket multiplied into millions and swept down upon the ripening fields of grain. All the ingenuity of man seemed powerless against this sea of black. For a time it seemed that the fight for human existence was lost—that the final chapter of a noble experiment at settlement was doomed. Men, women, and children labored with their might in the cause of life but also in the cause of civilization, as they beat and flayed the invading army, drowned them in ditches, drove them into fires, and buried them in trenches. And they prayed. Then came the gulls—in twos, in threes, in hundreds, in thousands—in great flocks that darkened the fields with their flying shadows. And the plague was stayed. They ate and gorged until they could hold no more—then disgorged, only to eat and disgorge again. When night settled over the scene, the two great forces retired—the gulls to their island home, the crickets to their rest from destruction. In early morning the conflict was resumed, day after day until the cricket army gradually disappeared and the green stocks of grain raised their heads again. John R. Young said of that epic battle:

> As the summer crept on, and the scant harvest drew nigh, the fight with the crickets commenced. Oh, how we fought and prayed, and prayed and fought the myriads of black, loathsome insects that flowed down like a flood of filthy water from the mountainside. And we should surely have been inundated, and swept into oblivion, save for the merciful Father's sending of the blessed sea gulls to our deliverance.
>
> The first I knew of the gulls, I heard their sharp cry. Upon looking up, I beheld what appeared like a vast flock of pigeons coming from the northwest. It was about three o'clock in the afternoon. My brother Franklin and I were trying to save an acre of wheat of father's, growing not far from where the Salt Lake Theatre now stands. The wheat was just beginning to turn yellow. The crickets would climb the stalk, cut off the head, then come down and eat it. To prevent this, my brother and I each took an end of a long rope, stretched it full length, then walked through the grain, hold the rope so as to hit the heads, and thus knock the crickets off. From sunrise till sunset we kept at this labor; for as darkness came the crickets sought shelter, but with the rising of the sun they commenced their ravages again.
>
> I have been asked, "How numerous were the gulls."
>
> There must have been thousands of them. Their coming was like a great cloud; and when they passed between us and the sun, a shadow covered the field. I could see the gulls settling for more than a mile around us. They were very tame, coming within four or five rods of us.
>
> At first we thought that they, also, were after the wheat, and this thought added to our terror; but we soon discovered that they devoured only the crickets. Needless to say, we quit drawing the rope, and gave our gentle visitors the possession of the field. As I remember it, the gulls came every morning for about three weeks when their mission was apparently ended, and they ceased coming. The precious crops were saved.[2]

It was a scanty harvest that the gulls had saved the Saints, insufficient for the many thousands who were now in the valley—

another winter with insufficient food, another winter on rations. Again in 1849, despite a good harvest, the food supply ran low because of the influx of Saints who had gathered to the mountains. Besides this, several thousand gold seekers bound for California passed through the valley, and many remained for the winter. But the Saints survived. The settlement was a success. A mighty struggle that tested the spiritual strength and physical fortitude of a great people had been won.

A Unique Colonization

When President Brigham Young issued his call for the Saints throughout the world to gather to the valleys of the mountains, he did not contemplate that they should all dwell in Salt Lake City or even in the valleys adjacent. The confines of Deseret, as the Saints called the territory to which they had come, were to embrace an area three times the present size of Utah. It was the dream of the Mormon leader to fill the habitable portions of this entire area with his people. The initial settlement at Salt Lake City had succeeded, and this success could be repeated in other valleys until the State of Deseret would become the envy of the world—and Zion a reality. The success of the Church's missionary activities gave President Young confidence in his plans, especially when converts by the thousands began gathering to Zion. The First Presidency wrote in 1850:

> The estimated population of 15,000 inhabitants in Deseret the past year, having raised grain sufficient to sustain the 30,000 for the coming year, inspires us confidently to believe that the 30,000 the coming year can raise sufficient for 60,000 the succeeding year, and to this object and end our energies will be exerted to double our population annually, by the assistance of the Perpetual Emigrating Poor Fund, and otherwise provide for the sustenance of that population.
>
> Viewing the gathering of Israel, which produces our increased population in the valleys of the mountains, an important part of the gospel of Jesus Christ, and one of the most important at the present time, we shall send few, or no Elders abroad to preach the Gospel this fall; but instruct them to raise grain and build houses, and prepare for the Saints, that they may come in

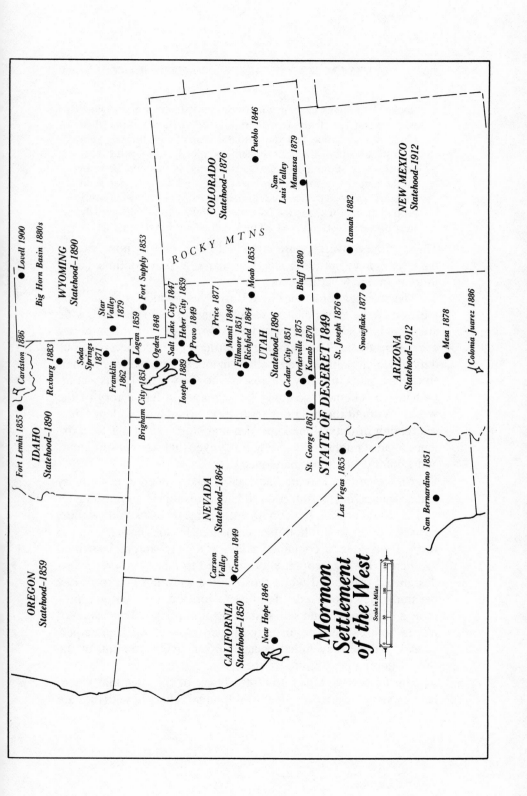

Mormon
Settlement
of the West

Scale in Miles

OREGON
Statehood—1859

CALIFORNIA
Statehood—1850

New Hope 1846

NEVADA
Statehood—1864

Carson
Valley
Genoa 1849

Las Vegas 1855

San Bernardino 1851

Fort Lemhi 1855

Cardston 1886

IDAHO
Statehood—1890

Rexburg 1883

Soda
Springs
1871

Franklin
1862

Brigham City 1851

Iosepa 1889

Big Horn Basin 1880s

Lovell 1900

WYOMING
Statehood—1890

Star
Valley
1879

Logan 1859

Ogden 1848

Salt Lake City 1847

Heber City 1859

Provo 1849

Fort Supply 1853

ROCKY MTNS

Price 1877

Manti 1849

Fillmore 1851

Richfield 1864

UTAH
Statehood—1896

Cedar City 1851

Orderville 1875

Kanab 1870

St. George 1861

Moab 1855

Bluff 1880

COLORADO
Statehood—1876

Pueblo 1846

San
Luis Valley

Manassa 1879

Ramah 1882

NEW MEXICO
Statehood—1912

STATE OF DESERET 1849

St. Joseph 1876

Snowflake 1877

ARIZONA
Statehood—1912

Mesa 1878

Colonia Juarez 1886

flocks, like doves to their windows; and we say: arise! to your
wagons and your tents, O scattered Israel! ye Saints of the Most
High! rich and poor, and gather to the State of Deseret, bringing
your plows and drills, your reapers and gleaners, your threshers
and cleaners of the most approved patterns, so that one man can
do the labor of twenty in the wheat field, and we will soon send
the Elders abroad by hundreds and thousands to a harvest of souls
among the nations, and the inhabitants of the earth shall speedily
hear of the salvation prepared by Israel's God for His people.[3]

Thus, as the converts poured into Salt Lake, the city now became
but a temporary outfitting place for many, as they continued their
journey into new settlements.

The colonization of the Great Basin was not left to chance. The
locations were determined by scouting parties, who traversed wide
areas, and the leaders for the colonies were called by the authority
of the priesthood. The founding of settlements became a religious
duty to which families were called, in much the same way as their
sons were called to carry the gospel into the world. It was a comprehensive scheme of colonization, unique in the history of the
world. Without the religious motive, it would have failed. Often
the feeling of duty alone kept men and women battling for existence against mighty odds. Sometimes even that was not sufficient,
and a colony would be abandoned.

An expedition leaving Salt Lake City to found a new colony
had an interesting organization. It had its bishopric, or presidency,
which would preside in the new settlement; its blacksmith, tailor,
harness maker, tinsmith, miller, carpenter, mason, farmers, and so
forth. If possible, it contained a doctor, a merchant, and a skilled
mechanic. It was a community prepared to labor at more or less
designated tasks, and while those called were not tied to follow
the trade they professed, the great majority did so, helping promote a harmonious and self-sustaining community. The few colo-
nizing failures were not usually the results of an inadequate personnel; rather, they failed because of an overestimation of the
life-sustaining possibilities of the site selected.

During the winter of 1847-48, many of the sites that would
later be settled were occupied by individuals charged with the care

of large herds of cattle. North of Salt Lake City, Thomas Grover settled on Deuel Creek, at what is now Centerville; Perregrine Sessions and Samuel Brown settled on East Mill Creek at what is now Bountiful; and Hector C. Haight, with one of his sons, wintered on the present site of Farmington.

In the spring of 1848, Captain James Brown, formerly of the Mormon Battalion, purchased the Goodyear tract of land at the mouth of Weber Canyon, some thirty miles north of the city, for $1,950 cash, which had been collected as battalion wages and authorized by the members for that purpose. On September 3, 1849, Brigham Young selected the site for the present city of Ogden. A wall was built to enclose the settlement. The number of settlers increased so rapidly that in 1851 it was divided into two wards. Also in 1851, the colonization movement to the north reached Box Elder Creek, where Brigham City was settled by Welsh and Scandinavian emigrants under Simeon A. Carter.

John Rowberry and Cyrus Tolman led a number of families west from Salt Lake City in 1849 to establish Tooele. Meanwhile, settlements were extending to the south. On March 17, 1849, a company of 150 persons, with John S. Higbee as president and Isaac Higbee and Dimick B. Huntington as counselors, moved into Utah Valley to a site two miles northwest of the present Provo City. Here they hastily built Fort Utah, as the Indians were gathering in large numbers and warnings were being received from Fort Bridger that an uprising was impending. In September the settlement was visited by the First Presidency, who selected the present site of Provo for a city. After a treaty of peace was negotiated with the Indians, the settlements of Battlecreek (Pleasant Grove), American Fork, Evansville (Lehi), Springville, and Payson were established.

Isaac Morley arrived in Sanpete County with 224 colonists in 1849, while Manti was selected a site for a city by Brigham Young in August 1850. George A. Smith led thirty families two hundred miles to the south, and on January 13, 1850, they began to settle Parowan in the Little Salt Lake Valley. Fillmore was settled by Anson Call in October 1851 and selected as the capital of the Utah territory. Also in the same year, Joseph L. Heywood established the town of Nephi.

At the general conference in October 1853, a number of men were called to gather families and strengthen the various settlements. George A. Smith and Erastus Snow were to take fifty families to Iron County; Wilford Woodruff and Ezra T. Benson, fifty families to Tooele County; Lyman Stevens and Reuben W. Allred, fifty families for each of the settlements in Sanpete County; Lorenzo Snow, fifty families to Box Elder County; and Orson Hyde, to raise a company and make a permanent settlement in Green River, Wyoming, near Fort Bridger.

By February 1856, the population of the Latter-day Saint settlements numbered 76,335.

Through the rest of that decade and the 1860s, additional settlements were established in southeastern and southwestern Utah. Some had to be temporarily abandoned in 1866-67 because of troubles with the Indians, but additional "missionary families" continued to be called to strengthen and reestablish those settlements as well as others.

The boundaries of Utah did not limit the ambitions of the Saints. In 1851 a settlement was made at San Bernardino, California, while several areas along the Little Colorado, Salt, Gila, and San Pedros rivers in Arizona were colonized. Some colonists were sent to Carson Valley, Nevada, while as early as 1854 there was a Mormon settlement in Wyoming. Extending northward, communities were established in Idaho at Fort Limhi on the Salmon River and at Franklin, in the northern end of Cache Valley.

Unsettled conditions in Utah Territory, due to the polygamy question, led to the establishment of colonies in Canada. In September 1886, Charles O. Card, president of the Cache Valley Stake, was sent to southern Alberta to investigate the possibility of establishing colonies there. He reported on favorable conditions, and the next year he led the establishment of a colony that came to be known as Cardston.

Another group of Saints who were seeking relief from persecution under U.S. anti-bigamy laws emigrated to Mexico in the late 1880s. They established such communities as Colonia Juarez,

Colonia Diaz, Dublan, Oaxaca, Pacheko, Garcia, and Chuichupi, where they tamed the barren lands, developed irrigation systems, and planted flourishing orchards and gardens. They also established industries and factories as well as an academy at Colonia Juarez.

Laws and Government

The Great Basin in 1847 was not formally a part of the United States, and no form of government had ever been provided for the territory. The Mormons, however, had five hundred of their men enlisted in the United States Army, and it was generally understood that sooner or later the Great Basin region would become a part of the United States. Brigham Young carried a United States flag across the plains in his wagon and raised it over the camp at the time of the enlistment of the Mormon Battalion. In late 1847, an American flag was raised over the fort at Salt Lake City.

No attempt was made to organize a civil government in the Salt Lake Valley until Brigham Young returned from Winter Quarters in the fall of 1848. On February 1, 1849, a call was issued for the people living in the valley to send delegates to Salt Lake City for the purpose of organizing a territorial government. Since the United States government had taken no step to organize the new territory, the inhabitants at the convention organized a state of Deseret to manage the affairs of the area until Congress should otherwise direct. The convention drafted a constitution patterned on the constitutions of the older states, with a governor, legislative body, and so forth.

The convention sent a memorial to Congress asking for admission to the Union as the State of Deseret. A few weeks later a petition signed by 2,270 individuals asking for a territorial form of government was prepared for forwarding to Congress. The reason for the petition was the belief that Congress would act more promptly in establishing some form of government if two alternatives were proposed.

Dr. John M. Bernhisel was sent to Washington on behalf of the Saints. He met Wilford Woodruff, then presiding in the Eastern States Mission, and they conferred with Colonel Thomas L. Kane.

Acting upon the advice of Colonel Kane, Dr. Bernhisel took no steps to present the petition for the territorial form of government to Congress, but earnestly labored for a State of Deseret. Congress, however, was in no mood to admit Deseret into the Union. Southern congressmen opposed the admission of every free (non-slave) state, and many northern congressmen, especially from Missouri, Illinois, and Iowa, opposed the admission of Deseret.

For a time it was proposed that Deseret and California be united under one state government for a period of two years, to offset the admission of Texas, a slave state. This proposition was advanced by General John Wilson in a private mission to California, which had already held a constitutional convention and was appealing for statehood. The southern states opposed the admission of California because of the slavery question, but despite the opposition, California was accepted as a state under Henry Clay's compromise bill of 1850. The entrance of California as a free state doomed the chances of the State of Deseret, as the South lined up solidly against the admission of another free state.

In September 1850, Congress passed an act creating not the State of Deseret but the Territory of Utah. The change in name from Deseret to Utah was a flat rejection of the desires of the Mormons. Utah, named after the Ute Indians living in the territory, had been used in earlier times by the mountain men.

So rapidly had the populations of Deseret and California increased, and so slowly did the wheels of government turn in providing a civil administration for them, that both territories had already formed provisional state governments and proceeded to manage their own affairs.

The creation of the provisional State of Deseret served a most useful purpose in the history of Utah. Brief as its existence was— 1849-1851—it nevertheless left its stamp upon the policies of the territory. The legislature and governor of Deseret assumed a paternalistic policy toward new communities and new industries. Money was voted to temporarily aid young industries, and this encouragement induced many men of means to begin manufacturing enterprises, which helped encourage the industrial independence of the region. Money was frequently voted to protect the settlements from Indian depredations, with the Nauvoo Legion revived for this purpose.

Further, the state government's policy adopted toward education was a far-sighted one, with the establishment of the University of Deseret and the allocation of state funds for its maintenance. Had Deseret been granted statehood, greater stress would have been laid upon that important phase of civilization than became the case later under territorial government.

Brigham Young was elected as governor of the provisional State of Deseret. So efficient was his administration of affairs that, with the organization of Utah Territory in September 1850, he was appointed by President Millard Fillmore as its first governor. He took the oath of office on February 3, 1851, and the provisional State of Deseret came to an end.

The majority of appointed officers for Utah Territory were non-Mormons from the East, men who were wholly unacquainted with the peculiarities of the Latter-day Saints and who failed to understand and sympathize with them. Appointment to the far-off Utah Territory was not considered an attractive assignment, and many able men, such as Joseph Buffington of Pennsylvania, who was appointed as chief justice, declined proffered positions.

Then, too, the Saints had a deep and abiding mistrust for the federal government, which had grown out of a feeling that the government, if not responsible for the outrages against them in Missouri and Illinois, had at least, by failing to act, consented to their persecutions. Thus, the Saints felt some antagonism against appointees to territorial offices, a feeling that was ill-concealed.

In the years following the organization of the Territory of Utah, there was a constant clash between federal appointees and the people of the territory. Some of the appointed officers came into the territory with their minds poisoned by slander against the Mormons. The moral standards of others were offensive to a people who had accepted the mission of bringing righteousness to all the world. Further, the Saints were attached to their religious leaders and followed their counsel, whether or not it coincided with the wishes and advices of civil government. No territorial official, regardless of his civil position, could possibly wield the same power and influence as Brigham Young. To the Saints, President Young was not only the founder of the State of Deseret, but also their prophet and president. Obedient as they wished to be to the law of the land, there was yet in their hearts the higher law of the gospel to which they owed the utmost allegiance and upon which they placed their reliance. Thus, the federal appointees from the East truly felt that they were outsiders, distrusted and unwanted. The ensuing bitterness and misunderstandings are an unfortunate chapter in the history of Utah.

29

A Self-Sustaining People

When the Saints moved into the Rocky Mountains, it was evident that such a large number of people must either supply their own wants or perish. They were, in a very literal sense, isolated from the world. They must not only supply themselves with sufficient food, but they must also produce their own building materials, manufacture their own clothing, provide for their own amusements, establish their own educational system, construct their own roads, and devise their own system of public communication. The isolation forced them to exercise an initiative that, for its accomplishments, has been rarely equaled in the world. Grim necessity developed a leadership and force of character that permeated the humblest household and made the founders of Latter-day Saint communities in the West a unique generation of men and women.

Fortunately for the Saints, the membership of the Church had been drawn primarily from the middle class of society, trained and inured to labor. It contained artisans from every walk of life. Especially was this true of the English converts. The system of apprenticeships in England had produced men efficient in the building trades, from architect to mason; shoemakers, harnessmakers, weavers, skinners, clothiers, cabinetmakers, millers, and skilled workers from every branch of industry. Even makers of musical instruments, builders of organs, composers, journalists, printers, and jewelers were found among them. Never have the people of Utah and the surrounding territory been so blessed with an array of trained laborers as in the first generation of pioneers who settled there. This was a vital factor in the success of the Latter-day Saints as colonizers.

The most enduring of their accomplishments was the erection of buildings. One is hardly accounted a world traveler today who has not visited Temple Square in Salt Lake City, entered the Tabernacle, and listened to a concert from the Tabernacle organ. Yet these attractions, together with the temple that stands upon the same block, were the work of a people who brought into the West little more than bare hands, fertile brains, and a mighty faith.

While less spectacular than the building program of the Church, the industrial accomplishments were the foundation of the commonwealth. When the water of City Creek was flooded over the adjacent land in the afternoon of July 23, 1847, the Saints began their economic independence. Irrigation grew rapidly from a mere flooding of the soil to a scientific method of farming, which soon made the Latter-day Saints independent of the entire world for their food supply. Irrigation became the key that unlocked the fertility of the soil and made possible the establishment of cities on a previously barren land.

The improvement of their herds of cattle and sheep and the raising of hogs and domestic fowls further strengthened the Saints' independence. The high cost of bringing freight across the plains and the great length of time involved in obtaining goods from the East forced the Saints to develop manufacturing and broadened their agricultural base.

As early as 1849, Brigham Young wrote to the elders in the various missions and asked them to investigate any industry that might be suited to the Latter-day Saints in their mountain home. They were also asked to urge converts with capital to migrate to Salt Lake Valley and enter the manufacturing field. A general epistle from the First Presidency in 1851 illustrates some of the accomplishments over a three-year period:

> "The Deseret Pottery" is in successful operation, some good light yellow ware was drawn from the kiln, June 27th, and white ware is soon expected. It is anticipated that the valley materials for making crockery and china ware will be equal to any other place; and that the pottery will soon be able to supply this market. Good potters are wanted. A carding machine is in operation and doing extensive business in this valley; also one in Utah [Valley], and others in progress.
>
> There are four grain and five saw mills in operation, or nearly completed in Great Salt Lake county; also two grain and two saw mills in Weber county; one grain and two saw mills in

Davis county; two grain and three saw mills in Utah county; one grain and two saw mills in San Pete county; one grain and one saw mill in Iron county; and one saw mill in Tooele county; and an increasing desire and exertion to promote domestic manufactures prevails throughout the territory.[1]

In his message to the territorial legislature in 1852, Governor Brigham Young gave the following information on the economic situation:

> Domestic manufactures, I am happy to state, are in a flourishing condition; considerable quantities of Leather and Crockery having found their way into market, and a large amount of clothing has been made, principally by the hands of the "*good housewife*," who thereby adds dignity to her station, and reflects credit, and honor upon her household. Specimens of Iron have also been forwarded from the works in Iron county, which, for the first run, was exceedingly flattering. It separates well, but owing to sulphur in the coal, not being sufficiently extracted, was thereby injured; but a little experience in combining material, and continued effort, it is believed, will soon produce that article in great abundance, and of good quality. . . . I am also happy to announce the arrival in our Territory, of the machinery for the manufacture of Sugar, from the Beet. The machinery, and operators, who have been accustomed to the manufacture of that article from the Beet, have come together from the "Old World," and being under the direction of energetic, enterprising, and able men, will doubtless soon furnish an abundant supply of that article, for the wants of the people.[2]

In the same message, the governor notes that a Mr. Gaunt was succeeding in establishing a woolen mill. "He is now weaving, and by another year, will be enabled to do an extensive business."[3]

Manufacturing by individual companies developed slowly, however, and paid small interest on the investments, due to the limited demand for manufactured articles in a new country that was lacking in population and money. This factor gave rise to cooperative manufacturing enterprises, which flourished until after the advent of the railroad. A brief study of the cooperative development at Brigham City will illustrate the nature and effect of such movements. Lorenzo Snow, who instituted and managed the enterprise, summarized its accomplishments in a letter to Bishop Lunt of Cedar City under date of October 1876:

> In accordance with your request, I send you the following brief account of the rise, progress and present condition of "Brigham City Mercantile and Manufacturing Association."
>
> We commenced over twelve years ago by organizing a mercantile department, which consisted of four stockholders, myself included, with a capital of about three thousand dollars. The dividends were paid in store goods, amounting, usually, to about twenty-five per cent per annum.
>
> As this enterprise prospered, we continued to receive capital stock, also adding new names to the list of stockholders, until we had a surplus of capital, or means, and succeeded in uniting the interests of the people and securing their patronage. We resolved, then, to commence home industries and receive our dividends, if any, in the articles produced. . . .
>
> We erected a tannery building, two stories, 45x80, with modern improvements and conveniences, at a cost of $10,000. Most of the materials, mason and carpenter work were furnished as capital stock by such persons as were able and desired an interest in our institution.
>
> The larger portion of this work was done in the winter season, when no other employment could be had, one-fourth being paid in merchandise to such as needed. We gained, by this measure, additional capital, as well as twenty or thirty new stockholders, without encroaching much on any one's property or business. This tannery has been operated during the past nine years with success and reasonable profits, producing an excellent quality of leather, from $8,000 to $10,000 annually. We connected with this branch of industry a boot and shoe shop; also, a saddle and harness shop, drawing our dividends in the articles manufactured in those departments.
>
> Our next enterprise was the establishing of a woolen factory, following the same course as in putting up the tannery—procuring the building materials, doing the mason and carpenter work in the season when laborers would otherwise have been unemployed. . . .
>
> With the view of probable difficulty in obtaining wool, we now started a sheep herd, commencing with fifteen hundred head, supplied by various individuals who could spare them, as

capital stock. They now number five thousand, and prove a great help to our factory in times like these, when money is scarce, and cash demanded for wool.

Our next business was the establishment of a dairy; and, having selected a suitable ranch, we commenced with sixty cows; erected some temporary buildings, making a small investment in vats, hoops, presses, etc., all of which have been gradually improved till, perhaps, now it is the finest, best and most commodious of any dairy in this Territory. The past two years we have had five hundred milch cows, producing, each season, in the neighborhood of $8,000 (eight thousand) in butter, cheese, and [milk].

Next we started a horn stock herd, numbering, at present, one thousand, which supplies, in connection with the sheep herd, a meat market, owned by our association. . . .

Also, we have a hat factory, in which are produced all our fur and wool hats. We make our tinware—have a pottery, broom, brush, and molasses factory, a shingle mill and two saw mills, operated by water power, and one steam saw mill; and also blacksmith, tailor and furniture departments, and one for putting up and repairing wagons and carriages. . . .

We have established a cotton farm of one hundred and twenty-five acres, in the southern part of the Territory, for the purpose of supplying warps to our woolen factory, where we maintain a colony of about twenty young men. This enterprise was started about two years ago, and has succeeded beyond our expectations. The first year, besides making improvements in building, making dams, constructing water sects, setting out trees, planting vineyards, plowing, scraping, leveling and preparing the ground, they raised a large crop of cotton, which produced in the neighborhood of seventy thousand yards of warp. More than double that amount has been raised this season.

We have a department for manufacturing straw hats, in which we employ from fifteen to twenty girls. Last year we employed twenty-five girls in our dairy, and have them in constant employ in our millinery and tailoring departments, also in making artificial flowers—as hat and shoe binders—as weavers in our woolen mills, and clerks in our mercantile department. . . .

The past two or three years we have paid our employees five-sixths in home products and one-sixth in imported merchandise, amounting in aggregate, at trade rates, to about $160,000.[4]

Utah's Dixie, so named because of the early cotton industry in that southern area, could have produced enough cotton to supply the entire territory. Mills for the spinning and weaving of cotton were established in St. George and Orderville, but the bulk of it was transported to Provo, Salt Lake City, and Brigham City. Southern Utah also became noted for its silk industry, built around silkworms imported from Japan and fed upon mulberry trees, which flourished in that part of the state. The cotton and silk industries were profitable while prices for hauling freight across the plains or from the Pacific coast continued to be high. With the coming of the railroad in 1869, however, both industries were doomed. Only the Saints' loyalty to their own establishments allowed the enterprises to survive at all in the next few years, and they were gradually abandoned.

The manufacture of paper was likewise a thriving business for a period. At the mouth of Big Cottonwood Canyon in the Salt Lake Valley may still be seen the remains of one of the mills. The granite walls survived a fire that gutted the buildings April 1, 1893, and the building was later restored.

Education

When the Saints made preparations for the exodus to the West in the winter of 1845-46, the future education of their children was considered. The eastern Saints who sailed for California on the ship *Brooklyn* carried with them a large quantity of books that had been gathered under instructions from Brigham Young. At Nauvoo, the Council of Twelve appointed W. W. Phelps to prepare and collect textbooks to be taken to the new gathering place. Some of the books he collected were used in schools conducted at Winter Quarters in the winter of 1846-47.

From Winter Quarters in December 1847, a "General Epistle" was sent to the Saints throughout the world, stating:

> It is very desirable that all the Saints should improve every opportunity of securing at least a copy of every valuable treatise on education—every book, map, chart, or diagram that may contain interesting, useful, and attractive matter, to gain the attention of children, and cause them to love to learn to read; and also every historical, mathematical, philosophical, geographical,

> geological, astronomical, scientific, practical, and all other variety of useful and interesting writings, maps, &c., to present to the General Church Recorder, when they shall arrive at their destination, from which important and interesting matter may be gleaned to compile the most valuable works, on every science and subject, for the benefit of the rising generation.[5]

These suggestions were followed by the Saints. As a result, a free public library was opened in Salt Lake City in 1850.

As soon as a portion of the Old Fort was completed in Salt Lake City in late October 1847, Mary Dilworth opened the first school in one of the newly constructed buildings. During the winter of 1848-49, a number of classes were conducted, many of them for missionaries. Before Utah was organized as a territory of the United States in September 1850, the legislature of the provisional State of Deseret passed an act for the creation of the University of Deseret, the forerunner of the present University of Utah. Orson Spencer, a graduate of the Theological Seminary at Hamilton, New York, was appointed to head the institution.

Though the founding of a university at such a time required greater means than the Saints possessed, the university managed to open in the Council House in November 1850. Dr. Cyrus Collins was the sole instructor. He was succeeded during the year by Orson Spencer and then by W. W. Phelps. But the university, which was underfinanced and had a limited patronage, had only a nominal existence until 1876. As a viable institution, the university really dates from the appointment of Dr. John R. Park as chancellor in 1880.

Elementary schools were conducted from the time of Mary Dilworth's school in 1847, although the school system throughout the territory was in a disorganized condition for many years, and the majority of the rising generation spent very little time in formal instruction. Several conditions retarded the development of the schools. First, there was the lack of school facilities and funds with which to hire teachers. Second, many communities, being isolated, could not find competent teachers. Those among the Saints who might have conducted schools were usually engaged in subduing the soil, building communities, or in carrying on the extensive missionary system of the Church.

"Men Are, that They Might Have Joy"

The philosophy of life as taught by the Prophet Joseph Smith
had nothing in it of asceticism. The body, in his opinion, was not a
prison for the spirit of man, but "spirit and element, inseparably
connected, receive a fulness of joy." (D&C 93:33.) The Book of
Mormon proclaimed, "Men are, that they might have joy." (2 Nephi 2:25.) The Prophet, quite to the dismay of many other religious
denominations of his day, introduced dancing, sports, and the
theater among the Saints. As the pioneers took their weary journey
to the valleys of the mountains, their load was lightened by song
and dance. It was well that these things became part of the life of
the Saints in the West, for they softened the hardness of life there.

In their isolation, the people had to provide their own entertainment. Every community, for example, developed a theatrical company. Nor did entertainment wait until homes were built. In 1848
plays were produced under the old bowery in Salt Lake City. In
1859 the Social Hall was erected for theatricals and dances. In
1861 Brigham Young ordered the construction of the Salt Lake
Theater. Within that historic building appeared almost every great
actor of America for more than half a century. The structure, designed by a Church architect, was a duplicate, outside and in, of
the famous Drury Lane Theater in London.

The theater was opened for dramatic performances March 8,
1862. For the first year, all of the plays presented there were prepared by the Deseret Dramatic Association. After the first year,
theatrical troupes crossing the continent furnished much of the
entertainment. The theater continued to be used until 1929, when
it was torn down to make way for commercial enterprises.

The example set by President Young in building and maintaining the Salt Lake Theater was followed to a lesser degree in other
Mormon communities. Nearly every community had a recreation
hall. In smaller communities, the building that served for worship
on the Sabbath day was often used for recreation during the week.

Communication

When the pioneers entered Salt Lake Valley, they found themselves cut off from the outside world. They knew nothing of what

The Salt Lake Theater in downtown Salt Lake City

was transpiring beyond the valley. Even the fate of the emigrating Saints upon the plains was unknown. Likewise, those emigrating companies knew nothing of the arrival of the early pioneers in the valley. There were but two ways to communicate: by sending a messenger on mule or horseback over the intervening miles or by entrusting letters to slow-moving caravans or trappers en route to the East or the West. There was no official mail service. Mail reaching the valley was distributed at the close of sacrament services each Sunday.

In the winter of 1849, the federal government established a post office in Salt Lake City and appointed Joseph L. Heywood postmaster. A bimonthly mail route was authorized between Kanesville and Great Salt Lake City, with Almon W. Babbitt authorized to carry the mail at his own expense. In 1850, the United States Postal Service was extended to the valley, and it gradually expanded to include other principal settlements.

A contract with the United States Postal Department to carry mail from the Missouri River to Salt Lake City was let to Samuel H. Woodson of Independence, Missouri, in 1850. The first mail arrived in the valley on November 9, 1850. Feramorz Little, a Mormon, subcontracted to carry the mail between Fort Laramie and Salt Lake City. In Brigham Young's journal we find this interesting entry:

> Brother Charles Decker arrived from Laramie with the eastern mail. He had to swim every river between this and Laramie. The mail coach and mules were lost at Hamm's Fork, where the mail lay under water from one to seven p. m.; the lead horses were saved by being cut loose. Brother Decker was in the ice water with the mail all the time, and then exhausted, had no resource but to wrap himself in robes and blankets, wet as water could make them, till morning, when he found himself in a free perspiration, fully relieved from a fever he had been laboring with under most of the time since he left the city.
>
> Brother Ephraim K. Hanks [about the same time had] proceeded as far as Bear river with the eastern mail. At Weber river the raft on which he and party crossed was sucked under, forcing them to swim for their lives: the mail was carried down the stream and lay in the water upward of two hours. After a great deal of trouble and at the risk of their lives they secured it, but in bad condition. On reaching Bear river, which was a foaming torrent, extending from mountain to mountain, they found it impossible to proceed.[6]

In 1859-60, the postal system improved with the introduction of the Pony Express. Under this plan, solitary horsemen carried the mail across the continent at the high rate of five dollars per ounce. Stations were located on an average of twenty-four miles apart, and fresh horses were kept at each station. Each rider would cover approximately seventy-two miles a day. The mail time from New York to San Francisco was cut to thirteen days, a remarkable achievement. The heroic riders covered their routes regardless of storm, heat, or Indian attack. The Pony Express was discontinued in 1861 for lack of patronage. Because of the high rate charged, the number of letters carried averaged fewer than two hundred per carrier. In addition, the overland telegraph was completed in 1861. Brigham Young was permitted to send the first message over the wire. On October 18, 1861, he sent the following to J. H. Wade, president of the Pacific Telegraph Company:

Sir:—Permit me to congratulate you upon the completion of the Overland Telegraph Line west to this city, to commend the energy displayed by yourself and associates in the rapid and successful prosecution of a work so beneficial, and to express the wish that its use may ever tend to promote the true interests of the dwellers upon both the Atlantic and Pacific slopes of our continent. Utah has not seceded, but is firm for the Constitution and laws of our once happy country, and is warmly interested in such useful enterprises as the one so far completed.[7]

The telegraph line from San Francisco was completed a few days later, and President Young had the privilege of sending the first wire to the Pacific coast. These courtesies recognized his great service in fostering the enterprise and also recognized the Mormon laborers who constructed much of the line.

A telegraph line connecting Salt Lake City with settlements south was extended as far as Pipe Springs, Arizona, in 1865-67. A Church enterprise, called the Deseret Telegraph, it was operated until 1900, when it was merged into the Western Union system.

30

The Utah War

It was unfortunate that the early applications of the people of Utah for statehood were rejected by the Congress of the United States. Under a territorial form of government, it was inevitable that antagonism would develop between a people so different as the Saints and government appointees sent into the territory.

The Saints were devoted primarily to the church of which they were members, and suspicious of a government that had been either unable or unwilling to protect them. Further, the majority of the Saints were of foreign birth. They had preferred The Church of Jesus Christ of Latter-day Saints to all else in life, including citizenship in their native lands. Having endured so much for the gospel they professed, the law of God was more important than the law of the land, although the latter would be observed so long as it did not interfere with the former. Under favorable circumstances the Mormons have been a people little understood. The peculiar circumstances that surrounded them in the early days of Utah inevitably led to mistakes and misunderstandings between them and those who came in contact with them.

These difficulties arose when the first appointments to federal offices in the territory were made by President Fillmore. Scarcely had the appointees taken their oath of office when three of them—Chief Justice Brandebury, Associate Justice Perry Brocchus, and Territorial Secretary Broughton D. Harris—refused to stay longer in the territory and returned to the East. There they spread the report that (1) they had been compelled to leave Utah because of the lawless and seditious acts of Governor Young, (2) Governor Young was wasting federal funds allotted to the territory, and (3) the Saints were immoral and were practicing polygamy.

Governor Young, anticipating the type of report these men would likely circulate, wrote to President Fillmore on September 29, 1851, setting forth facts that clearly contradicted the accusations. Other letters supporting his position were sent by Jedediah M. Grant, mayor of Salt Lake City, and Colonel Thomas L. Kane. Daniel Webster, United States Secretary of State, upon receipt of these letters, ordered the runaway officers to return to their positions or to resign. They resigned, and new appointees were named. Lazarus H. Reed of New York became Chief Justice; Leonidas Shaver, Associate Justice; and Benjamin G. Ferris, Territorial Secretary. These men were well received in Utah and became highly respected by the Saints.

Misunderstandings between the Saints and the federal appointees, and the subsequent ill feelings and abusive actions on both sides, fill many pages of Utah history. Some of these, however, led to greater consequences than others, and with these we are primarily concerned.

When Chief Justice Reed resigned in 1854, John F. Kinney was appointed to the position. He proved an honest and impartial judge, honored and esteemed by the Saints and others alike. But in 1855 there came to Utah as associate justices two men who were to arouse the resentment of the Saints and eventually cost the United States government forty million dollars. These men were William W. Drummond and George P. Stiles.

Judge Drummond was an immoral and unprincipled man. Leaving a wife and children without support in his own state of Illinois, he appeared in Utah accompanied by another woman, whom he introduced as his wife and who often sat upon the bench with him. Because of his drunken and dissolute habits, the Saints came to despise him, and their feelings were ill-concealed. When his immorality and neglect of his family were revealed, he left the territory in disgrace. In his letter of resignation, tendered to U.S. Attorney General Jeremiah S. Black, he spread a multitude of false accusations against the Saints. Judge Stiles sent an affidavit affirming some of these charges.

The federal government relied on the misrepresentations of these men as evidence of the Latter-day Saints' disregard for the law and as an excuse for the steps that followed. Denials of the accusations seemingly were disregarded, and without waiting for a federal investigation of the charges, President James Buchanan, the newly elected president, acted. On May 28, 1857, he ordered a portion of the United States Army to mobilize at Fort Leavenworth and proceed to Utah.

While the reports of Judge Drummond and others stirred President Buchanan to issue his drastic order, the real causes of the so-called war that followed were largely political. On June 17, 1856, the Republican party, meeting in Philadelphia, adopted a resolution that "it is both the right and the imperative duty of Congress to prohibit in the Territories those twin relics of barbarism—Polygamy and Slavery."[1] John C. Fremont was nominated at the Republican convention that year as the party's candidate. He was opposed by James Buchanan, the Democratic party candidate.

The Republican plan was to throw upon the Democratic party, which in its platform defended the right of the territories to determine for themselves the domestic problems of slavery, the position of defending also the right of a territory to determine for itself the domestic problems of marriage. So stirred up had the country become over the Saints and their doctrine of plural marriage that the Democrats had no desire to carry their platform to its logical conclusion. But the expedition against the Saints by the new Democratic administration would show to the voters of the nation that the Democrats, no less than the Republicans, were opposed to the Latter-day Saints and their practices.

John Taylor, who was editing an LDS paper, *The Mormon,* in New York City at the time, said later in the year during an address to the Saints in Utah:

> The republicans were determined to make the "Mormon" question tell in their favor. At the time they were trying to elect Fremont they put two questions into their platform, viz.: opposition to the domestic institutions of the South and to polygamy. The democrats have professed to be our friends and they go to work to sustain the domestic institutions of the South and the rights of the people, but when they do that the republicans throw polygamy at them and are determined to make them swallow that with the other [i.e., slavery]. This makes the democrats gag and they have felt a strong desire to get rid of the "Mormon" question.[2]

The sending of the expedition was encouraged by the proslavery group on the grounds that it would definitely curtail Utah's move for statehood, which had begun with renewed vigor and insistence in 1855. If it could be made to appear that the Saints were in rebellion against the United States, whether the facts supported that view or not, the danger of Utah as a new "free state" would be inevitably postponed. Thus it was that the charges of Judge Drummond were eagerly seized upon. An investigation was neither desired nor made, for fear that the true state of affairs might not warrant the political expediency offered.

Heeding the cries of conspirators in Utah for the removal of Governor Young, President Buchanan appointed new territorial officers. Alfred Cumming, who was appointed as the new governor, accompanied the expedition west from Fort Leavenworth.

The Saints Prepare to Defend Their Homes

On July 24, 1857, a large crowd of Latter-day Saints had gathered at Silver Lake, at the head of Big Cottonwood Canyon, thirty miles southeast of Salt Lake City. The occasion was the celebration of the tenth anniversary of the arrival of the Saints in the valley. Led by Brigham Young and other general Church officers, 2,587 people, including six large brass bands and several detachments of the Nauvoo Legion, were having a joyous celebration. Two United States flags waved from nearby peaks and two from the tops of adjacent pine trees. Three spacious board floors, with boweries built over them, were used for dancing.

At noon, Abraham O. Smoot, Orrin Porter Rockwell, Judson Stoddard, and Judge Elias Smith rode into the encampment and reported to Brigham Young and his counselors and associates that a United States army and supply trains were on the plains en route to Utah. The exact purpose of the army was unknown, but the rumors were that they were coming "to suppress the Mormons."

Not even the news of an approaching army could cause Brigham Young to spoil the celebration. But at the close of the day, he called an assembly to break the news. "Liars have reported that this people has committed treason," he said, "and upon their misrepresentations the President has ordered out troops to assist in officering the territory. We have transgressed no law, neither do we intend to do so; but as for any nation coming to destroy this people, God Almighty being my helper, it shall not be."[3]

Preparations for possible hostilities went forward quietly. Under date of August 1, 1857, Daniel H. Wells, commander of the Nauvoo Legion, reported to the officers and men of the Legion that an army was approaching Utah. He instructed the district commanders to hold their respective divisions in readiness to march at the shortest possible notice to any part of the territory. Word was also sent throughout the settlements that the Saints were to conserve the grain supply, to use none for the feeding of cattle, and to sell none to emigrant trains for that purpose.

Members of the Quorum of the Twelve who were presiding over missions were recalled home, as were nearly all the elders on missions. Samuel W. Richards was dispatched with instructions to Orson Pratt and Ezra T. Benson in the British Mission. En route he delivered to Colonel Thomas L. Kane a letter that was addressed to President Buchanan, protesting against the actions of the government and giving him a brief history of the Saints' treatment at the hands of the government from the beginning of the Missouri troubles.

Members of the Church in outlying settlements were ordered to dispose of their property and return to Salt Lake Valley. In addition, expeditions were sent out to locate the best places in the mountains for making a determined resistance to armed forces. On August 15 Colonel Robert T. Burton of the Nauvoo Legion was sent with a small detachment to the East, presumably to protect incoming Latter-day Saint emigrants, but in reality to learn the location, strength, and equipment of the approaching army and to send riders back each day with reports.

A volunteer company was called to go northward to establish a settlement near Fort Hall. This was in reality a detachment of militia to watch the northern route into Utah in the event the army attempted to enter from that direction. General Wells, with the main body of the militia, proceeded to Echo Canyon and fortified that natural barrier sufficiently to withstand a considerable force of troops.

Unfortunately, the purposes of the government in sending the expedition to Utah were not understood by the Church leaders. Had they known the nature of the splendid officers and personnel of the expedition and been aware of the instructions to them from the U.S. War Department, many of the complications that followed possibly would not have occurred. But the Saints had no way of knowing those facts, and the government had taken great pains to keep them in the dark rather than to inform them. Thus it was easy for a people who had endured so much in the way of persecution to believe the ribaldry of the rank and file of the camp.

Some of the scouts under Colonel Burton's command disguised themselves as California emigrants and mingled with the camps of the approaching army. They reported that the soldiers were boasting they would drive and plunder the Saints and "scalp old Brigham." John Taylor later told U.S. Vice President Schuyler Colfax, "We had men in all their camps, and knew what was intended. There was a continual boast among the men and officers, even before they left the Missouri River, of what they intended to do with the 'Mormons.' The houses were picked out that certain persons were to inhabit; farms, property, and women were to be distributed. 'Beauty and booty' were their watchword. We were to have another grand 'Mormon' conquest, and our houses, gardens, orchards, vineyards, fields, wives and daughters to be the spoils."[4] In the face of such reports and without an acquaintance with the sealed orders to the expedition commander, it was natural that the Saints expected the worst. Repeatedly they had been driven until there was no further place to which to flee. Now they would resist further persecution to the last drop of their blood.

Such was the situation when Captain Stewart Van Vliet, advance courier of the army, arrived in Salt Lake City in September. On the ninth he met with the Church authorities and told them he was seeking arrangements for food, forage, and other provisions for the army when it arrived in the city. His assurances that the army was not coming to make war did not convince the Saints.

They courteously informed him that no hostile army would be allowed to enter the territory, though federal officers would be welcomed without troops, if they came in peace. He reported to his superiors:

> In the course of my conversation with the Governor and the influential men of the Territory, I told them plainly and frankly what I conceived would be the result of their present course. I told them that they might prevent the small military force now approaching Utah from getting through the narrow defiles and rugged passes of the mountains this year, but that next season the United States Government would send troops sufficient to overcome all opposition. The answer to this was invariably the same: "We are aware that such will be the case; but when those troops arrive they will find Utah a desert. Every house will be burned to the ground, every tree cut down, and every field laid waste. We have three years' provisions on hand, which we will cache, and then take to the mountains and bid defiance to all the powers of the Government."
>
> I attended their services on Sunday, and, in course of a sermon delivered by Elder Taylor, he referred to the approach of the troops and declared they should not enter the Territory. He then referred to the probability of an over-powering force being sent against them, and desired all present who would apply the torch to their buildings, cut down their trees, and lay waste their fields, to hold up their hands. Every hand, in an audience numbering over four thousand persons, was raised at the same moment. During my stay in the city I visited several families, and all with whom I was thrown, looked upon the present movement of the troops toward their Territory as the commencement of another religious persecution, and expressed a fixed determination to sustain Governor Young in any measure he might adopt.[5]

Captain Van Vliet, impressed with the sincerity and orderliness of the Mormon people, felt convinced that the expedition was a mistake. His report to the Secretary of War, delivered personally at Washington, D.C., opened the way for a peace commission to be sent.

After Van Vliet's departure from Salt Lake City, Governor Young issued a proclamation declaring the territory under martial law. General Wells made his headquarters in Echo Canyon and commenced raising additional forces, amounting to 1,250 men at that place.

A Bloodless Conflict

The advance section of the expedition, under Colonel E. B. Alexander, crossed the border of the territory on September 29, determined to press on to Salt Lake City that fall. Acting upon advice previously given by Captain Van Vliet, Colonel Alexander waited at Hamm's Fork, in a place called Camp Wenfield, for the arrival of the main body of the army under the command of Colonel Albert Sidney Johnston.

While the troops were camped at Hamm's Fork, Governor Young sent a proclamation to the commander of the expedition demanding the removal of troops from the Utah Territory. Colonel Alexander gave the only reply possible: He was there by orders of the President of the United States, and further movements would depend upon "orders issued by competent authority."

The Utah militia now took the initiative. A council of war was held at Fort Bridger on October 3, and the council decided to begin operations against the expedition. The Saints had learned the methods of defensive war now used in their struggle for existence in the desert as well as in their experiences in crossing the plains; these methods were more effective than rifle fire or cannons. A copy of the instructions to the Utah militia officers was found upon the person of Major Joseph Taylor, of Weber County, when he was captured by United States troops early in October. From this document we get a picture of the Mormon campaign:

> You will proceed, with all possible despatch, without injuring your animals, to the Oregon Road, near the bend of Bear river, north by east of this place. Take close and correct observations of the country on your route. When you approach the road, send scouts ahead, to ascertain if the invading troops have passed that way. Should they have passed, take a concealed route, and get ahead of them. Express to Colonel Burton, who is now on that road and in the vicinity of the troops, and effect a junction

with him, so as to operate in concert. On ascertaining the locality or route of the troops, to proceed at once to annoy them in every possible way. Use every exertion to stampede their animals and set fire to their trains. Burn the whole country before them, and on their flanks. Keep them from sleeping by night surprises; blockade the road by felling trees or destroying river fords; where you can. Watch for opportunities to set fire to the grass on their windward, so as if possible to envelope their trains. Leave no grass before them that can be burned. Keep your men concealed as much as possible, and guard against surprise. Keep scouts out at all times, and communications open with Colonel Burton, Major McAllister and O. P. Rockwell, who are operating in the same way. Keep me advised daily of your movements, and every step the troops take, and in which direction.

God bless you, and give you success.

Your brother in Christ.
DANIEL H. WELLS.

P.S.—If the troops have not passed, or have turned in this direction follow, in their rear, and continue to annoy them, burning any trains they may have. Take no life, but destroy their trains, and stampede or drive away their animals, at every opportunity.[6]

Fort Bridger and Fort Supply, then owned by the Church, were burned to the ground to prevent their being utilized by the United States Army.

Before leaving Fort Bridger on October 3, General Wells sent Major Lot Smith with a small company of men to intercept the supply trains then advancing from South Pass and to either turn them back or burn them. Major Smith was successful in his mission and destroyed an immense quantity of supplies intended for the army. From the burning of supply trains, he turned to the business of running off cattle from the army encampments. As a result of his successive raids, one thousand head of cattle were sent into Salt Lake Valley. The government cavalry, which at times attempted to pursue his forces, were easily outrun because of the lighter equipment and better condition of his mounts. The only shots of the war were fired by a party of United States cavalry who came close to capturing Major Smith. The shots did no more damage than the killing of two horses, however.

Early in November 1857, General Albert Sidney Johnston arrived at the main camp of the U.S. Army troops on Hamm's Fork. He was a capable officer, and his enthusiasm revived the drooping spirits of the troops. For a time the troops considered turning north to enter Salt Lake Valley via Fort Hall. But for some reason that plan was abandoned, and the command moved toward Fort Bridger. Though the distance was less than forty miles, the army found it a barren desert. Grass for their stock was burned and no fuel could be found other than sagebrush. In addition, the troops faced one of the severest blizzards of the winter. The oxen weakened from lack of forage and many died. As a result of these problems, the forty-mile journey took fifteen days. And when the men reached Fort Bridger, they found it in ashes, as was Fort Supply twelve miles away. It was apparent that Salt Lake Valley could not be reached that year. General Johnston reluctantly returned to Black's Fork for the winter. This gave the Saints' militia an opportunity to return to their homes, leaving small squads of men to watch and report the army's movements.

Clearing Away Misunderstandings

The failure of the army to reach Salt Lake Valley in 1857 proved the undoing of the whole political scheme behind the expedition. The excessive cost of the expedition and the ill-conceived haste with which it had been begun aroused criticism over the entire nation. Senator Sam Houston, on the floor of the United States Senate, voiced the opinion of many:

> The more men you send to the "Mormon War" the more you increase the difficulty. They have to be fed. For some sixteen hundred miles you have to transport provisions. The regiments sent there have found Fort Bridger and other places, as they approached them, heaps of ashes. They will find Salt Lake, if they ever reach it, a heap of ashes. They will find that they will have to fight against Russia and Russians. Whoever goes there will meet the fate of Napoleon's army when he went to Moscow. Just as sure as we are now standing in the senate, these people, if they fight at all, will fight desperately. They are defending their homes. They are fighting to prevent the execution of threats that

have been made, which touch their hearths and their families; and depend upon it they will fight until every man perishes before he surrenders. That is not all. If they do not choose to go into conflict immediately, they will secure their women and children in the fastnesses of the mountains; they have provisions for two years; and they will carry on a guerrilla warfare which will be most terrible to the troops you send there. They will get no supplies there. You will have to transport them all from Independence, in Missouri. When the fire will consume it, there will not be a spear of grass left that will not be burnt. . . .

I know not what course will be taken on this subject. I hope it will be one of conciliation. As for troops to conquer the Mormons, fifty thousand would be as inefficient as two or three thousand; and in proportion as you send troops in that vast region, without supplies, and without the hope of them, with no means of subsistence after a certain period, unless it is transported to them, the greater will be your danger. Consider the facilities these people have to cut off your supplies. I say your men will never return, but their bones will whiten the valley of Salt Lake. If war begins, the very moment one single drop of blood is drawn, it will be the signal of extermination. Mr. President, in my opinion, whether we are to have a war with the Mormons or not, will depend on the fact whether our troops advance or not. If they do not advance; if negotiations be opened; if we understand what the Mormons are really willing to do; that they are ready to acquiesce in the mandates of the government, and render obedience to the Constitution; if you will take time to ascertain that, and not repudiate all idea of peace, we may have peace. But so sure as the troops advance, so sure they will be annihilated. You may treble them, and you will only add to the catastrophe, not diminish human suffering. These people expect nothing but extermination or abuse more intolerable than even extermination would be, from your troops, and they will oppose them.[7]

It became apparent in Washington before the winter was over that the administration was ready to withdraw peaceably from the whole affair, if a reasonable way was offered.

During the winter two rival governments of Utah Territory were in existence. Since Governor Young had received no official notice of his removal from office, and Governor Cumming had not been officially installed in office, the Latter-day Saint leader continued to function as territorial governor. Governor Cumming attempted to establish his authority from the army headquarters at Camp Scott, on Black's Fork, through a proclamation to the inhabitants of the territory in which he stated: "I come among you with no prejudices or enmities, and, by the exercise of a just and firm administration, I hope to command your confidence. Freedom of conscience and the use of your own peculiar mode of serving God, are sacred rights guaranteed by the Constitution, with which it is not the province of the government, or the disposition of its representatives in the Territory, to interfere."[8]

Governor Cumming's proclamation had little or no effect upon the territory, aside from creating a favorable attitude toward him as an individual. A court was set up at Camp Scott to deal with the numerous civil offenses among the teamsters attached to the army, while a grand jury returned indictments for treason against Brigham Young and sixty of his associates.

On February 25, 1858, Colonel Thomas L. Kane arrived in Salt Lake City. He had traveled from New York via the Isthmus of Panama to Los Angeles and thence by the southern overland route. From the beginning of the troubles in the territory, Colonel Kane had been kept informed of the situation by the Saints. During the winter of 1857-58, although in delicate health, he had made the long and dangerous journey at his own expense in order to aid his Latter-day Saint friends in their unfortunate situation. He brought with him convincing evidence that the U.S. Army's expedition was not to make war on the Saints; rather, it was to assure the citizens of the territory that Governor Cumming was a man of integrity and sterling character. Colonel Kane also assured the Saints that they had friends in Congress. His coming cleared away the clouds of misunderstanding and eventually resulted in a change of the viewpoint of the Saints.

Colonel Kane left Salt Lake City on March 8, 1858, with a letter from Brigham Young, "accrediting him [Colonel Kane] as a negotiator in the existing difficulties."[9] On March 12 he arrived at Camp Scott, where he was entertained by Governor Cumming and remained for three weeks. As a result, he was able to convince the Governor that he should accompany Kane to Salt Lake City and that he would receive a cordial reception. Accordingly Governor Cumming journeyed to Salt Lake City, where he was amazed at the hospitality shown him. In a letter to General Johnston he said: "I have been everywhere recognized as the governor of Utah; and so far from having encountered insults and indignities, I am gratified in being able to state to you that in passing through the settlements, I have been universally greeted with such respectful attentions as are due to the representative of the executive authority of the United States in the territory."[10]

A change of mind had come to the Saints after Colonel Kane's visit. Whereas they had previously been ready to fight to the end for their homes, now they had determined not to resist with arms but to burn their homes and flee south. Brigham Young had obtained from reports of trappers a mistaken idea that a large fertile area capable of supporting a half million population existed in the southwestern desert. Though two scouting parties sent out failed to locate such a place, the Saints were beginning to move southward. Daily the streets of Salt Lake City were thronged with wagons and stock starting the journey.

When Governor Cumming arrived, he found that a large portion of the inhabitants had deserted their homes, leaving only enough persons to fire the dwellings when the time arrived. He reported to Washington the true state of affairs and the deliberate falseness of Judge Drummond's charges. But even before news of Colonel Kane's accomplishments and Governor Cumming's report reached the East, a storm of protest was raging against President Buchanan and his course in sending out the Utah expedition. Senators and members of the House of Representatives openly demanded an investigation. The important newspapers of the East, especially the New York *Times, Tribune,* and *Herald,* took up the fight.

In April, President Buchanan appointed a peace commission, composed of L. W. Powell, former governor of Kentucky, and Major Ben McCullock of Texas. They carried with them a proclamation of pardon, dated April 6, 1858. It declared that Brigham Young was in a state of "rebellion" and "treason," yet in order to prevent the shedding of blood, a pardon would be granted to all who would submit to the authority of the federal government. When the peace commission reached Salt Lake City on June 7, they were astonished to find so large a city with its inhabitants fled. Even the Church leaders had joined in the move south.

When the commission members met with Brigham Young, he declared that the Church leaders were not guilty of treason or rebellion, but that they would accept the pardon. He also agreed to allow the army to pass through the city unmolested providing they did not stop and they would camp at least forty miles away. The commission forwarded a letter to that effect to General Johnston, and on June 26, 1858, the army entered Salt Lake Valley, passed through the city, and camped on the Jordan River. Three days later they marched southward and established a permanent camp, which they named Camp Floyd after the Secretary of War.

Thus was brought to a close an unfortunate chapter in the history of the Church and of the state of Utah. The army was maintained at Camp Floyd until the outbreak of the Civil War, when the camp was abandoned. While the camp remained, it was a social problem to Salt Lake City and the adjacent settlements. Immorality, gambling, drunkenness, and thievery accompanied the army and its hangers-on into the territory, and the Salt Lake City police force had to be increased fourfold as crimes heretofore unknown became commonplace.

The course taken by the Saints in the so-called Utah War was vindicated in the eyes of the nation. And the unwavering posture of Brigham Young, that with the help of the Lord the Saints could withstand the entire army of the United States, won the respect and admiration of the world.

31

Years of Conflict

The settlement of the Utah War enabled the Saints to return again to their homes and feel once more some sense of security. Work on the temple was resumed with vitality. But conflicts were to continue. The public announcement on August 29, 1852, that plural marriage was now an official doctrine of the Church would bring about a chain of antagonism in the nation that would shake the Church to its foundation. Although the practice was not in conflict with existing laws in the nation or in adjoining countries, it was nevertheless contrary to the well-established customs of Anglo-Saxon nations.

Orson Pratt, who was called upon by President Brigham Young to make the first public announcement of plural marriage, set forth the four necessary conditions under which a man could marry more than one wife. First, he must have the consent of his first wife. Second, he must have reasonable financial ability to support a second family. Third, he must be a member of the Church of moral integrity and good character. Fourth, the marriage must be authorized by the President of the Church, who held the keys of authorization for all celestial marriages. Where these requirements were fully complied with, a happy plural marriage usually resulted. That there were some violations and hence some unhappy marriages was inevitable. But plural marriage, so far as the Saints were concerned, accomplished its purposes. More women than men had joined the Church, and the practice absorbed the surplus females into good homes and an honorable position in the society. At the end of the first two years of migration to Utah, the number of women exceeded the number of men, 39,058 women to 37,277 men.[1] This difference in the sexes was to continue for the next fifty years.

Speaking again on this subject in 1869, Elder Pratt said: "If all the inhabitants of the earth at the present time . . . were righteous before God, keeping his commandments, and if, further, the numbers of the sexes were exactly equal, there would be no necessity for any such institution as polygamy. Every righteous man could have his wife, and there would be no surplus of females."[2] Under the circumstances of pioneer life, there was no alternative for single women except as house servants. It took only about two percent of the men of the Church to enter into plural marriage to absorb the surplus women. Church leaders taught that all young men should marry when they became of marriage age, and letters from Brigham Young to bishops urged them to take an active hand to bring this about.

Opposition Aroused

The Saints' practice of plural marriage created a considerable stir in the press and became the center of attack against the Church by its enemies. As Utah was a territory of the United States and as the laws for territories are passed by Congress, the discussion of polygamy was carried to that body and became the chief argument against the admission of Utah as a state. So bitter were attacks against the Church that Congress, under the influence of lobbyists and of the press, passed an antibigamy law in 1862, aimed at the suppression of polygamy among the Mormons. The bill, signed by President Abraham Lincoln on July 8, 1862, made the contracting of a plural marriage punishable by a fine of $500 or imprisonment for a term of five years, or both.

In the main the President and members of Congress were not hostile to the Mormons; rather, they were opposed to the practice of polygamy. The political platform upon which Lincoln was elected contained a plank condemning it. Out of friendship for the Saints, with whom he had become acquainted in Illinois, President Lincoln neglected to appoint officers to enforce the antibigamy law.

Enemies of the Church, however, were not content to let the issue drop. The law contained a provision forbidding a religious body in a territory to hold real estate in value to exceed $50,000. This was aimed directly at The Church of Jesus Christ of Latter-day Saints. Utah Governor Stephen S. Harding attempted in 1863 to have Brigham Young punished under this law, but the attempt failed, the constitutionality of the whole law being questioned.

Agitation against polygamy grew more bitter as the years passed, but it was not until 1874 that the constitutionality of the antibigamy law was tried and an attempt made to enforce it. The Saints were confident that the law was unconstitutional and that if a trial case was carried to the higher courts, it would be so declared and the uncertain state of affairs cleared up. Accordingly, George Reynolds, Brigham Young's private secretary, volunteered to test the law. Territorial officials seemed equally desirous of clarifying the matter by a friendly suit, and so Reynolds was indicted. He voluntarily appeared in court and furnished evidence that he had violated the law. Convicted, he was sentenced to one year's imprisonment and ordered to pay a $500 fine. When the case was appealed to the territorial Supreme Court, it was dismissed on the grounds that the grand jury that found the indictment against Reynolds was an illegal jury.

Antibigamy Laws Held Constitutional

The constitutionality of the law still being undecided, a second trial was held in 1875 before Alexander White, chief justice of Utah. The friendly nature of the previous trial was entirely lacking, the prosecution becoming bitter toward the accused, and the accused in turn refusing to furnish the evidence to prove a violation of the law. A conviction was obtained, however, and Elder Reynolds was sentenced to a $500 fine and two years in the penitentiary at hard labor. The Supreme Court of the territory confirmed the decree, and when the case was later appealed to the United States Supreme Court, that court upheld the constitutionality of the law. It was a stunning blow to the Church and the forerunner of a period of intense persecution. That decision was not given until January 6, 1879. In the meantime Brigham Young had died, and the Quorum of the Twelve Apostles became the presiding authority of the Church. An attempt to have the trial reopened and a petition to have Elder Reynolds pardoned met with failure. He was committed to prison on June 16, 1879.

In October 1880, the First Presidency was again organized

with John Taylor as President. Upon his administration fell the brunt of the antibigamy campaign. In March 1882, Congress passed the Edmunds Bill amending the antibigamy law of 1862. This new measure added to the punishable offense of plural marriages "polygamous living," which was defined as "unlawful cohabitation." The law abrogated the right of the traditional jury trial. Further, it deprived all who lived the polygamous relationship of the right to vote or hold public office. It declared all registration and election offices vacant in the territory and provided for federal appointees in their place, virtually depriving Utah of those rights of self-government which had become a definite factor in the government of territories. The law was made retroactive with regard to the franchise. No individual who had ever lived the law of plural marriage was allowed to vote, regardless of whether he was then living that law or not.

A campaign of bitter persecution began against those who had entered into plural marriage before or after the passage of the law. Hundreds of homes were broken up, the fathers and husbands being sent to prison. Women were sent to prison for contempt of court because they refused to testify against their husbands. Following a severe sentence given Rudger Clawson in October 1884, there developed what was termed the "segregation ruling." This ruling stated that separate indictments might be found against a man for every day he was found guilty of living with a plural wife. It was responsible for driving the leaders of the Church into exile, for it amounted to an announcement that a man who practiced polygamy or even attempted to provide for his wives might, by an accumulation of separate charges, be sent to prison for life. The policy was condemned by the Supreme Court of the United States in the case of Lorenzo Snow, which came before it in February 1887.

Edmunds-Tucker Law

In March 1887, Congress passed a still more rigid measure to suppress polygamy, known as the Edmunds-Tucker Law. This law provided for the disincorporation of The Church of Jesus Christ of Latter-day Saints and of the Perpetual Emigrating Fund Company.

The property of these corporations was to escheat to the federal government to be used for the benefit of schools in the territory. Buildings and grounds used exclusively for religious services, as well as burial grounds, were alone exempted from the law.

Frank H. Dyer, the United States marshal in Utah, took charge of the real and personal property of the Church. In order to retain the use of the tithing offices and the historian's office, the Church was forced to pay an annual rental of $2,400. High rental fees were also paid for use of the Gardo House and of the temple block. During this period the Church was under heavy financial stress. It could not borrow a dollar; only the faithful payment of tithes enabled it to weather the storm. The exiled First Presidency conducted the affairs of the Church from hiding places, generally called the underground. John Taylor died in exile July 27, 1887, at Kaysville, Utah. After his death, the crusade against polygamy continued, but with considerable tolerance on the part of the federal officers. President Grover Cleveland pardoned a number of men who had been given extraordinarily severe sentences.

Feelings against polygamy in Idaho and Arizona also became intense. In 1885 the Idaho Legislature passed a law that disfranchised *all* members of the Church, thus depriving all Mormons of the right to vote or hold office, regardless of whether or not they practiced polygamy themselves. The constitutionality of the law was questioned, but it was upheld by the United States Supreme Court on February 3, 1890. A similar bill was introduced in Congress for the Territory of Utah, called the "Struble Bill," but even prominent non-Mormons of Utah opposed it, and it was defeated.

The Manifesto

In the midst of these trying difficulties, Wilford Woodruff, who was sustained President of the Church on April 7, 1889, appealed to the Lord in prayer. In answer he received a revelation suspending plural marriage. On September 25, 1890, he issued his famous Manifesto, which declared an end to the contracting of plural marriages in the Church and called upon the members to obey the law of the land. In general conference on October 6,

1890, the Manifesto was sustained and thus became binding upon the Church. In that conference President Woodruff declared: "The step which I have taken in issuing this manifesto has not been done without earnest prayer before the Lord. . . . I am not ignorant of the feelings that have been engendered through the course I have pursued. . . . The Lord will never permit me or any other man who stands as the President of this Church to lead you astray. It is not in the programme. It is not in the mind of God. If I were to attempt that, the Lord would remove me out of my place."[3]

As a result of the Manifesto, there was a noticeable change in attitude toward the Church. On January 4, 1893, President Benjamin Harrison issued a proclamation of amnesty to those who had entered into plural marriages prior to November 1, 1890. The restrictions against voters were removed, and in 1893 the personal property of the Church was returned to its rightful owners. Three years later the real estate that had been confiscated was likewise returned to the Church. On January 4, 1896, Utah was admitted to the Union as the forty-fifth state.

The United Order

Brigham Young had not attempted to establish the law of consecration when he led the Saints into the valleys of the mountains. He seemed to be content with the spirit of cooperation that was generally manifest in the various communities. Survival in rural communities required cooperation in the building of roads, bridges, and irrigation canals. Because of the Saints' faith in the Church, in general there was little disagreement in local affairs. The very existence of the community usually depended upon the people's belief that they were doing the work of the Lord. Many a community in the Great Basin would have been abandoned but for the feeling of a religious duty to make it succeed.

The conditions of the 1860s and 1870s, however, gave rise to financial differences and a tendency to worldliness that disturbed President Young. In the winter of 1873-74 he started a reform movement to eliminate classes among the members. The movement was inaugurated at St. George while he was wintering there.

Rules of conduct were drawn up for those who entered the movement, which would be known as the United Order of Zion. The rules called for strict obedience to the commandments of God, for kindness and affection within the families, and for simplicity of dress and manner of living. They ended with this declaration: "We will combine our labor for mutual benefit, sustain with our faith, prayers, and words those whom we have elected to take the management of the different departments of the 'Order,' and be subject to them in their official capacity, refraining from a spirit of fault-finding. We will honestly and diligently labor and devote ourselves and all we have to the 'Order,' and to the building up of the Kingdom of God."[4]

On his return journey to Salt Lake in the spring of 1874, President Young preached the United Order at the various settlements. He also discussed it at general conference in April.

The development of the United Order was not uniform in the various settlements. Some did not start it at all. In communities where it was begun, the individuals were not required to enroll and some did not, resulting in community divisions. Because of advancing age and poor health, Brigham Young could not lend the movement his usual weight and vigor. Although there was some success in a few communities, such as Orderville and Glendale, the movement as a whole did not get a good start. By the time of President Young's death in 1877, the majority of the stakes had abandoned the United Order. The First Presidency officially ordered the total discontinuance in a letter dated May 1, 1882, and sent to stake presidents.

Cooperative Merchandising

Leaders of the Church anticipated effects the coming of the railroad to Utah in 1869 would produce on industry, and early in 1868 they initiated a movement to organize the Mormon merchants and purchasers into cooperative merchandising enterprises. This movement was designed to help the Saints to purchase articles manufactured in the East at reasonable prices without being subject to prices set by so-called gentile, or nonmember, merchants who were entering the territory. The capital for such enterprises was furnished in small amounts by a multitude of stockholders, a plan designed to encourage the people to go into merchandising and to share in the business profits, as well as to prevent concentration of wealth in a few hands.

The first of these cooperative merchandising organizations was begun in Provo in 1868. In 1869 the Zion's Cooperative Mercantile Institution, which was shortened to ZCMI, became a Church-wide institution, with local merchants invited to join the movement and to sell stock in their local concerns. In connection with the establishment of ZCMI, a boycott was urged against non-Mormon merchants. In the general conference in October 1868, Brigham Young announced: "I want to tell my brethren, my friends, and my enemies, that we are going to draw the reins so tight as not to let a Latter-day Saint trade with an outsider."[5]

Both of these movements were defensive. Enemies of the Church openly claimed that with the coming of the railroad, Mormonism would be overthrown. An influx of gentile merchants was expected. ZCMI and its branches throughout the territory proved, in the main, successful and served to level prices. However, they did contribute to bad feelings between Mormon and gentile merchants, which lasted until the end of the century.

Conflicts in Education

With the organization of Utah into a territory and the institution of public schools supported by taxation, there was bound to be some conflict. As the public schools came under the direction of federal officials, two directives were given: first, the scriptures were not to be taught in the public schools, and second, classes were not to be taught in church buildings. The Church fought against both edicts and lost. Private schools for the elementary grades, termed seminaries, were held in the wards of the Church for a few years in some localities, but the cost of supporting them, coupled with the taxes paid by all people to support the public schools, proved to be too heavy a burden, and the private schools disappeared in the course of a few years.

To add to the problem, Protestant churches, seeking to destroy the Latter-day Saints, found a new method of persuasion. While their preachers who had been sent among the settlements had failed to sway the Saints, now they set up secondary denominational schools in Latter-day Saint communities and invited all young people to attend. The teachers, primarily from the eastern states, were well-trained and able, and the Saints, who had no secondary schools of their own, found large numbers of their young enrolling in these denominational institutions. The first of these was the St. Mark's School, established in Salt Lake City in 1867 by the Episcopal Church. It was followed by the Salt Lake Seminary, a Methodist school, in 1870. Others followed in a number of the Latter-day Saint communities.

To offset what was happening, the Church began to enter the secondary school arena by setting up Church academies. The first of these was the Brigham Young Academy, established at Provo in 1875. This was followed by the Brigham Young Academy (College) in Logan. In 1888 the Church organized the Church Board of Education and appointed Dr. Karl G. Maeser, then president of the Provo Academy, to serve also as the first Superintendent of Church schools. In the same year the First Presidency sent instructions to stake presidents to organize an academy in each stake area. By 1907, some thirty-five academies had been established. A few of them, lacking buildings and finances, closed after a brief time. Twenty-two continued until public high schools were built in their communities. With the rise of the public high schools, the enrollment in academies declined. In 1880, public high schools in Utah enrolled only five percent of the secondary students of the state; by 1911 the public school enrollment equalled that of the academies, and by 1924, 90 percent of the high school students of Utah were attending state-operated schools. The Church retained and enlarged some of the academies as normal schools for the training of teachers. These included Brigham Young University in Provo; Brigham Young College, Logan; Weber Normal College, Ogden; Dixie Normal College in St. George, Utah; Snow Normal College in Ephraim, Utah; Ricks Normal College in Rexburg, Idaho; Mesa Normal College in Arizona; and Juarez Academy in Mexico. All other academies were closed by 1924.

John Taylor (1808–87)

Political Opposition

The Saints had been blessed with the wise leadership of President John Taylor, who succeeded Brigham Young and served as President from 1880 to 1887. From exile during most of his period as President, he kept the Church together during the trying times of persecution under the congressional acts passed to destroy polygamy. Wilford Woodruff, his successor, was likewise a bulwark of strength and, like John Taylor, had been an early associate of Joseph Smith. He did much to bring the Church out of its financial difficulties and to restore harmony with the civil government. He died September 2, 1898, and was succeeded eleven days later by Lorenzo Snow, then eighty-five years of age.

During President Snow's administration, opposition to the Saints flared afresh. Brigham H. Roberts, a member of the Church's First Council of the Seventy, was elected to represent Utah in Congress, but the non-Mormons in Utah's congressional delegation urged Congress to deny him a seat on the grounds that he was a polygamist. The dispute became nationwide, and Elder Roberts was finally excluded from Congress.

When Reed Smoot, a member of the Council of the Twelve,

was elected to the United States Senate in 1903, it was a signal for a
fresh attack against the Church. The Ministerial Alliance of Salt
Lake City petitioned the Senate to refuse him a seat on the grounds
that he believed in polygamy, though he was not a polygamist. The
case was before the Senate for two years, but after a full investigation he was seated February 20, 1907. And as the Church entered
the new century, persecution gradually ceased throughout the
United States and a more tolerant attitude was taken toward the
Saints.

A Temple Is Erected

Though the last half of the nineteenth century was a period of
great persecution and upheaval for the Latter-day Saints, it was
also a period of growth both spiritually and temporally. One of the
most remarkable symbols of the Saints' spiritual strength was the
completion and dedication of four temples, the most sacred buildings of the Saints.

Within a few days after the pioneers arrived in the Salt Lake
Valley, President Brigham Young designated the square where a
temple would be built. On April 6, 1853, he described the occasion:

> I scarcely ever say much about revelations, or visions, but
> suffice it to say, five years ago last July I was here, and saw in the
> spirit the Temple not ten feet from where we have laid the Chief
> Corner Stone. I have not inquired what kind of a Temple we
> should build. Why? Because it was presented before me. I never
> looked upon that ground, but the vision of it was there. I see it as
> plainly as if it was in reality before me. Wait until it is done, I will
> say, however, that it will have six towers, to begin with, instead
> of one. Now do not any of you apostatize because it will have six
> towers and Joseph built only one. It is easier for us to build six-
> teen, than it was for him to build one. The time will come when
> there will be one in the centre of Temples we shall build, and, on
> the top, groves and fish ponds. But we shall not see them here, at
> present.[6]

The occasion for these remarks was the laying of the cornerstone of the Salt Lake Temple. What a heroic enterprise—a
four-million-dollar structure commenced in a desert, while the ter-

The Salt Lake Temple under construction

rific struggle for existence was being waged, and by an impoverished people who, in the whole territory, numbered less than twenty thousand.

It took forty years of sacrifice and toil to complete the temple. By the time of its final dedication on April 6, 1893, three successive Presidents of the Church had had a hand in its building, and the Church's membership in the territory had grown to hundreds of thousands. Twice during that forty years the work came to a standstill. In 1857 the entire excavation was filled in and the mason work, which had not then risen above the ground, was completely covered up, the ground was plowed, and the whole plot presented the appearance of a cultivated field. Johnston's army was approaching Utah, and the entire population was preparing to destroy their homes and move to the south.

With peace and understanding restored, the Saints removed the soil from the foundations of the temple and set to work again, only to have a second interruption. The foundations were found insufficiently solid for the massive weight that was to rest upon them. Brigham Young ordered the entire foundation reset, announcing to the people, "This Temple must stand through the millennium."

And well might it stand for a thousand years, for the walls are built of solid granite blocks and are sixteen feet thick at the foundation, tapering to six feet thick at the top.

During the days of construction the temple block, which had been enclosed by a massive twelve foot wall, became a great workshop. The water of City Creek was converted into power, and airblast equipment, an iron foundry, and machine shops for metal and wood were in operation.

The granite for the building was obtained at the mouth of Little Cottonwood Canyon, twenty miles to the southeast, where the elements of an earlier epoch had loosened huge blocks from the massive granite walls and deposited them on the canyon floor. These boulders often weighed many tons and had to be divided by hand drills, wedges, and low explosives. Even many of the broken stones weighed several tons. These were hauled to Salt Lake City by ox teams, four or five yoke of oxen to a single stone.

The slowness with which the work progressed caused the workers to look for easier means of transportation. They finally decided to construct a canal from the mouth of the canyon to Salt Lake City and to float the great stones to the temple on barges rather than haul them with ox teams. The canal was begun, but before many miles were constructed, the Saints received assurance that a transcontinental railway would be built through Salt Lake City. As the railway promised a better solution to their problem, the Church contracted to construct a section of the proposed roadbed; work on the temple during 1868 and 1869 almost ceased, as Mormon laborers worked feverishly to complete the railway. Though the Saints had urged the construction of the main railroad line through Salt Lake City, company officials routed it through Ogden. But as soon as a branch line could be extended to Salt Lake City and then to the mouth of Little Cottonwood Canyon, the building of the temple proceeded at a faster rate. Even then, when Brigham Young died in 1877, the temple was only twenty feet above ground. The building continued during the troubled administration of President Taylor and was vigorously pushed to completion during the administration of President Woodruff.

Other Temples Are Built

Before the temple at Salt Lake City had been dedicated, three other temples had been completed in Utah. At St. George, a temple site was dedicated November 9, 1871. The temple was completed in 1877, and the dedication was held in connection with the forty-seventh annual conference of the Church held in the temple April 6, 1877.

In the same year that the St. George Temple was completed, two other temple sites were dedicated. The site for a temple in Logan was dedicated May 17, 1877, and the completed temple was dedicated May 17, 1884. A temple site in Manti was dedicated April 25, 1877, and the completed structure was dedicated May 21, 1888.

All of these temples were built while the Saints were still struggling to wrest a living in the harsh region and represent great sacrifice and cooperation of a whole people. The spirit with which the work proceeded at each temple is illustrated in the words of Brigham Young when he dedicated the site for the Manti Temple:

> We intend building this Temple for ourselves, and we are abundantly able to do it; therefore no man need come here to work expecting wages for his services. The neighboring settlements will send their men, and they can be changed whenever, and as often as desirable; and they can get credit on Labor Tithing or on Donation Account for their services, and we expect them to work until this Temple is completed without asking for wages. It is not in keeping with the character of Saints to make the building of Temples a matter of merchandise.
>
> We want to rear this Temple with clean hands and pure hearts, that we, with our children, may enter into it to receive our washings and anointings: the keys and ordinances of the holy Priesthood, and also to officiate in the same for our fathers and mothers and our forefathers who lived and died without the Gospel, that they with us may be made partakers of the fruits of the tree of life, and live and rejoice in our Father's kingdom. The Gospel is free, its ordinances are free, and we are at liberty to rear this Temple to the name of our Lord without charging anybody for our services.[7]

When we leave the account of the building of temples, we come to the most beautiful story of all—the story of what transpires inside the temple walls. In that story lie the reasons for the mighty sacrifice of millions of dollars and millions of hours of toil that have gone toward the erection and maintenance of those houses of God. Every member of the Church in good standing may, on reaching adulthood, enter the temple and receive his or her endowments, which are, according to John A. Widtsoe, courses of instruction relative to man's existence before he came on this earth, the history of the creation of the earth, the story of our first earthly parents, the history of the various dispensations of the gospel, the meaning of the sacrifice of Jesus Christ, the story of the restoration of the gospel, and the means and methods whereby joy on this earth and exaltation in heaven may be obtained.[8]

32

Constancy Amid Change

The twentieth century proved to be a century of change—change in the growth and prosperity of the Church, change in the industrial development of the nations, changes in fields of science, changes in the areas of philosophy and religion, changes brought about by a succession of wars that shook the stability and peace of mankind, the alignment of nations and of their political systems.

The Church had survived the conflicts attendant to the first fifty years in the Great Basin. Utah had finally achieved statehood. President Woodruff had made peace with the federal government, and all Church properties had been restored. The sugar-beet industry had become successful, with sugar factories humming, and farmers had found a cash crop to supplement the proceeds from livestock and wool.

Following the dedication of the Salt Lake Temple in April 1893, President Woodruff instructed the Saints regarding revelations he had received clarifying sealings done in temples. The sealing of individuals and families to prominent Church leaders, called the "law of adoption," was to be discontinued. Sealings were to be only to the family line—children to fathers, fathers to their fathers, and so forth. This change gave impetus to members to research their family lines, and to foster such research, the Genealogical Society was organized in 1894.

In 1893 President Woodruff instructed the Church to discontinue any rebaptisms as not being necessary for salvation. And in 1896, the monthly fast day of the Church was changed from the first Thursday of the month to the first Sunday.

President Lorenzo Snow, who succeeded President Woodruff upon his death in 1898, started a reform to stir the Saints to keep their vows, especially in the payment of tithes, that the Lord might bless them with prosperity. In the three short years of his presi-

Church Archives

Wilford Woodruff (1807–98)   *Lorenzo Snow (1814–1901)*

dency, he showed a vitality and leadership that belied his advancing years, a remarkable testimony to his divine calling.

Joseph F. Smith, who succeeded President Snow in 1901, was the last of the prophets who had known the first prophet, Joseph Smith. A son of the martyred Hyrum Smith, he had been only a lad when the Prophet died. His long experience in Church affairs, his unwavering faith, and his unique ability to explain the gospel of Jesus Christ in simple terms endeared him to the Saints. Under his leadership, the Church rose from debt to solvency, enabling it to begin a remarkable and much-needed building program. The Hotel Utah was completed in 1912; the beautiful Church Office Building was completed in 1917; and scores of ward chapels and stake buildings were erected.

Living Prophets of God

Of foremost importance to the study of Church history is the effect each living prophet of God has upon his generation. Each appears to have been chosen of God because of his preparation to meet the problems of his day. The Prophet Joseph Smith laid the enduring foundations. Brigham Young preserved the Church in isolation and built a great Rocky Mountain kingdom. John Taylor led a defense of this isolated commonwealth against a nation bent on its destruction or modification. Wilford Woodruff preserved the Church from political and economic disaster when defense was no longer feasible. Lorenzo Snow redefined and redirected the program and goals of the Church to make possible its survival, and in doing so ushered in a new era of history. Joseph F. Smith implemented this new program and, by his patience and kindliness, began the process by which the Church came to a position of respectability before a critical world. These great prophets belonged to the first century of the Church. All had known Joseph Smith. All but Joseph F. Smith had been his close associates.

The next president and prophet of the Church, Heber J. Grant, stood astride the first and second centuries of the Church's existence. During his twenty-seven years as the living prophet of God, he cemented together the achievements of the past and initiated temporal and spiritual growth in preparation for the great progress of the future.

Heber J. Grant became President of the Church on November 23, 1918, four days after the death of Joseph F. Smith. Several things marked the period of his leadership: the steady growth of the Church, the attaining of financial stability that survived the long depression of the thirties, the building of temples and many other church buildings, and the development of the Church welfare program. Membership between 1918 and 1945 grew from 600,000 to 900,000; the number of stakes, from 75 to 150. During the years following World War I, the Saints became prosperous, payment of the tithes increased, and the activities of the Church, especially in providing temples and other buildings, expanded.

The recordings of the revelations received by the prophets of God who followed Joseph Smith would fill volumes. They are found in the presidents' personal journals, wherein they relate their struggles with the problems of their day, their appeals to the Lord, and the inspiration that followed those prayers. They are found in minutes of First Presidency meetings and of meetings of the First Presidency and the Twelve in the Salt Lake Temple. They are found in letters from the First Presidency to stake presidents and other Church officers; they are found in special instructions to the Church in general conference reports.

Joseph F. Smith (1838–1918)   *Heber J. Grant (1856–1945)*

Because of continuous revelation, changes have continuously taken place within the Church. Instead of attempting to make the Church conform to the pattern given for the small membership of its formative years, the prophets have given directives under God's inspiration to meet the changing conditions of the world. In official handbooks, ward and stake officers receive instructions for performing their duties. In general conference reports and special letters to Church officers is a record of administrative changes and announced policies and doctrines. To have included these in a volume of scripture such as the Doctrine and Covenants would make an unwieldy volume, and each recurring edition would make preceding volumes obsolete because of incompleteness.

As to the plan of salvation proclaimed by Jesus Christ and the fundamental doctrines and principles as proclaimed by revelations to Joseph Smith in establishing the Church in this dispensation, there have been no changes. Here there has been a constancy among the successive prophets of the Church. This constancy in the midst of changes in society, not only among the leaders but quite generally among the membership of the Church, is a miracle of our time, and the result of the Spirit of God promised to the faithful members.

The Church Moves Outward

During the early part of the twentieth century, a number of factors have changed the makeup of the Church membership. First, there was a marked movement from the rural to urban areas. Some observers felt that this would weaken the Church, but it proved to be otherwise. Church activity increased. Tithes and offerings accentuated; the number of missionaries increased. This movement to the urban areas was not peculiar to the Latter-day Saints. It was a national movement due to development of farm machinery and methods that reduced the manpower needed to feed the nation. With populations moving to the cities, not only did the Saints change their occupations, but converts were more and more found among people in industry and the professions. In the main this resulted in a higher level of leadership and experience.

The great depression of the 1930s had a profound effect upon distribution of the Latter-day Saints. Unemployment in the Utah and Idaho areas reached undue proportions. Since the older and more populous centers of the nation offered work opportunities, many of the Saints left their homes to seek greener fields. Especially was this true of younger individuals and couples. The exodus was primarily in two directions—to California in the West and the Washington, D.C., area in the East. Those moving from farms did not return to farming in their new locations; they were absorbed in business and the professions. But they did not leave their religion behind. Their alignment to the gospel of Jesus Christ in the main was constant. New wards and stakes sprang up wherever they went, and a new era of Church growth began.

The depression affected the distribution of Church members in quite another way. The General Authorities, aware of the employment situation, ceased to urge converts in other sections of the United States or overseas to migrate to the center of the Church, but rather advised them to remain and build up the Church in their own localities. This led to the organization of stakes of Zion in many lands. The change did not signify a retreat from the principle of gathering; it was only a readjustment in the application of that principle. Changes in methods of travel and communication now made it possible for supervision of gathering places for the Saints in other parts of the world, and the stake became a gathering place, as it had been in the various communities in the Great Basin. With a stake organization, the Saints in any area of the world could find the unity of teaching, companionship, and programs that would fortify them from the ills of the world, which was the purpose of gathering from the beginning.

The Church Welfare Plan

The depression of the 1930s did not destroy the solidarity of the Church. Rather, it led to ways to preserve the faith of the members as well as assist them in surviving their economic problems. In 1934 the brethren began to gather the information concerning the people's needs and to pray for divine guidance. Out of work, study, and prayer came a plan that was announced to the Church in general conference in April 1936. The Welfare Plan, originally named the "security plan," was not a new philosophy; it revived the idea of a bishop's storehouse. Functioning through priesthood channels, it provided a system of voluntary production of food, clothing, and other necessities, to be stored in welfare centers and distributed to those in need. Harold B. Lee, then president of the Pioneer Stake, was appointed to head the program. A general welfare committee supervised by the First Presidency and the Presiding Bishopric gave instructions to the wards and stakes.

Priesthood quorums and Relief Societies within wards and stakes carried out the details of the program. Welfare farms were purchased, crops planted, dairies set up, and manufacturing quarters located. Goods were produced by voluntary labor, usually by those who had been unemployed. Their pay was work receipts redeemable in goods from a bishop's storehouse. As long as idle land or vacant buildings were available, there was no need for idleness. The Welfare Plan worked so well that it became a permanent institution to help care for the needy and keep them from being in want or dependent on a public dole. The plan brought favorable publicity from the national press and aroused favorable attitudes toward the Church.

Since the greater amount of Church income comes from the voluntary payment of tithing, the income sank to a low level during the great depression, and there was concern that if the depression continued too long, it might become necessary to close Church schools, restrict building programs, and minimize many other activities. Only a program initiated by President Heber J. Grant a few years prior to the depression saved the Church from such dire results. He foresaw the coming of the depression and, like Joseph in Egypt thousands of years before, began to divert a portion of the Church income annually into investments to provide for possible rainy days. Invested wisely, the income saved the Church from the threatening curtailment of its programs during the depression years.

The Effects of Worldwide Conflict

During the first half of the twentieth century, worldwide wars offered a further challenge to the unity of the Church. For the first time the Church found members engaged on both sides of bloody conflicts. Especially was this true in World Wars I and II. While other churches found bitterness among their members thus engaged in opposing forces, which resulted in many divisions of such churches, this did not happen among the Latter-day Saints. Assured by the living prophets that the wars were not the fault of individuals if they adhered to the peaceable principles of the gospel, the Saints were urged to support the respective nations in which they lived. They were admonished in a special message from the First Presidency on April 6, 1942: "On each side they believe that they are fighting for home, and country, and freedom. On each side, our brethren pray to the same God, in the same name, for victory. Both sides cannot be wholly right; perhaps neither is without wrong. God will work out in His own due time and in His own sovereign way the justice and right of the conflict, but He will not hold the innocent instrumentalities of the war, our brethren in arms, responsible for the conflict."[1]

Both world wars affected missionary work, reducing the number of the missionaries called and the countries to which they could go. Travel became difficult, and supervision of members in foreign lands nearly impossible. But amid all the conflicts the miracle was that the Saints who thus separated from the main body of the Church remained constant. They even called local missionaries to serve, and this brought about increased membership.

To help sustain Latter-day Saint servicemen in faithfulness to Christ, the Church organized a Servicemen's Committee during World War I under the direction of Elder Harold B. Lee of the Council of the Twelve to maintain contact as far as possible with men in service. To provide religious services, worthy elders were called and given authority to hold Church meetings and administer the sacrament. In addition, the Church obtained from the federal government the right to appoint Latter-day Saint chaplains for the several military services, in proportion to the respective numbers of Church members so enrolled. Not only did the majority of Church members in the military retain their faith, but many of their associates were converted and the way was paved for the opening of missions in many lands. Thus, the faith of the Saints remained constant and the Church continued its remarkable growth during wartime. Worldwide, attendance at meetings increased, missionaries responded to calls, and work in the temples multiplied.

A Milestone Is Reached

When a celebration was held in 1930 commemorating the first hundred years of the Church, the membership was recorded as 700,000. President Heber J. Grant reported: "We have at the present time: Stakes of Zion, 104; Wards, 930; Independent branches, 75; Total wards and branches in the stakes of Zion, from Canada to Mexico, 1039; Missions, 29; Mission branches, 800."[2] By the time George Albert Smith succeeded President Grant on May 21, 1945, the membership had reached some 900,000. At the time of his death six years later, the number had exceeded one million.

Remarkable as the growth of the Church had been in the first century, a growth that had more than equaled the total growth of Christianity in the first century after the death of Christ, it was still a long way from reaching its objective in carrying the gospel to all the world. The work of preparing its people to teach the multitudes occupying other lands with a diversity of languages, customs, and religious backgrounds had scarcely begun. Translations of even the standard scriptures existed in only a few languages, and translations of missionary tracts, Church magazines, and courses of study were virtually nonexistent. For youths, education in the scriptures was underway in the Primary, religion classes, and seminary, but it was limited to only part of the families of the Church, and the total enrollment was small.

Work for the dead was underway in existing temples, but the temples were few in number and quite unavailable to many in the growing membership of the Church. Genealogical work to furnish names to the temples was disorganized, and aids to those seeking after their dead extremely limited.

In all, it could be said that the Church had a clear vision of its goals but they seemed quite distant to a people unprepared except in spirit. It was the work of the next half century to develop a people ready and able to bring about a marvelous work and a wonder. During those years there was a renaissance of learning and the arts; a development of leadership through priesthood quorums and auxiliary organizations; a correlation of courses of study and of activities. The auxiliaries took the lead during much of this period in providing activities that promoted leadership, so much so, in fact, that correlation developed in the 1960s and '70s to curb the auxiliaries and bring leadership back to the priesthood.

Growth of the Auxiliaries

The Relief Society was originally organized by the Prophet Joseph Smith in Nauvoo on March 17, 1842. At that time it was known as the Female Relief Society. In 1892, it was renamed the National Woman's Relief Society, and in 1942, the Relief Society of The Church of Jesus Christ of Latter-day Saints. By the 1980s, membership had passed one million.

The Sunday School, which began in the winter of 1849 in the Old Fort in Salt Lake City, grew into a Churchwide movement. In 1866 it was organized as the Deseret Sunday School Union, with

Elder George Q. Cannon as president. From an initial membership of fifty, the enrollment now includes all Church members.

The Young Men's Mutual Improvement Association was first organized June 10, 1875, by Junius F. Wells acting under instruction from Brigham Young. The Young Women's Mutual Improvement Association had its origin in the Retrenchment Association, organized by Brigham Young at the Lion House on November 28, 1869. In 1880, general boards were set up for both associations, with the combined organization known as the Mutual Improvement Association. In November 1972, the MIA was realigned into Aaronic Priesthood and Melchizedek Priesthood MIA and placed directly under priesthood leadership. On June 23, 1974, Mutual Improvement Association was dropped from the name of Church youth programs and further modifications were implemented in the administrative structure of the Aaronic Priesthood and the Young Women.

The Primary originated at Farmington, Davis County, Utah, on August 25, 1878, under the direction of Aurelia S. Rogers, who perceived the need for religious education for young children. By 1980 the membership exceeded half a million children.

Genealogical Work

The Genealogical Society of Utah, which later became the Genealogical Department of the Church, was organized in the office of Church Historian Franklin D. Richards on November 13, 1894, "to be benevolent in collection, compiling, establishing and maintaining a genealogical library for the use and benefit of its members and others; educational in disseminating information regarding genealogical matters; and also religious."[3] At the time of incorporation the library consisted of a donation of eleven books and 300,000 films; by 1968 there were 80,000 volumes and 670,000 microfilms.

In the late 1960s the Church blasted into a granite mountain some twenty miles southeast of Salt Lake City, in the same general area as granite had been obtained for the Salt Lake Temple, to cut a huge storage vault for permanent storage of valuable Church and

George Albert Smith (1870–1951)   *David O. McKay (1873–1970)*

genealogical records. The Genealogical Department moved into the high-rise Church Office Building when it was completed in 1972, and by 1984 it had outgrown those quarters and work was progressing rapidly toward completion of a new research library for the public in the block west of Temple Square. Microfilming of church and government records throughout the world was adding many new records, making this the largest library of its kind in the world.

Arts and Letters

During the years in which Presidents Heber J. Grant and George Albert Smith led the Church, there occurred a renaissance of arts and letters, an area that had suffered during the long period of conflict. President Grant was a great patron of the arts. He purchased scores of paintings from promising young artists to help and encourage them; he could have covered the walls of the rooms in his home with such paintings. He had special editions printed of books that he loved, autographed them, and sent them to friends, Church leaders, and teachers at Christmastime. It is said that he gave away more than half a million books. He loved the theater. As a spindly lad of nine, when he had sold water to patrons on the third balcony of the old Salt Lake Theatre, he vowed that one day he would own that theater. And he did, for the day came when the advent of motion pictures doomed stage productions for a time and the Church could no longer maintain the theater, which had been built in 1861 by order of Brigham Young. To preserve the historic building, President Grant purchased it from the Church and personally operated it at a loss until, finding no public support for its preservation, he finally had to consent to the building's being razed in 1929 to make room for commercial enterprises.

George Albert Smith, who succeeded Heber J. Grant May 21, 1945, loved youth and won their love in turn by fostering Scouting and social activities in wards and stakes. His concern for all mankind, shown in his sermons and exemplified in his meetings with national leaders during his many travels, brought a new era of respect for the Church.

The Administration of David O. McKay

The presidency of David O. McKay, which began April 9, 1951, brought the Church worldwide recognition as an important institution. During his presidency, from 1951 to 1970, the membership increased from 1,111,000 to nearly three million. It was said that by 1970 half of the Church members had known no other prophet.

The Church entered a new era when President McKay announced in 1952 that sites had been selected for new temples in Bern, Switzerland, and London, England, and that stakes of Zion would soon be established worldwide. Throughout the first century of the Church the spirit of gathering prompted converts in foreign lands to gather to the headquarters of the Church and the various stakes in the Great Basin. Now, with the establishment of stakes throughout the world, there was no longer pressure for converts to emigrate to the central stakes. During the great depression of the 1930s, missionaries and mission presidents were told to urge converts to remain in their own native lands and build up the Church branches. This paved the way for the later establishment of stakes in those lands. While stakes had previously organized in Hawaii, in Canada, and in Colonia Juarez in Mexico to accommodate Saints who had gathered there, it was not until the 1960s and '70s that stakes were organized in all parts of the world where numbers justified. The new policy strengthened the Church in distant lands and also presented new challenges for taking the full program of the Church to the world.

33

Educating the Youth
of the Church

As public schools became increasingly available to the Latter-day Saints, it was not feasible for the Church to maintain a parallel system for secular training. The costs of doing so would be prohibitive. Beginning in 1913, with the abandonment of the Summit Academy in Utah, the Church gradually withdrew from much of the field of secular education. Church-operated elementary schools in the Rocky Mountain area were discontinued, and academies operating on the secondary level were disposed of by sale at a nominal price to state school districts or in some instances by outright gifts. In 1920 Horace H. Cummings, the Church superintendent of education, recommended the closing of all academies except those that had been changed to college level—Brigham Young University in Provo (1903); Brigham Young College in Logan, Utah; Weber Normal College in Ogden, Utah; Snow Normal College in Ephraim, Utah; and Gila College in Thatcher, Arizona.

By 1924 the only academy remaining, aside from those that had become colleges, was Juarez Academy in Colonia Juarez, Mexico. Adam S. Bennion, who became superintendent of Church schools in 1919, recommended that the junior colleges be transferred to the respective states on condition that the states continue to operate them as colleges. Between 1931 and 1934, Weber, Snow, and Dixie colleges were turned over to the State of Utah, with the above stipulation. In 1933 Gila College in Thatcher, Arizona, was transferred to the State of Arizona. Ricks College in Rexburg, Idaho, was offered to the State of Idaho, but the transfer was not made because the state would not accept the stipulation to continue the operation of the college. In 1931 the Latter-day Saint University in Salt Lake City was discontinued, but was allowed to continue as a business college.

As early as the turn of the century some weekday religion classes were being held after regular school hours for elementary students attending public schools. These were taught in ward chapels by teachers called by the bishop. In 1906 President Joseph F. Smith organized these classes under a general board of Religion Classes, with stake boards on the local level. The classes continued until 1928, when they were replaced by junior seminaries under the direction of the Church Department of Education. Junior seminaries were discontinued in 1938.

In 1912 the Church adopted a proposal to establish seminaries adjacent to high schools. The first such seminary was organized in the Granite School District in Salt Lake County, where students were released for one period during the day for religious instruction. A seminary building was constructed adjacent to Granite High School, and Thomas J. Yates was employed as the first teacher.

The program proved a great success, and the Utah State Board of Education passed a resolution to the effect that local boards of education governing public high schools could grant one credit toward graduation for courses in Bible history and literature. From that beginning, the program spread throughout Utah and Idaho, with some seminaries also established in parts of Arizona, Colorado, and Canada. In areas where school boards refused to grant released time or credit for seminary classes, classes were held in the early mornings before the start of the school day.

On a college level, an institute of religion was instituted at Moscow, Idaho, adjacent to the University of Idaho in 1926. The program, which provided daily religious instruction to students attending non-Church colleges, soon spread to other college campuses in Utah, Idaho, Wyoming, and California. A few universities accepted on transfer credits earned in Bible history and literature, but not credits earned in Church history or doctrine.

To provide both religious and secular instruction, schools conducted by missionaries had been established at various times on some of the islands of the Pacific, supervised by mission presidents. To provide for more centralized control, the Pacific Board of Education was organized in 1957, and missionary teachers were replaced by professional teachers. The last mission school was closed in 1963, after some sixty or so years of operation.

Expanding the Seminary Programs Worldwide

During the presidency of David O. McKay, the seminaries and institutes of religion became of vital importance in the Church's educational program. In 1951 Ernest L. Wilkinson was named to the position of president of Brigham Young University. Two years later, all Church schools except those in the Pacific were placed under President Wilkinson as administrator (later changed to chancellor) of the Unified Church Schools. William E. Berrett was appointed vice-president of BYU and vice-administrator of Church Schools, with responsibility for directing all weekday religious education, especially the seminary and institute programs.

The Church Schools' goals were, first to obtain from local school boards released time wherever possible for religious education on the high school level, and second, where released time could not be obtained, to organize early-morning seminary classes. During part of each summer Elder Berrett visited stake presidencies and bishops throughout the United States and Canada to obtain their consent and cooperation in starting early-morning seminaries until all established stakes were covered.

One of the major accomplishments was establishment of religious instruction among Indian students. The seminary program for the Lamanites had its beginning at the Intermountain Indian School in Brigham City, Utah. When the school opened in November 1949, six hundred Navajo students were enrolled, of whom six were Latter-day Saints. The numbers were small but their needs were great. Elder Spencer W. Kimball of the Council of the Twelve had a special assignment to foster Church programs among the Indians, and at his direction, J. Edwin Baird, a counselor in the Box Elder Stake presidency, and Boyd K. Packer, then a member of the North Box Elder Stake high council, were assigned to start a religious program for the LDS students at the school. A site was purchased, and a combined chapel and seminary building was erected in 1954. (Until that time, the students met in nearby homes.) The numbers of LDS students enrolled in the seminary program steadily increased, and some other students were converted to the Church as a result of the program.

During the fall of 1957, Boyd K. Packer and A. Theodore Tuttle, who were serving as general supervisors of seminaries and institutes of religion, surveyed Indian students in reservation schools in the United States and Canada. Their report to the administrator of the Unified Church School System recommended that:

1. Mission boards of education be organized where large numbers of Indian students were located.

2. An Institute of American Indian Study be organized at BYU.

3. The Department of Seminaries and Institutes of Religion be assigned to develop a curriculum and activity programs for use at federal Indian schools.

The survey disclosed that 632 Latter-day Saints were enrolled in off-reservation schools; 69 were attending six peripheral dormitories; 654 were attending reservation boarding schools; and 177 were enrolled at reservation day schools. The Church Board of Education approved the recommendations in September 1958, and Elder Berrett was assigned to develop the program, assisted by Elder Tuttle, by then a member of the First Council of the Seventy, and Elder Packer. They met several times with members of the Branch of Indian Education in the U.S. Bureau of Indian Affairs and obtained permission to establish buildings on Indian reservations for the purpose of religious instruction. J. Edwin Baird was appointed as the first coordinator of Indian seminaries in the LDS Department of Education. By 1961, Indian seminary enrollment had reached 3,528 students in 204 seminary classes in 85 federally operated schools in ten states and in two Canadian provinces. By 1970 enrollment had increased to 14,259 students in twenty-one states and Canada. The program had 49 full-time coordinators, 21 part-time coordinators, 113 part-time professional teachers, 110 voluntary teachers, and 398 missionary teachers.

In 1963 the First Presidency asked William E. Berrett to investigate the possibility of early-morning seminaries in England and Europe. After a survey was made of these areas, Elder Berrett reported that conditions were unfavorable for such a program at that time. In 1967 the Church Board of Education gave permission for a form of home-study seminary in parts of Iowa, Illinois, and Indiana. When the program proved successful, authorization was given for its expansion. Soon seminaries were started in England, Germany, New Zealand, and Australia, and supervisors had been appointed to begin seminaries and institutes of religion in Guatemala, Brazil, and Argentina. As a result of the experience in those areas, the Church Board of Education authorized the establishment of the programs worldwide wherever the Church was established.

With the three forms of seminaries—released-time or early-morning, Indian, and home-study—students of high-school ages could now be reached in every Latter-day Saint home.

The Institutes of Religion

Under the Unified School System, the program of establishing institutes of religion began a remarkable expansion. Existing institute buildings were enlarged or replaced with new buildings to accommodate rapidly increasing enrollments at colleges and universities in the United States and Canada where one hundred or more Latter-day Saint students were enrolled. A survey revealed that on the faculty of almost every college and university in the United States, a competent and faithful Latter-day Saint professor could be found who would be willing to gather the LDS students together in some available facility to discuss the gospel of Jesus Christ. Some of the teachers gave voluntary service while others received a small salary.

As early as 1960 the Church Board of Education had determined that it was impossible to establish Church universities and junior colleges throughout the many states and nations to which the Church was expanding, but that the seminary and institute programs could be so expanded within the financial ability of the Church. As expressed by Commissioner of Church Schools Neal A. Maxwell, when he took office in 1970: "The current international activity [of seminaries and institutes of religion] comes in the wake of an announcement by the Church Board of Education in November, 1970, which stated that the program of seminaries and institutes of religion should follow the growth and needs of the

Brigham Young University at Provo, Utah

membership of the Church throughout the world as quickly as feasible."[1]

By November 1970, the seminary and institute programs had been extended into all states of the United States, to several provinces of Canada, to England and Germany in Europe, to Guatemala in Central America, to Argentina and Brazil in South America, to New Zealand, and to Australia. The program was beginning to follow the Church into the world.

The Growth of Church Colleges

The Unified Church School System under administrator Ernest L. Wilkinson showed remarkable growth in many areas. One of them was in higher education, with Brigham Young University expanding and becoming the largest church-related university in America. The faculty was strengthened by men and women who had achieved success in their fields of expertise and who were firmly committed to Church doctrines and policies. The institution became unique as a university, teaching secular disciplines while adhering to and teaching the religious principles and doctrines of

Jesus Christ. It won the respect of the world, and its graduates were eagerly sought by the business and professional world.

The decades of the 1950s and '60s under President Wilkinson's direction saw the building of a new campus with excellent buildings and facilities. Dr. Wilkinson was followed by Dallin H. Oaks and then Jeffrey Holland, both of whom were equally committed to excellence in facilities as well as teaching. Limited by the Church Board of Education to a full-time enrollment of 25,000, the university admitted students of exceptional talent and the faculty was able to tighten study requirements.

Under the direction of Dr. Harvey L. Taylor, who succeeded Dr. Wilkinson as administrator of all Church schools except BYU, institutions that had been established in the Pacific to teach both secular and religious subjects were reorganized and strengthened with professional teachers and principals. These consisted of two colleges, the Church College of Hawaii, which would later become a branch of BYU, and the Church College of New Zealand, as well as high schools in American Samoa and Western Samoa, and elementary schools in American Samoa, Western Samoa, Tonga, Tahiti, and Fiji.

Ricks College at Rexburg, Idaho, continued to grow, eventually becoming a leader among junior colleges in America. With an enrollment ceiling of 7,500 students, the college now serves students not only from Idaho but from a wide area of states and nations as well. Many go on to pursue their education at four-year colleges and universities.

Church Schools in Mexico and South America

During Harvey Taylor's administration with Church Schools, elementary schools were established in Mexico for some 6,000 Latter-day Saint students who were being deprived of any educational opportunities. The largest school was built at Benemerito on the outskirts of Mexico City. This complex included a primary school, six secondary-school classroom buildings, student resident cottages, vocational shops, and other facilities, with a total enrollment of some 2,000 students.

In Chile, four elementary schools and one high school were established, with both secular and religious subjects taught. An elementary school was also established for Latter-day Saint Indian children in La Paz, Bolivia.

In 1971, the Church reorganized the educational system and united all Church schools under a commissioner, Neal A. Maxwell. A general policy to govern the future establishment of Church schools was also adopted. It included the following recommendations:

1. Religious education is to have primary emphasis in the future expansion of the Church Educational System.

2. No additional universities or colleges are presently planned and the enrollment limitation at Brigham Young University and Ricks College is 25,000 and 7,500, respectively. New elementary and secondary schools will be developed only in areas not adequately served by existing school systems.

The general policy for governing the Church Educational System rests on the assumption that non-religious education is usually provided by the state. Since members contribute taxes to support their local, state, and national governments around the world, they are entitled to and should participate fully in those systems of education. However, where other educational systems are non-existent, seriously deficient, or inaccessible to the Latter-day Saints, the Church may elect to provide basic education for its members under carefully established criteria.[2]

These policies have continued to govern the Church's educational programs under Elder Maxwell's successors, Jeffrey R. Holland and then Henry B. Eyring. The Church continues to pursue the same goal expounded by the Prophet Joseph Smith in the early days of the Church: "Study and learn, and become acquainted with all good books, and with languages, tongues, and people." (D&C 90:15.)

34

To Strengthen the Saints

To his chief apostle, Peter, Jesus Christ gave the command, "When thou art converted, strengthen thy brethren." (Luke 22:32.) The Lord gave similar instructions in 1835 through the Prophet Joseph Smith: "Strengthen your brethren in all your conversations, in all your prayers, in all your exhortations, and in all your doings." (D&C 108:7.)

Thus, the Church has as its primary responsibility the strengthening of its members. Those who have been converted by the Spirit and who have been baptized may succumb to the forces of evil and error in the world unless they continue to study the word of God and remain in close association with family members and their brothers and sisters in the gospel. The first duty of the priesthood is to strengthen the members, and upon the success of this duty depends the success of two other major objectives: to carry the gospel to all peoples and to save our dead. Through the years the Church has adopted programs designed to instruct the Saints in the principles of the gospel and encourage them to live these principles. The programs have undergone changes to meet changing times, but the underlying purposes remain the same: to strengthen the members.

Correlating the Church Programs

One of the key efforts of the Church to help strengthen the basic unit, the family, has been to correlate various priesthood and auxiliary programs. At general conference in April 1906, President Joseph F. Smith stated:

> We expect to see the day, if we live long enough (and if some of us do not live long enough to see it, there are others who will), when every council of the Priesthood in the Church of Jesus Christ of Latter-day Saints will understand its duty, will assume its own responsibility, will magnify its calling, and fill its

place in the Church, to the uttermost, according to the intelligence and ability possessed by it. When that day shall come,
there will not be so much necessity for work that is now being
done by the auxiliary organizations, because it will be done by
the regular quorums of the Priesthood. The Lord designed and
comprehended it from the beginning, and He has made provision
in the Church whereby every need may be met and satisfied
through the regular organizations of the Priesthood. It has truly
been said that the Church is perfectly organized. The only trouble
is that these organizations are not fully alive to the obligations
that rest upon them. When they become thoroughly awakened to
the requirements made of them, they will fulfill their duties more
faithfully, and the work of the Lord will be all the stronger and
more powerful and influential in the world.[1]

A general Church Correlation Committee was organized in
1908 to coordinate activities and curricula of the auxiliaries and the
priesthood. In 1920 this committee was combined with an advisory
committee comprised of representatives of the general boards. The
combined committee reviewed programs, lesson manuals, and
other activities sponsored by various Church organizations and
made some recommendations concerning elimination of overlap-
ping of lesson materials as well as defined responsibilities of the
various auxiliaries. Many of the committee's recommendations
were implemented, while others were not.

Other efforts were made over the years to correlate the Church
programs, but no sweeping changes were made in either the priesthood or auxiliary responsibilities. Then, in 1960, the Melchizedek
Priesthood Committee, under the chairmanship of Elder Harold B.
Lee of the Council of the Twelve, was given the following charge
in a letter from the First Presidency:

> We of the First Presidency have over the years felt the need
> of a correlation between and among the courses of study put out
> by the General Priesthood Committee and by the responsible
> heads of other Committees of the General Authorities for the in-
> struction of the Priesthood of the Church.
>
> We have also felt the very urgent need of a correlation of
> studies among the Auxiliaries of the Church. We have noted
> what seemed to be a tendency toward a fundamental, guiding

concept, particularly among certain of the Auxiliary organizations, that there must be every year a new course of study for each
of the Auxiliary organizations so moving. We questioned
whether the composite of all of them might not tend away from
the development of a given line of study or activity having the ultimate and desired objective of building up a knowledge of the
gospel, a power to promulgate the same, a promotion of the
growth, faith, and stronger testimony of the principles of the
Gospel among the members of the Church. . . .

We would therefore commend to you Brethren of the General Priesthood Committee the beginning of an exhaustive,
prayerful study and consideration of this entire subject.[2]

The letter was signed by David O. McKay, J. Reuben Clark, Jr.,
and Henry D. Moyle, members of the First Presidency.

Antone K. Romney, dean of the College of Education at
Brigham Young University, headed a committee to review all that
had previously been done to correlate the Church's programs. The
Correlation Executive Committee was to include seven members
of the Council of the Twelve and the three members of the Presiding Bishopric. Three correlation committees were set up, one
each for the children, youth, and adult areas, with a member of the
Twelve presiding over each. Their goal was to consolidate and
simplify all Church programs. Managing directors were also appointed for four phases of priesthood activity: home teaching, missionary, welfare, and genealogy. These directors were three Assistants to the Twelve and one of the presidents of the First Council of
the Seventy, with a member of the executive committee assigned
to serve as chairman of each group. Professionally trained men
were called to be general secretaries. Elder Lee continued to direct
the program until he became President of the Church in July 1972.

Gradually the correlation program brought about changes
that accomplished its purposes. Home teaching and family home
evening programs were coordinated with the programs of the
priesthood and auxiliaries. A unified magazine, which drew material from the various English-language magazines of the Church,
was established in 1967 for publication and distribution in non-
English-speaking areas. Separate magazines for the auxiliaries
were discontinued in 1970, and on January 1, 1971, three new

magazines appeared: the *Friend* for children; the *New Era* for youth; and the *Ensign* for adults.

In 1972 effective steps toward correlation of curriculum were taken with the organization of a department of instructional materials, which was to coordinate all manuals and instructional items for the auxiliaries and priesthood committees. By 1972, the writing of manuals had been completely removed from the auxiliaries.

Home Teaching

Some of the most important changes in correlating the Church programs were made with regard to home teaching. One of the major responsibilities of the priesthood was given by the Lord in section 20 of the Doctrine and Covenants: "The teacher's duty is to watch over the church always, and be with and strengthen them; and see that there is no iniquity in the church, neither hardness with each other, neither lying, backbiting, nor evil speaking. And see that the church meet together often, and also see that all the members do their duty." (D&C 20:53-55.)

For many years representatives of the ward or branch, called "ward teachers," visited assigned families each month to present a message. Under correlation, the name of this function was changed to "home teaching," with priesthood representatives assigned to help parents in their efforts to teach their families. President Marion G. Romney of the First Presidency has explained:

> Home teaching, properly functioning, brings to the home of each member two priesthood bearers divinely commissioned and authoritatively called into the service by their priesthood leader and bishop. These home teachers—priesthood bearers—carry the heavy and glorious responsibility of representing the Lord Jesus Christ in looking after the welfare of each member and of encouraging and inspiring every member to discharge his duty, both family and church.
>
> Among the specific responsibilities of home teachers, the following may be listed:
>
> First and foremost, to so live that they always enjoy the companionship of the Holy Ghost and act under his inspiration in the discharge of their home teaching responsibilities.

Second, to encourage and inspire every member to do his or her part to make and keep the home a truly Latter-day Saint home.[3]

Under the new program, priesthood quorums rather than the bishop became responsible for supervising home teaching. Home teachers were to become personally acquainted with all family members assigned to them and make visits whenever necessary to contribute to the families' spiritual welfare and Church activity. Monthly lessons were no longer to be given, and the home teachers were to be more responsible for taking their own initiative in determining what was best for each individual family. Later it was suggested that the message of the First Presidency in the *Ensign* each month might be used effectively as the home teachers called on their assigned families. Home teachers were also counseled to make visits as necessary to help each family to full activity. The head of each family was to be honored and consulted as to any message to be given and the needs of his family.

Family Home Evening

Under Church correlation, renewed emphasis was given to family home evening. The concept was not new, for in November 1831 the Lord had commanded: "Inasmuch as parents have children in Zion, or in any of her stakes which are organized, that teach them not to understand the doctrine of repentance, faith in Christ the Son of the living God, and of baptism and the gift of the Holy Ghost by the laying on of the hands, when eight years old, the sin be upon the heads of the parents. . . . And they shall also teach their children to pray, and to walk uprightly before the Lord." (D&C 68:25, 28.)

In the early days of the Church, families met together often, with few outside influences or activities to draw them away. But by the twentieth century, many forces were competing for attention, and changing social conditions found families too often divided by occupation, school, and church activities, until most rarely met as a family for discussion, counsel, and instruction. The concept of a regular family home evening was introduced by the First Presidency in a letter to the Saints in 1915: "We advise and urge the inauguration of a 'Home Evening' throughout the Church, at which time fathers and mothers may gather their boys and girls about them in the home and teach them the word of the Lord. . . . If the Saints obey this counsel, we promise that great blessings will result. Love at home and obedience to parents will increase. Faith will be developed in the hearts of the youth of Israel, and they will gain power to combat the evil influences and temptations which beset them."[4]

In January 1965, a formal family home evening program was introduced by the First Presidency. Elder Harold B. Lee noted in an address to the priesthood two years later, "Family home evening manuals with lessons for each week have been prepared and placed in the hands of every parent throughout the Church. Each year's theme of the home evening lessons has been correlated with the Melchizedek Priesthood and the Relief Society lessons, and the Sunday School general board has instituted a special class each week for parents to aid in their weekly family home evening and to help the parents to be better teachers of their children."[5]

Monday evening was the evening designated for families, with no Church-sponsored activities to be scheduled that would conflict with family activities. Family home evening manuals were distributed to Latter-day Saint homes where English was spoken, and eventually the manuals were translated into many other languages until the program was in operation worldwide. The lessons provided for flexibility, with suggestions given for teaching little children and youth, as well as ways to adapt the material for older persons. The success of the program was quickly evident, and many other churches and family-oriented organizations have expressed interest in the concept.

Social Services

To help the Saints meet some of the social problems that face them in living "in the world, but not of the world," LDS Social Services have been established. In the early days of the Restoration, most Latter-day Saints lived in rural settlements where everyone knew his neighbor, and people looked out for one another. Elderly relatives often lived with their younger family members, with ex-

tended family members in close proximity. There were fewer social problems, and the entire community could sometimes be
called upon to help with wayward or errant persons and those
who had special needs, such as the physically and mentally handicapped.

Life in the twentieth century is much more complex. Families
are often separated by long distances; people change residences
more frequently; and outside influences, such as modern media
and entertainment, have invaded the home and to a great extent
changed family life. Thus, the Church has adapted its programs
and adopted new programs to help families and individuals cope
with their problems.

Through priesthood channels, LDS Social Services offers assistance and counseling to alcoholics, drug abusers, homosexuals,
unwed mothers and fathers, and those who are in trouble with the
law. There are family counseling specialists, adoption agencies,
foster-child care facilities, day camps for children with special
problems, and programs for Indian students. Persons with mental
and physical disabilities can find special programs designed to help
meet their needs. "Family members should make every effort to
care for an individual with special needs within the family environ-
ment," the *Welfare Services Handbook* recommends, adding that
"after the individual and family have done all they can, the Church
stands ready to help."

Each ward has a welfare services committee that meets regularly to consider the needs of ward members. Under the direction
of the bishop, the committee looks for resources. Resource
"teams" composed of qualified ward and stake members may be
tapped. These include persons who have professional backgrounds
in such fields as medicine, nursing, law, accounting, banking,
and finance. If quorum and ward resources are insufficient, state,
regional, and even general Church or community resources may be
used.

The Church's concern for the individual may be summarized in
the commandment given through the Prophet Joseph Smith: "Remember in all things the poor and the needy, the sick and the af-

flicted, for he that doeth not these things, the same is not my disciple." (D&C 52:40.)

The gospel of Jesus Christ is a gospel of love, and needed help is to be given with love, to soften burdens, and to promote unity and happiness.

35

God Prepares the Way

"I will go and do the things which the Lord hath commanded, for I know that the Lord giveth no commandments unto the children of men, save he shall prepare a way for them that they may accomplish the thing which he commandeth them." (1 Nephi 3:7.)

God commanded the apostles at Jerusalem to carry the gospel to every nation and people. Likewise, to the apostles of this dispensation of the fulness of times, he has commanded that they carry the gospel to all nations. The Church has never deviated from this objective even though critics have pointed out that for every new member of the Church, thousands more people have been born into the world. In addition, many of the nations of the world have been closed to the preaching of the gospel, and among those nations open to missionaries, a very minimal number of persons have actually come in contact with The Church of Jesus Christ of Latter-day Saints. But despite the seeming odds, the Latter-day Saints have become even more certain that the Lord will prepare the way and that the commandment to carry the gospel to every nation will be fulfilled in the Lord's own time. And there is growing justification for this belief.

In 1930 the Lord declared that he would shorten the time—and this has been done. In the days of Joseph Smith it took a man on a good horse some eight days to travel from Boston to Washington, D.C. It generally took six weeks by ship to journey from Liverpool, England, to New Orleans. From the time that Robert Fulton plied the Hudson River with the first steamboat and John Watts invented the first steam engine, a marvelous work began among the children of men. Now we measure in hours the distance between continents. When the Saints first traversed the vast plains from the Mississippi to the Rocky Mountains, it took weeks and even months to carry letters from one point in that trail to its beginning or end. The telegraph quickly shortened the time, and that was just the beginning. The amazing thing is that this spectacular shortening of the days occurred in a time that roughly paralleled the work of the Lord in again establishing his church among men. It is not surprising that the latter-day prophets link the one series of events to the other, that God is moving in the minds of men in the scientific world as he has moved the minds of men in spiritual realms.

In 1962 the Mormon Tabernacle Choir took part in a program at Mount Rushmore, South Dakota, during which both the words and music and the visual image were broadcast to a satellite 18,300 miles above the earth and relayed by television in the satellite to Europe. That event was the forerunner in a revolution that signaled the beginning of the end of barriers between nations. By 1984 a single satellite could relay 33,000 telephone conversations and two television programs between the United States and Europe at the same time. And scientists tell us that the time is near when every person can carry a small instrument in his pocket that would enable him, almost at will, to communicate with another person who is similarly equipped anywhere in the world.

What seemed impossible a century ago has now become commonplace. To carry the gospel to all men suddenly is within the realm of possibility. To preach the gospel from the air has become a reality.

The new program of the Church to carry the gospel to all peoples in their own tongues would not have been possible had God not prepared the way. But it has become feasible through developments in rapid travel and communication, enabling Church officials to keep in constant and immediate contact with all areas of the world.

Reaching the Greater Audience

By the beginning of the twentieth century, it was becoming apparent that the general conferences held in the Salt Lake Tabernacle were reaching only a small percentage of the Latter-day Saints. Even the additional use of adjacent buildings provided but a temporary answer, for only a small percentage of officials from wards and stakes and just a handful of the general membership could be accommodated.

For a brief time the building of a larger tabernacle to hold some fifty thousand members was contemplated. But the Church found an answer to prayer that brought about the cancellation of all such plans. There was a better alternative. God had opened the door to methods of carrying the Church to the members wherever they might live in the world.

Radio was first used by some Latter-day Saints in the 1920s. In March 1922 a demonstration showed that radio transmission from Salt Lake City could reach a listening audience in a thousand-mile radius. The Church purchased a station that year, and in 1924 general conferences were first broadcast. In 1925 the Tabernacle Choir commenced broadcasting religious programs, and in 1929 such broadcasts became a permanent weekly feature on radio. This was the beginning of the use of technical devices to carry the message of the Church to the world.

By the 1970s the Church owned several radio and television stations in various parts of the world, which were administered by Bonneville International, a holding company for Church broadcasting facilities. With these stations plus voluntary services of thousands of private radio and television stations, general conference speakers found themselves addressing millions of unseen listeners and viewers.

In October 1981 the Church established satellite receiving disks at five hundred stake centers throughout the United States, a program that is planned to reach, in time, similar listening centers throughout the world. This enables the General Authorities to be both seen and heard by vast audiences.

New Administrative Offices

From the time the Church was organized in this dispensation and the priesthood bestowed upon leaders, the organization under that priesthood authority has been expanded and changed as needed. By the time of the Prophet Joseph Smith's death, the organization had reached a stage that was to prove adequate for a hundred years. Joseph Smith at one time added two additional counselors to the First Presidency of three, and Brigham Young, David O. McKay, and Spencer W. Kimball also added counselors when the press of duties proved heavy. Otherwise, the offices of First Presidency, Council of the Twelve, and Patriarch to the Church continued without change. The First Council of the Seventy directed the various quorums of seventy, which were organized on a multistake, and later on a stake, basis. Members of the Twelve, who had spent considerable time in leading colonization, were replaced as leaders of the various settlements by stake presidents so that the apostles were now available for regular counsel with the First Presidency and for the other duties to which the Lord had called them.

On April 6, 1941, President Heber J. Grant announced that a new office of "Assistant to the Twelve" had been established. Five men were initially called to that position and given authority to carry out any assignments as made by the Twelve. President Grant also gave special authority, when needed, for a member of the First Council of the Seventy to be sent by the Twelve to organize a new stake or reorganize an existing one. This was a temporary authority only for a specific duty.

With the rapid growth of the Church during the administration of President David O. McKay, and especially following the decision to organize stakes and wards throughout the world, the need for additional officers with authority to organize stakes and set the Church in order became apparent. President McKay strengthened the General Authorities by calling additional Assistants to the Twelve. He also increased the authority of members of the First Council of the Seventy. When a new member was called to fill a vacancy in that quorum, the new member was first ordained to the office of seventy and then to the office of high priest. In time all members of the quorum were so ordained.

On September 29, 1967, the First Presidency announced the establishment of a new priesthood calling, Regional Representative of the Twelve. Sixty-nine high priests were initially called to that position; the number was later increased as needed. The appointments were for a brief period of years. Stakes were formed into regions, usually with three to five stakes in each. One of the primary responsibilities of the Regional Representatives was to provide leadership training and correlation between the stakes and to act as a liaison between the stake presidents and the General Authorities. These responsibilities have increased as needed.

On October 3, 1975, President Spencer W. Kimball announced that the First Quorum of the Seventy was to be fully organized, with an eventual membership of seventy members. On October 1, 1976, Assistants to the Twelve were released from that calling and were ordained as members of the First Quorum of the Seventy. From time to time additional members are added to the quorum. A policy was also begun to retire members of the Seventy as well as some who had been Assistants to the Twelve from active duty when they reached an advanced age or were incapacitated by ill health. Those thus retired were given the title Emeritus.

At general conference in April 1984, the First Presidency announced that new members called to the First Quorum of the Seventy would hold office only for a certain period of years, as needed, and would then be replaced by others. Existing high priests in the Church could now be called directly and ordained seventies. This change greatly enlarged the number of General Authorities and also brought into Church government men already trained in leadership and proven in faith.

In June 1984 the First Presidency announced a change in the administration of thirteen geographical areas, with the new assignments to be effective July 1, 1984. Members of the First Quorum of the Seventy were assigned to serve as members of area presidencies, with each area presidency consisting of a president and two counselors, all members of the First Quorum of the Seventy. They were made accountable to the First Presidency and Council of the Twelve for building up the Church and regulating its affairs in their respective areas. The new organization provided for periodic rotation of assignments. During the initial evaluation period, presidencies residing overseas were given the responsibility for not only the ecclesiastical work of the Church, but also temporal affairs. These include the functions of the Church Educational System, the Pre-

*Spencer W. Kimball,
twelfth president of
the Church*

siding Bishopric's international offices, printing services, physical facilities, translations, and public communications.

Revelation on the Priesthood

One of the most significant and far-reaching events for the Church in the twentieth century occurred on June 8, 1978, when President Spencer W. Kimball announced that worthy men of all races were now eligible to receive the priesthood. The First Presidency sent a letter to "all general and local priesthood officers" in which they stated:

> As we have witnessed the expansion of the work of the Lord over the earth, we have been grateful that people of many nations have responded to the message of the restored gospel, and have joined the Church in ever-increasing numbers. This, in turn, has inspired us with a desire to extend to every worthy member of the Church all of the privileges and blessings which the gospel affords.

Aware of the promises made by the prophets and presidents of the Church who have preceded us that at some time, in God's eternal plan, all of our brethren who are worthy may receive the priesthood, and witnessing the faithfulness of those from whom the priesthood has been withheld, we have pleaded long and earnestly in behalf of these, our faithful brethren, spending many hours in the Upper Room of the Temple supplicating the Lord for divine guidance.

He has heard our prayers, and by revelation has confirmed that the long-promised day has come when every faithful, worthy man in the Church may receive the holy priesthood, with power to exercise its divine authority, and enjoy with his loved ones every blessing that flows therefrom, including the blessings of the temple. Accordingly, all worthy male members of the Church may be ordained to the priesthood without regard for race or color. Priesthood leaders are instructed to follow the policy of carefully interviewing all candidates for ordination to either the Aaronic or the Melchizedek Priesthood to insure that they meet the established standards for worthiness.

We declare with soberness that the Lord has now made known his will for the blessing of all his children throughout the earth who will hearken to the voice of his authorized servants, and prepare themselves to receive every blessing of the gospel.[1]

Reaction within and without the Church was far-reaching. On September 30, 1978, members attending general conference accepted the revelation by unanimous vote as being the mind and will of the Lord.

The prophets in all ages have called upon their people to whom light and understanding has been given to repent and escape from condemnation. Through the Prophet Joseph Smith the Lord set forth the law: "Of him unto whom much is given much is required; and he who sins against the greater light shall receive the greater condemnation." (D&C 82:3.)

And again, referring to those who have entered into covenant with the Lord: "Whoso breaketh this covenant after he hath received it, and altogether turneth therefrom, shall not have forgiveness of sins in this world nor in the world to come." (D&C 84:41.)

Concerning the priesthood, the Lord said:

This greater priesthood administereth the gospel and holdeth the key of the mysteries of the kingdom, even the key of the knowledge of God.

Therefore, in the ordinances thereof, the power of godliness is manifest. And without the ordinances thereof, and the authority of the priesthood, the power of godliness is not manifest unto men in the flesh; for without this no man can see the face of God, even the Father, and live.

Now this Moses plainly taught to the children of Israel in the wilderness, and sought diligently to sanctify his people that they might behold the face of God; but they hardened their hearts and could not endure his presence; therefore, the Lord in his wrath, for his anger was kindled against them, swore that they should not enter into his rest while in the wilderness, which rest is the fulness of his glory. Therefore, he took Moses out of their midst, and the Holy Priesthood also. (D&C 84:19-25.)

In all ages and times, the Church of Jesus Christ has been open to all peoples, and those entering have been blessed. Those seeking the greater blessings need to be brought into the full program of the Church. Until that full program could be carried into all nations and until God had provided the means and organization whereby his prophets and apostles could reach and teach and unite his people, the time had not arrived for extending his priesthood to all men. When the final history of God's dealings with his children is written, it will be discerned that his love has governed all his actions in giving or withholding his power and light to men.

36

Taking the Church to the People

For a hundred years converts to the Church had anticipated leaving their homes in distant lands and gathering to Zion to be near the center of Church activity, a place of safety, a place of instruction from a prophet of God. Accordingly, no wards or stakes were established in mission areas, and the Saints were urged to immigrate to Utah. The only exception to this policy involved converts in the isles of the Pacific. For a time these converts were also expected to gather to the Church center, and a colony of Polynesians, chiefly from Hawaii, was established in Skull Valley, some fifty miles west of Salt Lake City. But these settlers from the lush green lands of the Pacific could not adjust to the desert, and in a few years most of them returned to their old homes. In 1935 the first stake of the Church outside North America was organized in Oahu, Hawaii, and the natives of the Pacific Isles were instructed to remain in their homelands.

Organizing Stakes and Wards

The fundamental organization to uphold the central Church structure is the stake with its several wards and branches. The word *stake* was taken from the simile of pegs or stakes used to uphold a tent. The Prophet Joseph Smith organized the first stake at Kirtland, Ohio, on February 17, 1834. The organization of other stakes followed as the Church moved into Missouri and Illinois until eleven stakes had been organized. All of these were dissolved as the Saints were driven to the West. In the West, stakes were organized as needed wherever the Saints settled in sufficient numbers.

During the great depression of the 1930s converts in other lands were advised to remain where they were and to build up local branches, but stakes were not organized and the complete program of the Church was not available. However, as the Church con-

Top: A typical Latter-day Saint chapel in the United States.
Bottom: Chapel in Meridan, Venezuela

tinued to grow, there came a time for change. The year 1960 might well be considered a turning point in Church history, for in that year President David O. McKay instructed the Council of the Twelve to organize stakes throughout the world. In 1960-61, fifteen stakes were organized in nations outside the United States and Canada, and during the decade of the sixties, forty-six stakes were organized in seventeen countries. In the following decade the number of such stakes doubled and redoubled as the Church reached out to some ninety nations.

With the organization of stakes and wards, the way was paved to carry the full program of the Church to the people. This included not only the needed priesthood authority and quorums, but also the auxiliary organizations and programs in full, the welfare program, and, as far as feasible, Church publications.

An Expanding Building Program

As wards and stakes have been established throughout the world, new buildings have begun to dot the landscape wherever the Church may be found in sufficient numbers. The style and size of each building is adjusted to meet local needs and climatic conditions. Many ward buildings are small but adjustable to permit expansion as needed. During the great chapel-building decade from 1970 to 1980, three buildings were completed on an average each day. By the 1980s, a slowdown in the building of chapels in some areas occurred as meeting schedules were adjusted so several wards could meet in a single chapel.

As a result of the organization of stakes and wards in many nations, local Church members have responded with increased vigor in Church attendance and proselytizing activity. Further, the Church has acquired new status in the eyes of the civil governments in the respective countries and in the local press.

In Their Own Language

During the early period when converts from the many countries were urged to immigrate to the headquarters of the Church, no great effort was made to translate Church literature and courses of study into non-English languages. Translations were chiefly limited to the Book of Mormon, a few pamphlets, and some courses of study for the auxiliary organizations.

The diverse languages spoken by Saints who had migrated to the Great Basin in the United States had always presented a problem. The scriptures and courses of study in America were available only in English. Brigham Young tried a novel experiment in a hope to unify at least the written languages. In 1853, a committee consisting of Parley P. Pratt, Heber C. Kimball, and George D. Watt

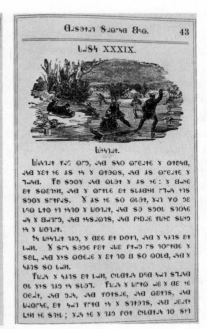

The Deseret Alphabet, developed in 1850s

was called to devise an original alphabet and spelling system that all could learn and use more quickly and conveniently. Elder Watt, an English convert, was chiefly responsible for the development of what was called the Deseret Alphabet. The commission produced its work, an alphabet of thirty-eight characters, early in 1854. In 1855 the Territorial Legislature voted a sum of $2500 for the casting of type, and attempts were made to teach the people the new alphabet. A "First Primer" and a "Second Primer" were published. A small-sized edition of the Book of Mormon was brought out in 1859. The *Deseret News* did not use the new type until 1859, when, beginning with the issue of February 9 and continuing for six months, excerpts from the Bible and Book of Mormon were published. Despite President Young's repeated insistence on the wisdom and utility of the system, it dropped out of sight during the 1860s.

As stakes and wards were organized and missions established throughout the world, there was a need to translate the scriptures and courses of study into many languages. During the period when converts to the Church were encouraged to immigrate to the United States, it was expected that all would learn English, and no other language was taught in school or church. But as Church units were established in other countries, few converts, in other than English-speaking nations, could speak or read English. The Lord had declared that the gospel should go to every people in their own language. Accordingly, in the 1960s the Church entered into an extensive program of fulfilling that commandment by setting up a translation department to provide not only the scriptures, but all manuals, courses of study, handbooks of instruction, and other Church publications in the languages of the peoples to whom the Church had gone.

A reorganization of translation efforts was effected in 1965. In 1967 translation services were combined with the Distribution Department, which supervised distribution centers in areas where there were large numbers of Latter-day Saints, such as Germany, England, Tokyo, and Mexico City. The department also began supervising the printing of most of the translated materials in local centers. In 1972 both departments were brought under the Department of Internal Communication, together with the correlation committee. The translation of scriptures, manuals, courses of instruction, and other materials became a great program, increasing as the Church extended into new lands and cultures. Experts were brought into full-time employment to facilitate and perfect the work.

New Editions of the Scriptures

In 1979 the Church published a new 2,432-page edition of the King James Version of the Bible containing many special features and a revolutionary footnote system that would enable Church members to correlate the teachings of the Bible with the other standard works. A combination Book of Mormon, Doctrine and Covenants, and Pearl of Great Price followed in 1981, with similar study aids. The new footnote system correlated the teachings of the latter-day scriptures with those of the Bible. The effects of these publications were an increased interest in the scriptures, a new proficiency in study, and a greater awareness of how each book of scripture strengthens and establishes the truth of the others.

In introducing the new edition of the Bible to the Saints at general conference on October 8, 1982, Elder Boyd K. Packer declared that the recently completed scripture project had produced "the most comprehensive compilation of scriptural information on the mission and teachings of the Lord Jesus Christ that has ever been assembled in the history of the world." He termed this work "the crowning achievement in the administration of President Spencer W. Kimball."[1]

Elder Thomas S. Monson of the Council of the Twelve, chairman of the Scripture Publication Committee, explained:

> Those who use the new Bible become its strongest advocates. . . .
>
> The widest use so far has been in the Church seminary system where the edition was made available to students at low cost. The price was made possible by the volume of new Bibles produced.
>
> As students in the seminary system become familiar with the new Bible, a whole generation will become better Bible scholars than the previous generation.
>
> In the past, people tended to be specialists in one of the standard works (Bible, Book of Mormon, Doctrine and Covenants, Pearl of Great Price) and neglected the corroborating and supporting evidences in the other standard works.
>
> The new system of footnotes and cross-references will make more well-rounded scholars on all the standard works instead of neglecting some.
>
> Teachers will find new sources that will help immeasurably in providing a broader perspective through all of the standard works. The footnote system (since included in all the standard works) gives a better, broader interpretation of particular passages.[2]

Area General Conferences

The time: August 27, 1971. The place: Manchester, England. The occasion: the first Area General Conference of the Church. At this historic meeting, President Joseph Fielding Smith, prophet of the Lord, declared:

Joseph Fielding Smith (1876–1972) Harold B. Lee (1899–1973)

It is a matter of great satisfaction to me, and I am sure to my Brethren, that the Church has now grown to the point that it seems wise and necessary to hold general conferences in various nations. And what could be more appropriate than to begin this new advancement here in the British Isles, the place from which so much of the strength of the Church came, in the early days of this dispensation. . . .

We are members of a world church, a church that has the plan of life and salvation, a church set up by the Lord himself in these last days to carry his message of salvation to all his children in all the earth.

The day is long since past when informed people think of us as a peculiar group in the tops of the Rocky Mountains in America. . . . We are coming of age as a church and as a people. We have attained the stature and strength that are enabling us to fulfill the commission given us by the Lord through the Prophet Joseph Smith that we should carry the glad tidings of the restoration to every nation and to all people.

And not only shall we preach the gospel in every nation before the second coming of the Son of Man, but we shall make converts and establish congregations of Saints among them.[3]

Another important step had been taken toward accomplishing the Lord's work. In subsequent years area conferences were held in Asia, the South Pacific, Australia, various areas of North America,

South America, South Africa, and other countries of Europe. New
Zions—new gathering places for the pure in heart—have been es-
tablished as the Church and its programs have been taken to the
people in their own cultures, lands, and languages. At the first
Mexico and Central America area conference held at Mexico City
on August 1972, Elder Bruce R. McConkie of the Council of the
Twelve explained the gathering of Israel in the contemporary
Church. He spoke of many lands of promise and inheritance:

> Any person . . . who has accepted the restored gospel, and
> who now seeks to worship the Lord, in his own tongue, and
> among his own people, and with the Saints of his own nation has
> complied with the law of gathering. . . . The place of gathering
> for the Mexican Saints is in Mexico; the place of gathering for the
> Guatemalan Saints is in Guatemala; the place of gathering for the
> Brazilian Saints is in Brazil; and so it goes throughout the length
> and breadth of the whole earth. Japan is for the Japanese; Korea
> is for the Koreans; Australia is for the Australians; every nation is
> the gathering place for its own people.[4]

At general conference in April 1973, President Harold B. Lee
expanded upon this theme, stating:

> [Zion's] boundaries are being enlarged, her stakes are being
> strengthened. In the early years of the Church specific places to
> which the Saints were to be gathered together were given, and the
> Lord directed that these gathering places should not be
> changed. . . . No longer might this church be thought of as the
> "Utah church," or as an "American church," but the membership
> of the Church is now distributed over the earth in 78 countries,
> teaching the gospel in 17 different languages at the present time.
> This greatly expanded Church population is today our most chal-
> lenging problem.[5]

Multistake Conferences

In 1984 another step was taken to bring the messages and influence of the General Authorities closer to Church members in all
lands. Because the number of stakes and missions had increased so
dramatically in recent years, it was becoming rare for a stake to
have a General Authority visitor except when the stake presidency
was to be reorganized. Even an increase in the number called to

serve in the First Quorum of the Seventy did not provide for more frequent visits. Thus, the average Church member had fewer opportunities to see and hear in person the Church leaders. When the number of stake conferences in each stake was reduced from four to two a year, the burden on the General Authorities was lessened but not solved. The responsibility for helping individual stakes fell increasingly on Regional Representatives of the Council of the Twelve.

In early 1984, the first multistake conferences were introduced. On January 15, 1984, some fifteen thousand Latter-day Saints from eight adjacent stakes met in the Tabernacle on Temple Square in Salt Lake City. The attendance represented 58 percent of the membership of those stakes. Several General Authorities addressed the Saints at the conference. Other multistake conferences followed this initial one.

The first such conference in South America was held at Lima, Peru, on March 24-25, 1984, with nearly eleven thousand Latter-day Saints from a nine-stake area in attendance. It was reported at the conference that the Church in Peru had grown from one hundred members in 1957 to more than seventy thousand in 1984, an increase of some seven thousand percent. There were now sixteen stakes in Peru.

Through such conferences, as well as increased missionary efforts and the organization of wards and stakes as needed, the Church was continuing to find ways to bring to pass the Prophet Joseph Smith's prophecy that "every man shall hear the fulness of the gospel in his own tongue, and in his own language."

The Language Training Mission

For many years newly called missionaries attended training sessions at a missionary home in Salt Lake City, where they learned discussions to be presented to contacts in the mission field as well as heard special messages from General Authorities and others. All of the instruction was in the English language, and those called to labor among non-English-speaking peoples had to master the new languages after they arrived in the mission field.

In 1961 instruction and training at Brigham Young University was begun in two languages. This was increased in 1963 with construction of a multibuilding complex that could accommodate more than three thousand persons at a time. Intensive programs were developed for almost all languages in which the gospel would be taught, and the rapidity with which missionaries acquired the ability to communicate in new languages attracted much attention from governments and others involved in language training. The availability of returned missionaries attending Brigham Young University and members of the faculty who could be drawn into teaching service became important factors in the program's success.

Eventually the mission home in Salt Lake City was closed, and all missionaries—including those who were to serve in English-speaking missions—attended the center in Provo or similar centers set up in other parts of the world. The success of this training program exceeded all expectations, as missionaries were able to begin productive proselytizing almost as soon as they reached the mission field.

The Longer Stride

Spencer W. Kimball, newly called of the Lord as President of the Church after the death of President Harold B. Lee, humbly declared on April 6, 1974, "We would not have had it thus but now the only thing for us to do is to press forward firmly." President Lee had proclaimed on more than one occasion that Spencer W. Kimball was "no ordinary man." His was a vigor born of the Spirit, a vigor that belied his age and physical condition. Tried in the fire, he had come out purified. He led the way in both word and deed when he pronounced to the Church that the time had come when "we must lengthen our stride."

"Change our sights and raise our goals" became the watchword of the Church. Within the next two years the number of full-time missionaries doubled. When the Council of the Seventy reported to President Kimball that the number had passed the 27,000 mark, the response was, "Now go and double it."

Church Office Building,
Salt Lake City

There was a feeling of urgency apparent in the Church—a feeling that God had prepared the way but that the people of the Church were not traveling the way fast enough. Stakes and wards were asked to call more missionaries. A special call was also made for older, experienced couples, who were needed to train and advise the multitude of officers and teachers being called to positions almost immediately after becoming members of the Church. To a great extent, it was young people, the majority between eighteen and thirty years of age, who were being converted. In many areas the majority of bishops were in their early twenties, while stake presidents were often in their thirties and forties. They were not called to their positions because of their knowledge of the duties and the responsibilities involved; rather, they were called because of their faith.

The great growth of the Church in the sixties is shown by a few statistics. Church membership increased by one million, going from 2,800,000 to 3,800,000. A total of 206 new stakes were organized and 2,158 chapels constructed. Membership in Latin America grew from 18,000 to 135,000.

The decade of the 1970s showed even greater growth. Church membership grew to nearly five million. Symbolic of this growth, a new 28-story office building was erected in Salt Lake City to house administrative offices for the many departments responsible for keeping track of financial and membership records and directing the work of the building program, auxiliaries, Church publications, Church Educational System, and other phases of activity. The building was dedicated in 1972, and in a matter of only a few years it was completely filled—and plans were being made to house some of the organizations in additional quarters.

During the 1970s, missions, wards, and stakes were extended into eighty-six countries. The greatest growth continued to be in Latin America and Asia. But even in the eastern United States, particularly in large cities, many new converts were swelling the rolls of Church membership. This was due in part to missionary lessons being taught in non-English languages among minority groups of Americans and immigrants. A missionary who was assigned to learn Italian, Spanish, Japanese, or even Russian in the Missionary Training Center might find himself laboring in New York City, Chicago, Miami, or Los Angeles among these minority groups.

Missionary Work Among the Indians and Polynesians

The translation and publication of the Book of Mormon by Joseph Smith led to early efforts by the Church to convert the American Indians and the Polynesians of the Pacific. This ancient record revealed that certain Israelites had migrated from Palestine to the Americas and to the islands of the sea some six hundred years before Christ. The Book of Mormon contains many promises of the Lord for these peoples, promises that will be fulfilled in the day when the Church of Jesus Christ shall be established among the Gentiles. Early attempts by the Church to teach the Indians, or Lamanites, as they are sometimes called, met with only sporadic success, due in part to language barriers, lack of sufficient numbers of missionaries, and opposition from Indian agents of the federal government.

It is estimated that there are approximately half a million Indians living on United States Indian reservations, with another third of a million in Canada. In total, however, these Indians comprise but an estimated half of one percent of the total number of Lehi's descendants. The main body of those descendants lives south of the United States border. According to one study, the total may be approximately 177 million, most of whom are Mestizo, or of mixed European and native bloodlines. Another 36 million pure-blooded Indians live in South America and 24 million in Mexico and Central America.[6]

The Polynesians in Hawaii, Tonga, Samoa, New Zealand, the Cook Islands, Tahiti, and many smaller islands are thought by some to be descendants or followers of Hagoth, a Nephite shipbuilder of 55 B.C. (See Alma 63:3-8.) Other scholars suggest a connection with other immigration from Palestine at about the time of Lehi's journey. In either case, the Polynesians are apparently of Israelite origin.

In 1925 Elder Melvin J. Ballard of the Council of the Twelve made this statement in Buenos Aires, Argentina, when he dedicated South America for the preaching of the gospel: "The work of the Lord will grow slowly for a time here, just as an oak grows from an acorn. It will not shoot up in a day as does the sunflower that grows quickly and then dies. But thousands will join the Church here. It will be divided into more than one mission and will be one of the strongest in the Church. . . . The day will come when the Lamanites in this land will be a power in the Church."[7]

In the decade of the 1970s, more than 750,000 Lamanites joined the Church. By 1980, there were more than 600,000 Church members in Latin America, a great number of whom were of some Indian blood, with more than 7,000 persons being baptized each month. Some 2,500 missionaries were serving that year in Latin countries. The growth promises to be even greater during the last two decades of the twentieth century.

President Kimball's Vision

At an area conference in Mexico on February 20, 1977, President Spencer W. Kimball spoke of the future for the Lamanites as he had envisioned it in 1946:

As I looked into the future, I saw the Lamanites from the isles of the sea and the Americas rise to a great destiny. I saw great numbers of Lamanites and Nephites in beautiful homes that have all the comforts that science can afford.

I could see you children of Lehi with your herds and flocks on a thousand hills, and instead of working for others I could see you getting the management of the positions of responsibility. I saw you the owners of many farms and ranches and homes and gardens.

In my dream I no longer saw you the servants of other people. I saw you the employers. I saw you the masters, owners of banks and businesses . . . as engineers and builders . . . in great political positions and functioning as administrators over the land . . . as doctors and lawyers. Many of your people I saw were writing books and magazine articles and continuing to have a powerful influence on the thought of the country. . . . I saw the Church growing with rapid strides and I saw them organized in wards and stakes. . . . I saw a temple and expect to see it filled with men and women and young people in the temple of God.

Now, that was my dream. Maybe it was a vision. Maybe the Lord was showing to me what this great people would accomplish.[8]

The Church in the Dominican Republic

An example of how the Church became established in one area is found in an account of John A. Davis, who served a mission with his wife, Ada, in the Dominican Republic. When they arrived on January 13, 1978, there was one small branch of twenty-four members. They later returned to preside over the mission, and when they completed that assignment in July 1983, he wrote,

we left over 6,000 members in 32 branches located in 28 major cities. Over 600 had received patriarchal blessings. We had processed over 40 local missionaries who had or were then serving in 13 other missions. . . . We had welcomed back 17 who had filled honorable, outstanding missions. Twenty-two families had received their endowments in the Atlanta Temple and 100 families were scheduled to go to the Atlanta Temple in July of that year, and a few to the Salt Lake Temple.

During our two-year mission presidency, we bought building sites and buildings and saw 12 chapels built, plus two complete buildings purchased for chapels, a gorgeous mission home, and a complete home for the mission office.

We saw the seminary program grow to be larger and stronger than anywhere else in the Caribbean. An ex-Catholic priest was fully employed by the Church Educational System to supervise the seminary and institute program, and when we left he was the first counselor in the mission presidency.[9]

Similar accounts could be cited showing like development of the Church in other countries of the world.

The Church in Africa

The first Church branch in Africa was organized in Cape Town, South Africa, on May 23, 1853. The missionaries assigned there, however, met with great opposition. Growth of the Church was so slow and discouraging that the mission was closed in 1865. A few small branches continued, but with little growth.

After the South African Mission was reopened in 1903, a number of branches were organized in various cities. In January 1954 President David O. McKay visited the mission, the first Church President to visit that land. His visit gave impetus to the missionary program there. It was not, however, until 1970 that a stake, the Transvaal Stake, was organized in South Africa. A second stake, the Sandton South Africa Stake, was formed in October 1978. The total Church membership in Africa by that time was less than 10,000.

In Nigeria, Northern Africa, a group of black Nigerians in the 1950s became acquainted with the Book of Mormon, believed in it, and sought contact with the Church. Early in 1960 President McKay appointed Elder LaMar S. Williams to head a mission to Nigeria. Two older couples were assigned to go with him. However, civil authorities in Nigeria refused to issue visas to the missionaries on the basis that the Church did not give blacks the same rights to the priesthood as extended to other people. Elder Williams did obtain a tourist visa and visited that land, but he could do nothing for the people but to counsel them to wait. It was not until the important revelation of 1978, which declared the priesthood available to all worthy men, that the way was at last opened to missionary work in Nigeria and neighboring countries.

After the revelation was announced, Rendell N. Mabey was appointed president of the Nigerian Mission. His efforts and those of Edwin Q. Cannon and A. Bruce Knudsen resulted in the establishment of many branches.

Anthony Obinna, the first president of the first native black branch in Africa, writes:

> Dear Brethren,
>
> The entire members of the Church of Jesus Christ of Latter-day Saints in this part of Nigeria have the pleasure to thank you and the Latter-day Saints throughout the world for opening the door for the Gospel to come to our people in its fullness.
>
> We are happy for the many hours in the Upper Room of the Temple you spent supplicating the Lord to bring us into the fold. We thank our Heavenly Father for hearing your prayers and ours and by revelation has confirmed the long promised day, and has granted the holy priesthood to us, with the power to exercise its divine authority and enjoy every blessings of the temple. . . .
>
> There is no doubt that the Church here will grow and become a mighty centre for the Saints and bring progress enough to the people of Nigeria as it is doing all over the world.[10]

A Commitment to the Work

The growth of the Church and the commitment of the members to carry out the commandments of Christ was set forth by President Kimball in an address at general conference on October 2, 1982. He declared:

> I am gratified with the growth of the Church around the world, for the nearly fifty new stakes which have been approved or created since we were in general conference last April, and for the groundbreakings that have occurred for the building of five more temples. They are important indicators of the growth of the kingdom. . . .
>
> The day for carrying the gospel to ever more places and people is here and now. We must come to think of our obligation to share the message rather than of our own convenience. . . .
>
> The parting words of the Master to His Apostles just before His

Ascension were, "Go ye into all the world, and preach the gospel to every creature. He that believeth and is baptized shall be saved; but he that believeth not shall be damned." (Mark 16: 15-16.) . . .

I thrill to the words of the Prophet Joseph Smith in a letter that he sent to the Church from Nauvoo on September 6, 1842: "Shall we not go on in so great a cause? Go forward. . . . Courage . . . and on, on to the victory!" (D&C 128:22.)[11]

In the decade 1973-1983, during the administration of President Kimball, remarkable growth took place. Church membership soared an estimated 64 percent, from 3,321,556 members to 5,450,000. The number of stakes jumped an estimated 133 percent, from 630 stakes to 1,465. The number of temples dedicated worldwide rose a dramatic 74 percent, from 15 operating temples to 26, with 16 additional temples in stages of planning and construction. The number of full-time missionaries surged 59 percent, from 17,258 to 27,400. The number of missions rose 62 percent, from 108 to 175, and the number of converts increased 140 percent, from 79,603 in 1973 to an estimated 191,013 in 1983.[12]

37

New Temples Are Built

In April 1981, President Spencer W. Kimball announced that nine new temples would be built: in Chicago, Illinois; Dallas, Texas; Guatemala City, Guatemala; Lima, Peru; Frankfurt, Germany; Stockholm, Sweden; Manila, Philippines; Johannesburg, South Africa; and Seoul, Korea.

This was not the first such announcement of new temples to be built or planned during President Kimball's administration. There had been earlier ones, and there were later ones. But this announcement was in a particular setting—a meeting of 250 General Authorities, Regional Representatives, and stake presidents from each temple district named. The meeting preceded the general conference sessions. It is recorded that a stake president from each of the new temple districts had an opportunity to speak. Their gratitude and testimonies were punctuated with sobs. The Korean exclaimed, *"Komansumnida, komansumnida"* (Thank you, thank you) when President Kimball's words were translated for him. "We have been praying and crying for years for a temple," was the reaction of Han In Sang, a Regional Representative from Korea.

"Going to the temple has been a great sacrifice for the members in South Africa," said Louis Hefer, Regional Representative from Johannesburg, South Africa, after hearing of the announcement. "I walked around—on cloud 25; I didn't stop at nine! We felt that we would someday have a temple, but we didn't think it would come this soon. We are grateful."

These reactions were typical of those that have followed every announcement concerning a new temple. Members of the Church throughout the world are hungry for the opportunities temples bring to them.

A Glimpse at a Dedication

On August 9, 1983, at Tonga in the South Pacific, President Gordon B. Hinckley, second counselor in the First Presidency of

Temple in Apia, Samoa, dedicated in 1983

the Church, officiated in the laying of the cornerstone of a temple on this far-distant Pacific island. The temple was now ready for dedication, and the people had gathered to witness a historic event. A temple of God, the heart and core of the Church of Jesus Christ, was to be dedicated and opened to them, that they might come forth and save their dead.

The people came from a number of islands to be there for the dedication services August 9 through 11. Many sold personal belongings in order to raise the necessary funds. Although they suffered from the cold of winter in this southern hemisphere, many stayed for days in tents. Some four hundred came from Tonga's northern island, Vava'u, traveling two days by boat. President Mosese H. Langi recalled, "Some sold their produce, pigs, and other animals for the boat fare, which is about 18 Pa'anga (about $15.40). It takes two weeks to earn that amount."

The joy expressed by the people on this historic occasion was beyond the joys the world has come to know. These humble people love one another. They have an intense love and concern for their ancestors who are dead, especially those who had no opportunity to hear about Jesus Christ. These people have embraced the gospel of Jesus Christ. They know that their ancestors have the joy of salvation only if they come unto Jesus through the door of baptism, which requires knowledge of God, repentance of their sins, and forgiveness. They know that their dead families cannot be united unless they are sealed by the power and authority of Christ. Now they can enter into a temple of God and have the necessary ordinances performed by proxy for the salvation of their loved ones who have passed into the spirit world.

The history of the Church cannot be understood apart from temples and what goes on within them. Without that knowledge, the actions of people at a newly dedicated temple are meaningless. With that knowledge, the dedication becomes an outstanding historical event.

The dedication ceremony in Tonga was but one of many similar events as the Church entered into the greatest temple-building era in the history of the world. It was an outcome of obedience to the commandments of Jesus Christ. Temple building, as we have seen, started in the earliest days of the Church. Work for the dead has been a fundamental program of the Church in every era, but until recent years, temples were available only in a few areas, and many of the Saints had to travel great distances to have the temple ordinances performed for themselves and those who had passed on.

Temples in Many Lands

Joseph Smith predicted that in time, the Church would have thousands of temples, and that the great purpose of the Saints' work during the millennium would be to save the dead and provide the justice of God for all His children from Adam to the end of time. But conditions were not ripe for expansion of temples throughout the world until the period when the Church was so organized that temples in many lands were now possible.

In April 1984, President Hinckley announced that additional temples would be built in San Diego, California; Portland, Oregon; Las Vegas, Nevada; Toronto, Canada; and Bogota, Colombia. This brought to forty-seven the number of temples operating, under construction, or in planning stages. Concerning this work, President Hinckley said that to "every faithful Latter-day Saint, a temple occupies a position of special affection and offers special blessings that can be obtained in no other place. Temples, and that which occurs within them, are the very essence of the gospel of Jesus Christ. The work that goes on in these sacred houses is, for the most part, concerned with eternity, and the things of eternity. And the great selfless labors carried on by the Saints wherever these Houses of the Lord are found represent, in my judgment, more nearly the spirit of the Son of God, who gave His life as a vicarious sacrifice for all of us, than any other work which I know.

"We are living now in a great temple-building era of the Church," he said, noting that six temples were dedicated in 1983, six were scheduled for dedication in 1984, and six more were scheduled for dedication in 1985. "This will mean that within a period of three years we will have dedicated as many temples as were built and dedicated in all the previous history of the Church.

"To carry on the great mandate given by President Spencer W. Kimball, we go forward with this work of taking the temples to the people of the Church, building smaller temples, and more of them, so that the Latter-day Saints will not have to travel so far to take advantage of the great blessings offered in these Houses of the Lord."[1]

In this temple-building era, the program of the Church is to take the Church with all of its activities to the people, with temples to be located where they will be convenient for the Saints. Many of the new temples are smaller than those built in earlier years, but they are designed for more efficient use of space to accomplish the ordinance work to take place in them.

President Hinckley expressed the importance of temples at the time of dedication of the Atlanta Temple, June 1, 1983:

> To the Latter-day Saints who will have the privilege of entering these portals this building will represent visible, tangible expression of their conviction that life is eternal, that death is not the end but only a portal through which we pass to another sphere of action. Oh that we had the power, the gift of tongues, the spirit of persuasion, to portray to those who criticize us the beauty, the peace, the spirit which comes of Christ, all of which are felt in these holy places. If we had that capacity, their unfriendly

Washington Temple in Kensington, Maryland, dedicated in 1974

tongues would stop, their vicious accusations would end, and they would long for the privilege of enjoying the blessings of this and similar holy houses.[2]

Growth in Number of Temples

More work was done on temples in the 1970s than in any previous ten-year period—construction and remodeling equaling temple work for all previous decades of the Church combined. Five older temples were extensively remodeled and rededicated, two new temples were built, and construction started on five others. The Washington Temple, with its seven floors and 294 rooms, was dedicated in 1974 after receiving international attention while it was opened to the public. The Sao Paulo Temple, the first in Latin America, was dedicated in 1978.

But the 1980s were to prove even more remarkable in temple building. Three temples were completed in 1980—in Tokyo, Japan; Seattle, Washington; and American Samoa.

In 1981, the Jordan River Temple in Salt Lake County was completed and dedicated. In 1982, the Mexico City Temple was completed and dedicated.

In an address to Regional Representatives of the Twelve on April 6, 1984, President Hinckley said:

> We are building temples on a scale never before experienced in all of the history of the Church. I know that the power of the Lord was acting upon President Kimball when he moved so affirmatively in the direction of constructing new temples. Over a period of three years we will have dedicated eighteen new Houses of the Lord. What a tremendous thing that is! These are smaller temples than were built in earlier years, but they are much more efficient in the use of space to accomplish the ordinance work that takes place therein. They are not monuments of grandeur; they are, rather, sacred houses of God in which his eternal work may be performed as efficaciously and as beneficially as that done in any temple built at any time.
>
> These sacred buildings have great capacity. More and more they are being conveniently located so that the people may use them.
>
> The duty of temple work has been laid upon this people. But it is more than a duty. It is a blessing. I am satisfied that if our people would attend the temple more, there would be less selfishness in their lives. There would be less absence of love in their relationships. There would be more fidelity on the part of husbands and wives. There would be more love and peace and happiness in the homes of our people. There would come into the minds of the Latter-day Saints an increased awareness of their relationship to God our Eternal Father and of the need to work a little harder at the matter of living as sons and daughters of God.[3]

Developments in Genealogical Research

To further promote the unique program of the Church in doing work for the salvation of the dead, great strides were made in the 1970s and 1980s in obtaining and housing the necessary genealogical data needed for that work.

The Granite Mountain Records Vault, located at the mouth of Little Cottonwood Canyon eighteen miles southeast of Salt Lake City, and dedicated in 1966, became the repository of microfilmed genealogy records gathered from members of the Church and from the archives of city, county, and national sources throughout much of the world.

The Church sponsored the first World Conference on Records in 1969 in Salt Lake City. The conference attracted some ten thousand genealogists from all parts of the world. A second such conference was held in Salt Lake City August 12-15, 1980, and was attended by more than eleven thousand genealogists from 32 nations.

Lord Teviot, a member of the House of Lords in England, praised Latter-day Saints for their interest in preserving records long before most of his countrymen cared that much about the subject. "Mormons are more concerned with British records than the British generally are," he said. "This interest has been helpful for British, as well as American, researchers."[4]

The Spirit of Family Research

While nothing so arouses the spirit of doing research for one's ancestors as actually doing work for the dead in the temple, some important steps have been taken to awaken the spirit of research. In the building of each temple, Latter-day Saints in the designated temple area are invited to volunteer freely of their time and money. The result, in every instance, is a flurry of interest in genealogical research and in temple attendance.

In the late 1970s and continuing into the 1980s, members of the Church participated in a four-generation program in which they were to submit records of the past four generations of their families. These records then became part of the Church's genealogical repository. The purpose of the program was twofold: to add to the Church records the names of family ancestors and to stir an interest among the members in genealogical work and salvation for the dead. The Genealogical Department also began setting up in many stakes microfilm machines on which specially called individuals could search through the records of various nations. Elder J. Thomas Fyans of the First Quorum of the Seventy explained these new approaches to genealogical research:

> A number of years ago, if you wanted to do genealogical research, it was necessary to travel to the locality where you thought the records of your ancestors would be and receive per-

mission from the vicar, priest, or custodian of the records to
search them in pursuit of your ancestry.

The Church recognized the tremendous burden to Church
members of the cost in time and money of international travel,
and it was determined that the Genealogical Department would
send someone to secure permission to microfilm the records and
then let the Church members use these microfilms in a setting
much more convenient to their homes. . . . The stakes will soon
be introducing a process whereby we can take all the names from
a microfilm, place them on a card, and the computers will arrange them alphabetically. This is called records extraction.
These alphabetized name lists will be like a telephone book
which can be the basis for not only temple work but also other future references.[5]

The records extraction program soon proved successful and
came to be the chief source of names for ordinance work in the
temples.

38

The Great Melting Pot

The year, 1982. The place, Wilshire Ward, Los Angeles. The occasion, a typical Sunday sacrament meeting. Arnold J. Irvine, staff writer for the *Church News,* describes what he saw—an example of the Church as the great melting pot of races and nations:

> A black sister led the singing. Presiding at the sacrament table were white and black priesthood holders. Among those passing the sacrament were an Oriental brother and a seventy converted from Judaism. Polynesians and Latin Americans were in the congregation.
>
> A black sister bore testimony to the truthfulness of the Book of Mormon, and others bore testimonies including an Oriental brother from Hawaii and several Caucasians including a blind man.
>
> The older members have, as a general rule, accepted the new people well. . . .
>
> The building, now known as the Los Angeles California Stake Center, is used for more than just meetings of the Wilshire Ward. At the same time as the Wilshire meetings, the Los Angeles 2nd Branch, composed entirely of Korean members, meets in another part of the complex. Yong Il Ko presides over the approximately 100 branch members, some of whom travel 30 miles to attend meetings.
>
> As Wilshire Ward members leave the building, members of the Spanish-speaking Los Angeles 3rd Ward arrive. They are presided over by a native of Peru, Bishop Rafael N. Seminario. His membership clerk is his father, Victor A. Seminario, and the bishop's mother, Betty, is Primary president. . . .
>
> As the Spanish language services got underway another service began in the baptistry where the Los Angeles 5th Branch was holding a baptism for two young Chinese converts.[1]

This is but one example of how the Church, in one of the older wards of the Church in the Pacific Coast area, is promoting the brotherhood of all the children of God.

In thousands of wards throughout the world, this panorama of nationalities worshiping together may be observed. The Church of Jesus Christ of Latter-day Saints has become the great melting pot. Black and white, bond and free, rich and poor, the business executive and the day laborer, the college professor and the underprivileged—all are joined together in a common brotherhood in the kingdom of God on earth.

In the Church schools, the same mingling of nationalities and cultures may be observed. The seminaries especially produce a great mingling together of many nationalities five days a week. Hundreds of thousands train to be leaders in the Church, becoming immersed in a love of the gospel of Jesus Christ—and ready upon graduation to go forth as missionaries to any part of God's vineyard. In the institutes of religion, Latter-day Saints attending colleges throughout the world meet together each day to study the gospel. They are of all races, but they are becoming one.

A Melting Pot in the South Pacific

Responding recently to questions in an interview regarding the mixture of races and cultures at the BYU–Hawaii campus, President Jeffrey Holland praised the unity of students and faculty at the school:

> We believe that all education should strengthen desirable character traits and should also strengthen a conviction of spiritual principles and practices. We also want to provide an intercultural experience, to help students gain a knowledge of their own and others' cultures. . . . We enroll 20 percent of our students from the South Pacific area—New Zealand, Tahiti, Samoa, Tonga, Fiji, and other island areas. Another 20 percent of our students come from Asian rim countries, including Singapore, the Philippines, Hong Kong, Taiwan, Japan, Korea and the People's Republic of China. Thirty-five percent of our student body comes from Hawaii, and the rest from the U.S. mainland, Canada, South and Central America and Europe.

In response to a question on dress standards, President Holland replied:

> Although the standards are the same on both campuses [BYU at Provo and BYU–Hawaii], the multicultural nature at

Young Latter-day Saints in the South Pacific

BYU–Hawaii presents many different challenges. At either BYU or BYU–Hawaii, for example, one may see a young man and a young woman walking hand in hand, one of them wearing blue jeans and the other wearing a skirt. However, at BYU–Hawaii, it may be the young woman wearing the blue jeans and the young man wearing a lava-lava, which is essentially a skirt.[2]

The same mingling of nationalities may be observed in all Church schools, not just in classwork, which would be found quite common in most universities, but in worship meetings in the many Church wards that meet on campus. A camaraderie may be observed, a unique brotherhood among the various nationalities mingling in daily campus life.

Throughout the world, wherever Latter-day Saints may be found, the Church is demonstrating how the principles of the gospel, when properly observed, produce the oneness that God desires among his children. The members are putting into practice the commandment Jesus Christ gave to his disciples in the early church: "A new commandment I give unto you, That ye love one another; as I have loved you, that ye also love one another. By this shall all men know that ye are my disciples, if ye have love one to another." (John 13:34-35.)

All Are Alike Before the Lord

Diversity of race has always been a problem in society. It has produced social classes with barriers between races and nations that have prevented the establishment of real brotherhood. In India, diversity of racial origins has resulted in a caste system, which well-meaning national leaders have tried to eliminate but without any marked success. In Africa, tribal differences have produced a perpetual state of discontent and political unrest that has left African nations constantly on the verge of revolution. In South Africa, apartheid has prevented unity in social activities and in work, church, and government. None of the long-established churches has been able to break down the social barriers.

As The Church of Jesus Christ of Latter-day Saints finds converts in such societies, it faces this age-old problem of differences in race and culture. Can the Church produce the needed brotherhood that can bring unity and peace among such divergent peoples? Will the Church become the great melting pot that unites all mankind?

The Church has distinct advantages over all other organizations that have attempted to do so. First, members have the knowledge that all the inhabitants of the earth are literally God's children, and as such, they are entitled to his love and the joy that comes from obedience to his laws. God has given his prophets an understanding of his plans for his children and the commandments to carry them out. This entails teaching all people the principles of the gospel and the ordinances necessary for their entrance into a kingdom of brotherhood. "He denieth none that come unto him, black and white, bond and free, male and female; and he remembereth the heathen; and all are alike unto God, both Jew and Gentile." (2 Nephi 26:33.)

Second, the Church makes no distinction between races and nations. All the offices in the Church are open to all, as God might direct. There is no priestly class. All worthy males may hold the priesthood. All females may hold membership and office in the Relief Society. Male and female are equal in the sight of God. They have equal voice in sustaining or refusing to sustain appointed officers. Men and women rise together to their exaltation, for "neither is the man without the woman, neither the woman without the man, in the Lord," said the apostle Paul. (1 Corinthians 11:11.)

Third, there is no distinction in dress worn by members of the Church. There are no robes or vestments designating class or office. There are no priestly classes, no monasteries or nunneries. There are no salaries that go with office to which men or women might aspire. All are alike before the Lord. Those whose offices require their full time, such as General Authorities, are sustained with their families out of the income of the Church to the extent of their normal needs. All others, such as ward and stake officers, serve on a voluntary basis without salary, sustaining themselves and their families with the labor of their own hands. Hence, jealousy and envy of position does not occur to divide God's people. Further, there is work for all. There is a multitude of services to be rendered, and nearly all become involved. And all can be involved if they so desire.

Equality in the Priesthood of God

God has always loved his children. Any other postulate is unacceptable. Because of his love, his judgment of his children is based on the individual's opportunities, knowledge, and understanding as well as the deeds done on earth. Those without the law are judged without the law. Those who know the law are held accountable for that knowledge. Hence, Christ said to the Pharisees: "If ye were blind, ye should have no sin: but now ye say, We see; therefore your sin remaineth." (John 9:41.) At another time he said concerning the Jewish leaders: "If I had not come and spoken unto them, they had not had sin: but now they have no cloke for their sin. . . . If I had not done among them the works which none other man did, they had not had sin: but now have they both seen and hated both me and my Father." (John 15:22, 24.) Because they knew the laws of God, they were held accountable for the crucifixion of their Lord. But the Roman soldiers who nailed the Christ to the cross did not know that they were crucifying the Son of God; hence, Christ could pray, "Father, forgive them; for they know not what they do." (Luke 23:34.) The Jewish leaders were not so forgiven.

Latter-day Saint family in South America

This law of accountability for one's actions must be understood if the history of the Church of Jesus Christ is to be understood. In God's dealings with his children from the time of Adam, those who have received the knowledge and the power of the priesthood have been required to observe strictly the covenants entered into, or to suffer dire consequences for failure to do so. "Of him unto whom much is given much is required," the Lord has declared. (D&C 82:3.) Out of love for his children, he has withheld the power of God (his priesthood) from the greater number of his children because they were not prepared to receive it; in other words, they were not able to meet the requirements, and if allowed to enter into covenants with God, they would have fallen under condemnation. He would have given the Holy Melchizedek Priesthood to the children of Israel who were led by Moses into the wilderness, but they were not ready; thus, out of love for them, that they might not come under condemnation for their failure to live the requirements, the Lord withdrew the higher priesthood from them.

The priesthood had been promised to the righteous descendants of Abraham, and the Jewish priests and scribes proclaimed superiority by virtue of being children of Abraham, but Jesus said unto them: "Think not to say within yourselves, We have Abraham to our father: for I say unto you, that God is able of these stones[3] to raise up children unto Abraham." (Matthew 3:9.) Faithful men today who are not descendants of Abraham may receive the priesthood, for God so revealed: "Whoso is faithful unto the obtaining these two priesthoods of which I have spoken, and the magnifying their calling, are sanctified by the Spirit unto the renewing of their bodies. They become the sons of Moses and of Aaron and the seed of Abraham, and the church and kingdom, and the elect of God." (D&C 84:33-34.)

Diversity Among God's Chosen Servants

As the Church has become worldwide, leaders called to preside over it have been drawn from many nations and races. The first General Authority of Japanese descent, Adney Y. Komatsu, was called as an Assistant to the Twelve in April 1975; the next year he became a member of the First Quorum of the Seventy. Two men from outside the United States were called to the First Quorum of the Seventy in 1975: Charles A. Didier, Belgium, and Jacob de Jager, the Netherlands. Also called that year was George P. Lee, a Navajo. F. Enzio Busche of Germany and Yoshihiko Kikuchi of Japan were added to the quorum in 1977; Derek A. Cuthbert of England and Ted E. Brewerton of Canada in 1978; and Angel Abrea of Argentina in 1981.

These calls have helped give the Church a cosmopolitan flavor in race, culture, and experience. They have brought to the Saints in many countries the realization that the Church is their church; it has no boundaries of race or nation. The message taught by these leaders is the same, for the gospel taught is the universal gospel of Jesus Christ.

The Indian Student Placement Program

The desire of parents to promote the welfare of their children is perhaps nowhere so apparent as in the operation of the Indian Student Placement program. In 1947 Golden Buchanan, a member of the Sevier Stake presidency in Utah, became touched by the predicament of transient Indian youths hired to work in the sugar-beet fields. He implored Elder Spencer W. Kimball of the Council of the Twelve to consider the possibility of placing these youths in Latter-day Saint homes during the school term, allowing them to attend school and live as members of the foster family. Elder Kimball became enthusiastic about the idea and obtained the sanction of the First Presidency to help develop such a program. Eventually thousands of youths from the Indian reservations were transported by the Church to foster homes in Utah, Idaho, Oregon, and other areas.

While some problems were encountered in acquainting the youths with the white culture and some opposition came from other churches and from the U.S. Bureau of Indian Affairs, the program grew, with great beneficial results to the Indian students and their families. Indian parents were so anxious for the development of their young children that they were willing to part with them for the long school year, and usually to repeat the separation for one school year after another. Indians have a deep love for their children; they are family oriented. But love for the gospel of Jesus Christ brought them to sacrifice for the welfare of their children.

The Fruits of the Tree

"Every tree is known by his own fruit. For of thorns men do not gather figs, nor of a bramble bush gather they grapes." (Luke 6:44.)

The works of The Church of Jesus Christ of Latter-day Saints are visible to the world, and the fruit thereof is good. To taste of it is to desire more, for those who do so find happiness and peace. The tree is still young and its branches have yet to reach out to all who might desire to partake of its fruits, but the tree is sturdy. Its roots are deep; it is nourished with the spirit of truth, and its destiny is great.

The story of the unfolding of the Church from its American beginnings into a world church is a great saga, presently written but piecemeal and perhaps never written in completeness, for it will never be wholly completed. Events recorded upon the pages of history never catch up with the momentum of the "stone cut without hands" as it rolls forth to crush out error and promote truth in the world.

To look into the future, we need to read again the words of Jesus Christ when he organized his church in this dispensation and gave a preview of its work and destiny:

> The voice of the Lord is unto all men, and there is none to escape; and there is no eye that shall not see, neither ear that shall not hear, neither heart that shall not be penetrated. And the rebellious shall be pierced with much sorrow; for their iniquities shall be spoken upon the housetops, and their secret acts shall be revealed. And the voice of warning shall be unto all people, by the mouths of my disciples, whom I have chosen in these last days. And they shall go forth and none shall stay them, for I the Lord have commanded them. . . .
>
> And verily I say unto you, that they who go forth, bearing these tidings unto the inhabitants of the earth, to them is power given to seal both on earth and in heaven, the unbelieving and rebellious; yea, verily, to seal them up unto the day when the wrath of God shall be poured out upon the wicked without measure— unto the day when the Lord shall come to recompense unto every man according to his work, and measure to every man according to the measure which he has measured to his fellow man. . . .
>
> And again, verily I say unto you, O inhabitants of the earth: I the Lord am willing to make these things known unto all flesh; for I am no respecter of persons, and will that all men shall know that the day speedily cometh; the hour is not yet, but is nigh at hand, when peace shall be taken from the earth, and the devil shall have power over his own dominion. And also the Lord shall have power over his saints, and shall reign in their midst, and shall come down in judgment upon Idumea, or the world. (D&C 1:2-5, 8-10, 34-36.)

This brief review of the evidences of the Church's growth and a few glimpses of its effects among the individuals and nations of the earth are necessary to an understanding of what has happened in the closing years of the twentieth century. When Joseph Smith was in jail in Liberty, Missouri, the Lord gave him—and us—a look at the Church's destiny:

> God shall give unto you knowledge by his Holy Spirit, yea, by the unspeakable gift of the Holy Ghost, that has not been revealed since the world was until now; which our forefathers have awaited with anxious expectation to be revealed in the last times,

which their minds were pointed to by the angels, as held in reserve for the fulness of their glory; a time to come in the which nothing shall be withheld, whether there be one God or many gods, they shall be manifest.

All thrones and dominions, principalities and powers, shall be revealed and set forth upon all who have endured valiantly for the gospel of Jesus Christ.

And also, if there be bounds set to the heavens or to the seas, or to the dry land, or to the sun, moon, or stars—all the times of their revolutions, all the appointed days, months, and years, and all the days of their days, months, and years, and all their glories, laws, and set times, shall be revealed in the days of the dispensation of the fulness of times—according to that which was ordained in the midst of the Council of the Eternal God of all other gods before this world was, that should be reserved unto the finishing and the end thereof, when every man shall enter into his eternal presence and into his immortal rest.

How long can rolling waters remain impure? What power shall stay the heavens? As well might man stretch forth his puny arm to stop the Missouri river in its decreed course, or to turn it up stream, as to hinder the Almighty from pouring down knowledge from heaven upon the heads of the Latter-day Saints. (D&C 121:26-33.)

In an address to Regional Representatives of the Twelve on September 29, 1978, President Spencer W. Kimball summarized the vast work awaiting the Church in which the righteous of all nations shall be one:

The Lord is moving upon the affairs of men and of nations to hasten the day of readiness when leaders will permit the elect among them to receive the gospel of Jesus Christ and when the gospel will be preached "for a witness" among all nations. . . .

We can bring the gospel with its healing balm and its powerful program to countless numbers, not only to introduce the gospel to them but to show them in our communities how we live and how they can live and better their lives. . . .

There are almost three billion people now living on the earth in nations where the gospel is not now being preached. If we could only make a small beginning in every nation, soon the converts among each kindred and tongue could step forth as light to their own people and the gospel would thus be preached in all nations before the coming of the Lord.

President Kimball then issued a challenge: "There seems to be a great movement afoot in many nations to prepare people for the further light and knowledge that only we can give them. The Lord by his Spirit is preparing people for the day when the gospel will be taught them in plainness. We must be ready!"[4]

Footnotes

Chapter 2: A Remarkable Vision

1. This account is taken from Joseph Smith, *History of the Church* 1:2-6. This writing was begun by Joseph Smith in 1838, eight years after the organization of the Church, and was first published in 1843, commencing in volume 3, number 10, of *Times and Seasons,* a Mormon newspaper in Nauvoo, Illinois. A briefer history was included by the Prophet in a document called the Wentworth Letter, which was written for John Wentworth, editor and proprietor of the *Chicago Democrat.* The Wentworth Letter was published in *Times and Seasons* 3, no. 9 (March 15, 1842).
2. Joseph's father, the boy's playmates, and the Methodist minister of the village all indicated that they noticed the change.
3. *HC* 1:7-8.

Chapter 3: Why a Restoration

1. Neander, *General History of the Christian Religion and Church* 1:250.
2. Philip Smith, *Students' Ecclesiastical History* 1:49.
3. *Eusebius' Ecclesiastical History,* Book VIII, chapter 1.
4. Mosheim, *Institutes,* Century II, vol. 1, chapter 4.
5. Mosheim, *An Ecclesiastical History, Ancient and Modern,* Century I, vol. 1, part 1, p. 74.
6. Gibbon, *The History of the Decline and Fall of the Roman Empire,* p. xv.
7. See Acts 2:37-41; 8:26-39. Talmage, *The Great Apostasy,* 1950 ed., note, pp. 93-95; also Talmage, *The Articles of Faith,* 1924 ed., chapters 6 and 7.
8. Talmage, *Articles of Faith,* chapter 6, note 2.
9. Talmage, *The Great Apostasy,* pp. 94-95; B. H. Roberts, *Outlines of Ecclesiastical History,* p. 133.
10. Mosheim, *Ecclesiastical History,* Century XI, part 2, chapter 2:2.
11. Talmage, *The Great Apostasy,* pp. 105-8.
12. Josephus, *Jewish Wars,* vol. 3, book V, chapter 8.

Chapter 4: A Field Ready to Reap

1. *HC* 3:304.
2. Ray, *Textbook on Campbellism,* p. 29.
3. Roberts, *A Comprehensive History of the Church* 1:5-6.
4. Lucy Mack Smith, *History of Joseph Smith, by His Mother,* p. 46.
5. Ibid., pp. 35-36.
6. Whitney, *Life of Heber C. Kimball,* p. 14.
7. Cowley, *Wilford Woodruff,* pp. 14-15.
8. Pratt, *Autobiography,* p. 19.
9. Snow, *Biography and Family Record of Lorenzo Snow,* pp. 2, 3.
10. Roberts, *Life of John Taylor,* pp. 31-32.

Chapter 5: Moroni's Mission to Joseph

1. Joseph Smith–History 1:27-50. See also *HC* 1:9-15.
2. This historic site is now owned by The Church of Jesus Christ of Latter-
   day Saints. The monument, dedicated in the summer of 1935, is the
   work of Torlief Knaphus, a Norwegian convert to the Church.
3. *HC* 1:16.
4. For the feelings and thoughts of the Prophet during this visit, and for the
   words of the angel to him, we are indebted to Oliver Cowdery, whose
   written account of these matters appeared in a series of eight letters first
   published in the *Latter-day Saints' Messenger and Advocate,* vols. 1 and
   2. The letters have been reproduced several times in Latter-day Saint
   publications, including *Improvement Era* 2, no. 11 (September 1899):
   807-9. Since Joseph was editor of the *Messenger and Advocate* and this
   edition bore his approval, it can be considered authentic, as if coming
   from his own pen.
5. *Messenger and Advocate* 2, no. 1 (October 1835): 192-93.
6. Joseph Smith–History 1:54; *HC* 1:16.
7. Joseph Smith–History 1:59-60; *HC* 1:18-19.

Chapter 6: The Book of Mormon Comes Forth

1. *HC* 1:282-83.
2. *HC* 1:339.
3. Extract from the Wentworth Letter, written by Joseph Smith to John
   Wentworth, editor of the *Chicago Democrat,* March 1, 1842.
4. See Exodus 28:30; Ezra 2:63; Nehemiah 7:65.
5. Lucy Mack Smith, *History of Joseph Smith, by His Mother,* p. 107.
6. *HC* 1:19.
7. A sheet of paper with characters from the plates of the Book of Mormon
   was found in March 1980 by Mark Hofmann in a 1668 Cambridge edi-

tion of the King James Bible that had orginally been in the Smith family. The manuscript, now called the "Hofmann Manuscript," is thought by Church experts to be the original Anthon transcript that Martin Harris took to New York for verification. It harmonizes with two descriptions of the documents made by Dr. Anthon in correspondence with E. D. Howe, dated February 17, 1834, and the Reverend T. W. Coit, April 3, 1841. A handwritten note signed by Joseph Smith on the reverse side of the document reads as follows: "These caractors were dilligently coppied by my own hand from the plates of gold and given to Martin Harris who took them to new york Citty but the learned could not translate it because the Lord would not open it up to them in fulfilment of the prop[h]cy of Isa[i]h written in the 29th Chapter and 11 verse." See Danel W. Bachman, *BYU Studies* 20 (Summer 1980): 321-45; Bachman, *Ensign,* July 1980, pp. 69-73.

8. *Messenger and Advocate* 1 (1834): 14. Champollian's work on Egyptian grammar did not appear until 1836, and it is the basis, along with his other works, for all study on Egyptology.

9. *HC* 1:48-49.

10. The original manuscript was in the handwriting of several persons who had acted as scribes, although the greater part was by Oliver Cowdery. A statement that Oliver made later, that he had written with his own hand the entire Book of Mormon manuscript save only a few pages, could only have referred to the *copy* of the original, which he retained. The original manuscript remained in the hands of Joseph Smith and was subsequently buried in the cornerstone of the Nauvoo Temple. A portion of this manuscript came later into the hands of Joseph F. Smith, then a member of the Quorum of the Twelve Apostles (see *Deseret News,* December 23, 1899). The copy from which the Book of Mormon was typeset remained the prized possession of Oliver Cowdery. At the time of his death in 1850, the manuscript came into the possession of David Whitmer. It is now owned by the Reorganized Church of Jesus Christ of Latter Day Saints.

11. J. M. Sjodahl, author of *An Introduction to the Study of the Book of Mormon,* once sent to several learned linguists seven lines of characters that are generally considered to be a genuine copy of Nephite characters from the plates. Although the characters were declared genuine, none of the linguists could read them.

12. See Exodus 28:30; Leviticus 8:8; Numbers 27:21; Deuteronomy 33:8; 1 Samuel 28:6; Ezra 2:63; Nehemiah 7:65.

13. Most of the mistakes in grammar and spelling were corrected by Joseph Smith in the second edition of the Book of Mormon. The style of expression and the meaning of the sentences have, however, remained unaltered. Orson Pratt, a member of the Quorum of the Twelve, divided the book into chapters and verses in 1879. The most recent edition of the Book of Mormon, published by the Church in 1981, contains a number

of corrections, based upon an examination of the original manuscript as
well as corrections subsequently made by the Prophet.

14. Lucy Mack Smith, *History of Joseph Smith, by His Mother*, pp. 99-101.

Chapter 7: Authority Is Restored

1. In an article in *Messenger and Advocate* 1 (October 1834), pp. 14-16,
   Oliver Cowdery ends the quotation thus: "Which shall remain upon the
   earth, that the Sons of Levi may yet offer an offering unto the Lord in
   righteousness."
2. Joseph Smith–History 1:70-73; *HC* 1:39-42.
3. Cowdery, *op. cit.*
4. *HC* 1:44.
5. *HC* 1:52.
6. *HC* 1:54-55.
7. *HC* 1:64.

Chapter 9: The Church Is Organized

1. *HC* 1:77-78.
2. "The name of the new church, as given in an April 6 revelation, was the
   Church of Jesus Christ, and until 1834 the members called it either that
   or the Church of Christ. The use of the term 'Saints' came gradually, but
   as early as August 1831 members of the Church were referred to as
   Saints in a revelation. . . . On May 3, 1834, a conference of the Church
   in Kirtland, Ohio, accepted a resolution proclaiming that thereafter the
   Church would be known as The Church of the Latter-day Saints. . . .
   Finally, on April 23, 1838, another revelation designated the name as
   The Church of Jesus Christ of Latter-day Saints. This has been the official title ever since." James B. Allen and Glen M. Leonard, *The Story of
   the Latter-day Saints*, p. 47. For examples of early use of the phrase
   "Church of Latter-day Saints," see William E. Berrett and Alma P. Burton, *Readings in L.D.S. Church History* 1:75-76.
3. D&C 65:2. See also Daniel 2:34-35, 45.

Chapter 10: Missionaries Go Forth

1. *HC* 1:81.
2. Pratt, *Autobiography*, p. 51.
3. Ibid., p. 52.
4. Ibid., p. 54.
5. Ibid., p. 56.
6. Ibid., p. 57.
7. Backman, *The Heavens Resound*, pp. 56-57.
8. Backman, *Joseph Smith's First Vision*, p. 116.

Chapter 11: The Church Moves West

1. This refers to the line separating the whites and the Indians, the Indians being referred to here as Jews.
2. *HC* 1:197.
3. Whitmer, *The Book of John Whitmer*, p. 6.
4. Roberts, *A Comprehensive History* 1:255.

Chapter 12: Other Scriptures Come Forth

1. In recent years the Book of Commandments has been published by the Church of Christ (Hedrickites) at Independence, Missouri.
2. *HC* 2:235.
3. Roberts, *A Comprehensive History* 2:126.
4. *HC* 2:286.
5. *HC* 2:334. See also *Millennial Star* 15:519, 550.
6. *Messenger and Advocate* 2 (December 1835): 234.
7. See Cannon, *Life of Joseph Smith*, p. 182.
8. The wood engravings for the facsimiles were done by Reuben Hedlock, an engraver from Canada. John Taylor, a worker in wood, was also present and working on the *Times and Seasons* at that time. For years after publication of the facsimiles, the original documents remained in the possession of the Joseph Smith family. After the Prophet's death, they were retained by his widow, Emma. She later sold them to a museum at St. Louis, and they were subsequently found in the Museum of Chicago. In the great Chicago fire of 1871 the museum was destroyed, as were most of the precious ancient manuscripts it housed.
9. See the introduction to section 88 in the 1981 edition of the Doctrine and Covenants.
10. For additional information on the School of the Prophets, see Backman, *The Heavens Resound*, pp. 264-68.

Chapter 13: Conflict in Missouri

1. Constitution of the United States, Article I, section 9, para. 1.
2. George Q. Cannon, *Life of Joseph Smith*, p. 155.
3. *HC* 1:392.
4. *HC* 1:375-76.
5. *HC* 1:390-91.
6. *HC* 1:423-24.
7. The Lord's word on such matters had been received by Joseph Smith in a revelation on August 6, 1833, but this was not generally known in Zion. See Doctrine and Covenants, section 98.
8. Pratt, *Autobiography*, p. 112.
9. *HC* 2:461-62.
10. *HC* 1:455.

Chapter 14: The Calling of Leaders

1. *HC* 1:243n.
2. *HC* 2:186-200 and notes.
3. *HC* 2:201-3.

Chapter 15: The Beginning of Temple Building

1. *HC* 1:342-43.
2. *HC* 1:352.
3. *HC* 3:353-54.
4. *HC* 3:366.
5. Whitney, *Life of Heber C. Kimball,* p. 68.
6. *Journal of Discourses* 14:273.
7. *HC* 3:349-50.
8. Backman, *The Heavens Resound,* p. 153.
9. Whitney, *Life of Heber C. Kimball,* p. 90.
10. Bancroft, *History of Utah,* p. 112.
11. *HC* 2:410-18.
12. *Backman, The Heavens Resound,* pp. 298-99. See *HC* 2:427-28; *Messenger and Advocate* 2 (March 1836): 281; diary of Joseph Smith, 1835–36, pp. 184-85; diary of Stephen Post, March 27, 1836; Autobiography of Truman O. Angell, p. 5; Heber C. Kimball in *Journal of Discourses* 9:376; George A. Smith in *Journal of Discourses* 2:10; journal of Edward Partridge, March 27, 1836; Autobiography of Heber C. Kimball.
13. *HC* 2:427-28.
14. *HC* 2:435-36; D&C 110, preface and verses 1-7, 11-16.

Chapter 16: The Saints Are Driven Out of Missouri

1. General H. G. Parks to the Governor, published by order of the General Assembly of Missouri, p. 32.
2. *HC* 3:158.
3. Roberts, *A Comprehensive History* 1:463.
4. *HC* 3:175.
5. *HC* 3:188.
6. *HC* 3:190-91n.
7. *HC* 3:203.
8. *HC* 3:250.
9. Pratt, *Autobiography,* pp. 210-11.
10. *HC* 3:182.
11. *HC* 3:303-4.

Chapter 17: A Faith Stronger Than Steel

1. *HC* 4:3-4n.
2. Whitney, *Life of Heber C. Kimball,* pp. 265-66.
3. Cowley, *Wilford Woodruff,* p. 118.
4. Ibid., p. 134.
5. Pratt, *Autobiography,* p. 325.
6. Ibid., p. 328.
7. Letter from Orson Hyde to Parley P. Pratt in England, dated November 22, 1841; *HC* 4:457.
8. *HC* 4:249.
9. *HC* 4:273.
10. Brodie, *Route from Liverpool to Great Salt Lake Valley,* pp. 205-6.
11. Roberts, *Life of John Taylor,* pp. 107-8.
12. *HC* 4:80.
13. For a full account, see *HC* 4:154-57; also Joseph Fielding Smith, *Essentials in Church History,* pp. 247-48.

Chapter 18: The Temple in Nauvoo

1. *HC* 4:595-96.

Chapter 19: A Clash of Social Orders

1. *HC* 6:188.
2. *HC* 6:197-209.
3. *HC* 6:268.
4. *HC* 5:500-507. See also D&C 132.
5. Discourse at Provo, Utah, July 14, 1855. See Roberts, *A Comprehensive History* 2:102-3.
6. Roberts, *Life of John Taylor,* p. 100.
7. *HC* 5:85.
8. *HC* 6:222.
9. *HC* 6:225.
10. *HC* 6:275.
11. *HC* 6:152.
12. *HC* 6:443-44.
13. *HC* 6:448.

Chapter 20: Martyrs for the Church

1. *HC* 6:499.
2. *HC* 6:537.
3. *HC* 6:540.

4. *HC* 6:545-46.
5. *HC* 6:549-50.
6. *HC* 6:552.
7. *HC* 6:554.
8. *Millennial Star* 24:775.
9. *Millennial Star* 24:358. For the fulfillment of this prophecy, see Roberts, *A Comprehensive History* 2:270n.1.
10. A person arrested for a crime must be taken before a justice of the peace or other court officer. If the justice believes there is reasonable cause for trial, the prisoner is committed to jail or released on bail until a trial can be held.
11. *HC* 6:600-601.

Chapter 21: The Church of Christ or of Man?

1. Pratt, *Autobiography,* p. 331.
2. In the fall of 1844, at Emma Smith's request, the bodies were secretly removed and reburied in a spot near the Nauvoo Mansion overlooking the Mississippi River. The spot remained unmarked for many years. In 1928, because of the rising waters of the Mississippi, backed up by the Keokuk Dam, the bodies were unearthed by members of the Reorganized Church of Jesus Christ of Latter Day Saints and, together with the remains of Emma Smith, reburied in higher ground and the plot enclosed by an iron fence. A suitable monument has been erected in their memory by their descendants.
3. See Far West Council Record, March 15, 1838; also *HC* 3:31-32n.

Chapter 22: The Persecution Resumes

1. *HC* 6:498.
2. *HC* 7:204.
3. "Jack Mormons" was a term applied to nonmembers of the Church who showed special friendship for the Saints. It later came to be applied to inactive Mormons who did not live the Word of Wisdom or keep the other commandments.
4. Ford, *A History of Illinois,* p. 364.
5. Roberts, *A Comprehensive History* 2:477.
6. Joseph Fielding Smith, *Essentials in Church History,* pp. 326-27.
7. *HC* 7:449-51.

Chapter 23: The Exodus from Nauvoo

1. *Memoirs of John R. Young, Utah Pioneer,* p. 14.
2. Little, *From Kirtland to Salt Lake City,* pp. 47-48.
3. Roberts, *A Comprehensive History* 3:45-46.

4. *Millennial Star,* vol. 8, nos. 7 and 8.
5. Pratt, *Autobiography,* p. 342.
6. Cowley, *Wilford Woodruff,* p. 247.
7. Gregg, *History of Hancock County, Illinois,* pp. 345-46.
8. Conyers, *A Brief History of the Leading Causes of the Hancock Mob, in the Year 1846,* p. 54.
9. The exact number is not known. Governor Ford placed it at 150, but others gave the higher figure.
10. Ford, *A History of Illinois,* pp. 424-25.

Chapter 24: The Mormon Battalion

1. Roberts, "History of the Mormon Church," *Americana,* March 1912, p. 288.
2. Quaife, *The Diary of James K. Polk* 1:444.
3. Roberts, *op. cit.,* pp. 293-94.
4. Journal History, July 13, 1846.
5. Brigham Young, Manuscript History, 1846–47, 2:222.
6. Ibid., p. 226.
7. Thomas L. Kane, "The Mormons," address delivered before the Historical Society of Pennsylvania on March 26, 1850, in Daniel Tyler, *A Concise History of the Mormon Battalion,* p. 80.
8. Ibid., pp. 80-81.
9. Journal History, July 1-2, 1846.
10. Roberts, *op. cit.,* p. 310.
11. Journal History, 1846, pp. 30-34.
12. Journal History, September 26, 1846.
13. Tyler, *History of the Mormon Battalion,* p. 181.
14. Roberts, *The Mormon Battalion,* p. 2.

Chapter 25: Pioneers

1. Kane, "The Mormons," in Tyler, p. 92.
2. Letter of Brigham Young to Elders Hyde, Pratt, and Taylor, dated July 6, 1847, in *Millennial Star* 12:18.
3. Bancroft, *History of California* 4:268-71.
4. This route was later followed by the Union Pacific between Omaha and Laramie.
5. The Indians fired the old grass of the prairies every spring so that the new growth would entice the buffalo herds to their hunting grounds during the summer. Along the Oregon Trail, the trappers fired the prairies in the fall so that the spring burning by the Indians would not hinder an early growth of grass to feed their pack-train animals.
6. Little, *From Kirtland to Salt Lake City,* pp. 82-83.

7. For an illustration and a description of William Clayton's odometer, see Roberts, *A Comprehensive History* 3:174 and 3:190-91n.3.

8. For an illustration of a buffalo skull used as a bulletin by Brigham Young, see Roberts, *A Comprehensive History* 3:184.

9. Ibid.

10. Brigham Young, Manuscript History, 1847, p. 557.

11. Orson Pratt, Journal.

12. Brigham Young, Manuscript History, 1847, p. 559.

13. The ferry was designed especially for the use of the large caravans of Saints that would come later in the season. Between June 18 and July 1, five hundred wagons with 1,553 persons left the Elkhorn River to follow the trail blazed by the earlier company. These companies had 2,213 oxen, 124 horses, 887 cows, 358 sheep, 716 chickens, and a number of pigs.

14. Orson Pratt, Journal, entry for June 26, 1847.

15. Ibid.

16. Erastus Snow, "Discourse on the Utah Pioneers," July 24, 1880, in *The Utah Pioneer,* pp. 44-45.

17. Orson Pratt, Journal, entry for June 28, 1847.

18. Brigham Young, Manuscript History, 2:561.

19. Snow, "Discourse," p. 43.

20. Wilford Woodruff, Journal, entry for June 28, 1847.

21. *Millennial Star* 12:161.

22. Snow, "Discourse," p. 45.

23. Orson Pratt, Journal, entry for July 21, 1847.

24. Brigham Young, Manuscript History, entry for July 24, 1847, 2:564.

25. Snow, "Discourse," p. 23.

Chapter 26: The New Gathering Place

1. Tyler, *History of the Mormon Battalion,* p. 315.

2. Talmage, *The Great Salt Lake, Present and Past,* p. 88.

3. Brigham Young, Manuscript History.

4. *HC* 7:616-17.

5. Kanesville was the name given in 1848 to the original Mormon settlement at Miller's Hollow. It was later named Council Bluffs.

6. Brigham Young, Manuscript History, entry for April 26, 1848; *HC* 7:625.

Chapter 27: The Spirit of Gathering

1. *Deseret News,* July 24, 1852, p. 2.

2. *Millennial Star* 10:85.

3. Ibid., p. 86.

4. Ibid.

5. Snow, *Biography and Family Record of Lorenzo Snow*, p. 108.
6. Letter dated October 16, 1849, in Little, *From Kirtland to Salt Lake City*, p. 216.
7. Hubert Howe Bancroft, *History of Utah*, p. 397.
8. *Millennial Star* 15:618.
9. Tullidge, *History of Salt Lake City*, p. 100.
10. *Millennial Star* 17:219.
11. Larson, *History of the Perpetual Emigrating Fund Company*, p. 92.
12. *Millennial Star* 14:325.

Chapter 28: Conquering the Desert

1. John R. Young, *Memoirs*, p. 64.
2. Ibid., pp. 64-66.
3. Little, *From Kirtland to Salt Lake City*, pp. 229-30.

Chapter 29: A Self-Sustaining People

1. Roberts, *A Comprehensive History* 4:24.
2. *Deseret News*, December 25, 1852.
3. Ibid.
4. Snow, *Biography and Family Record of Lorenzo Snow*, pp. 291-95.
5. *Millennial Star* 10:85.
6. See Roberts, *A Comprehensive History* 4:29-30.
7. *Deseret News*, October 23, 1861.

Chapter 30: The Utah War

1. Roberts, *A Comprehensive History* 4:223.
2. *Deseret News*, September 2, 1857.
3. Joseph Fielding Smith, *Essentials in Church History*, pp. 409-10.
4. Ibid., p. 412n.
5. Ibid., pp. 410-11.
6. Roberts, *A Comprehensive History* 4:279-80.
7. Roberts, *A Comprehensive History* 4:294-95.
8. Roberts, *A Comprehensive History* 4:315.
9. Roberts, *A Comprehensive History* 4:349.
10. Roberts, *A Comprehensive History* 4:384.

Chapter 31: Years of Conflict

1. Roberts, *A Comprehensive History* 3:488.
2. Evans, *Joseph Smith, an American Prophet*, p. 267.
3. *Deseret News*, October 11, 1890, p. 2.

4. Roberts, *A Comprehensive History* 5:228.
5. *Journal of Discourses* 12:286.
6. *Millennial Star* 15:488.
7. *Millennial Star* 39:373.
8. Widtsoe, *A Rational Theology*, pp. 124-27.

Chapter 32: Constancy Amid Change

1. Clark, *Messages of the First Presidency* 6:159.
2. *Conference Report*, April 1930, p. 176.
3. Lofthouse, *A History of the Genealogical Society*.

Chapter 33: Educating the Youth of the Church

1. Maxwell, "Seek Learning Even by Study and by Faith," pp. 6-7.
2. Ibid., p. 3.

Chapter 34: To Strengthen the Saints

1. *Conference Report*, April 1906, p. 3.
2. Lee, *Stand Ye in Holy Places*, pp. 294-95; *Improvement Era*, January 1968, p. 26.
3. Marion G. Romney, "The Responsibilities of Home Teachers," *Ensign*, March 1973, p. 12.
4. *Improvement Era*, June 1915, pp. 733-34.
5. Lee, *Improvement Era*, January 1968, p. 27.

Chapter 35: God Prepares the Way

1. This letter has been published in the 1981 edition of the Doctrine and Covenants as Official Declaration–2. For remarks given by President N. Eldon Tanner, first counselor in the First Presidency, when the revelation was presented to the members of the Church for their sustaining vote, see *Ensign*, November 1978, p. 18.

Chapter 36: Taking the Church to the People

1. Boyd K. Packer, "Scriptures," *Ensign*, November 1982, p. 53.
2. *Church News*, November 14, 1981, p. 3.
3. Report of the British Area General Conference, August 27-29, 1971, p. 5.
4. Report of the first Mexico and Central America Area General Conference, August 25-27, 1972, p. 45.

5. Harold B. Lee, "Strengthen the Stakes of Zion," *Ensign*, July 1973, pp. 4, 5.
6. *Church News*, February 26, 1984, p. 7.
7. Ibid.
8. Ibid.
9. From a copy of the dedication prayer, in the possession of President John A. Davis.
10. Spencer W. Kimball, "The Lord Expects Righteousness," *Ensign*, November 1982, pp. 4-5.
11. "A Decade of Growth," *Ensign*, January 1984, p. 10.

Chapter 37: New Temples Are Built

1. Report of an announcement made in a meeting prior to the first session of general conference, April 7, 1984, in *Ensign*, May 1984, p. 102.
2. *Church News*, June 5, 1983, p. 3.
3. "News of the Church," *Ensign*, May 1984, p. 99.
4. *Church News*, August 16, 1980.
5. J. Thomas Fyans, "Ours Is a Shared Ancestry," *Ensign*, November 1978, p. 29.

Chapter 38: The Great Melting Pot

1. *Church News*, January 1, 1983.
2. *Church News*, February 19, 1984, p. 10.
3. The King James Bible uses the word *stones*. However, in a sermon delivered July 23, 1843, the Prophet Joseph Smith used the term "stony Gentiles." Thus, God is literally raising up children of Abraham from the Gentiles who enter the Church and prove faithful. See *Teachings of the Prophet Joseph Smith*, p. 319.
4. Spencer W. Kimball, "The Uttermost Parts of the Earth," *Ensign*, July 1979, pp. 2-9.

Bibliography

Books and Theses

Allen, James B., and Glen M. Leonard. *The Story of the Latter-day Saints*. Salt Lake City: Deseret Book, 1976.

Backman, Milton V., Jr., *Joseph Smith's First Vision. The First Vision in Its Historical Context*. 2nd ed. rev. Salt Lake City: Bookcraft, 1980.

_____ . *The Heavens Resound: A History of the Latter-day Saints in Ohio, 1830–1838*. Salt Lake City: Deseret Book, 1983.

Bancroft, Hubert Howe. *The Works of Hubert Howe Bancroft. History of California*. 7 vols. San Francisco, 1886. *History of Utah, 1540–1886*. San Francisco, 1890.

Berrett, William E. *The Restored Church*. Rev. ed. Salt Lake City: Deseret Book, 1974.

Berrett, William Edwin. *Doctrines of the Restored Church*. Salt Lake City: Department of Education, The Church of Jesus Christ of Latter-day Saints, 1941.

Berrett, William E., and Alma P. Burton, comps. *Readings in L.D.S. Church History from Original Manuscripts*. 3 vols. Salt Lake City: Deseret Book, 1953–58.

Brodie, Fawn M., ed. *Route from Liverpool to Great Salt Lake Valley . . . from Sketches Made by Frederick Piercy*. Cambridge, Mass.: Belknap Press of Harvard University Press, 1962.

Cannon, George Q. *Life of Joseph Smith*. Salt Lake City: Deseret Book, 1958.

Clark, James R., ed. *Messages of the First Presidency of The Church of Jesus Christ of Latter-day Saints*. 6 vols. Salt Lake City: Bookcraft, 1965–75.

Conyers, Josiah B. *A Brief History of the Leading Causes of the Hancock Mob, in the Year 1846*. St. Louis, 1846.

Cowley, Matthias F. *Wilford Woodruff: History of His Life and Labors as Recorded in His Daily Journals*. Salt Lake City: Deseret News, 1909. Reprinted by Bookcraft, 1964.

Eusebius' Ecclesiastical History. Grand Rapids, Mich.: Baker House, 1976.

Evans, John Henry. *Joseph Smith, an American Prophet*. New York: Macmillan Company, 1933. Reprinted by Deseret Book, 1946.

Ford, Thomas. *A History of Illinois*. Chicago, 1854.

Gibbon, Edward. *The History of the Decline and Fall of the Roman Empire*. 1887. Preface by Dean Milman.

Gregg, T. H. *History of Hancock, Illinois*. Chicago, 1880.

Jessee, Dean C., ed. *Personal Writings of Joseph Smith*. Salt Lake City: Deseret Book, 1984.

Josephus. *Works of Josephus*. Vol. 3, *Jewish Wars*.

Larson, Gustive O. *History of the Perpetual Emigrating Fund Company*. Unpublished master's thesis. University of Utah, 1926.

Lee, Harold B. *Stand Ye in Holy Places*. Salt Lake City: Deseret Book, 1974.

Little, James A. *From Kirtland to Salt Lake City*. Salt Lake City, 1890.

Lofthouse, Merrill S. *A History of the Genealogical Society of the Church . . . to 1970*. Unpublished master's thesis, Brigham Young University, 1971.

Mosheim, John Lawrence. *An Ecclesiastical History, Ancient and Modern*.

_____ . *Institutes of Ecclesiastical History Ancient and Modern*.

Neander, Augustus. *General History of the Christian Religion and Church*. Trans. Joseph Torrey. 1871.

Pratt, Parley P. *Autobiography of Parley Parker Pratt*. Salt Lake City: Deseret Book, 1964.

Quaife, Milo Milton, ed. *The Diary of James K. Polk*. 4 vols. Chicago, 1910.

Ray, D. B. *Textbook on Campbellism*. Memphis, 1867.

Roberts, B. H. *A Comprehensive History of the Church of Jesus Christ of Latter-day Saints, Century I*. 6 vols. Salt Lake City: The Church of Jesus Christ of Latter-day Saints, 1930.

_____ . *The Life of John Taylor, Third President of the Church*. Salt Lake City: Bookcraft, 1963.

_____ . *The Mormon Battalion*. Salt Lake City, 1909.

_____ . *Outlines of Ecclesiastical History*. Salt Lake City: Deseret Book, 1979.

Sjodahl, J. M. *An Introduction to the Study of the Book of Mormon*. Salt Lake City: Deseret News Press, 1927.

Smith, Joseph. *History of the Church of Jesus Christ of Latter-day Saints*. 7 vols. Edited by B. H. Roberts. Salt Lake City: The Church of Jesus Christ of Latter-day Saints, 1920–22.

Smith, Joseph Fielding. *Essentials in Church History*. Salt Lake City: Deseret Book, 1973.

_____ , comp. *Teachings of the Prophet Joseph Smith*. Salt Lake City: Deseret Book, 1961.

Smith, Lucy Mack. *History of Joseph Smith by His Mother*. Edited by Preston Nibley. Salt Lake City: Bookcraft, 1979.

Snow, Eliza R. *Biography and Family Record of Lorenzo Snow*. Salt Lake City: Deseret News, 1884.

Talmage, James E. *The Great Salt Lake, Present and Past*. Salt Lake City: Deseret News, 1900.

Talmage, James E. *Articles of Faith*. Salt Lake City: The Church of Jesus Christ of Latter-day Saints, 1924.

_____ . *The Great Apostasy*. Salt Lake City: Deseret Book, 1978.

Tullidge, Edward. *History of Salt Lake City*. Salt Lake City, 1886.

Tyler, Daniel. *A Concise History of the Mormon Battalion in the Mexican War, 1846–47*. Salt Lake City, 1881.

Whitmer, John. *The Book of John Whitmer: Kept by Commandment*. Independence, Mo.: Library Archives, Reorganized Church of Jesus Christ of Latter Day Saints.

Whitney, Orson F. *Life of Heber C. Kimball*. 2nd ed. Salt Lake City: Stevens and Wallis, Inc., 1945. Reprinted by Bookcraft, 1967.

Widtsoe, John A. *A Rational Theology*. Salt Lake City: Deseret Book, 1937.

Young, John R. *Memoirs of John R. Young, Utah Pioneer*. Salt Lake City, 1920.

Articles and Speeches

Backman, Danel W. "A Look at the Newly Discovered Joseph Smith Manuscript," *Ensign*, July 1980, pp. 69-73.

———. "Sealed in a Book: Preliminary Observations on the Newly Found 'Anthon Manuscript'." *BYU Studies* 20 (Summer 1980): 321-45.

Kane, Thomas L. "The Mormons." Discourse delivered before the Historical Society of Pennsylvania, March 26, 1850. Text reprinted in Daniel Tyler, *A Concise History of the Mormon Battalion*, pp. 64-106.

Maxwell, Neal A. "Seek Learning Even by Study and by Faith." Report for 1971 from the Commissioner of Education in The Church of Jesus Christ of Latter-day Saints.

Roberts, B. H. "History of the Mormon Church," *Americana*, March 1912.

Snow, Erastus. "Discourse on the Utah Pioneers." *The Utah Pioneer*, July 24, 1880.

Journals and Diaries

Angell, Truman O. Autobiography. Microfilm of holograph, Church Archives. Typescript, Brigham Young University.

Journal History of the Church. Church Archives.

Kimball, Heber C. Autobiography. Church Archives.

Partridge, Edward. Journal. Church Archives.

Post, Stephen. Diary. Holograph, Church Archives.

Pratt, Orson. Journal. Holograph, Church Archives.

Smith, Joseph, Jr. Diary, 1835–36. Church Archives.

Woodruff, Wilford. Journal. Church Archives.

Young, Brigham. Manuscript History, 1846–47.

Periodicals and Miscellaneous Publications

Area Conference Reports. The Church of Jesus Christ of Latter-day Saints, 1971– .

Conference Reports. The Church of Jesus Christ of Latter-day Saints, 1898– .

Contributor. Salt Lake City, 1879–1896.

Deseret News. Salt Lake City, 1850– .
Far West Council Record. The Church of Jesus Christ of Latter-day Saints.
Journal of Discourses. 26 vols. London: Latter-day Saints Book Depot,
    1854–1886.
Millennial Star. Manchester, Liverpool, and London, England, 1840–1970.
Times and Seasons. Commerce (Nauvoo), Illinois, 1839–46.

Index